Founder of Hasidism

Contraversions
Critical Studies in Jewish Literature, Culture, and Society

Daniel Boyarin and Chana Kronfeld, General Editors

Founder of Hasidism

*A Quest for the Historical
Ba'al Shem Tov*

Moshe Rosman

UNIVERSITY OF CALIFORNIA PRESS
Berkeley · Los Angeles · London

University of California Press
Berkeley and Los Angeles, California

University of California Press
London, England

Library of Congress Cataloging-in-Publication Data

Rosman, Murray Jay.
    Founder of Hasidism : a quest for the historical
Ba'al Shem Tov / Moshe Rosman.
        p.   cm. — (Contraversions ; 5)
    Includes bibliographical references and index.
    ISBN 0-520-20191-4 (alk. paper)
    1. Ba'al Shem Tov, ca. 1700–1760. 2. Ha-
sidism—Ukraine—Biography. 3. Rabbis—
Ukraine—Biography. 4. Hasidism—History—
18th century. I. Title. II. Series.
BM175.I8R66   1996
296.8'332'092—dc20
    [B]   95-35641
                                                  CIP

Printed in the United States of America
    2 3 4 5 6 7 8 9
The paper used in this publication meets the minimum requirements of American National Standard
for Information Sciences—Permanence of Paper for
Printed Library Materials, ANSI Z39.48–1984 ∞

For My Parents
Norman Rosman and Elayne Chimerinsky Rosman

Contents

Acknowledgments

In my first book I emphasized the paramount contribution of my teachers to my work. While their influence continues, and Professor Jacob Goldberg continues to be of active help, this time around critical input has come from colleagues in two main contexts. The first is the lively interchange that takes place formally on the Israeli academic conference circuit and informally in and around the Jewish National and University Library in Jerusalem and at Bar Ilan University where I teach. The many opportunities I have had to hear and present lectures and to discuss with colleagues topics relating to this book constitute an extended postgraduate seminar.

The second context is the University of Michigan, where I spent the spring 1989 semester as a guest of the History Department and the Frankel Center for Jewish Studies. There I learned about developments in historical thinking and writing that changed my perspective, influenced my style, and made me explore new approaches to research and writing. I thank Todd Endelman, then director of the Frankel Center, for making this experience possible.

My students have prompted me to formulate in coherent form many of the components of the analysis contained here. They have asked questions, pointed to contradictions, and demanded that I refine my thinking.

In a more specific way, I am grateful to the staffs of the Biblioteka Czartoryskich in Cracow, the Archiwum Glowny Akt Dawnych in Warsaw, the Central State Historical Archives of Ukraine and the Vernadsky Library Jewish Division, both in Kiev, the Central Archive for the History of the Jewish People in Jerusalem, the University of Michigan Graduate Library in Ann Arbor, the Bar Ilan University Library, the Jewish National and University Library, and the Gershom Scholem Collection for all of their help. Yuri Khoderkovsky of Kiev drew the maps.

Chapter 5 is a significant revision and enlargement of "Social Conflicts in Międzybóż in the Generation of the Besht," in *Hasidism Reappraised*, ed. A. Rapoport-Albert, published by the Littman Library of Jewish Civilization (Oxford, 1996).

Daniel Boyarin took a special interest in my research and worked with integrity to have it published. Stanley Holwitz, Michelle Bonnice, Diana Feinberg, Sheila Berg, Susie Guttman, and the rest of the staff of the University of California Press have shown a sincere—and appreciated—concern for this project and have done their best to have it appear in a worthy form. Gershon Bacon, Israel Bartal, Rahel Elior, Immanuel Etkes, Gershon Hundert, Moshe Idel, Anita Norich, Elhanan Reiner, Shaul Stampfer, and Khone Shmeruk each read parts or all of the manuscript and made specific suggestions. Robert Binder served as a conscientious consultant on style. While they are not responsible for how I applied their advice, I am grateful to all of these colleagues for their kind attentions.

I have dedicated this book to my parents, who not only gave me life but also gave me the tools I needed to live and to assume a career in scholarship and who have never ceased sharing in my life. My parents-in-law, Emil and Eda Reed, have believed in me even when I made mistakes. My children, Elisheva, Tamar, Yaacov, Michael, Avital, and Meir, have made a vital contribution to this book by putting it into perspective. Lynne, my wife, has graciously and lovingly given this project the space it demanded in our life.

Note to the Reader

Translations of biblical texts generally follow the new Jewish Publication Society translation (Philadelphia, 1962–1982), with appropriate modifications. Other translations are original unless otherwise noted. Depending on the context, personal names are written according to the way they appear in Polish sources or are transliterated from Hebrew or Yiddish according to the system suggested by the *Encyclopaedia Judaica*. Geographic names generally follow the spelling of the country in which the place was located during the eighteenth century. "Hasidism," "Hasidic," "Hasid," when capitalized, refer to the movement usually associated with the Ba'al Shem Tov. When not capitalized, these terms refer to the old-style, mystical-ascetic hasidism discussed in detail in chapter 2.

Page from August Alexander Czartoryski's 1760 register of the Jewish residents of Międzybóż and their property tax (*czynsz*) obligations. Number 93 is "Balszam Doktor . . . Liber" (Dr. Ba'al Shem . . . Exempt). One of only a few mentions of the Besht in Polish documents, it confirms that the Besht lived and that he was supported by the Jewish communal establishment which gave him a communally owned house to live in tax free. Some of the Besht's relatives and associates also appear in this register. See chapter 10 for a discussion of this document. Courtesy Biblioteka Czartoryskich (Gospodarcze 308).

Introduction

For more than one hundred fifty years the biography of the putative founder of Hasidism, Israel ben Eliezer, the Ba'al Shem Tov, has been on the agenda of Jewish studies and, indeed, the history of religion. Hasidism has had a tremendous impact in both the spiritual and social realms. In Hasidism the mystical ethos became part of everyday religion; Kabbalah was turned into a tool for intensifying communal life, rather than for encouraging isolation; emphasis was placed on the need to relate to God through joy, instead of abnegation; and addressing the individual's needs became a major religious objective. In short, Hasidism created a unique sort of pietism that captured the imagination of the masses of eastern European Jewry in the nineteenth and early twentieth centuries. After a period of decline, marked especially by the tragic fate of virtually all Hasidic communities during the Holocaust, Hasidism has proven it has the power to flourish in modern democratic societies. Today we are witnessing tremendous growth of Hasidic groups in Israel, America, and Europe.

Socially, the Hasidim, devoted to their charismatic leaders (*zaddikim* or *rebbes*), found a means of organization that successfully bridged many of the gaps between the elite and the rank and file. They formed disciplined, yet entirely voluntary, communities where the interconnectedness of members' souls was manifest. Issues of social justice and economic welfare were as central to the *zaddik*'s concern as were prayer and ritual observance. In our own time, the moral and religious teachings of famous zaddikim and the Hasidic style of worship with its singing and dancing inform, to some degree, the ideology and practice of all streams of Jewish religion and exert an influence on certain non-Jewish circles as well. Moreover, the Hasid in his caftan and fur-trimmed hat, fervently at prayer, has been adopted the world over as a stereotypical emblem of traditional Jewish life.

As the progenitor of this movement that has been so central to the development of modern Judaism, the Besht (the common Hebrew acronym of Ba'al Shem Tov, employed by Israel himself) arouses keen interest. There is a tacit assumption among researchers that to understand the Besht is somehow to understand Hasidism, and with it much of modern Jewish religion and experience. Writers have treated the patterns of his life as directly responsible for the movement's ideology and institutions, as an adumbration of what was to unfold, or as a standard for measuring the later movement's break of faith with its founder's noble intentions.[1]

Beyond his connection to Hasidism, the Besht is perceived as one of the great figures in the history of Jewish spirituality. Alongside the Vilna Gaon and Moses Mendelssohn, he is popularly viewed as one of the eighteenth-century personalities responsible for forging the ethos and visage of modern Judaism. If the Gaon represents traditional scholarship and observance and Mendelssohn encodes rationalism and enlightenment, it is the Besht who is often credited as the chief spokesman for the humane, warm side of Judaism, as against its supposed impersonal legalism. He is seen as stressing genuine communion with God, while minimizing ritual punctiliousness. He respected the individual and taught the infinite worth of each person. He insisted that Jewish worship and observance should be a joyous service of the heart.[2] This being the general belief, historians great and small have tried their hand at depicting the Besht.

The Besht is also important for reasons of methodology. He represents a classic example of one of the most vexing problems in historiography: recovering the biography of a legendary leader. Like the quest for the historical persons behind the mythologies of other cultural heroes—the most famous example being Jesus[3]—the attempt to reconstruct the course of the Besht's life has proven to be an elusive task. At the root of this type of scholarship lies a powerful desire to discover as much detail as possible about a figure credited with starting a successful, new direction in religious belief and practice or in political and social life. Typically, this desire is frustrated by a dearth of sources. There is little or no material written by the figure himself, and there is only chance, fragmentary mention of him by contemporaries. However, the movement tracing its origins to a central figure but following him by a generation or more may have used oral traditions of what the figure did and said to produce compilations of stories about him and sayings spoken by him, yielding a detailed account of his life. For early Christianity, this compilation is the Gospels; for Hasidism, it is *Shivhei Ha-Besht* (In Praise of the Ba'al Shem Tov).[4]

Lacking collateral material, scholars must depend primarily on their ability to interpret this compilation, the shortcomings of which are obvious: it is based, at best, on memories more than a generation old; these memories may have been filtered through many people before being recorded; these memories have been altered by editors intent on serving the interests of the movement at a relatively advanced stage of its development, many years after the central figure's death; the compilation contains material that is patently unhistorical. Given such circumstances, how can the historicity of any individual datum be evaluated? With little material to compare with the stories of the compilation, it is difficult for a scholar to penetrate beyond what the editors wanted their readers to know and to arrive at what a historian wants to know.

In the case of the Besht, the source material has been so scanty and so exceptionally equivocal that many descriptions of him have been overshadowed by the describers' ideological proclivities. All historical accounts are based on situated vision and, as such, are constructions of the contents of the sources, according to the interpretive rules of the community of historians.[5] In light of the highly problematic nature of the Besht sources usually employed, most Besht descriptions are constructions of constructions with only a light anchor in the sources. The scholarly imagination can run virtually free because the pickets of the sources are so few and far between. Consequently, as Albert Schweitzer found to be true of Jesus and Daphna Golan of Shaka Zulu:[6] to every scholar, her or his own blatantly projected, ideologically self-serving Besht. The act of describing the Ba'al Shem Tov has often served as a means of reifying various—sometimes competing—conceptions of Jewish culture.[7] Chapter 12 offers one example of how the image of the Besht has been pressed into the service of ideology and politics.

On one level this book is a methodological case study of possible approaches (context, text, and image analysis) to the recovery of the historical person behind the legends. It may serve as an antidote to the ideologically weighted approach by focusing more on the materials that can be drawn on to construct a description, rather than on the description itself. My main purpose is to call attention to materials, interpretations, and methodological considerations that should now be taken into account when portraying the Besht. By summarizing the issues and results of previous Ba'al Shem Tov research, presenting contexts within which the Besht lived his life, and examining the primary texts that contain information about him, I hope to create a foundation that will serve as a basis for future research and biographical depiction.

In the course of critically synthesizing previous treatments, various issues are reconsidered here. In most instances this is done with a view toward contributing new information, a new perspective, or a new interpretation. In some cases—such as the discussions of the meaning of Ba'al Shem Tov or the thesis of Yaffa Eliach—my presentation does not revise generally accepted conclusions, even if it augments them. I raise these topics because from my experience in teaching students and lecturing before audiences of nonspecialists, I have found that many scholarly conclusions have still not penetrated popular consciousness and mistaken notions have yet to be laid to rest.

I understand that my presentation of the context and texts of the Besht's life contains within it my own notion of the Besht. In the penultimate chapter I have attempted to make this image explicit via a brief constructed description of the Besht, admittedly utilizing many inferences, implications, and even conjectures. I am much less comfortable with this tentative presentation than with the material in the first ten chapters. It is offered both as a gesture of good faith and to crystallize a conception that can stimulate others in their research.

My description is more limited in scope than what can be read elsewhere. It is, however, more closely tied to sources that, as best as can be determined, were actually connected to the Besht, either as products of his pen or as descriptions of his behavior by people who were witness to his activities. With the source material available at the present time, it is impossible to write a conventional, full-scale biography of Israel ben Eliezer, Ba'al Shem Tov. Those who have done so have allowed their imaginations to run ahead of their research.

To construct the story of the Besht's life, the first step is describing context. Recent work has clarified many topics in the history of Ukraine and the Polish-Lithuanian Commonwealth as a whole, in the history of the Jews in these lands, in the history of Jewish mysticism, and in the history of Hasidism. The history of the Jews can now be integrated in a much more meaningful way with other vectors in the history of the Commonwealth. The universe of intellectual and spiritual discourse and political and social institutions in which the Besht participated is clearer.

Most significant, some of the archives of the town of Międzybóż, the place where the Besht was active for most of his career as a public personality, have survived and are available at the Czartoryski Library in Cracow. In addition to mentioning the Besht and some of his followers, these archives enable us to become acquainted with the town, its demography, its economic situation, its social structure, its Jewish community, and its problems. We can, in a way, meet the people with whom the Besht interacted, become aware of the contours and rhythms of the society in which he lived, and observe some of the situations and constraints he faced in life. We can attempt to place him in the community's constellation of institutions and relationships.

Context imparts meaning to details. A feature seen in isolation carries a signification different from one shown as part of a face. In studying history, our response to the question "Why?" often is to place a phenomenon in a broader context, to relate it to as many other phenomena as possible. By clarifying more aspects of the context of the Besht's life, we are able to interpret the older sources more intelligently. There are more facts to compare, more criteria for evaluation. It is easier to separate the probable from the fantastic. In some cases, traditional stories and partisan opinions can be challenged, confirmed, or supplemented. Details, formerly dismissed, now take on importance. Actions can be understood in a new light. Chronology may be approximated. There will be mysteries solved, others posed.[8]

The power of context as a substitute for extensive documentation is limited. It can be used to wring more information out of the sources, but it cannot create new sources. Whatever image of the Besht emerges from this study will be based on relatively sparse material and, in part, on methodological assumptions that can be defended but not proven beyond a reasonable doubt.

The alternative is to say nothing—a path guaranteed to avert criticism, but at a price. To give up the study of the Besht because of its problematic nature is to neglect sources with some obvious historical value, to abandon a problem of considerable historical importance, and to abdicate the field in favor of popularizers and ideologues whose Ba'al Shem Tovs will be much less connected to reality.

> One of the most peculiar traits of postmodern literature, or the literature of the period since the Second World War, is its emphasis upon the limits of literature, and indeed upon the apparent impossibility of there being a literature commensurate with the complexity of contemporary experience . . .

[However,] the contemporary biographer seems trapped in a nineteenth-century time-lapse in which the exigencies of "a serious job of good scholarship" have yet to be tempered by the postmodern cult of self-conscious failure. While innumerable novels, from Faulkner's *The Sound and the Fury* to Robbe-Grillet's *Le Voyeur,* exploit the absence of central pieces of information, and while such novels as Samuel Beckett's *Watt* exploit the use of multiple inconclusive explanations of the same event, the biographer appears reluctant to admit the absence of vital data or the inadequacy of overall analyses.[9]

The Ba'al Shem Tov provides an excellent opportunity to make the required admissions. With the shortcomings more obvious, though not necessarily different in kind, than is the case with other subjects, it is clear from the outset that there will be no continuous narrative and the relationship between the image and the original will require continual refinement long after this book is closed. This is no "definitive" work.

It is rather, after the discussion of context, an analysis of sources, with the conclusions offering glimpses into how the Besht's public career developed, what he did at some points in his life, how he was received, and what his connection was to the movement with which he has been associated in both popular and scholarly discourse. I hope that the more critical and more textual nature of this contribution will compensate for its modesty.

My fundamental argument with most previous writers is that they chose to concentrate on sources—legendary stories and sayings—that have the least likelihood of communicating information on the Besht and are the most susceptible to ideological interpretation. In contrast to these writers, I have deemphasized the stories about the Besht, using them primarily as a supplement to information gained in other ways. I have been even more circumspect in crediting the sayings.

As I point out in chapter 6, this approach has prevented me from contributing in more than a general fashion to the intellectual biography of the Ba'al Shem Tov. Others, with greater confidence in the stories and sayings and in the possibility of interpreting them accurately, have in the past, and continue at present, to explicate the Besht's Torah or way.[10] My focus is on the Besht's place in life rather than in theology.

I do not deny that my construction of the Besht's life and activity, limited as it is, contains projections of my own preconceived notions and predilections, although, in the nature of things, I am blind to them. Critics will likely identify them and succeed in connecting what I have written to my own biography and biases—those of a committed, observant

Jew, born in the United States, who chose together with his wife to settle in Israel and raise six children. My claim, however, is that I have subjected the sources to more rigorous criticism than has been done previously and have even discovered a few new ones, notably Polish sources that mention the Besht explicitly (see chap. 10). Also, I do try to keep faith with the canons of the interpretive community of academic, "moderately objectivist" historians to which I would like to think I belong. My hope is that these conditions will result in a strong connection between my limited description and the historical Ba'al Shem Tov.

PART I

Context

CHAPTER ONE

Ba'al Shem Tov

Scholarly biographical descriptions of Israel ben Eliezer contain a few points on which there is at least a consensus. Most writers agree that he lived from approximately 1700 to 1760 and was a person of humble origins who eventually merited the appellation Ba'al Shem Tov (the Besht), which translates as "Master of the Good Name" (the precise meaning of this title has been the subject of some discussion; see below).[1] The Besht had certain mystical powers and was known as a nonascetic, pneumatic-ecstatic who projected charismatic appeal. He involved himself in the problems of everyday life and communicated with people through folksy discussion and the telling of stories. He was in some sense the founder of the movement that became known as Hasidism.[2] Beyond these basic points, however, there is little agreement about most aspects of the Besht's biography.

Scholars dispute whether the Besht became prominent as a result of the spiritual devotion he personified and inspired or as a result of his healing and magical abilities. Some denied that he claimed or utilized magical or theurgic abilities, while others theorized that at some point he ceased to employ them. There were those who called him a vulgar ignoramus and those who styled him a profound and original religious figure comparable to Buddha, Jesus, or Spinoza. With regard to the details of his activity, there are many questions with multiple answers, and each implied answer has had its proponents.[3]

Did the Besht create a new movement, or redirect an existing movement, or have nothing to do with a movement? Did he establish institutions? Was his stance toward the rabbinic/communal establishment approving or disapproving, and did his position change over time? Were his followers marginal people, the "common people," second-class intelligentsia and clergy, or first-rank mystics and scholars? Was the Besht's public activity primarily religious, or did it focus on social and political issues as well? Did he inaugurate a new path in religious life or simply realize traditional ideals in a more successful way? Was he populist or elitist or some combination of the two? How much attention did he attract, and was there significant opposition to him in his lifetime? Did he try to emigrate to the Land of Israel? If he did so, did his failure to reach that destination have an effect on his public activities and doctrines? To what extent was he involved in a struggle against the Sabbateans and Frankists?[4]

My contention is that the confusion and contradiction concerning the Besht are largely a function of the exceedingly small number of sources available and the highly equivocal nature of many of those that exist. The corpus of Besht sources lends itself to a broad range of interpretation. Moreover, most writers paid scant attention to the context of the Besht's life and this allowed room for even freer interpretation. For example, the question of whether the Besht founded a movement depends to a large degree on whether a hasidic movement of some sort already existed. Understanding the nature of his relationship to the communal establishment would seem to be contingent on having an idea of the structure and functioning of that establishment. The process of determining which issues the Besht addressed would probably benefit from a knowledge of which issues were on the agenda of the community in which he lived. Moreover, details gleaned from information about the context might bear directly on the interpretation of sources that mention the Besht.

Consideration of some aspects of the context of the Besht's life, together with a viable characterization of the form and content of the sources that relate to him, can establish a perspective from which to identify and assess various images constructed by biographers of the Besht. It can also lay the foundations of a new, more authoritative construction of aspects of the Besht's life.

Chapters 6 through 10 present and assess key texts relating to the Besht. The rest of this chapter and the next four offer a construction of the context of his activities.

BA'AL SHEM

Despite the findings of academic researchers over the past two generations,[5] there still persists a certain amount of confusion in popular explanations of the title by which Israel ben Eliezer was known: Ba'al Shem Tov. In rabbinic literature and Jewish folklore, the term *shem tov* is usually employed in the sense of "a good reputation." There is, for example, the famous saying of the second-century Talmudic sage, Rabbi Simeon: "There are three crowns: the crown of Torah, the crown of the priesthood, and the crown of royalty, but the crown of a good name [*shem tov*] exceeds them all."[6] The word *ba'al* literally means master, often with the connotation of owner or possessor. Thus one common, popular rendering of Ba'al Shem Tov has been Man of a Good Reputation.[7]

This interpretation reflects a fundamental misunderstanding of the term and an ignorance of Jewish cultural history. Many men[8] in Jewish history were referred to interchangeably as *ba'al* (pl. *ba'alei*) *shem, ba'al (ha-)shemot* (*shemot* is the plural of *shem*) or *ba'al shem tov*. The "tov," or "good," is therefore not essential to the title. What is essential is the "shem," the name. What all *ba'alei shem* had in common was the ability to employ magical techniques for manipulating the name or names of God to achieve practical effects in everyday life. They were masters of *The* Name—God's name—and dealt in what was termed practical Kabbalah.[9]

Ba'alei shem share many of the characteristics of what Mircea Eliade dubbed "shaman," an ancient type of holy man appearing in various forms in many of the world's religions up until modern times. The shaman is a master of the techniques of ecstasy, whose soul, during his trances, passes from one cosmic region to another: ascending to the realm of the holy, descending to the netherworld, and communicating with the spirits. His ability to move beyond the world of physical experience makes him a specialist in matters of the human soul. He can see the soul, discerning when it is possessed by spirits or wanders away from its rightful place in the body. The shaman can liberate a possessed soul or chase an errant one and return it to its normal state. Such liberation is manifested in exorcism, while restoration of the soul is seen as curing of illness. Often the shaman serves as a psychopomp who conducts souls to the afterworld.[10]

As traveler through the geography of the mystical, the shaman mediates between God and humanity and challenges the dangers posed by the spirits. In recognition of his direct experience with the supernatural, the shaman is entrusted with magical defense on earth; in addition to curing disease and exorcising demons, he protects against sorcerers' spells, enemies' designs, and other calamities, points out thieves, controls the weather, and places the particular requirements of his society before God. Among his techniques, in addition to ecstatic trances and mystical ascents, are usually to be found the capacities to become invisible, to fly or cover long distances in a flash, and to foretell the future. He normally employs a special costume and instruments to effect communication with the world of the spirits. He can also combine his shamanistic qualities with other magical techniques and his role as shaman with other religious functions.[11]

Ba'alei shem, from ancient times through the seventeenth and eighteenth centuries, fit Eliade's typology in many respects.[12] They were ecstatic mystics whose main technique in communicating with the supernatural was the magical employment of the names of God, particularly as written in inscriptions placed in amulets. In his book-length, autobiographical ethical will written about 1760, the Besht's contemporary, Pinhas Katznellenbogen (1691–1767?), referred to such ba'alei shem and their use of God's names and other techniques to help people cope with reality. Katznellenbogen's description of one such ba'al shem, Joseph from Jerusalem, whom he met in 1720, echoes significant aspects of Eliade's characterization of shamans.

> He was expert in the holy names, knew how to foreshorten distance,[13] and was expert in chiromancy and metoposcopy.[14] . . . He told me about wondrous acts by which, having had the opportunity to perform them with the help of God, he did something helpful. He said that I would encounter a worthy match, the daughter of great people, and through her I would become great, with the help of God, and our material circumstances would be ample—all of this he saw via metoposcopy.[15]

Another ba'al shem who lived at the turn of the eighteenth century was Rabbi Hirsh Frankel (1662–1740), Landesrabbiner of Ansbach as of 1709. In 1713 he was sentenced to life imprisonment for blaspheming the Christian religion and for practicing "Kabbalistic arts."[16] An official report on the investigation into his case indicates that through adjurations and written incantations, Rabbi Frankel employed twenty-seven different Kabbalistic skills. These included such things as communicating with Satan, demons, and the dead, coercing people to reveal secrets, forcing robbers to return stolen goods, freeing prisoners, killing or foiling enemies by means of curses or incantations, facilitating sexual intercourse for sexually dysfunctional couples, inducing fertility and birth, extinguishing fires, immobilizing individuals, making government officials do his bidding, and transferring money magically from one person to another. Among his Kabbalistic techniques were the classic shamanistic capabilities of becoming invisible and foreshortening distance.[17]

Probably the most famous practical Kabbalist of his time was Rabbi Jonathan Eybeschuetz (1690–1764), whose disciples reportedly publicized his shamanistic talents. They claimed that he could perform miracles, revive the dead, know the intentions of the wicked, and punish—even kill—them by his word. He could ensure that any barren woman would give birth, reveal whose soul was reincarnated in whose body, and read people's sins on their foreheads. In sum,

> according to them he had the power to command in heaven and on earth and everything which he decreed would be quickly done and fulfilled. . . . As a result he gained a reputation as a divine man throughout the world, even in every village and settlement in Ashkenaz and Poland. The [German Jewish] villagers could tell of Eybeschuetz's novel miracles and wonders, and so it was in the land of Poland.[18]

While many more seventeenth- and eighteenth-century ba'alei shem are reported,[19] these examples adequately convey a sense of the range of ba'alei shem activities among the Ashkenazic Jews of central and eastern Europe in the generation of the Besht. As masters of God's names they communicated with the supernatural realm and induced theurgic effects. Their techniques included written incantations, exorcism, chiromancy, metoposcopy, invisibility, distance vision, distance foreshortening, and herbal medicine. Their mission was to protect people from adversity, whether stemming from human beings, natural forces, or supernatural entities. They also lent support in the normal pursuit of health, material sustenance, and success in marriage and procreation. "Magical security" is a felicitous description of their general function in Jewish society. While ba'alei shem may have acquired good reputations, this had nothing to do with the title ba'al shem. ⟵

Another common misunderstanding, challenged by Gershom Scholem, is to try to distinguish between Israel Besht and other ba'alei shem by insisting that he differed from them: while most were called ba'al shem (Master of the Name), he was called "Ba'al Shem *Tov*," understood as "*Good* Master of the Name." Such an interpretation implies that while other ba'alei shem were common sorcerers who worked their magic—

white or black—arbitrarily, the Besht was a cut above them and used his powers only in the service of good and spirituality.[20]

This reading of the title is untenable for several reasons. Eliade contrasted shamans with sorcerers, noting that sorcerers are often adversaries of shamans and that, as opposed to sorcerers, shamans always play a positive role in society.[21] The foregoing summary of ba'al shem activities demonstrates this to be true of these Jewish shaman types as well. They were dedicated to serving people's legitimate needs, not to making mischief. Even Rabbi Frankel's accusers noted that he never used his Kabbalistic powers to do harm.[22] Moreover, Scholem, Mendel Piekarz, and Gedaliah Nigal all proved that the terms "ba'al shem" and "ba'al shem tov" are interchangeable and the Besht was not the only, or even the first, ba'al shem *tov*.[23]

The Besht himself was sometimes referred to as "Ba'al Shem" only. Even in the three references he made to his title in signatures to his letters, twice he signed himself "Besht" and once as Besh (the acronym for Ba'al Shem).[24] The correct rendering of Ba'al Shem or Ba'al Shem Tov, then, is "Master of the (Good, Divine) Name," because no name represents goodness more than God's.

The misinterpretations of the term "Besht" might seem to be unworthy of mention because they are so patently mistaken. They are significant, however, as indicators of regnant popular perceptions of the Besht and as crude reflections of more sophisticated scholarly attempts to play down, explain away, or even deny the Besht's being a ba'al shem. It should be noted at the outset, however, that to deny that the title "Besht" implies anything other than the fact that Israel ben Eliezer was a theurgic ba'al shem does violence to the meaning of the term during his lifetime. Any uncoupling of the Besht and his title bears a heavy burden of proof that to date has not been met.

Moreover, all evidence does indicate that the Ba'al Shem Tov was indeed a ba'al shem in the manipulative, theurgic sense of the term. The stories in *Shivhei Ha-Besht* portray him as using practical Kabbalah to perform quasi-miracles, exorcisms, and other magical acts in the spirit of protection and service discussed above. The descriptions of the Besht by himself and by his contemporaries, Jews and Christians, refer to him as being a Kabbalist and healer—the main attributes of a theurgic ba'al shem.[25]

Other interpretations of the significance of the title "Besht" remove Israel ben Eliezer from the eighteenth-century context and seem to be attempts to make the image of the Besht conform to the values of the writers. They represent an excellent example of shaping the image of the Besht to reflect current ideology, whether it be antispiritualism, the idealization of rationalism, or the enthronement of early Hasidism as a culturally "modern" movement.

BA'ALEI SHEM AND JEWISH SOCIETY

A prevalent assumption about the status of ba'alei shem in eighteenth-century Jewish society has been a key component in at least two of the important historiographical images of the Besht that have developed. The assumption is that ba'alei shem had low status. They were supposedly disparaged as superficial mystics, cheap magicians, and quack doctors. Members of the rabbinic elite and communal oligarchy dismissed them, and they found their constituency among the superstitious, uneducated poor.[26]

This understanding of the position of ba'alei shem was one basis for the claim, alluded to above, that the Besht was not merely a ba'al shem. If he were, how could he have reached prominence? Rather, the story of his career is in large part the story of his demonstrating that he was more than a ba'al shem. Initial dismissal on the part of the establishment gave way to respect and devotion as he proved to his prestigious adversaries that he possessed profound knowledge and that his ba'al shemism was only a way to make a living or a means of hiding his true holy identity.[27]

Another Ba'al Shem Tov image nourished by the low-status ba'al shem assumption is the idea that the Besht was a populist rebel. The rabbinic-aristocratic establishment was insensitive to the impoverished masses and ran the community according to its own interests. The man who stood up to them and galvanized opposition to the elite was a man of the people. His spirituality was not the arid, irrelevant Talmudic casuistry of the rabbis but the vital, popular mysticism that led to direct involvement in the lives of the masses. As a member of the disenfranchised majority, he could represent their interests and create an alternative to the corrupt elite.[28]

The question of the social status of ba'alei shem is significant, then, for reaching an understanding of the Besht's position in society and the nature of his public activity. If ba'alei shem were not scorned by normative, or even elite, society, it becomes much more difficult to sustain an image of the Besht as only partially a ba'al shem or as a populist rebel.

The idea that ba'alei shem were held in low esteem is based primarily on the stories in the hagiographic collection *Shivhei Ha-Besht* (discussed in detail in chapter 9). One motif in these stories is how prominent people refused to believe in the Besht until he demonstrated to them his superior mystical knowledge. Most telling in this connection is the famous episode depicting the Besht's rise to leadership in the town where he spent the bulk of his public career, Międzybóż.

> A story: When the Besht came to the community of Międzybóż, he was not important in the eyes of the hasidim, that is, R. Zev Kutzes and R. David Purkes,[29] because of the name which people called him, "Besht." This name is not fitting for a *zaddik*.[30]

The story then tells how one of the students of the skeptical "hasidim" became ill and wanted to send for the Besht to treat him. His teachers refused until his situation became desperate. When the Besht met with the student, he informed him that he was to die. He also assured the fellow that despite his failure to correct a sin committed during his life, he would enter paradise with the Besht as his guide.[31] In heaven the now-deceased student met up with the Besht in a palace where the Besht was teaching Torah. The Besht was raising questions that the assembled Yeshiva students could not answer, and he had to provide the answers himself.

A dream appearance of the paradise-inhabiting student provided the two "hasidim" with proof of the Besht's knowledge of both the ways of heaven and the complexities of Torah. And so, "From that day on they followed the Besht."

This story has been interpreted to imply that to gain acceptance by respected members of society—as exemplified by the "hasidim" (a term to be examined in the next chapter)—the Besht had to demonstrate that he was not just a ba'al shem but also a psychopomp and Torah scholar. The story might mean that the title Ba'al Shem Tov aroused derision, not respect, among those who were keepers of the norms of society and tradition. A mere ba'al shem apparently could not be "important."

The first to question the veracity of this low-status image of ba'alei shem was Piekarz. He brought two examples of prominent rabbinic figures, both contemporaries of the Besht. One, Rabbi Abraham Abish, occupier of prestigious rabbinic posts in Lublin and later Frankfurt, dealt in practical Kabbalah and even wrote a guide to the use of incantations and charms for healing purposes. The second, Joel Halpern of Zamość, explicitly dubbed "Ba'al Shem," was a respected scholar and authority of his time, as evidenced by the appearance of his endorsements alongside those of other honored rabbis in three books of the period.[32]

Nigal described five men—Naftali Katz of Poznań, Ephraim Reisher, Samuel Essingen, Jonathan Eybeschuetz, and Hirsh Frankel—ranging from as far east as Ostrog in Ukraine to as far west as Amsterdam, who held rabbinical positions in respectable communities and were at the same time practical Kabbalists who manipulated names. Two of them, Essingen and Reisher, were specifically called "Ba'al Shem" and "Ba'al Shem Tov," respectively.[33]

Moreover, the ba'al shemism of these men was not covert or incidental to their "regular" rabbinic activity. These men were praised by other rabbis and their own descendants for their ba'al shem powers, and at least two of them—Essingen and Eybeschuetz—published accounts of their Kabbalistic exploits, which appear to be aimed at spreading their reputations and widening their followings. For them, being a ba'al shem was a virtue that enhanced their standing.[34]

This implies that among the rabbinic elite of the Ashkenazic communities from Ukraine to western Europe, the title "Ba'al Shem" did not necessarily denote that the bearer was on the margins of spiritual life. It can no longer be disputed that at least some ba'alei shem were very much a part of normative communal existence and even attained positions of spiritual leadership.[35]

The possibly high status, as well as the apparently increasing number, of ba'alei shem at the turn of the eighteenth century may be connected to recent discoveries about the spread of Kabbalah. In the late seventeenth and early eighteenth century, popular, practical Kabbalah was making inroads in the consciousness of Ashkenazic, particularly Polish, Jewry. Zev Gries has pointed out that in the period following the failure of the messianic movement of Shabbetai Zvi, there was a large increase in the number of popular, Kabbalah-based books of moral conduct.[36]

This was a genre of ethical literature that epitomized Kabbalistic theology and codified Kabbalistic ritual and theurgy for the masses. These cheap books—which allowed for self-study—found their way into many homes. Prayer services and ritual behavior at central events in the life cycle—birth, circumcision, marriage, illness, death, and burial—were more and more governed by the dictates of Kabbalah, which found expression in these tracts. In addition, the art in many synagogues of the time was apparently rooted in popular, conventional, mystical knowledge as expressed in graphic mythological allusions.[37]

These books and pictures brought many to the conclusion that they could at least stand at the threshold of holiness. Even the illiterate could see how important Kabbalah was and could learn some of its principles through ritual observance, listening to popular sermons, colloquial conversation, and viewing the decoration in the synagogue. The discussion and practice of popular Kabbalah informed daily discourse in Jewish eastern Europe of the early eighteenth century, perhaps analogously to the way in which the commonplace tenets of psychology are ever-present in contemporary popular, intellectual culture.

Popular Kabbalistic literature both exemplified and promoted the conviction that, of all areas of Jewish study and observance, it was Kabbalah that held the deep secrets and true meaning of the Torah and pointed the way to Redemption. While not all rabbis were Kabbalistic adepts, they were generally admirers of the masters of Kabbalah and believers in its theurgic efficacy.[38] Common people could assure themselves that by following Kabbalistic ritual they were doing the proper thing.

If popular, practical Kabbalah was assuming such a central role in people's lives, then it is not surprising that there was a respectable place in society for the experts in this Kabbalah, whether formally called ba'alei shem or merely known as Kabbalistic adepts. They were among the chief promoters of the adoption of Kabbalistic ritual.[39] For example, in a manuscript that is now lost, the eighteenth-century wine merchant Ber of Bolechow related how a spiritual revolution took place in his study hall in the town of Tysmienica in the late 1730s.[40] Prompted by their reading of the Kabbalistic book, *Hemdat Yamim*,[41] and guided by "*ba'alei ha-shemot*," the young married men who devoted themselves to full-time Torah study began reading Kabbalistic works and observing Kabbalistic rituals, especially ascetic ones: fasting, flinging themselves on the ground, hitting their chests with stones, and so on.

This development seems to parallel what was happening in Fürth more than thirty-five years earlier. Pinhas Katznellenbogen described the visit of the crypto-Sabbatean Abraham Rovigo in 1701:[42] "All of the hasidim and ascetics from among the scholars went to him to draw from his well, a well of living water, of the wisdom of the Kabbalah; it was his glory. My father of blessed memory also became his disciple." Rovigo was renowned as one of the outstanding Kabbalists of his day, and he exercised a profound effect on the Jewish scholarly elite of Fürth. By the early eighteenth century, then, in Fürth—as later in Tysmienica, Brody, and many other places—the scholarly class included people who combined Torah study with Kabbalistic study and practice.[43] They received the Kabbalist, Rovigo, with great enthusiasm.

Even more interesting, in the context of the question of the role of

eighteenth-century ba'alei shem in Jewish society, is what Katznellenbogen had to say about Rovigo's assistant, Mordecai Ashkenazi.

> And his disciple who served him was called our teacher and rabbi Mordecai
> from Lwów. He so cleaved to the teaching and the faith of his master that he
> was privileged to have a maggid revealed to him in the form of his master,
> the perfect sage, Abraham Rovigo. [The maggid] learned with him the wis-
> dom of Kabbalah and revealed secrets to him until he wrote a book on sev-
> eral of the passages of the Zohar and it was called, *Eshel Abraham*, after his
> master. My father, the hasid, revealed all of this to me, for I knew that
> *R. Mordecai was not a scholar, expert in the study of the Talmud;* but from
> heaven he was rewarded because he served the great sage of the generation,
> the pillar of the world, our master and teacher Rabbi Abraham of blessed
> memory. From my youth I knew [Mordecai] whose face was like an angel of
> God, who had a beard, and was very old. I went to receive his blessing every
> Sabbath.[44] (Emphasis added.)

Katznellenbogen did not call Mordecai a ba'al shem, but his description of him indicates that he was at least a similar type of Kabbalistic
adept. Like many ba'alei shem, including, apparently, the Besht, Mordecai was not a Talmudic or even a Kabbalah scholar. Rovigo wrote that
until they met in 1695, Mordecai could not even read the Zohar.[45] Even
the pubescent Katznellenbogen was aware of Mordecai's scholarly limitations. Rather, Mordecai learned the "secrets" of Kabbalah from a representative of the spiritual realm[46]—not from Abraham Rovigo but from
an otherworldly being in his form. What made Mordecai a figure of ven-
eration who gave out blessings every Sabbath was not his mediocre intellectual, Torah study achievements but his close contact with the great
Rovigo, his communication with the divine realm, and his inspiring appearance. Like the ba'alei shem referred to by Ber of Bolechow, Mordecai promoted Kabbalistic study (his commentary on the Zohar) and
Kabbalistic ritual (he was evidently involved in Katznellenbogen's search
for a verse that began and ended with the letters of his name, to be recited during prayer as a common Kabbalistic ritual). He serves as an indication that there was a respectable place in eighteenth-century Ashkenazic society for nonrabbinic, spiritualist figures. Such men, regarded as
possessing both a special relationship with the divine and Kabbalistic
knowledge not available simply by virtue of rabbinic studies, could exercise a powerful spiritual influence over Talmudists and plebeians alike.

In a society awash in the ethos of Kabbalah, ba'alei shem were needed
not only to teach Kabbalistic doctrine and the proper observance of rit-

ual but also to apply their expertise where lay people were inadequate. If Kabbalah held the secrets, it was ba'alei shem who held the key to at least the practical, applied part of Kabbalah. This was the part that could smooth the path through the exigencies of life while awaiting collective Redemption. In this, too, the ba'al shem was useful—and not only to the poor or the ignorant. Katznellenbogen, a member of one of the most prominent Ashkenazic rabbinic families,[47] and himself a communal rabbi, made a number of references to ba'alei shem and his encounters with them.[48]

Joseph of Jerusalem was one ba'al shem from whom Rabbi Katznellenbogen learned. Another was one of the most famous ba'alei shem of the early eighteenth century, Benjamin Beinish Ha-Kohen of Krotoshin.[49] Katznellenbogen was particularly close to him. His description of one of Beinish's amulet ceremonies illustrates the kind of prescriptions ba'alei shem gave to people to help them with their problems and indicates the mind-set that facilitated belief in the efficaciousness of ba'alei shem.

> Then the Kabbalist, the aforementioned, our Teacher and Rabbi, Beinish of blessed memory[50] came to me and I requested from him that he give me something as a charm for a woman having difficulty in childbirth, for I had done several of the things mentioned in his *Amtahat Binyamin* [Beinish's book] and none helped. So he gave me two things; one, names bound up in a white linen case, approximately five thumbs wide and seven fingers long. He wrote in his own handwriting on one side "inside," to say that that side should be placed inwards, towards the birthing woman's navel. On the other side he wrote "outside," as a sign that it should face outwards. At the two ends of the binding he himself made two linen loops so as to put a linen cord through them as ties. This binding with the names is to be placed on the woman's navel and tightened with the cords by pulling them back and tying them there in order that the name binder be tied tightly to her body so that it doesn't slip and fall from her belly. One must be very careful not to place the name binder too early; only when the infant is ready to come out. The midwife who knows how to determine the time will know precisely when it is necessary.
>
> One must also be very careful that the woman herself or the women standing there with her remove the binder immediately as the child comes out since the woman herself is occupied with her pains and the midwife is busy with taking the child out, so the main responsibility falls on the women standing there with her that they be very, very careful to remove the name binder at the time when the child begins to come out, for there is a danger, God forbid, that the woman's intestines will also come out after the child. Once this actually happened; the woman's intestines came out and she died, God save us. So this must be watched very well and there is a great warning to remove the binder in time and then the woman and child will be safe and sound with help of God of awesome praise.[51]

Pinhas Katznellenbogen, who grew up in a rabbinic home, received an intensive, advanced rabbinic education, and served as rabbi of several communities,[52] reported his resort to the ba'al shem with a complete lack of self-consciousness or defensiveness.[53] There was nothing amiss in a bona fide rabbi employing the services of a bona fide ba'al shem.[54] The efficacy of the practical Kabbalah was so taken for granted even by this member of the rabbinic elite that for Katznellenbogen the failure of published remedies to bring relief could only mean that a special, custom-made amulet was required. He had only respect for the ba'alei shem he encountered and never put them to any embarrassing tests.[55]

That there is strong evidence to indicate that ba'alei shem could enjoy high status and be spiritually influential should not lead to the conclusion that all did so. As Piekarz put it, "The ba'alei shem's trade was fertile ground for the activities of imposters and scoundrels, and it is no wonder that they also engendered criticism and ridicule . . . but the reality was, as usual, complex."[56] This complex reality includes different sorts of criticism leveled at ba'alei shem.

One critique—call it rational rejection—argued that ba'al shemism was nothing more than magic and therefore contrary to the idea of an omnipotent God and illegitimate as part of Jewish religion. It should be rejected, even punished, out of hand. As might be expected, this critique was common in periods of rationalism such as the time of Maimonides or in the late eighteenth century and seems to have influenced even Hasidic circles. Thus we shall see in the next chapter that the founder of the Habad Hasidic group distanced himself from practical Kabbalistic practices, claiming not to have read anything about them, not to have met anyone who dealt in them, and not to have any knowledge of the Besht employing them.[57] An antipractical Kabbalah attitude is shared by most academic scholars and is largely responsible for their efforts to minimize the Besht's ba'al shemism. Interestingly, all of the stories that portray the Besht as something other than a full-fledged ba'al shem are found in sources dating from at least a generation after his death, that is, from the late eighteenth century or later.[58]

A second critique of ba'alei shem entailed the rejection of the practitioners but not the art. There were those in the eighteenth century who, in principle, believed in practical Kabbalah but considered many ba'alei shem to be sorcerers or charlatans. Jacob Emden, for example, practiced practical Kabbalah, using a gold ring with holy names inscribed on it to cure a sick girl.[59] Yet this did not prevent him from criticizing ba'alei shem.

Teetering between two lies are the miracles of the ba'alei shemot who are in the land; false magicians and seers of mendacity; dross covering a shard. They hear but do not speak in praise of the world of perfection, but rather of the world of chaos. Their entire thought is to return the world to the state of chaos. Yet they want to lay hold of the name like the name of the great ones, the people of reputation, the people of distinction. . . . I have seen wicked heretics come and from out of a holy place (the wisdom of Kabbalah) change the word of the living God to heresy.[60]

Emden was of the opinion that prominent ba'alei shem were the biggest supporters of his nemesis, Jonathan Eybeschuetz.[61] He charged that the ba'alei shem affirmed the non-Sabbatean nature of Eybeschuetz's amulets, as a quid pro quo for Eybeschuetz encouraging people to believe in the ba'alei shem, consult them, and make them wealthy.[62] This may have had something to do with Emden's antipathy toward many of the ba'alei shem of his day because of their sympathy for his enemy. However, he was also aware that some of them failed to be effective. He dwelled particularly on the failures of Samuel Essingen, who apparently caused the death of one of his patients and impoverished others who continued in their desperately persistent fashion to throw good money after bad believing Essingen's promises that he would eventually find the right formula to cure them.[63]

A third criticism is found in the doctrine of the Ari and continues in hasidic tradition. This is the idea that magical manipulation of names is an ancillary mystical activity concerned with minor ontological phenomena. It distracts from the essential objective of mysticism, which is to commune with the Divine.[64]

A fourth type of anti-ba'al shem critique was apparently the most common in the early eighteenth century.[65] This was not actually a criticism per se but rather a caveat: dealing in names can be a dangerous business; perhaps one should stay away from it. This attitude lay behind the ambivalence toward the manipulation of divine names in Jewish tradition from at least the Middle Ages.[66]

This ambivalence resonated in Katznellenbogen's family. In his will, Katznellenbogen's paternal grandfather, Saul, had forbidden his children to use names for mystical purposes. Pinhas appreciated the reason why: "I also know *ba'alei shem* today who would deal in names in these times; and I know that virtually all of them did not end up well. Some hurt themselves, some shortened their lives, some failed to have children."[67] Contact with the Divine, while helpful to others, can be dangerous to the practitioner. One can be easily consumed in the fire of holiness.

Yet while the use of names might be dangerous, and therefore unadvisable, Katznellenbogen still felt that it was important to be familiar with the names and their powers, in order—as he cited in the name of Menahem Azariah da Fano—"to know the greatness of God and to be destined for the world to come . . . but not in order to do anything." According to Katznellenbogen, this was the policy of his own father, Moses, who was adept at the names but not prepared to employ them. He did make an exception of two name-inscribed rings that he made according to the instructions of the famous Rabbi Zvi Hirsh Kaidanover. One of these rings was intended to be worn as a protective pendant by a child; the other was for adults, to avoid nocturnal emissions.[68]

Pinhas Katznellenbogen himself apparently decided that the safest and most efficient path was to consult professional ba'alei shem such as Joseph of Jerusalem and Benjamin Beinish,[69] although he, too, seems to have made the occasional exception, as when he attempted to apply, unsuccessfully, the birth techniques in Beinish's book and concocted a magical home remedy for his sick daughter, who had actually requested a consultation with doctors in Vienna.[70]

To at least three generations of the Katznellenbogen family—grandfather Saul, father Moses, and son Pinhas—the issue of holy name manipulation and practical Kabbalah was a central one. Whether or not they actually practiced this art, they were fascinated by it and surrounded by its practitioners. It is a sign of the growing popularity of practical Kabbalah that each generation of this prominent family, from the late seventeenth century through the early eighteenth century, felt it necessary to set forth a position with regard to the proper place of practical Kabbalah. It also seems that as time went on, in the spirit of the times, the members of the family were drawn progressively toward mystical and magical practices, whether implemented by themselves or through the medium of ba'alei shem. The grandfather was aware, but he shied away. The son was informed and dabbled. The grandson incorporated Kabbalistic considerations and practices into his life on a routine basis. In 1758, a member of the fourth generation, Pinhas's daughter, Rachel, seems to have been influenced by a new trend when she requested a consultation with a specialist doctor in Vienna.[71]

One can well imagine that if the Besht had come to the town where Pinhas Katznellenbogen was rabbi, or to any of the many towns in Poland-Lithuania and the lands of Ashkenaz where the Kabbalistic ethos was prevalent, he would have been received similarly to Mordecai Ashkenazi: as a holy man with special qualities from whom people could learn the secrets of Kabbalah, receive instruction in ritual, and benefit from his blessings. This does not mean that he would have been universally accepted or that his techniques would have been regarded by all as efficacious. People like the hasidic skeptics in the *Shivhei Ha-Besht* story may indeed have had reservations about his use of the divine name. Their doubts, however, do not mean that he was held in general derision. He may not have been "important in the eyes of the hasidim," but in such a community the title Besht would certainly have qualified him as an important man, whom even the doubters would have to contend with (as they do in the story) and not dismiss out of hand. There were many righteous people who were also ba'alei shem. People from all walks of life— artisans, merchants, rabbis, and even some hasidim—availed themselves of the services of ba'alei shem. There is no basis for assuming that Międzybóż was less hospitable to such Kabbalists than other Ashkenazic Jewish communities, even if some important members of the community entertained reservations. In the first half of the eighteenth century, the efficacy of ba'alei shem may have been a controversial subject; but conventional wisdom had not yet resolved the issue. Their claim to participate in the arena of holiness had to be taken seriously, even if rejected by some.[72]

Shivhei Ha-Besht was compiled in the late eighteenth century, when attitudes, generally, toward practical Kabbalah were changing. Its presentation of the story about the doubting hasidim in such a way as to indicate that ba'alei shem were generally marginal, without indicating the great popularity and acceptance they often enjoyed, may reflect a later sensibility.

CHAPTER TWO

Hasidism before Hasidism

The story in *Shivhei Ha-Besht* about the two hasidim who were skeptical about the Besht may not accurately reflect early eighteenth-century attitudes toward ba'alei shem. It does raise a logical question: If the Ba'al Shem Tov was the founder of Hasidism, how is it that this story dubs as "hasidim" people who were in Międzybóż before him and who were unwilling to accept him? Were there hasidim before Hasidism?[1]

The answer to this question is "Yes." The once dominant, and still popular, view is that the Hasidic movement arose de novo, in contrast and opposed to normative rabbinic Judaism as it was believed and practiced in eighteenth-century Poland. Scholars specializing in the field of Hasidism have abandoned this notion.[2]

The word *hasid* in Hebrew has a long history. Its root, *hesed,* is usually translated as "love" or "lovingkindness"; hence a hasid can be someone who practices lovingkindness or compassion. In the Book of Jeremiah (3:12), God Himself is described as "hasid" in this sense of being compassionate. In the Bible, human beings who love God and are loved by Him are also referred to as "hasid." Such love is expressed by fulfilling the obligations God has imposed. Therefore, "hasid" often appears in parallel with the word *zaddik,* a righteous person. A person who is righteous is particularly close to God; thus another connotation of the word became someone who has a special relationship to God. By the rabbinic period, "hasid" came to denote a person who was especially strict and careful in the performance of religious obligations: a pious person.[3]

In addition to these generic meanings, "hasid" also has acquired significance as a technical term through the course of Jewish history. Prior to the Hasmonean Revolt against Seleucid rule in the Land of Israel in the second century B.C.E., those people who first organized resistance to Hellenization were referred to as Hasidim.[4] In Germany of the late twelfth century, an ascetic, ethical, mystic group that became institutionalized and wielded considerable influence, both in its time and through its spiritual legacy, was called "Hasidei Ashkenaz" (lit. the Pious of Germany). Their leader was Rabbi Judah Hasid.[5]

In late sixteenth-century Safed in the Land of Israel, groups of mystics called "holy associations" flourished. These groups focused on mysticism as propounded by Moses Cordovero (1562–1625) or Isaac Luria (1534–1572), referred to by the acronym Ari (Lion). They aimed to make their hearts dwelling places for the Shekhina (God's presence). To this end they were supposed to keep their thoughts continually on Torah and holiness. They would meet with fellow adepts every day to discuss matters mystical and spiritual and on Fridays to review the activities of the preceding week. They visited the graves of famous rabbis together, confessed their sins before meals and on going to sleep at night, and rebuked each other for wrongdoings. They were extremely careful about ethical matters and stayed away from all luxuries. They spoke in Hebrew among themselves as well as to other people on the Sabbath.[6]

In a series of letters that were widely circulated in Ashkenazic Europe, a Moravian Jew, Solomon Shlumel of Dresnitz, who came to Safed in 1602, wrote descriptions of the city and its mystics, representing them as ideal types to be emulated. Solomon told, for example, how on Tuesdays the mystical adepts rose four hours before dawn to study and meditate. On Thursdays, after regular morning prayers, these hasidim would gather in one synagogue and lament the destruction of the Temple and the exile of the Shekhina, along with the exile of the people of Israel. "And all of them prayed the entire service with great weeping and a broken heart. . . . Then two men of the Yeshivot of the great Hasidim . . . would begin to pray with awe and fear and great reverence and tears would stream from their eyes as if from two fountains of water." On the Sabbath these men recited special psalms and an original poem welcoming the mystically imagined Sabbath bride. They also practiced mystically meaningful Sabbath rituals such as immersion in a ritual bath, wearing white, smelling spices, and displaying twelve loaves of bread.[7]

In general, members of these holy associations, the hasidim, were committed to a certain ethical-spiritual way of life that included many ascetic and mystical practices, group rituals, and study obligations, far beyond those required of the regular Jew. These were elitist groups who constituted the spiritual vanguard of the Jewish people. Such holy associations were one of several varieties of mystic conventicles that existed in Jewish—and Christian and Muslim—communities in many periods and places.[8]

In the Ashkenazic Jewish communities of Germany and Poland, the seventeenth century marked a renewed commitment to the penitential ideals and practices of the Hasidei Ashkenaz. While these precepts and rituals had never lost their moral force, they were now adopted by more people as a way of life, reinforced by ideas appropriated from Sephardic sources and by the influence of Lurianic Kabbalah, with its emphasis on asceticism.[9] Those who combined devotion to mysticism and ascetic practices were often found attached to two types of associations that served as forums for study and mystical fellowship, the *bet midrash* and the *kloyz*.

The bet midrash and the kloyz were basically institutions for advanced Torah study by people who were no longer students but independent scholars. The fundamental difference between them was that the bet midrash was supported by communal funds and was a public forum, while the kloyz was typically founded as an independent, private academy with an endowment from a wealthy individual.[10] While both institutions were established primarily as places of Torah study, in practice many of the people who joined them were—in addition to being Torah scholars—hasidim. By the second half of the seventeenth century in Poland, this term denoted those who were mystical adepts, being both scholars of Kabbalah and practitioners of Kabbalistic, particularly ascetic, ritual customs. In at least some *batei midrash* and *kloyzim,* the leading figures were charismatic hasidim such as Hayyim Zanzer and Moses Ostrer in Brody and Moses of Kutów. These figures were accorded respect and status, in addition to their stipends, by the larger community. Alongside regular Torah study, batei midrash and kloyzim dominated by hasidim served as places for mystical study, prayer and contemplation, fellowship, and intensive Kabbalistic ritual practice.[11]

In this connection, Pinhas Katznellenbogen's will is helpful. In it there is a concise description of a hasid, Pinhas's uncle, Sa'adia Isaiah.

> He was a great hasid. Veritably, his mouth did not cease from study day and night. He would observe fasts. At the time when I was there I knew that he fasted before Rosh Ha-Shana from Sabbath to Sabbath and on Monday night he was very weak and could not sleep and I remained awake with him all that

night. Even though he was very weak and suffering greatly from his fast, still
he did not stop studying. How great was the degree of hasidism and asceticism that he practiced! One thing which I know is that he would wait twenty-
four hours between eating meat and milk or the opposite.[12]

This hasid was also evidently a believer in practical Kabbalah. Katznellenbogen described how his hasid uncle once cut open a plum and found
a worm. He took this to be an omen that he had probably already eaten
plums that year and had made the requisite blessing on eating a fruit for
the first time each season. The worm was a signal to him not to pro-
nounce the blessing unnecessarily. Because of this doubt, he then refrained from eating plums. In that way he avoided the dilemma of either
pronouncing an unnecessary blessing or failing to say one that was required.

In his autobiography, in part intended to demonstrate the silliness of
traditional Jews and the traditional way of life, Solomon Maimon
(1754–1800) gave a vivid description of some extreme practitioners of
hasidic asceticism.

> Simon of Lubtsch had undergone the severest exercises of penance. He had
> already carried out the *Teshuvat Ha-Kana,* which consists in fasting daily for
> six years, and avoiding the use of anything that derives from a living being
> (meat, milk, honey, and the like) for the evening meal. He had also practiced
> *Galut,* that is, a continuous wandering, in which the penitent is not allowed
> to remain two days in the same place. In addition he had worn a hair shirt
> next to his body. But he felt that he would not satisfy his conscience unless
> he further observed the *Teshuvat Ha-Mishkal,* which requires a particular
> form of penance proportioned to every sin.[13] But as he found by calculation
> that the number of his sins was too great to be atoned for in this way, he took
> it into his head to starve himself to death [and succeeded].
> [. . .]
> Yossel of Kleck proposed nothing less than to hasten the advent of the Mes-
> siah. To this end he performed strict penance, fasted, rolled himself in the
> snow, undertook night watches and similar austerities. By pursuits of this sort
> he believed he could accomplish the overthrow of the legion of evil spirits who
> kept guard on the Messiah and obstructed his coming. To these exercises he
> added many Kabbalistic fooleries[14]—fumigations, conjurations and similar
> practices—till at length he lost his wits and believed that he really saw spir-
> its and called each of them by name.[15]

As was the case with Katznellenbogen's uncle, Maimon indicated a link
between hasidic asceticism and Kabbalah. For Yossel of Kleck, his ascetic
observances were to have a direct effect on the world of the spirits. The
Kabbalistic rituals he performed were not only, or even primarily, to induce repentance in himself; rather, these rituals had a theurgic intent.

These hasidim were elitist and separatist. They often conducted their own prayer services apart from the community synagogue, held themselves to a stricter standard of kashrut (dietary laws), so that they would not eat the meat normally sold by the community butchers, and restricted access to their group.[16] Yet in eighteenth-century Ashkenaz and Poland, the number of hasidim and the groups that gravitated toward conventicles was growing. Paradoxically, perhaps, their devotion to a strict spiritual regimen gained them material support as well as prestige in the Jewish communities in which they were located. They could exercise a significant influence on the community in general. Scholem interpreted reports about apparently unlearned people who dabbled in Kabbalah and ethical literature and prayed with special devotion (devekut) in an ecstatic, uncontrolled manner (including crying, rejoicing, singing, and movements) as evidence for the popularization of certain hasidic practices around the second quarter of the eighteenth century.[17]

The social influence of the hasidim derived from the strictness of their position. By demanding more nearly perfect adherence to the generally accepted societal norm of fulfillment of the law, which was conventionally regarded as the expression of God's will, they were hard to attack. They did not, however, bear responsibility for the implementation or consequences of their demands; that belonged to the official leadership. In the absence of responsibility, they had little incentive to compromise on what any member of their community would presumably admit, if pressed, was the right code of behavior.

A good example of hasidic prestige and influence in communal religious affairs was the predicament faced by Pinhas Katznellenbogen, about 1722, when he was the rabbi in Leipnik.[18] In this community the rabbi had an assistant (moreh zedek) who handled minor questions of ritual law (observance of kashrut, Sabbath, prayer rituals, etc.) whom Pinhas considered to be "prodigious in hasidism and strict with himself" in matters of religious observance. He coveted control over shehita (ritual slaughtering).[19]

Holding the economic and religious leverage of making expensive meat fit for consumption, the shohet (ritual slaughterer) was often the focus of public scrutiny and a lightning rod for public controversies. In the late eighteenth century, for example, the question of who was the shohet could be symbolic of who controlled the community—Hasidim or their opponents.[20]

In 1722, the rabbi's assistant, who was a hasid, complained repeatedly to the community's rabbi, Katznellenbogen himself, that the official shohet was not punctilious enough in the performance of his all-important task. The community council rejected these charges as motivated by a desire to take over the shohet's job. If the moreh zedek's accusation was true, then his criticism of the shohet was not necessarily cynical. This hasid may have felt that the only way to ensure that the meat supply of the community met the highest standard of kashrut—the standard to which he himself was committed—would be to do the slaughtering himself. Moreover, the shohet's job would also have afforded the hasid a practical way to impose his views on the community, putting him in a much more central position. As shohet with a priori control over the meat supply, he could raise the standard of kashrut and with it the price of meat. This may be what was behind the community's resistance to replacing their old shohet, who had had the job for more than thirty years, with this strictly observant person.

The shohet, for his part, protested vociferously that he was knowledgeable, experienced, and faithful to his task. Rabbi Katznellenbogen was in a quandary. He respected the hasid as a pious man and supported his bid to become shohet. However, the rabbi, too, was a communal employee and subject to the orders of the *kahal* (community council). Although he tried to convince the kahal that it would be better to have the hasid as shohet, in the end he had to respect their wishes. Finally, after Katznellenbogen had already left Leipnik and assumed the rabbinate in Mark-Breit, the hasid filed a formal complaint with him concerning a specific act of slaughtering. He held a hearing in which each of the antagonists presented his case. The evidence came down to one person's word against the other, and the rabbi could not come to a decision, although he tried to convince the shohet to resign voluntarily. The denouement came when Katznellenbogen had a dream in which the shohet's soul had migrated into the body of a dog—a punishment for having fed nonkosher meat to the people of the community. On hearing this apparently divine communication, the shohet agreed to give up his post.[21]

This episode shows the mystical-ascetic hasid cast in the role of conscience of the community. Both as moreh zedek and would-be custodian of kashrut, he had the moral authority to set standards. While the rabbi had to be concerned with communal politics and balancing interests, the hasid could make uncompromising religious demands. In this case, at least, the rabbi respected him both for his lifestyle and his principled position and worked to apply the hasid's standards and enhance his power in the community.

In Leipnik, the kahal seemed willing to grant their resident hasid limited power in the community as rabbi's assistant, but not as shohet. The most famous case of a community refusing to accept a mystical-ascetic hasid in an important executive function took place in Szarogród, in Ukraine.

Rabbi Jacob Joseph of Polonne is well known as the Besht's disciple and the author of the first hasidic books, published in the 1780s. Around the time he was forming his relationship with the Besht in the 1740s, Jacob Joseph was the rabbi of the sizable community of Szarogród. At some point, he took up the ways of mystical-ascetic hasidism: fasting, secluding himself every morning in order to contemplate and study, refusing to eat the standard kosher meat, and insisting on praying in a small elite group rather than with the entire community. As he explained it, this behavior on his part aroused opposition among the householders of the Szarogród Jewish community. They wanted their rabbi to be available for consultation and adjudication and to be accessible as a spiritual leader. Rabbi Jacob Joseph's behavior removed him both physically and psychologically from involvement with the community. His contention was that his immersion in divine matters was more important and did more good for the community than would his mundane participation in the routine life of his flock.[22]

The Jewish householders of Szarogród felt that the mystical-ascetic hasidic lifestyle was not appropriate for a communal rabbi who was supposed to be an active leader and an accessible model. Jacob Joseph's attempt to mix the role of rabbi with that of resident mystic could not succeed. In the end, he lost his position and was forced to leave the town on a Friday, shortly before the onset of the Sabbath.[23] Such a hasty departure implies that the situation had reached a crisis.

Later traditions and many scholarly accounts assert that it was Jacob Joseph's association with the Ba'al Shem Tov that led to his removal.[24] By the rabbi's own account, this was not so. Jacob Joseph's problems were engendered by his inclination toward the path of mystical asceticism. There is no hint of a connection to the Besht. The controversy was not over his suddenly advocating a new, unconventional style of being Jewish that his community perceived as revolutionary and therefore strongly opposed; the hasidism to which Jacob Joseph turned was—certainly by the 1740s—traditional and accepted. The members of the Szarogród community did not object to mystical-ascetic hasidic practices per se; they were opposed to their own rabbi behaving like a resident mystic.[25]

Like the skeptical Zev Wolf Kuces and David Purkes, in the story about the Besht's arrival in Międzybóż,[26] Rabbi Jacob Joseph was already a hasid—of the mystical-ascetic type—when he became associated with the Besht. He did not need the Besht to convert him to hasidism. The best evidence documenting their relationship suggests that the Besht's influence on the rabbi was to temper his asceticism, substituting other, less physically draining, mystical practices.[27]

The same is true for other associates of the Besht. In *Shivhei Ha-Besht,* Nahman of Horodenka is quoted as follows: "When I was a great hasid I went every day to a cold *mikveh*. . . . [D]espite this I could not rid myself of wayward thoughts until I turned to the wisdom of the Besht."[28] Not asceticism, but following the advice of the Besht, is what brought Nahman closer to spiritual perfection.

The conflict between the demands of the rabbinate and Rabbi Jacob Joseph's desire to lead the life of a mystical ascetic point up a further differentiation of professional religious roles in the Ashkenazic Jewish communities of the eighteenth century. Alongside rabbis and ba'alei shem stood mystical-ascetic hasidim. While the boundaries among these types were fluid—we have seen examples of ba'alei shem who were also rabbis—the functions were distinct. There was room for more than one type of religious leadership to flourish.

In Poland by the eighteenth century, hasidim and their conventicles, or *havurot,*[29] were accepted fixtures. When so-called Beshtian Hasidism made its appearance, contemporaries saw in it not so much an innovation vis-à-vis normative Judaism as a change in hasidism. In his autobiography, Solomon Maimon,[30] who witnessed the rise of "Beshtian Hasidism," explained the new group thus:

> About this time I became acquainted with a sect of my people called the New Hasidim, which was then coming into prominence. Hasidim is the name generally given by the Hebrews to the pious, that is, to those who are distinguished by the exercise of the strictest piety. From time immemorial men such as these have freed themselves from worldly occupations and pleasures and devoted their lives to the strictest observance of the laws of religion and to penance for their sins. They sought to attain this object . . . by prayers and other exercises of devotion, by chastisement of the body and by similar means.
>
> But about this time some among them set themselves up as founders of a new sect. They maintained that true piety by no means consists in chastisement of the body, by which the spiritual quiet and cheerfulness necessary to the knowledge and love of God are disturbed. . . . Instead of spending their lives in separation from the world, suppressing their natural feelings, and deadening their powers, they believed that they acted much more to the purpose in seeking to develop their natural feelings as fully as possible, to bring their powers into exercise, and constantly to widen their sphere of activity. . . .
>
> Those sects were not in fact distinct sects of religion; their difference con-

sisted merely in the mode of their religious exercises. But still their animosity went so far that they condemned each other as heretics, and indulged in mutual persecution.[31]

Maimon expressed his view that the new Hasidim were just that: a new style in *hasidic* practice. They grew out of, and coexisted with, the groups of traditional mystical-ascetic hasidim; they did not arise de novo. Opposition to them was concentrated among the old-style hasidim, whose doctrines they were altering, and not necessarily "the rabbis," a diverse group.[32]

Maimon's description of the old hasidim as seeking to attain the strictest standard of piety "by prayers and other exercises of devotion, by chastisement of the body and by similar means," while the new Hasidim "maintained that true piety by no means consists in chastisement of the body" dovetails with the description of the new Hasidim by their outstanding exponent in White Russia in the late eighteenth century, Shneur Zalman of Ladi (1740–1813).

Shneur Zalman was the leader of the White Russian Hasidim, known as Habad. In 1798, he was arrested by the Russian authorities on suspicion of forming his group with the intention of starting a new religious sect—somehow connected to the Freemasons—and of plotting to aid Napoleon and the French Revolutionary forces. After his mid-September arrest and subsequent interrogation, Shneur Zalman was released, together with the other Hasidim who were arrested with him, on 25 November 1798 by order of the tsar. In November 1800, he was arrested once again on the renewed charge of leading a new, heretical sect, related to Sabbateanism. Once again, after a thorough investigation, he was released, in early April, on the direct order of the tsar.[33]

Recently, copies of documents connected with Shneur Zalman's arrests and interrogations have been published. Included in the published documents are Shneur Zalman's own written answers to questions posed by his interrogators.[34] One of the main things the authorities were trying to determine was whether or not the Hasidim did constitute a new, heretical sect. To this end they pressed the zaddik to define the differences between Hasidism and "regular" Jewish practice.[35]

In his answers, Shneur Zalman took the approach that there was nothing novel or untraditional about Hasidic practice. Rather there were always people called hasidim in Judaism. Their hallmark was

that they prayed at length and with devotion and have been called "hasidim" from time immemorial. . . . All who burden themselves to pray with devotion—both young and old—are a minority of a minority within the mass of the people, and the masses call them, in all of the regions of White Russia and Poland and virtually all of Lithuania, "Hasidim," after the ancient Hasidim who would pray with devotion as explained above, although the current Hasidim are not as great as the ancient ones. . . . It is well known that we [i.e., today's Hasidim] fulfill the commandments of God much more punctiliously than ordinary Jews, and even more than some of the ones learned in Torah.[36]

Maimon emphasized piety, devotional prayer, and asceticism as the signs of old hasidism, while new Hasidism left out the asceticism. Shneur Zalman indirectly confirmed Maimon's analysis in his insistence that devotional prayer was the continuing feature of hasidic practice from ancient times until his own day and that current Hasidim were committed to a stricter standard of observance than the average Jew or even many of the rabbis.[37]

Against this background it is understandable why opposition to the new-style Hasidim in the late eighteenth century was so strongly associated with Elijah ben Solomon, the Gaon of Vilna.[38] The Vilna Gaon— as he is usually referred to—is popularly known for his prodigious Torah scholarship. By reputation and scholarly legacy undoubtedly one of the greatest virtuosos of Talmudic scholarship who ever lived, he was totally immersed in his studies. This view of the Gaon is reinforced by apocryphal anecdotes. For example, when after several decades his sister came to visit him, the Gaon is reputed to have said a brief hello and quickly returned to his studies.[39]

Popular perception, developed through the nineteenth and twentieth centuries, contrasted the Gaon with a man he never met and about whom he probably knew little, if anything—the Ba'al Shem Tov.[40] In the popular mind, the Gaon was a severe, aloof, rigorous authoritarian who was the polar opposite of the merry, inspiring, nonjudgmental, lenient Ba'al Shem Tov. The Gaon lived his life within the four cubits of strictest halakhic interpretation, interested only in his own pursuit of Torah knowledge, sternly oblivious to the exigencies people faced in real life. In contrast, the Besht was a warm mystic, given to heavenly encounters, emphasizing the importance of joyful prayer, song, and spiritual experience, involved with the problems of the people around him, and willing to give them the halakhic benefit of the doubt.[41]

The late eighteenth- and early nineteenth-century sources,[42] however, reveal striking similarities between the construction of the Gaon's life by his children and disciples writing in the years following his death in 1797 and the construction of the Besht's life at around the same time in

Hasidic tradition, as expressed in the hagiographic collection *Shivhei Ha-Besht,* which is discussed at length in chapter 9. The Besht was a faith healer who derived his powers from a knowledge of practical, theurgic Kabbalah and folk medicine. The Gaon, too, at one point in his life tried his hand at practical Kabbalah and even started fashioning a golem. He was tempted in his youth to learn the secrets of herbal medicine from Christian villagers, until his father forbade him to do so. According to the stories, the Ba'al Shem Tov put great stock in music; so did the Gaon. He is reputed to have said that it facilitated understanding of the esoteric and held the power of life and death. The Ba'al Shem Tov specialized in controlling the name of God for theurgic purposes. The Gaon claimed that by employing one of God's names he could reproduce the solar system on a tabletop and disprove "Aristotelian" notions about the autonomy of the universe. Both the Besht and the Gaon were reputed to care little about money; both practiced periodic isolation during at least some part of their lives. Both prayed impressively. When the Besht prayed, according to tradition, "everyone saw that the water was rippling. The Shekinah hovered over him and as a result the earth trembled."[43] The Gaon "stood to pray, word by word, with pleasant sounds and a subtle melody. Whoever heard him . . . melted like wax before the flame of his concentration. For he concentrated on every single word of the service and produced each sound and utterance with a pleasant tune and with power."[44] People came from far away just to be inspired by the experience of being close to him when he prayed. "They gazed in wonder at how a person could reach such a level of love of God."[45]

As we will see in chapter 10, the Besht was a sort of mystic-in-residence, having no formal public responsibilities in the community, but serving as a spiritual leader through his example and learning with the other members of the bet midrash. The Gaon, too, performed no official function in Vilna. For close to half a century the community supported him while he studied mostly in splendid isolation or with an elite group of those close to him—a kloyz.[46] Stories about both men have them supporting the poor, dowering indigent brides, and ransoming prisoners. Both were also involved in controversies over the rabbi serving their community (in both cases taking the side of the party opposed to the rabbi). Finally, both the Besht and the Gaon were said to have attempted and failed to settle in the Land of Israel.

In short, both Elijah Gaon and Israel Ba'al Shem Tov were held by those who revered their respective memories to have represented a standard ideal type that resonated in Jewish society of their age: the mystical-ascetic hasid. Ironically, and perhaps not coincidentally, the Gaon was actually called "hasid" by his contemporaries.[47] The Ba'al Shem Tov apparently did not perpetuate all aspects of the old-style hasidic practice. This is implied by Pinhas of Koretz who commented that the essence of Hasidism began with the Besht because he abrogated many of the customs instituted by Rabbi Judah Hasid in the Middle Ages and observed up until the eighteenth century.[48] In other words, the Besht emerged from the mystic-ascetic-hasidic tradition but changed it significantly.

The Gaon was the more complete embodiment of the traditional mystical-ascetic hasid because his way included several features that lay at the heart of the old-style hasidism. First and foremost, the Gaon placed tremendous emphasis on rabbinic erudition, believing that it was the chief path to achieving communion with God and ultimate Redemption.[49] In addition, according to accounts by those close to him, the Gaon maintained a subsistence diet, deprived himself of sleep, spent much time in gloomy isolation, and spent a period of his life in self-imposed wandering. He not only dabbled in practical Kabbalah, he was intimately familiar with the great works of contemplative Kabbalah.[50] It was erudition, asceticism, and conversance with the profundities of Kabbalah that made the Gaon the hasid par excellence.

The new Hasidim who, according to Maimon, rejected the identification of piety with suffering and sought instead "to develop their natural feelings as fully as possible, to bring their powers into exercise and constantly widen their sphere of activity" directly threatened ascetic, erudite, elitist hasidism. They were not necessarily opposed to or by the communal establishment or normative rabbinic Judaism as a whole. The Gaon's reaction to the new Hasidim can perhaps be explained by the parallels between the ideal image of the Besht and of himself. The two models were so close that the danger of the false hasid being mistaken for the real one was all too likely. The nonasceticism, lack of emphasis on rabbinic erudition, and deficient Kabbalistic profundity in Beshtian Hasidism were easy to overlook, and for some even to embrace; but they were, for the Gaon, the essential, negative aspects.

It is noteworthy that the opposition forces to the new Hasidim in Vilna insisted on calling them Mithasdim (those who make themselves as if they are hasidim) and "Karliner" (those who come from Karlin)[51]—a practice that the Hasidim themselves interpreted as a refusal to recognize their legitimacy and as an insult.[52] Might it be that those who withheld the name "hasid" from the new Hasidim were thereby expressing the view that they had no right to claim this title, which really belonged to a different set of people?

During the Besht's lifetime, all of this was in the future. The definitions and polemics of the late eighteenth century do demonstrate, however, that there was an ongoing institutional and doctrinal context within which Beshtian Hasidism developed and from which it was gradually differentiated. The polemics that began in the 1770s and the attempts by Solomon Maimon and Shneur Zalman of Ladi in the 1790s to define the Hasidic movement all imply that the process of differentiation of Hasidism from hasidism did not culminate until the last third of the century.

Hasidism, then, was an outgrowth of an already existing religious orientation and not, as many have suggested, a radically new phenomenon that came as history's response to a crisis of Judaism or of Jewish society.[53] Hasidism was probably connected to the growing popularization of mysticism inspired in large part by the example of the traditional mystical-ascetic hasidim and ba'alei shem and made practicable through the spread of inexpensive, unsophisticated Kabbalah-based literature.[54]

Earlier I stated that by the eighteenth century many nonscholarly Jews were convinced that they could at least stand at the threshold of holiness. Perhaps the new Hasidism's attraction was the promise to take them across the threshold. It made every Jew into a candidate for Hasid, by abolishing the daunting ascetic requirements and obliging the leader of the group, the zaddik, to focus his efforts on the individual. The zaddik was to be a mentor whose goal was to communicate the esoteric. Rather than permitting the masses only the spillover of mystical doctrines that they could glean from a secondary source like the hanhagot (moral conduct) literature or a passive one like synagogue art, the zaddik saw it as his responsibility to instill these doctrines directly, by whatever means he deemed appropriate, in virtually all individuals. To paraphrase Martin Buber, Hasidism was to further the process through which Kabbalah turned into a mode of life for the community, an ethos for the masses.[55]

With this as a working hypothesis, it is useful to consider more of the statements in the testimony of Rabbi Shneur Zalman of Ladi.[56] When questioned about his training and activities, Shneur Zalman made it clear that Kabbalah was a very important element of Hasidism. For one thing, both he and his interlocutors emphasized that he was knowledgeable about Kabbalah, in implied contrast to other rabbis.[57] Also in

contrast to others, he spread Kabbalistic doctrines among the masses:
When asked what his title was, Shneur Zalman answered and his Jewish interpreter paraphrased,

> He is rabbi in the town of Liozna and explicates the Holy Scripture and the
> ethical writings . . . to those who come to him, he relieves their doubts con-
> cerning the Jewish Torah, teaching them how to serve God in public. In his
> homilies he explains the ancient Kabbalah. . . . The thing that is different
> about his teaching is that there are rabbis who claim that Kabbalah should
> not be taught to people who are under forty years of age. While he does not
> teach Kabbalah, in his interpretations of the Torah he interweaves explana-
> tions of difficult passages that are actually Kabbalah.[58]

Moreover, Shneur Zalman indicated to the Russian authorities that
the important difference between the prayers of the Hasidim and those
of the rest of the Jews was "only this, that we customarily add the additions to the prayer service according to the directions of the teaching
of the Kabbalah with combinations of letters and alternations of letters."[59] He carefully enumerated the Kabbalistically influenced prayer
books that the Hasidim used.[60] So suffused with the tenets of Kabbalah
was Shneur Zalman's conception of Judaism that in order to defend Hasidic theology during his second interrogation, he treated the Russian authorities—who obviously knew less Kabbalah than the average Jew—to
a short Kabbalistically based discourse: "With humility I beseech Your
Merciful Honor's forgiveness that I dare to bother him with such wide-
ranging citation from the ancient books of Kabbalah."[61] This was apparently a standard explanation that he had used, in various versions,
on different occasions.

For Shneur Zalman, then, the distinctive part of Hasidic ritual was
prayer; the distinctive component in its spiritual content was Kabbalah—
but, significantly, not practical Kabbalah. As he wrote,

> But there is another thing which some people mistakenly call Kabbalah, this
> is to adjure holy or unholy angels to perform some sign. Behold I have not
> seen any book on this nor any person who did this. I only heard that they
> used to do it in the first generations. Also that Rabbi [the Maggid of Mez-
> erich] did not know anything about this and in this knowledge there is no
> benefit whatsoever for the service of God.[62]

Shneur Zalman's notion of the essentials of Hasidism is probably an
accurate statement of how Hasidism was perceived by its practitioners,
at least in White Russia, circa 1800. We must recall, however, that
Shneur Zalman never met the Besht. He was a disciple of Dov Ber, the
Maggid of Mezerich, and knew of the Besht only from the reports of oth-

ers. The Besht is conspicuously absent from Shneur Zalman's account of the rise of Hasidism, while his disowning of practical Kabbalah seems to put more than temporal distance between himself and the Besht. The only statement he had to make about the Besht in his testimony, in response to a direct question on the subject, implied that the Besht was indeed a practical Kabbalist: "That R. Israel Ba'al Shem Tov did not write books nor did he leave [writings] after himself, therefore the acts of the angels and demons are not known to me."[63] The essential point is that whatever the Besht was, it had nothing to do with Shneur Zalman, the disciple of the Maggid, who himself claimed to know little about practical Kabbalah.[64] Shneur Zalman's view of Hasidism may be an accurate representation of the essence of the maturing movement in his day; its links to the essence of the Besht's "Hasidism" are unclear.

To what extent, then, does Shneur Zalman's explanation of the maturing movement circa 1800 serve as an accurate description of the Besht's new way in Hasidism? What was the Besht's role in the process of moving along the continuum from old-style mystical-ascetic hasidism to the new popular variety? Many have claimed that essential features of mature Hasidism—including the apparent rejection of practical Kabbalah and the social role of the zaddik—were already implicit in the doctrines and behavior of the Ba'al Shem Tov.[65] This assumption bears closer examination. It is possible that the Ba'al Shem Tov innovated a new style in hasidism without actually founding Hasidism. This is, I suggest, a useful organizing perspective from which to read the texts that relate to the Besht.

CHAPTER THREE

A Country in Decline?

It is self-evident that the course of the Besht's life was affected by the geopolitical and sociocultural-economic milieu in which he lived. Yet the Ba'al Shem Tov has often been portrayed in popular works with only superficial attention to his surroundings, as if his life transcended time and space. The interest in connecting his activities and teachings to later history has frequently obscured the relationship of the Besht to the place and period in which he actually lived.[1] In more historically oriented scholarly writing there were attempts to relate the patterns of his life to conditions in Poland and its Jewish community in a general way.[2] A clearer perception of the country and the region within it where the Besht lived can help to establish the parameters of his existence and contribute to an understanding of the range and nature of his activities.

THE POLISH-LITHUANIAN COMMONWEALTH

The Besht lived his entire life (1700?–1760) during the period when the Polish-Lithuanian Commonwealth, as Poland was then called, and the Duchy of Saxony were united in the person of common rulers, the two Wettin kings, August II (1697–1732) and August III (1733–1763). The fact that Polish kingship was acquired by the ruler of a foreign country is emblematic of the general limitations of Poland's polity in determining its own fate through the eighteenth century.[3]

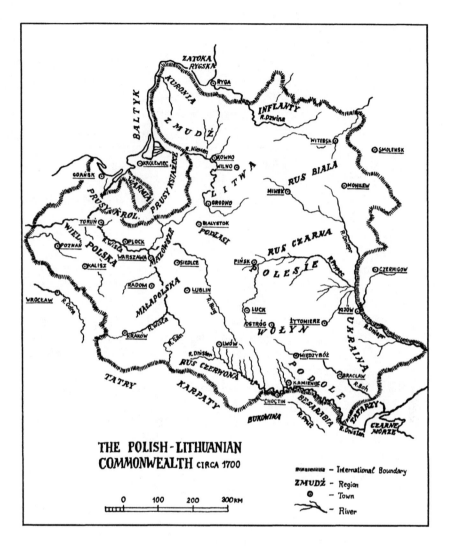

THE POLISH-LITHUANIAN
COMMONWEALTH CIRCA 1700

ᴍᴜᴜᴜᴜᴜᴜᴜ — *International Boundary*
ZMUDŻ - *Region*
⊙ — *Town*
— *River*

0   100   200   300 KM

Poland had entered the seventeenth century as a contender for the position of dominant power in northern Europe. Since the time of Casimir
the Great (1333–1370), the Commonwealth had been expanding its bor-
ders in all directions. In 1610, a Polish army stood at the gates of the
Kremlin, poised to conquer Muscovy. Poland's political institutions were
evolving democratic forms, with a parliament (Sejm) and king elected—
after a fashion—by the nobility, which numbered approximately 10 percent of the population. It was both relatively and absolutely the largest

electorate in Europe at the time. The agrarian economy was booming as the international grain trade turned Poland into the breadbasket of western Europe.

This vast state of some ten million inhabitants in 1648 comprised— in addition to its 40 percent ethnic Poles—Ukrainians (Ruthenians), White Russians, Lithuanians, Letts, Estonians, Germans, Turks, Armenians, Italians, Scots, and Jews. Its non–Roman Catholic religions included several varieties of Protestantism, Eastern ("Greek") and Armenian Orthodoxy, Ukrainian Catholicism, Islam, and Judaism. The country was overwhelmingly agrarian, with more than 90 percent of the Christian population living on the land as peasants. A large majority of Jews lived in small towns and cities.

The Commonwealth had managed its great ethnic diversity and religious pluralism largely without resort to overt repression. Muslims and Armenians were rather small groups concentrated in areas of Red Russia and Podolia near the Turkish border. They were left to their own devices, the Armenians even enjoying a measure of autonomy.[4]

This was also true of the large Jewish minority.[5] The Poles' tradition of toleration and the compelling utilitarian reasons for admitting Jews to Poland and granting them wide-ranging economic freedom meant that the Jews would enjoy other freedoms as well. In the realm of religion and internal communal affairs, the Jews' social, cultural, and theological distance from Christians made it possible to give the Jewish community a very high degree of authority and freedom without fear of encroachment on Catholic church prerogatives or sensibilities.[6] Non–state-sanctioned violence against Jews was a constant phenomenon that ebbed and flowed according to the complex interaction of economics, politics, and religion. While the general level of security in daily life was not high, specifically anti-Jewish actions inspired by lower clergy, peasant leaders, petty noblemen, townspeople, bandits, or rebels were common enough to produce an undercurrent of insecurity in Jewish consciousness.[7]

Once, during the Cossack-Peasant Revolt that began in the Ukrainian provinces of the Commonwealth in 1648, anti-Jewish violence reached a peak unprecedented in Europe for ferocity and number of victims. This revolt, originally fomented by the Cossacks to protest their treatment at the hands of the Polish government, eventually took on the character of a full-scale, popular peasant uprising, fought over a range of ethnic, religious, social, and economic divides. The revolt was initially directed at Polish noblemen and Church—in some cases, even Orthodox—institutions. Yet the identification of the Jews with the Poles, their large number, the heritage of anti-Jewish violence, and the Jews' over-whelmingly predominant urban and civilian status guaranteed that they would be the primary victims.[8]

The Polish government's more or less laissez-faire policies with regard to the Armenian and non-Christian minorities did not obtain when it came to Eastern Orthodox and Protestant dissenters from the Catholic faith, which was dominant among the Polish political class. Theological differences with the relatively numerous Protestants and Orthodox had potential ramifications for the "true faith" and "true Church." They also had political significance. Under certain conditions, Protestants might gravitate to the side of covetous Protestant German states to the west, and the Orthodox naturally looked eastward to the Moscow-based hi-erarchy of their Church. While violent suppression of these "dissenters" was an option, the pious Catholic king, Zygmunt III (1587–1632), pre-ferred to combat Protestantism and Eastern Orthodoxy among his sub-jects with a combination of Jesuit polemical activity, administrative ha-rassment, and unofficial discrimination.[9]

With education concentrated in the hands of the Jesuits and appoint-ments and royal land grants made chiefly to Roman Catholics, the pres-sure on members of the elites of society both to convert and to Polonize was strong. Eventually, "Polish nobleman" and "Catholic" became in-separable attributes. As the seventeenth century progressed, the more po-litically powerful and wealthy a nobleman was, the less likely he was to be Protestant or Orthodox. If his family had been non-Catholic earlier on, then along with their religion they had probably changed their name from something like the Ukrainian Vyshnevetsky to the Polish Wis-niowiecki. Conversion of non-Polish noblemen was less a matter of faith than of assimilation into the power elite.[10]

In the eastern parts of the country, where Poles and Catholics were a small minority, the goal of Christian church union was invoked and brought to fruition at Brest in 1596. The resulting Uniate, or Greek Catholic, church preserved the Orthodox rites and liturgy while subor-dinating the Commonwealth's Orthodox hierarchy to the authority of the pope, both administratively and in matters of faith and dogma. Po-litically, the union was intended to sever the religious tie between Mus-covy and the Orthodox inhabitants of the eastern areas of the Com-monwealth.[11]

For Poland, the end of the seventeenth century showed the promise of its onset to be unfulfilled. A series of Cossack revolts beginning in 1591 culminated, in 1648, in the general revolt of the peasantry in the Ukrainian regions of the Commonwealth. This was followed by invasions by Muscovy (1654), Sweden (1655), and Turkey (1671). Poland lost so-called Left Bank Ukraine (east of the Dnieper) and Zaporozhe to Muscovy and the Cossacks (1667), while Cossack Right Bank Ukraine (Kiev and Braclaw provinces) became a Turkish protectorate and Podolia was ceded to Turkey (1672), along with an annual tribute. Altogether almost one-third of the Commonwealth's territory had been taken away. When some of these losses were regained as part of the Treaty of Karlowitz (signed at the end of the Ottoman War in 1699), the compensation paled beside King Jan Sobieski's (reigned 1674–1696) original plan of conquering Moldavia and Walachia and wiping out the Tatar threat once and for all. Compared to Austria's gains from the same treaty, Poland's repossession of Podolia seemed but a consolation prize for a junior ally, not a sign of the renewal of Polish power.[12]

The treaty had officially restored both Podolia and Right Bank Ukraine to Polish rule, but Peter the Great refused to allow the Poles to take over the Right Bank area until the Turks made it his least unpalatable option after the Treaty of Prut (1711). Beginning with the election of two foreigners to the kingship in 1697, continuing with episodes such as the delay in occupying the Right Bank, and in view of the constant presence of foreign troops, through the eighteenth century it became apparent that someone else's interest would increasingly influence Poland's circumstances.[13]

The loss of territory, the devastation of the war campaigns, and the expenses incurred by Sobieski's military exploits played havoc with the Commonwealth's economy. Population decreased, and agricultural production and export were a fraction of what they had been before 1648. Town commercial life contracted, and some towns virtually disappeared. Taxes were raised to overcome the diminished population, production, commerce, and income, but smaller total sums of money were collected. Short on revenue, the state treasury resorted to continual currency devaluation via coin debasement as a means of financing deficits.[14]

By the late seventeenth century, the country's democratic political institutions were seriously impaired. The Sejm's ability to act was fundamentally undermined by the custom of *liberum veto,* by which any one member could dissolve the house by casting a lone vote of no confidence. The king—dependent on parliament to raise money, maintain military forces, and approve appointments—could neither rule unilaterally nor work effectively with a parliament liable to dispersal at the whim of his opponents. This led to near political paralysis. King Jan Casimir was so frustrated by the checks on his power, held in the hand of so capricious a partner, that he abdicated (1667).[15]

The elected monarchy itself was originally conceived as an expression of the power of a polity based on free, privileged, and strong noblemen. When in 1574 Henri Valois forsook the Polish throne for that of France, his erstwhile subjects taunted him for preferring to be the king of slaves who might revolt and assassinate him at any time. The Polish king was the freely chosen leader of free and noble men who, once having chosen him, would willingly die for him.

In an era when the Commonwealth was wounded and threatened on all sides, the election of the king was a golden opportunity for meddling in Poland's internal affairs by foreign powers who sought to subordinate the Commonwealth to their political plans. Foreign kings viewed the Polish throne as a means of cementing alliances or frustrating enemies in the service of their own interests. They nominated the candidates and then lobbied, bribed, or fought for their election. The dual election, in 1697, of two rival foreigners, Prince Conti of France and Frederick August of Austria, was much more the function of international politics and domestic intrigue than of a considered view of Poland's interests by Poles.[16] A few years later, in 1704, Swedish machinations resulted in the election of a new rival to August II, Stanislaw Leszczynski, and Swedish pressure resulted in the temporary resignation of August II (1706). It was the Russians who supported both Wettins against their various antagonists.[17]

In its weakened state, Poland spent the beginning of the eighteenth century "in the shadow of the Northern League."[18] Not officially a party to the Great Northern War (a contest pitting Sweden against Russia and her allies, Denmark and Saxony), Poland found that most of the war's battles were fought on her territory. The combatants' diplomatic initiatives wound up determining the contours of Poland's domestic politics. As noted, Russia supported August II while Sweden supported Leszczynski. The nobility split its loyalty between these rival kings, and the maneuvering between the two camps continued until Leszczynski retired to France in 1735.[19]

The result of the Great Northern War was that Russia succeeded in humbling Sweden, but at the cost of devastating much of the northern half of Poland, wrecking its economy, and politically splintering the nobility. With Sweden defeated, so was—for the moment at least—Leszczynski. Again, it was Russia that in part enabled August II's reinstatement as king of all of the country (1709), made August into a client,

and reinforced his reign over the resistance of a significant proportion
of the nobility during the 1717 Silent Sejm, at which the Russian-
sanctioned agreement was approved without debate. Yet again, in 1733,
Russia determined the selection of August's son as successor. Historians
are virtually unanimous in judging the Wettin period as the time when
Poland slid into its status as a Russian protectorate.[20] This slide was aided
by a movement within Poland toward assimilative Polish-Catholic
nationalism, which resulted in active discrimination against and even persecution of non–Roman Catholic Christians, quite unlike the more light-
handed Counter-Reformation policies of Zygmunt III in the early seventeenth century. The Polish anti-"dissenter" campaign of the eighteenth
century presented neighboring, non-Catholic countries, especially Russia, with an excellent pretext for deepening their involvement in Poland's
internal affairs in the name of protecting their coreligionists.[21]

While the end of the Great Northern War (1721) did eventually lead
to a significant upturn in economic activity, the improvement in large part
skipped over the big, royally chartered cities like Cracow and Lublin. The
new prosperity was concentrated mainly in the holdings of the aristocratic magnates. These leading twenty or so families owned tremendous
estates (latifundia), located primarily east of the Vistula, which collec-
tively dominated Poland's most basic industry, its agricultural export.
By dispensing economic opportunities, the magnates also controlled
blocs of noblemen who voted in the *sejmiki* (dietines), Sejm, and royal
elections and who filled the military levies, which did the fighting. On
their latifundia with their vast wealth, private armies, and supreme political and judicial authority, these magnates were the equal of most German princes.[22]

Their tremendous economic and political power created a conflict of
interest for these individuals. Whether to serve the *raison d'etat* of
Poland, meaning the will of the Sejm and king, or to advance the interests of their own virtual ministates was a constant dilemma, usually resolved in one's own favor. Foreign powers were able to exploit this
dilemma by offering to make the national interest identical with that of
a particular magnate by rendering him a powerful role—and great personal reward—in reshaping Poland. Magnates began to represent the interests of a given power, or group of powers. Through the first two-thirds
of the eighteenth century, the Czartoryskis, for example, were protégés
of Russia, while the Potockis represented the French-Austrian axis. It was
difficult to discern to what degree a magnate spoke for himself, for a foreign patron, or for Poland.[23]

As central authority in Poland became progressively weaker with part-time and competing kings, ineffectual Sejm, foreign enforcers, the dislocations of the Great Northern War, and a series of natural disasters, the aristocratic magnates filled the vacuum. Their latifundia expanded and increasingly became the locus of economic activity, wealth, and political power. They held direct legislative, juridical, and administrative authority over the millions of people who inhabited their properties. With their private armies they defended whole sections of the country and determined the strength of the national army as well. In national politics they played the role of political boss and kingmaker, often aspiring to the big prize themselves. It is understandable that some historians have dubbed this period of decline the time of "Polish magnate oligarchy." While it is tempting to dismiss summarily—but unjustifiably—the power of the king in eighteenth-century Poland, it is difficult to exaggerate the power and importance of the aristocratic magnates.[24]

These parameters of the Commonwealth composed the framework on which much of the circumstances of life developed throughout the country. The Besht's region, Podolia, was no exception. It was directly affected by the political developments of the seventeenth century. The wars, conquests, and reconquest had far-reaching implications for the lives of the people who resided there, most obviously in modulating migration and settlement trends. The weakness of the central government and the dominance of the aristocratic magnates were nowhere more pronounced, making this region more a collection of gigantic feudal estates than a constituent unit of the royal administration. The latifundium economy was in full operation there, and most people earned their livings directly or indirectly from latifundium enterprises. The ethnic pluralism of the Commonwealth was in strong evidence: Poles, Ukrainians (Ruthenians), and Jews (and their various religious groupings) were all well represented. The particular versions of the Commonwealth's structure and problems that were found in Podolia formed the substratum of the life of the Besht, and it is important to examine them to understand the possibilities and limitations that governed the evolution of his activities.

PODOLIA

Originally part of medieval Rus and ethnically identified with the historical lands of Ukraine,[25] Podolia (Ukrainian Podillia; Polish Podole) was officially annexed by Poland in 1434. This was 135 years before the Union of Lublin brought Lithuania, White Russia, and what later became

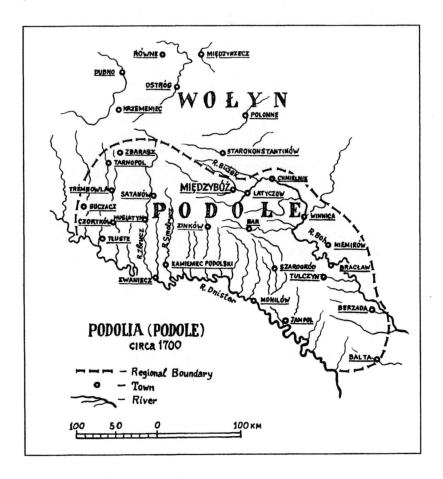

PODOLIA (PODOLE)
CIRCA 1700

- - - - — Regional Boundary
o — Town
~ — River

100   50   0   100 KM

known as Right and (part of) Left Bank Ukraine under Polish sovereignty. The economic potential of this fertile but sparsely settled territory, under perennial threat of Tatar and Ottoman attack, was obvious. To realize its wealth, the territory had to be protected, settled, and organized. This was effected by the granting of large tracts of land—the foundation of the latifundia—to (mainly Ukrainian) noblemen. In return for guaranteeing defense and security, the king allowed the noblemen to set up manors and towns. The lands were to be worked by peasants who, after an initial exemption period, would be liable for various feudal dues in labor, money, and kind. After 1538, the peasants lost their right of judicial appeal to the king, and their lord gained effectively absolute power over them.[26]

Ukrainian peasants were the primary element of the rural village population. A few of them settled in the new towns that the magnates set up and that attracted settlers mainly from the west: Poles, Germans, Greeks, Armenians, and Jews. These people created the commercial infrastructure for linking Podolia to the rest of Poland and Europe beyond. The Jews were also heavily involved in administration of the magnates' latifundia through the institution of leasing.[27]

The fundamental problem of Polish rule in this region—as in all of the Ukrainian territories—was how to convert formal ownership into real control. These areas were originally ethnically and linguistically Ukrainian, Orthodox in religion, and free peasant in terms of social organization. I have already alluded to the process of Polonization of the local nobility by offers of land and political power in return for assimilation and loyalty. The creation of the Uniate church was intended to serve as a halfway house for those (particularly peasants) whose stake in the new Polish order was not large enough to tempt them to convert outright. The establishment of the feudal estates, with initially trivial feudal dues, was an attempt to bring the peasantry under Polish hegemony without pain. Colonists from Poland proper, including both the town dwellers referred to above and some Polish peasants as well, strengthened the economic and social ties between Podolia and the western Polish territories. Owing their existence to the Polish lords, they could be counted on to demonstrate their loyalty.[28]

Defense was arranged by hiring Cossacks to staff the magnates' private armies and to fill out the ranks of the kings' forces as well. While these people were, in the main, ethnically and religiously similar to the peasants, as fighters they expected to be included in the ranks of the nobility. The gap between their expectations of political and financial rewards and the Polish authorities' attempts to keep them in their place resulted in a series of revolts. Dissatisfaction among the Cossacks had its complement among the peasant population at large. As the feudal burden gradually increased through the first half of the seventeenth century, peasants, having become serfs, sometimes displayed resistance to their Polish overlords. Some ran away to latifundia with lower taxes, joined the Cossacks, or mutinied.[29]

By the middle of the seventeenth century, most of the nobility and the high clergy in the Ukrainian territories, particularly Podolia, had undergone a high degree of polonization, although the Orthodox church, always weaker in Podolia than in the surrounding regions, still maintained a presence. The towns, dominated by Poles, Jews, and other non-Ukrainian elements, had become the commercial, administrative, and military foci of the region. Culturally, the farther west they were, the more they tended to be polonotropic.[30] Still, the Polish hold over the Ukrainian territories was not completely secure. The dependence on the non-Polish Cossacks for defense and on the unassimilated and ever more pressed peasants for labor and income made for a fragile structure that periodically displayed acute weakness. Finally, the 1648 uprising led by Bogdan Chmielnicki synergized Cossack and peasant resistance and brought the system of Polish hegemony crashing down. Rather than fight against the Tatars, the Cossack army allied with them against the Polish landlords. After this force's initial military successes, the serfs turned on their masters. Cossacks and peasants chased the leaseholders from the countryside and then attacked them and the other people in the towns.[31]

The treaty ending the fighting in 1649 restored full Polish control of Podolia. Unlike the Right Bank territories immediately to the east, where sovereignty remained in dispute and fighting continued sporadically for several years, the situation in Podolia stabilized. Within about a generation, however, the 1672 Treaty of Buczacz ceded this territory to the Ottoman Empire. The outcome was a twenty-seven-year occupation, which is traditionally referred to by Ukrainians as "the Ruin." Tatar raids and running Polish-Turkish battles throughout the period resulted in the destruction of land and property, loss of life, and many refugees fleeing either west and north to Poland or east across the Dnieper to Russian-controlled Left Bank Ukraine. The latifundia ceased to produce, towns emptied, and the population was drastically reduced.[32]

The ruin of Podolia in the last third of the seventeenth century put it on a different course from much of the rest of Poland. From the mid-1680s, King Jan Sobieski began regaining parts of Podolian territory from Turkish control, culminating in complete recovery in the 1699 Karlowitz Treaty, under August II. As the reconquest progressed, there was a reprise of the Polish colonization project of some two centuries earlier. With the Russians blocking a Polish return to the areas farther east, new settlement efforts were concentrated on Podolia. Once again the magnate latifundia owners promised fifteen- or twenty-year exemptions to peasants willing to settle down. They solicited Jews and other townspeople to come and reestablish life and commerce in the towns. The Jewish-dominated leasing system was revived in modified form with the scope of leases somewhat curtailed.[33]

In a bid to change the social and political dynamics of the region, the Sejm decided to disband the Polish-sponsored Cossack army. The goal was to remove the agent that fifty years earlier had served as the precipitant for the peasant uprising. The effect, however, was the opposite. In 1702, displaced Cossacks, under Semen Palii, decided to fight rather than accept assignment to oblivion, and the cycle of Cossack revolt followed by peasant uprising seemed to begin again. The rebels quickly occupied many Podolian towns. In a campaign in early 1703, the Polish Hetman, Adam Mikolaj Sieniawski, systematically recaptured most of the towns and pushed Palii and his forces into the Right Bank territories. There the leader of the Russian-sponsored Hetman state, Ivan Mazepa, defeated and arrested his potential rival, effectively ending the revolt.[34]

Given this respite, the Podolian landowners continued their rebuilding, while the Great Northern War was being fought mostly in other areas of the Commonwealth. The defeat of Palii and later of Mazepa at the battle of Poltawa, together with the continuing weakness of Turkey and the actual return of Polish control to the Right Bank Ukraine areas, created a security zone for Podolia. For the moment both of the two great traditional threats to Polish rule in the region, the Tatars and the Cossacks, were subdued. Moreover, as the central government was both occupied elsewhere and continually weakened by foreign intervention, the magnates were relatively free to consolidate absolute rule over their latifundia.[35]

Thus, while in the first two decades of the eighteenth century the rest of Poland contended with the havoc and destruction sown by the Great Northern War, Podolia was being reconstructed from the ruin it suffered in the previous century. As Podolia was traditionally less dependent on the grain export trade than the provinces to the west and north,[36] the war-induced disruption of international trade via the Baltic had a relatively light impact. Podolian grain was mostly consumed locally as liquor or feed, or used to supply other regions of Poland ravaged by the war. Podolia's active overland cattle trade with central Europe continued along the southern routes that had been followed for centuries.[37]

Circumstances in the early eighteenth century—weakness of the Cossacks and Turks, a measure of insulation from the adverse economic effects of the Great Northern War, people looking for a safe political and economic haven in which to settle—made it possible for the magnates to reconstitute their Podolian estates and the feudal relationship with their serfs. They even succeeded in finally uprooting the Orthodox church. Between 1691 and 1720, all Orthodox dioceses and Church hierarchy in Podolia and the other western Ukrainian areas (Red Russia, Wolhynia) became officially Uniate. The Uniate church experienced rapid growth. Of particular note is the strong development of the Bazylian monastic order, which served as the elite of this church. The order controlled the higher Church educational institutions and much Church property and held the exclusive right to be candidates for investiture as bishops.[38]

Despite Polish achievements on the Podolian political, economic, and religious fronts, the fundamental opposition between the Polish or Polonized elites and the enserfed, still mostly Ukrainian, Orthodox (or Uniate) peasantry was not resolved. In 1717, just at the time when the feudal tax exemptions granted at the beginning of the recolonization period were starting to run out and, under Russian pressure, the Polish standing army was limited to 18,000 men with a mere 4,000 deployed in Ukraine, the word *Haidamak* begins to appear in the sources.[39] A Turkish word literally meaning "flight" and employed semantically as "robber" or "vagrant," the term was applied by the Poles to runaway serfs who hid in the forests and emerged in small groups to rob travelers and attack towns or noble estates.[40]

With no large, organized Cossack forces within easy political or geographic reach to serve as an organizing base, the Haidamaks remained a minor phenomenon operating in disparate bands, mainly in Right Bank Ukraine. In 1734, however, in the disorganized aftermath of the interregnum and the election—under Russian tutelage—of August III, Verlan, a Cossack officer in the private army of Jerzy Lubomirski, mutinied and organized Cossack-style units of some one thousand peasants. He raised the standard of revolt against the Polish lords, promising—like Chmielnicki and Palii before him—the removal of Jews, Polish landlords, and Catholic institutions from Ukrainian lands. Verlan claimed, falsely, that he was charged with this mission by the Russian tsarina, Anna. His exploits inspired other Haidamaks, and similar roving bands sprang up, raiding as far as the eastern parts of Podolia. A combination of Polish, Russian, and turncoat Haidamak efforts succeeded in scaling back the revolt and reducing Haidamak resistance to sporadic attacks.[41]

In 1750, however, Haidamaks began attacking regional centers from Kiev Province as far west as Latyczow in Podolia, the area where the Besht lived. A special nobility-based militia was formed to put down this latest attempt at revolt. Once again, Haidamak resistance retained a low profile until the most famous and well-organized Haidamak rebellion, centered around Uman in Bracław Province, in 1768—eight years after the Besht's death.[42]

The periodic Haidamak uprisings were a salient fact of life in Podolia.

It is evident from the stories in *Shivhei Ha-Besht* about the Ba'al Shem Tov and his associates that Jews fled their towns when the Haidamaks were on the move and the violent outbreaks served as benchmarks for dating prior and subsequent events (e.g., "two years before the flight"). The Besht himself may have fled before the attacks linked with the 1734 Verlan Revolt, when he lived in Tluste or elsewhere, and the threat of Haidamak collective punishment of Jews was evidently a serious concern for him.[43]

In the 1730s and 1740s, another type of social outlaw appeared, primarily in Podolia and Red Russia. These were the Opryshky, bandits who never actually organized a revolt but proved to be a security nightmare for noblemen and Jews.[44] While in Ukrainian folklore they were romanticized as Robin Hood types, Jewish sources—reflecting the viewpoint of their victims—were far less sanguine.[45] One of the most famous Opryshky raids, led by Ivan Boychik at the head of a twenty-eight-man gang, was on the town of Bolechow in 1759.[46] The Jewish wine merchant Ber of Bolechow's family was there; he described the attack in vivid and violent detail in his memoirs. The Jews of the town were robbed and looted, and seventeen Gentiles were forced to hand over their horses. The casualties were three Jews killed (one woman, two men), four wounded (two Jewish women, one Jewish man, and one Gentile man), and one of the Opryshky killed and two wounded (including Boychik himself), all three by a Jew shooting out of his fortified cellar.[47]

The robbers rode out of town, Ber wrote, "triumphantly . . . dressed in silk ladies' dresses which they had stolen in the town. . . . The chief of the band put on himself the white Leibserdak [traditional Jewish fringed garment] of my brother which he had had made for Passover. . . . The bandits also made a flag from an apron of brocade of very fine silk, embroidered with gold and silver, which they put on a stick, and this flag they carried in front of their chief."[48]

Another source of insecurity in the eighteenth-century Commonwealth, which Jews did not share with Polish noblemen or the Catholic church, was religious libel.[49] During the first half of the eighteenth century, blood and desecration of the host libels increased in number throughout the country, including Podolia. Libels were less frequent than attacks by Haidamaks and Opryshky, but the threat was ever-present and mounting a defense against an accusation was difficult. These libels were one more compelling reason for Jews to maintain strict communal discipline, keep lines of communication and influence open to the authorities, and remain vigilant.[50]

Culturally, eighteenth-century Podolia was a crossroads. Each of the three dominant ethnic groups—Poles, Jews, and Ukrainians—had its own language, religious ritual, and elite culture.[51] The difference in the ways the Jews and the Opryshky used expensive ladies' clothing may indicate a significant difference (at least between peasants and Jews) in material culture as well. While there was superficial familiarity with each other's rituals and idioms and a high degree of de facto toleration for the practice of other people's "false" religions, there was no ideology of ecumenicism or equality.[52] Jews, for example, were routinely termed "nonbelievers" or "infidels" in many official documents and remained politically disenfranchised. Polish administrators and even high noblemen displayed familiarity with, and tolerance for, Jewish customs connected with the Sabbath, holidays, kashrut, and prayers. They also employed Jewish technical terms such as *becherem* (ban), *bachur* (youth or student), *treif* (nonkosher), and *ba'al shem*. Their lexicon included expressions like "Jewish tricks," "sly Jews," and "haughty Jew," which indicate that they shared anti-Jewish stereotypes.[53] With regard to other groups, Orthodox, even Uniates, met with continuing discrimination, and worse, when it came to officeholding, municipal regulations, and treatment at the hands of officials. There were also anti-Ukrainian stereotypes. Just as administrators spoke of "Jewish tricks," they mentioned "Ruthenian [Ukrainian] tricks."[54]

On the level of popular culture, however, there is reason to believe that rather close ties existed between the groups. The best evidence to come to light for this is in the realm of popular religion. Tobias Kohn, a Jewish physician who spent a good part of his youth in Cracow, wrote in 1707 concerning the cultural level of the Commonwealth, "Even if demons had never been created they would have had to have been created for the people of this country; for there is no land where they are more occupied with demons, talismans, oath formulas, mystical names and dreams."[55] Kohn did not specify which segment of the Commonwealth's population he was describing, but it is likely that he meant everybody. Certainly in Podolia the belief in the occult and the existence of an unseen world of goblins and demons that posed a constant threat to human life was common to Jews and Christians alike.[56]

Stanislaw Vincenz, in describing the spiritual life of the Hucul mountain people of the northern Carpathians, put it this way:

> Protection against sorcery—whether it is sent from afar or imposed secretly; whether it is in the form of illness, or a visitation of the soul, or injury to animals, barrenness, or only one of the more petty injuries in everyday life—

protection from all this is just as important as protection against the irruption of mighty powers and the intrusion of forest apparitions or ordinary illnesses. Children and cattle are protected in advance by purifying them with living fire, or washing them with spring water, and also with the aid of all kinds of amulets and tokens. But all these things must have eyes, must have consciousness and purpose. This is the object of the incantations, curses, and prayers, which are all covered by the generic term of spells.[57]

If Jews employed ba'alei shem to communicate with this supernatural world and protect them from it, Christians had their *charivnyky, znakhari,* and *vorozhbyty* who served similar purposes. When it came to fending off supernatural predators, religious lines could be crossed. Ba'alei shem were not averse to learning cures from Gentiles, and the stories in *Shivhei Ha-Besht* and Ukrainian folklore indicate that Christians might avail themselves of the services of the Jewish holy men and vice versa. At least sometimes, members of each group viewed the holy individuals of the other as possessing theurgic power.[58]

In this connection, the non-Jewish population apparently referred to the Besht in Międzybóż as *kabalista* and *doktor.*[59] Conversely, in *Shivhei Ha-Besht,* there are several stories that demonstrate a belief in the theurgic power of certain Gentiles. For example, once the Besht is said to have declared concerning a particular priest, "I do not want to provoke him because he is a great sorcerer; he will sense it the moment that I begin to deal with him."[60]

Common beliefs about the occult and mutual respect for each other's theurgic powers suggest that cultural alienation among these groups was not as thoroughgoing as the distinctive and boundary-marking practices of elite religion might suggest. Kashrut rules made it very inconvenient for Jews and Christians to share a meal or celebration together. Different Sabbaths, holidays, and, indeed, calendars gave the members of each group a different rhythm in their life cycle. Different rituals, embodying differing beliefs, defined characteristic lifestyles.

Yet alongside these and other well-rehearsed distinctions there was a core of beliefs about the nature of reality and the methods for dealing with the vicissitudes of life that was common to all "common" people. Recent research on Jewish popular culture in other regions of Europe indicates that such common belief systems and common behaviors are to be expected.[61] On the social plane, they could serve as a countervailing force to separatist rituals, offering contexts for acceptable settings for social contact.

Jewish-Christian social encounters can be schematized as occupying a spectrum ranging from antagonistic encounters during wars, riots, raids, holdups, and casual street physical and verbal violence through more or less acrimonious but controlled confrontations in law courts to mildly negative, neutral, or friendly business, neighbor, and health (or spirit) care relationships and culminating in real individual friendships and group wartime alliance and cooperation.[62] Perhaps an important factor in creating this spectrum was the dialectic between the explicit attitude of the elite sources of religion that encouraged alienation from outgroups[63] and the implied attitude of shared fate inherent in the common understanding of the nature of reality. As one moves along the continuum, alienation weakens and shared fate strengthens.

Interestingly, *Shivhei Ha-Besht* includes a strain that encourages a feeling of shared moral obligation between Jew and Gentile. In one story, the Ba'al Shem Tov's disciple, Jacob Joseph of Polonne, has a dream in which he enters a palace in paradise. There Satan accused an arrendator of defrauding villagers in his area. This sin was deemed to outweigh the fact that the man "studied constantly" and gave money to charity. A punishment was decreed, and on earth the lord of the estate confiscated the arrendator's possessions and put him and his family in jail. The moral of the story is then spelled out: "From this it can be seen that one should refrain from robbing Gentiles, since, as it is written in the books, Satan deducts this sin from one's holy merits, God forbid." In another story, the Besht warns his disciples how "he saw that in heaven Jews who live in the villages were accused of cheating Gentiles in their accounts."[64] While, as we shall see in chapter 9, these stories do not necessarily express the Besht's actual attitudes, they probably do indicate trends in popular culture.

Other aspects of religious experience that made an impact in Podolia are sectarianism and mysticism. Orthodox schismatic and mystical groups such as the Old Believers, the Khlysty, and the Dukhabory were represented there; and the Starchy mystical sect originated in the Carpathians just over the Moldavian border.[65] On the Jewish side, Podolia proved receptive to the recrudescence of the remnants of the mystical, messianic Sabbatean movement. In western Podolia in the 1750s, Jacob Frank succeeded in reincarnating Sabbateanism in a more radical, antinomian form than his seventeenth-century predecessors.[66]

Several scholars have noted the coincidence that the Besht, putative founder of a Jewish mystical sect, appeared in a region where such types were fairly common.[67] In 1968, Yaffa Eliach published a sensational article[68] that, while disdained in the strongest terms by leading scholars in the fields of mysticism, Hasidism, and Polish-Jewish history, has made a lasting impression among historical buffs and nonspecialized historians alike.[69] Eliach claimed, "There are significant ritual and sociological similarities between the Hasidism of the Besht and the Dissenting sects of the Russian Church. The striking similarities plus the battles waged by the Jewish scholars of that period [against Hasidism] leave little doubt that the Besht's Hasidism was directly influenced by these Raskol [schismatic] groups."[70]

The first sentence of this citation positing significant similarities between Hasidism and Russian dissenting sects may be true, although all of the evidence adduced so far, by Eliach and others, is superficial and more research needs to be done.[71] Gershon D. Hundert has pointed out how in the mid-eighteenth century pietistic movements with significant ritual and sociological similarities to Hasidism were popular in western Europe and North America as well.[72] This should serve as a caution that even if there is a correlation with regard to the characteristics of all of these sects, theorizing a causative relationship, as Eliach did, is a case of falling into the trap of a very common logical fallacy. What seems more likely is that all of these geographically and culturally widespread phenomena were similar reactions to similar conditions obtaining in a world whose religious foundations had been shaken very hard over the previous century or so. The elusive concept of zeitgeist gains meaning when applied to this combination of like circumstances and like, yet diffuse, reactions.

One can find parallels between the contemporaries Judah Hasid and Francis of Assisi in the twelfth century, or Muslim Ayatollahs and certain ultra-Orthodox rabbis in the twentieth, but there are no direct links that prove flow of influence. Similarly, Eliach could point to parallels, but not to a single piece of evidence demonstrating that the Besht, or any Hasidic leader, was in contact in more than a superficial way with any Christian theologian. Her assertion to the contrary is purely speculative, and her certitude as to the presence of direct influence of the Raskol groups rests on nothing more than apparent, superficial ritual similarities, temporal coincidence, and hyperinterpretation of legendary details, seeing in them references to actual events.

Moreover, basic points in Eliach's argument are demonstrably wrong. First, blithely unaware of the history of the text and apparently choosing to ignore its hagiographic character, she relied mostly—and completely uncritically—on *Shivhei Ha-Besht* for information on the Besht's life and behavior. For example, she considered the first story in *Shivhei*

Ha-Besht, purporting to recount incidents in the life of the Besht's father prior to his birth, to be "the oldest account of the Besht's origins."
I have shown elsewhere that the first story is a development of the second—but earlier—story describing an episode in the life of the Besht's
father. The first story's version probably originated among Habad Hasidim in the first decade of the nineteenth century. Moreover, even the
earlier, second story is obviously stereotypical and legendary and originally may not even have been told about the Besht's father.[73] Second, Eliach's attempt to link opposition to early Hasidism with opposition to
the Russian schismatic groups does not stand. As we shall see, it is doubtful that the Besht met with active opposition during his lifetime. Later
opponents of Hasidim accused them of being Sabbateans and Frankists
or even, rarely, Quakers, Mennonites, and Freemasons, but never Russian Orthodox schismatics.[74] Third, the Adam from whom the Besht was
said to have received his holy writings was proven by Khone Shmeruk—
five years before Eliach's article was published—to be the semimythical
Adam Ba'al Shem of sixteenth-century Prague. Eliach's supposition that
he was the Christian Orthodox religious figure Adam Zernikov is untenable.[75] Fourth, Eliach's completely unsupported assertion that the
Besht's behavior was determined by his "addiction to his pipe" in which
he "smoked something other than tobacco" displays a refusal to accept
the possibility of a non-drug-induced mystical-ecstatic experience and, I
would posit, the influence of the American drug culture that in 1968 was
moving into high gear.

The relationship between Hasidism and new mystical-ecstatic sects in
other religions is an important issue. It can reveal much about the *mentalité* of eighteenth-century European society. This subject awaits an expert in the requisite fields to investigate it fully.

The multidimensional crisis of the Polish-Lithuanian Commonwealth
in the eighteenth century has been duly noted by at least some historians of the Besht and early Hasidism. The most familiar is S. M. Dubnow's account at the beginning of his *History of Hasidism,*[76] which depicts early eighteenth-century Poland as mired in political and economic
chaos. According to Dubnow, this chaos left the Jews exposed to violence and exploitation. Their sole recourse was to seek comfort within
the confines of the in-group for all of the insults showered upon them by
the surrounding society.[77]

As we have seen, sporadic violence was a strong feature of this society and Jews were particularly liable to become its victims in a number
of ways. It should be emphasized, however, that the weakness of the cen-

tral government of the Commonwealth did not mean that law and order were everywhere correspondingly weak. To a large extent, especially in Podolia, the political vacuum was filled by the aristocratic magnates. Contrary to their image in Dubnow's account, and those of many Polish and Ukrainian historians as well, the high nobility were not all drunken, irresponsible playboys. Allowing for individual differences, magnates (some of the active managers were women) were by and large capable of providing their subjects with a stable and, by the standards of the time, reasonably safe environment. This included their Jews. The successful recolonization of Podolia in the first half of the eighteenth century is testimony to their political power and administrative talents.[78]

The Podolian recolonization is also relevant when evaluating the economic context of the Besht's life. While the country as a whole was in an economic downturn, Podolia was developing and growing. Population growth was up, new towns were established and old ones revitalized. External trade was stable, and urban commerce was on the rise. Podolia was probably one of the more attractive places to live in Poland, especially after the Great Northern War ended. At that point the North was just beginning reconstruction, while in Podolia it had been going strong for a generation, ever since the reconquest from Turkish rule. Jews responded to the new opportunities in Podolia by moving there as part of the recolonization movement, reaching, by 1764, a population of almost forty thousand—some 6 percent of the overall Jewish population of the Commonwealth. To see Podolia and its Jewish community as suffering the effects of a debilitating crisis fails to take into account steady growth and development during the first half of the eighteenth century.[79]

Culturally, Jewish alienation was not as absolute as is often assumed. While elite Jewish and Christian cultures shared little in common, both produced mystical-ecstatic sects. Close physical proximity, familiarity with each other's lifestyles, business and other utilitarian considerations, and subtle, shared assumptions about reality and the means for contending with it, all contributed to a situation in which Jews and Christians found the opportunities and the means to communicate with each other.

Dubnow drew a line from the 1648 Persecutions accompanying the Chmielnicki Uprising and the effects of their attendant depradations to the activities of the Besht some one hundred years later. He implied that the catastrophe of 1648 gave rise to problematic circumstances that defied resolution until the Ba'al Shem Tov came along. This view became the conventional one and can be read even in recent books.[80]

This collapsing of one hundred years of history has not withstood scholarly scrutiny. Mordecai Nadav and Hundert demonstrated convincingly how the effects of the persecutions were dissipated within one or two generations. West of the Dnieper most of the destroyed communities were eventually reestablished, the population was replenished, the economy was restored, even if changed, and life returned to a state of normalcy.[81] The year 1648 was not the determining context for the socioeconomic reality or even the mentalité of the Besht's era.

The portrayal by Dubnow, and the many who followed in his path, of the Jews of "Poland" as living a bleak, alienated, dangerous existence, relieved only by their rich, internal, spiritual life, does not seem to be an apt description of Podolia's Jews. The horrible events of 1648–1660 were a vivid historical memory, but not still present in the conditions of everyday life.

Along with everyone in the region, the Jews benefited from the moderate degree of stability afforded by magnate rule and the economic boom that was the effect of recolonization. They also knew how to cooperate with their neighbors in areas of life where cooperation was deemed appropriate by both sides, such as physical and supernatural defense. In Podolia, Jews and Christians shared the physical, social, cultural, and economic environment, even if they did not operate in the same universe of discourse.

As we shall see, the Besht both attracted the attention of his Christian neighbors and paid attention to them. The authorities he dealt with were administrators of the magnates. The common belief in a bustling supernatural world made his shamanesque activities plausible to Jew and Gentile alike and brought him into contact with Christian theurgists. On occasion he was called on to respond to anti-Jewish libels and the general atmosphere of violence and insecurity. Conversely, the relative prosperity and organization of Podolia and his town, Międzybóż, within it, provided the modicum of law, order, and economic prosperity necessary for the Ba'al Shem Tov to function.

CHAPTER FOUR

Międzybóż

A Place in Time and Space

The development and relative prosperity of Podolia during the Besht's lifetime is partially illustrated by the circumstances in the three Podolian locales with which his life is most closely associated: his reported childhood home and perhaps even his birthplace, Okopy;[1] his later residence, Tłuste;[2] and the place where he spent most of his public career, Międzybóż.[3]

The Okopy mentioned in *Shivhei Ha-Besht* as the Besht's early hometown was probably Okop Góry Swięty Trojcy (Hill Fortification of the Holy Trinity).[4] This position just north of the Moldavian border, some three miles from the city of Kamieniec Podolski, was founded in 1692 as a forward military base from which Jan Sobieski's forces could conduct reconnaissance and raid the Turks occupying the city. By the time the Poles regained Kamieniec Podolski in 1699, Okopy had become a civilian settlement, owned by the Wojewoda of Kiev, Marcin Kątski, who received a charter for the town in June 1700. The charter specified that in the town, officially called Swięty Trojcy (Holy Trinity), there would be a weekly market and two commercial fairs annually.[5]

Okopy owed its existence to the Polish recapture and resettlement of Podolia. Like dozens of similar new, small commercial centers, it must have attracted a complement of commercially inclined Jews, although as late as the 1764 census the Jewish population of Okopy and vicinity was listed as only 230.[6] The Ba'al Shem Tov's parents were probably among those Jews who were drawn to the newly established town when its Jewish community was presumably even smaller. The Besht was apparently born around the time the small town made the transition from army base to civilian settlement.[7]

According to traditions reported in *Shivhei Ha-Besht,* the Besht worked in Tłuste as a *melamed* (elementary teacher) and there underwent his original revelation and early experiences as a ba'al shem healer. On two of the surviving letters he signed, the Besht himself indicated Tłuste as his home or place of origin. Tłuste was a minor commercial center, founded originally in the mid-sixteenth century. The 1764 census listed 355 Jews resident in it and its associated villages. Its participation in the wave of development in early eighteenth-century Podolia is symbolized by the new Catholic church built there in 1717. It suffered from a visit by passing Muscovite troops in early 1741.[8]

One of the Podolian towns most abundantly documented in extant archival sources is, fortuitously, Międzybóż,[9] the place where the Besht was most active following his revelation as a ba'al shem. In reading both Hasidic traditions about the Besht and modern descriptions of his life, it is easy to gain the impression that Międzybóż, where the Besht lived from 1740 until his death in 1760, was a small, outlying hamlet (Yiddish *shtetl;* Polish *miasteczko*). Save for his presence there, it seems, Międzybóż would have had no significance. According to conventional accounts, it also had little impact on the course of the Besht's life. Living in Międzybóż is usually viewed as incidental to the Besht's achievements.[10]

Detaching the Besht from the context of most of his public activity makes it easier to construct a description of him that meets the requirements of ideology. It does not help in strengthening the reality-based component of that description. An understanding of the context of the Besht's public and private life in Międzybóż will provide new criteria for linking and assessing the sources about him and evaluating the information they provide. Hundreds of documents relating to Międzybóż in the late seventeenth century and first half of the eighteenth century have been preserved in the archive of the families that owned the town, the Sieniawskis and Czartoryskis. This archive is housed in the Czartoryski Library (Biblioteka Czartoryskich) in Cracow. Some of these archival sources facilitate understanding of the circumstances in Międzybóż, and within its Jewish community, during the period the Besht lived there. There is even a small amount of material relating directly to the Besht himself (see chap. 10).

Międzybóż was not a small, poor, unremarkable hamlet. Already

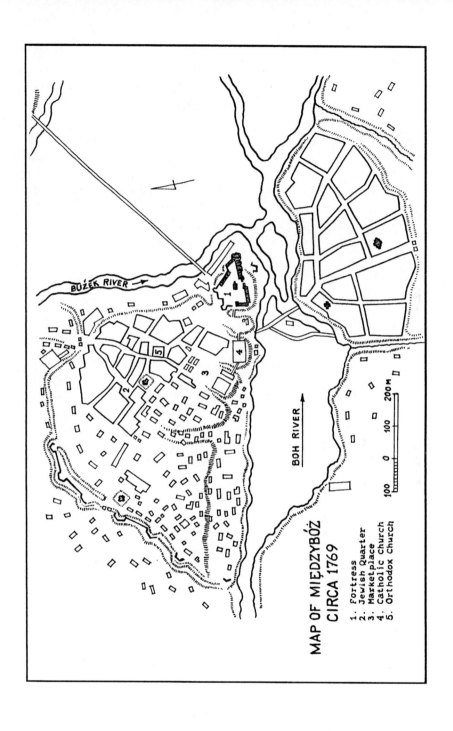

BUŻEK RIVER →

BOH RIVER ↑

MAP OF MIĘDZYBÓŻ
CIRCA 1769

1. Fortress
2. Jewish Quarter
3. Marketplace
4. Catholic Church
5. Orthodox Church

200 M

100

0

100

settled in the twelfth century, it was one of the main population and commercial centers of Podolia. As a fortress town, Międzybóż was the last line of defense against Tatar attacks aimed at Crown Poland.[11] It was part of an unofficial border area, marking the eastward extent of "Polishness" in Ukraine. For example, from Międzybóż westward, the Uniate church held sway over the peasantry; to the east, Orthodoxy was still viable. Likewise, only to the east of Międzybóż was there strong evidence of Cossack political influence and freedom movements. In the eighteenth century, Międzybóż served as a haven for refugees—particularly Jews—fleeing Cossack and Haidamak attacks in towns to the east.[12]

Before the 1648 war, Międzybóż reportedly reached a peak population of more than ten thousand inhabitants. During the war, however, Chmielnicki occupied Międzybóż four times, destroying it in March 1649. The Sieniawski family, Międzybóż's owners, returned to their possession after the 1658 Treaty of Hadiacz. The Turkish war of 1672 and the subsequent Treaty of Buczacz drove them out again, as Międzybóż was taken over by Tatars and Janissaries. In less than a year (October 1672), Mikołaj Sieniawski retook his town but under the terms of the 1676 Treaty of Żurawno was obligated to evacuate it. He finally did in 1678, at which time the Turks occupied the town.[13]

Polish rule returned to Międzybóż in the spring of 1686 when the Turks staged a strategic retreat in the face of a new Polish offensive. By 1691, Adam Mikołaj Sieniawski, the owner of the town, was leasing out the *arenda*.[14] A Christian wood-carver named Roman Skaminski noted that he arrived in Międzybóż with his parents in 1699 when "there were still only a few people" there but prices had already begun to rise—presumably as part of the general phenomenon of development.[15] Incipient prosperity was interrupted when Palii occupied Międzybóż during his revolt in 1702. Adam Mikołaj Sieniawski, who was also the Polish Hetman, drove him out in 1703, restoring Międzybóż to its trajectory of building and rapid growth.[16]

By 1740, around the time of the Besht's arrival there, Międzybóż was one of the largest towns in Ukraine. While never regaining its pre-1648 size, the population had increased by some 50 percent over the previous twenty years and enjoyed a construction boom as well. It now consisted of 764 potential taxpaying households (545 Christian and 219 Jewish), or approximately five thousand people (about one-third Jews).[17] Situated in Podolia, midway between Lwów and Kiev, near the Bóg River, which empties into the Black Sea, Międzybóż was an administrative center for the Czartoryski latifundium as well as an important trade emporium where merchants of the region and from the West gathered to buy and sell. It was also a point of origin for organized trade caravans that crossed the steppes to Kiev. There was a permanent garrison there to provide security for the town and the trade routes. Międzybóż merchants could be found in Polish commercial centers like Lwów and Lublin, but also as far away as Kiev to the east and the mercantile cities of Germany and Silesia to the west.[18]

There are several signs that Międzybóż was generally orderly and thriving around the time the Besht settled there in 1740. In 1738, a plague ravaging the region skipped over Międzybóż, probably a testimony to the relatively high level of nutrition and cleanliness of the town—both attributes associated with a measure of prosperity and good administration.[19] As an indicator of aggregate wealth, it is noteworthy that in the late 1730s and early 1740s the three main religious communities, Catholic, Orthodox, and Jewish, all undertook major building or restoration projects of their houses of worship.[20]

Another indicator of the degree to which Międzybóż was flourishing was the value of the general arenda of the town, which awarded its holder the lease on income derived from liquor manufacture and sale, various market and product taxes, operation of local mills, and customary payments from some of the guilds.[21] The price of the Międzybóż arenda increased more than fourteenfold (from 2,000 zl. to 28,800 zl.)[22] from the period of resettlement until the period of the Besht's arrival there some fifty years later, including a moderate 12 percent rise between 1736 and 1743. The pattern of steep rises in the late seventeenth and early eighteenth century, followed by smaller increases later on, cannot be ascribed to arbitrary demands on the part of the Polish landlords or simple inflation. It should rather be seen as reflecting the market for this lease as the town's economy and population grew dramatically with the return of Polish rule and then more moderately from the late 1720s.[23]

The overall economic situation was characterized in a 1745 letter written by the Polish administrator, Rynkiewicz, who reported to his superior, Walicki, concerning the villages attached to the Międzybóż latifundium that "the economy of the Międzybóż *klucz* [latifundium administrative unit] is following the usual course and, with God's grace, everything is good."[24] Some Jews were also conscious of Międzybóż's relatively fortunate situation. When, in 1745, due to other pressing financial obligations, the Jewish community of Żinków sought to delay paying a certain levy, they requested that "Jews who have it better, as in Międzybóż," advance the money on their behalf, temporarily.[25]

Generally positive economic circumstances do not mean that the Międzybóż economy was problem-free or always registering positive growth. Arrendators, for example, were sometimes forced to buy latifundium products such as cattle and fish. These forced sales were economically unproductive, constituting a subsidy given by the arrendators to unprofitable latifundium businesses. This subsidy had to be passed on in higher arenda collection fees or absorbed as a loss by the lessees.[26] Like other places, Międzybóż had to put up with economically damaging events such as floods that destroyed mills and crops, occasional Haidamak attacks, and costly visits by Muscovite army units that constituted part of the growing Russian political and military influence on the Commonwealth. The Haidamaks and Muscovites were especially harmful to village arrendators, who had to supply provisions free and were often the target of casual violence and worse at the hands of the raiders. Sometimes, as in 1734 and 1735, the city of Międzybóż itself suffered incursion.[27]

In the realm of the business cycle proper, there is evidence that around 1744, a few years after the Besht's arrival, Międzybóż experienced what might be termed a recession. In his letter cited above, Rynkiewicz implied that the serf population was able to meet its feudal obligations and was not suffering badly enough to defect. At the same time, however, arrendators were complaining that the serfs were not honoring debts to them. As a consequence, some arrendators were having difficulties paying their own obligations. When arenda renewal time came around, bidders were not willing to pay as much for leases, competition for leases decreased, and bargaining between the administrators and potential lessees became more protracted and contentious.[28]

The result was that from 1744 to 1745, the price of the Międzybóż area village leases held steady or dropped by up to 17 percent.[29] In the city itself, between 1744 and 1746 the general arrendators were also having problems collecting what was owed them and, in turn, paying their debts. In June 1744, they tried to cancel their contract. In early 1746, deep in debt, with no credit and no cash, the Międzybóż arrendators were arrested by the administrator in charge, Obrębski. He then changed his mind, released them, and helped them collect from their debtors so they could honor their financial commitments.[30]

Another probable indicator of recession circa 1744 is the reduction that year in the amount of excise tax collected from self-employed Jews. According to a register compiled by the kahal and translated into Polish,[31] in 1744—as compared with 1743—the total assessment was reduced by almost 18 percent, from 4,853 to 3,991 zloty. While some of this reduction may have been the result of a reform in the method of assessment,[32] it seems likely that part of it resulted from an economic downturn.

Downturn does not, however, mean crisis. It is true that sixteen of those who were assessed in 1743 did not pay in 1744, probably due to death, migration, impoverishment, or—in the case of the two women omitted from the second list—remarriage. Against this trend, ten people were dunned an increased amount in 1744. Twenty new taxpayers (more than 12 percent of the total and a net gain of four) were added to the roll in 1744. Such a large number of new taxpayers argues for the fundamental economic strength of the town.

The Jewish community of Międzybóż was reestablished around 1660, after it had been destroyed in the Chmielnicki Revolt of 1648–1649. Jews reappear in the records by 1662. By 1666 the community was large enough to employ a *szkolnik* (bailiff) who represented it in dealings with the municipality and for a nobleman named Czarnowodski to sue it for harboring a Jew who had lodged a false accusation against him.[33] In 1681, under Turkish rule, there were 88 Jews in Międzybóż (out of approximately 1500 in all Podolia).[34] By the mid-eighteenth century, following the period of the town's accelerated development, Międzybóż, with a reported 2,039 Jews, was one of the fifteen largest Jewish communities in all of the Polish-Lithuanian Commonwealth. Between 1722 and 1740, while the town's population as a whole was growing by 50 percent, the number of Jews had increased by 67 percent. Jews owned the majority of the better, stone houses in the town as well as most of the stores on the marketplace. There was no ghetto in Międzybóż, and close to a third of the Jews had at least one Christian neighbor.[35]

Międzybóż was "on the map" before the Ba'al Shem Tov made it his home. When he settled there in 1740, he was joining a community that was large, secure, and generally prosperous. It offered the promise of a large clientele for his ba'al shem services and a budget that could support religious institutions. The financial problems of the mid-1740s may have encouraged some people to seek out spiritual guidance and moral support that a figure like the Besht could provide.

Hebrew sources on Międzybóż are few. Because the Polish overlords of Międzybóż were very concerned about preserving order, guaranteeing the smooth functioning of town life, and gaining revenues from their properties, the extant Polish sources are particularly rich with regard to fiscal matters and conflicts within the community that came to the attention of the Polish authorities. From these it is possible to gain rare, detailed, partially quantifiable information on the life of this eighteenth-century Jewish community that was the Besht's home.

From the available tax information it is possible to divide the community's population into rough categories. The poorest people permanently resident in the Jewish community of Międzybóż were those who owned no homes and do not appear on the list of potential real estate taxpayers. It is difficult to determine their number. There is a list of more than thirty Jews (some are referred to only as unspecified *sąsiędzi*, literally "neighbors," but in this context apparently boarders or guests in the homes of others), who were designated for expulsion from the Między-bóż community in 1743. Presumably, they were denied the right of permanent residence by the kahal because they were too poor to participate in the tax burden. None of them had their own homes. Of the twenty-eight people listed by name, five were women, two of them called "widow." Fourteen of the men and one of the women were designated artisans or semiskilled workers.[36]

The next category of people were those who had permission to live in the community on a permanent basis but owned no homes. They boarded or rented rooms in the homes of wealthier people. Many of them were probably servants, and a high percentage of these were single women.[37] There is no way to gauge their number in Międzybóż.[38]

Another group includes those who are listed as real estate owners liable to pay the *czynsz* (an annual fee) on their property. The people listed are, roughly, those who were heads of households. This number fluctuated from year to year, usually rising. Thus, as mentioned, in 1740 there were 219 such people. By 1742, after more people had married and established homes and some had migrated to the town, the number stood at 230.[39]

Nearly 14 percent (32) of this group of household heads were women. As is to be expected, based on precedents from elsewhere in preindustrial Europe,[40] almost all of these women were widows; twenty-seven were specifically termed *wdowa*. Inheritance of the house and devolution of the identity—and apparently the responsibility—of the household did not necessarily pass to these women merely as a result of the absence of a male candidate. For five of these widows, the document specifies—as it does for several male householders as well—that a son-in-law or (married) son was living in their home. This implies that despite the presence of a young married man whose mention signals that he probably had a family and was old enough to be a householder himself, the woman owned the house and was considered the head of the household. This recalls the type of businesswoman-widow represented by the famous Gluckel of Hameln (1648–1724). Having been involved in business matters all along, she took over management of the family business and property on her husband's death and had a strong hand in guiding the matches and careers of her maturing children.[41]

As with women in European preindustrial society generally, the Jewish woman had no political rights, could not participate in the elections or deliberations of the kahal, and was subject both by Jewish tradition and European custom to the authority of her father, husband, or—in the case of a servant girl—master. Independent widows, however, who controlled significant economic resources and wielded familial authority were everywhere a partial exception to this restrictive framework. In some cities they even continued to enjoy their husbands' political and economic privileges.[42] In Międzybóż, this unenfranchised, but potentially powerful, group would have made an ideal constituency for the Ba'al Shem Tov. His areas of specialization—medicine and the occult—were traditionally associated with women. There are hints in *Shivhei Ha-Besht* and elsewhere that it was women, in particular, who recognized his powers.[43]

The people on the czynsz tax roll, men and women, while not the poorest in the community, did represent an economic range. To understand the parameters of this range, it is useful to compare the 1742 czynsz tax list with the list of excise tax payers in 1743 and 1744. As noted above, the excise list names 154 and 158 people, probably household heads, for each year.[44] The approximately seventy householders[45] who appear on the czynsz roll, but not on the excise tax lists, were either poor people, employees of others, or butchers and bakers whose excise tax was figured according to a different method (see chap. 5) and who were generally classed with the poorer people. With the exception of the relatively well paid rabbi, who in the early 1740s earned more than 600 zloty per year, and the cantor, who was paid approximately half that,[46] those who were gainfully employed but not among the excise tax payers were probably just above the poverty line.

The excise tax assessment for those who do appear on the list was, in principle, proportional to their income. Obligations ranged from as low as 3 zloty to as high as 350. What percentage of a taxpayer's income did this represent? We do not know what the precise relationship was between tax and income. A tax schedule from Stara Sieniawa near Międzybóż, dated October 1741, specified that merchants would have to pay

24 groszy per 100 zloty worth of retailed merchandise, or 0.75 percent.[47] Similarly, a 1744 schedule specified that arrendators of outlying villages owed the excise arrendators 2 percent of gross revenues on the first thousand zloty they took in and 7 percent thereafter.[48] The value of merchandise sold or of gross revenues is normally many times greater than net profit. The lower the profit margin, the higher the actual tax. If, for example, merchants' or arrendators' net profits were as much as 10 percent, then the actual tax rates they paid based on the two schedules mentioned would soar to 7.5 percent, 20 percent, and 70 percent. Until further research clarifies profit margins, the tax data can serve only as a relative indicator of income.

Relatively speaking, the more than hundredfold difference in the excise tax payments of the richest and poorest taxpayers (3 zl.–350 zl.) indicates that there was a wide gap in income and, presumably, standard of living in Jewish Międzybóż, even without taking into account those who were poor and exempt from this tax.

Table 1 illustrates the size of the various taxpaying groups, with the assumption, based on the 1742 czynsz tax roll, that there were at least seventy householders who paid no excise tax at all.

TABLE 1   EXCISE TAXPAYERS IN MIĘDZYBÓŻ
IN 1743 AND 1744
According to Amount Paid

Cohort (amount paid in zl.)	Number in Cohort in 1743	Percentage of Total Number of Taxpayers in 1743 (Total = 224)	Number in Cohort in 1744	Percentage of Total Number of Taxpayers in 1744 (Total = 228)
a (0)	70?	31	70?	31
b (≤10)	50	22	68	30
c (≤20)	37	16	28	12
d (≤30)	22	10	21	9
e (≤40)	9	4	13	6
f (≤50)	5	2	9	4
g (≤60)	10	4	3	1
h (≤70)	6	3	4	2
i (≤80)	2	1	1	*
j (≤90)	4	2	2	1
k (≤100)	1	*	3	1
l (≤200)	7	3	4	2
m (>200)	1	*	1	*

SOURCE: BC EW 41 Regestr Taxy . . . 1744.
Note: An asterisk indicates less than 0.5 percent. Percentages are approximate.

This table shows that the economic structure of Międzybóż's Jewish community was pyramidlike, not elliptical. Most of the Jews working in Międzybóż were lower class, rather than middle class. Assuming that the conservative estimate of seventy exempt householders is reasonably correct, in 1743 more than 50 percent and in 1744 more than 60 percent of the householders (cohorts a and b) paid little or no excise tax. The middle-size sums of 11 to 40 zloty were paid by approximately 25 to 30 percent (c, d, e), while 10 to 15 percent of the householders were in the upper cohorts (f–m). The pyramid had a slight bulge at the top, with those paying more than 100 zloty (l, m) approximately equal to the number in the three cohorts paying between 71 and 100 zloty (i, j, k). The number of very rich people in Międzybóż was somewhat out of proportion to the number in the other economic categories.

When the economic situation worsened in 1744, it is interesting to observe that it was not only the poor who were affected. Only four (b, e, f, k) of the thirteen cohorts increased in number.[49] Their spacing suggests that they served as the main basins for "catching" those who fell from the cohorts above them, and taxpayers fell from as high as cohort l. Even the sole member of cohort m, the richest taxpayer, Moszko Charyton, went from an assessment of 350 zloty to one of only 280 zloty, a decline of 20 percent—slightly more than the 18 percent average. This suggests that when times worsened, virtually everyone was affected.

Based on czynsz tax rolls,[50] it is possible to characterize the general areas of Jewish economic endeavor in Międzybóż. One category is commerce. In addition to the storekeepers and occasional vendors listed above, there were merchants, probably like Charyton, whose businesses had international connections.[51] Many of the Jewish storekeepers, as well as those who sold in the marketplace from a stand or a sack, traveled to surrounding villages on buying trips and to neighboring towns for fairs.[52] While no one is explicitly identified as a moneylender, it is likely that, as in other places, this was an active sideline for some Jewish merchants, arrendators, and clergy.[53]

Another occupational category that entailed commerce was artisanry. Male and female petty artisans usually sold their own wares, although most of their time was spent in producing a product or providing a service. Apparently the most common of these occupations were the needle, fur, and shoemaking trades. While women were prominent in the first of these, they are not identified in the other two.[54] Międzybóż Jews were also engaged in metalworking trades,[55] including goldsmithery, in glaziery, in papermaking, and in bookbinding.

Food preparation trades constituted a significant occupational sector. There were both female and male bakers and even at least one cake specialist (male). Butchers and slaughterers were also an important component of the occupational structure. Because of Jewish ritual requirements and the potential in tax revenue for the community from the slaughter and sale of meat, these men were closely supervised and their trade carefully regulated. While their product was sold in high quantities at relatively high prices, they belonged to the lower-paid segments of the population. They had a clearly defined identity in the town that was expressed in the establishment of their own association and synagogue. In the 1730s and 1740s, the meat men played a political role, opposing the wealthy Icko Ognisty and Wolf Abramowicz, both closely tied to the Polish administration, who wielded significant authority over the Jewish community.[56]

Another branch of the comestible sector was liquor preparation and sale. Jews worked as brewers and distillers as well as bartenders.[57] Many families served liquor in their homes as a sideline, with the wife and children taking primary responsibility for this enterprise.[58]

Services provided by Jews included medicinal preparation and barbering, which in the eighteenth century encompassed quasi-medical responsibilities such as tooth-pulling and leeching. Jews were also teamsters, musicians, and household servants. The service sector also included communal workers and clergy. There was a rabbi, a person who appears to be a rabbi emeritus, cantor, "bass singer" (assistant cantor), preacher, bath attendant, sextons, teachers, a Kabbalist, and various unspecified "clergymen" (duchowny).[59]

The most financially rewarding of the Międzybóż Jewish occupations was commerce. Of the nine highest taxpayers, paying more than 100 zloty in excise tax in either 1743 or 1744, eight were definitely store owners and the ninth may have been one. Of the twenty-nine people who paid between 40 and 100 zloty in at least one of these two years, nineteen were definitely store owners. Three were tailors, two were notions dealers, one was a furrier, and one was a goldsmith. From this information it appears that an artisan selling his own products from his workshop could potentially work his way into what might be termed an upper-middle-class economic position. To be among the richest people in town, however, it was necessary to have a store selling a range of merchandise such as cloth, foodstuffs, or finished goods, purchased wholesale from a variety of sources.

The leading commercial family was the Charytons. Moszko Charyton, his sons, Leyzor and Mordha, and his son-in-law, Manaszko, owned
five stores among them and paid a combined total of 1,188 zloty in excise tax in 1743 and 1744.[60] Representing 2.5 percent of the excise taxpayers, they paid almost 13.5 percent of the total tax. Other prominent
commercial families were the Zelmanowiczes, the Gierszonowiczes, and
Nota and his son, Leybka. Szaja Froimowicz, Symha Bunem Moszkowicz Kowelski, Wolf,[61] and Szmoyło, son-in-law of Gielman,[62] round out
the top commercial taxpayers in 1743 and 1744.

There was an overlap between the commercial, store-owning class and
those who held the most important arenda leases. Judka and Jankiel Gierszonowicz, Moszko and Leyzor Charyton, and Chaim Illowicz can all
be definitely identified as both store owners and arrendators at various
times;[63] they are probably just examples of this phenomenon. This coincidence is to be expected since bidding on lucrative leases required a
goodly amount of capital, which the wealthiest store owners could ac-
cumulate. Once the arenda gained momentum it, in turn, could provide
cash for financing commercial ventures.[64]

Another area of positive correlation with the Jewish economic elite of
Międzybóż was community politics. The town's Jewish community was
organized in typical fashion with responsibility for the autonomous functions of Jewish life—tax collection, adjudication, education, and charity; membership, housing, and fiscal policy; and regulation of economic,
religious, social, and family life—in the hands of the community council, the kahal. In the typical Polish community, the kahal was an oligar-
chal body that was dominated by a few families who were wealthy and
well connected, especially with the Polish authorities. Political rights in
the community's institutions were limited to male householders who paid
a minimum tax. As was true in Polish and European municipalities in
general, poorer people, such as artisans, were not allowed to participate
in elections.[65]

Regulations from Międzybóż around 1745 specify that home own-
ing—implying a minimal tax contribution—was a sina qua non for political participation. Arrendators, who might qualify financially to participate in the elections, could only do so if they owned a house in
Międzybóż and lived in it or elsewhere in the Międzybóż district. If they
lived in Międzybóż or its environs but did not actually own a house in
the town, they had no vote. Likewise, two householders who shared a
home could not both vote for the elders of the community; only the

official owner of the house was entitled to vote. With regard to office-holding, anyone who was exempt from taxes could not become a *rosh* (elder), although he could serve in a lower position on the kahal.[66]

Limited information on the officeholders in Międzybóż allows for some insight into the political organization of the community. The offices in Międzybóż consisted of the following: four *roshim* (Polish *kwartalny*), who rotated as the chief executive officer; four *tuvim* (Polish *ławnicy*), assistants to the rosh whose specific duties are not explained; four *ne'emanim* (Polish *wiernicy*), usually people entrusted with overseeing some financial function such as tax collection; six *gabaim* (Polish *tytory*), who would be in charge of various communal services and welfare functions such as charity dispersal and maintenance of the synagogue; and five *electorowie* (no Hebrew equivalent is given). The last term normally referred to electors (Hebrew *borerim*) who would choose the officeholders after they themselves had been selected by the electorate. It is evident that in Międzybóż the electors, rather than choose tax assessors, did the assessing themselves, in addition to their electoral duties.[67]

For eight of the years between 1726 and 1743 there are complete or partial lists of officeholders,[68] which shed some light on the question of the degree to which the communal organization of Międzybóż was, as is the case elsewhere,[69] a self-perpetuating oligarchy. The sample is admittedly small, but it does suggest the parameters of the phenomenon.

For the years documented, there were thirty-two roshim to be elected. Twenty people actually filled the office, with Wolf Abramowicz serving four times, Kielman Bieniaszewicz Luczynski three times, and Boruch Czarny, Nyson Majerowicz, Aron Zelmanowicz, Chaskiel Rabinowicz, Symcha Bun Moskiewicz Kowelski, and Szaja Froimowicz twice each.[70] This ratio of 1.6:1 for offices to officeholders implies more turnover and less repeat incumbency than is usually assumed on the basis of information from places such as Cracow in the seventeenth century. There Majer Bałaban found an offices-to-officeholder ratio of 4:1 for the first eight years documented (1622–1626, 1631–1633). Over the longer period of twenty years, the top offices in Cracow rotated among a small group numbering only thirteen people (a ratio of 6.15:1).[71] This compares with twenty people in Międzybóż for the eight years documented.

Considering all sixty-nine offices filled in Międzybóż for the three years—1739, 1740, and 1742—for which information is complete, the ratio of offices to officeholders was still 1.6:1 and far below the Cracow precedent.[72] Of the forty-three individuals who held some office, ten held as many as three offices. The highest number of offices held by the members of one family (the Zelmanowiczes) was seven, or around 10 percent of the total offices available and more than two per year.

The structure suggested by these numbers is of an oligarchy composed of several factions, probably based mainly on family ties. Each faction had to be accommodated, and therefore no single group could commandeer all the offices year after year, merely exchanging titles among themselves, as was the case in seventeenth-century Cracow. In Międzybóż, apparently, the offices had to rotate through the factions, a process that took several years.

The existence of strong factions both inside and outside the kahal is demonstrated by the role played in Międzybóż by the *pospólstwo*. The *pospólstwo* (Hebrew *yehidei segula*) comprised all of the male householders in the Jewish community whose tax level entitled them to participate in the political process but who were not currently holding office.[73] For the kahal to be run year after year by the same small group of people, the pospólstwo would need to be weak and easily dominated by them.

In Międzybóż, however, this was not the case. The pospólstwo played an active role, serving to monitor kahal decisions and activities and preventing the kahal from becoming the domain of one group. Important measures, such as allotting arenda contracts, settling accounts with the community's arrendators, determining community membership, petitioning the lord or lady, and dispensing major punishments, required the participation of pospólstwo representatives, alongside the members of the kahal.[74]

Factionalism was the probable underlying cause of the controversy, around 1714, when members of the new kahal attempted to exclude the pospólstwo from major decisions and perpetuate their own incumbency. The pospólstwo declared its preference for the old kahal and registered a vociferous and effective protest against the new one with the Polish authorities. In 1726, in response to demands by the pospólstwo, the Polish authorities prohibited roshim and tuvim from serving consecutive terms in their posts.[75]

Communal regulations restricting the power of elected officials—even symbolic power—was another means by which the pospólstwo attempted to keep a rein on whichever faction happened to be in power. The granting of honors in the synagogue on the Sabbath is a prime example. In general, synagogue management was the responsibility of the elected gabbaim. They were to handle the budget, collect the donations, and distribute the Sabbath synagogue honors. As elsewhere, the basis for rationing these honors was money. In Międzybóż, however, honors were sold during the course of the preceding week to those who were willing to pay for them. They were not to be given out on the Sabbath itself, in front of the entire congregation, in exchange for the promise of a donation or at the discretion of one of the gabbaim. This system of deciding in advance on the basis of payment discriminated against the poorer people. It did, however, decrease the discretionary power of the gabbaim, permit time to protest questionable decisions, and prevent the synagogue service itself from turning into an auction or a public test of power and prestige among the wealthy. Honors would not be limited to the faction that held office but would remain available to whomever could pay.

To cut off the likeliest avenue of abuse of these rules, the rosh of the month was prohibited from claiming honors for his relatives or himself. If the rosh were detained on communal business, however, the synagogue service would be delayed until he arrived, and he did have the right to grant one honor to one guest each week.[76]

While by the late 1730s the prohibition on consecutive offices was not observed, there was at least some change in the composition of the roshim every year. This turnover was encoded in law by 1741 when the instructions from the Polish administration mandated that of the four roshim, one was to be chosen by the administration (apparently the general arrendator), one by the outgoing kahal, and two by the pospólstwo. The election results and other sources demonstrate that people named as part of the pospólstwo in some years were indeed members of the kahal in other years.[77] Members of the pospólstwo were, then, potential members of the kahal in reality, not merely by legal definition. Whatever factions were in power had to take into account the will of those that were out of power, since they were likely to exchange places in the near term.

The complexity of the division of political power in Międzybóż is even more obvious when we examine the identity of those who held the offices. Money was not the single overriding consideration. While the affluent Zelmanowiczes were well represented, the even wealthier Charytons appear only once, with Moszko Charyton as rosh in 1737, during the few years recorded. Assuming that they were interested in political power—if only to further enhance their economic position—their near-total absence in the documented years is consistent with a factional structure. Perhaps when the Zelmanowiczes were in, the Charytons were out. The impression of rivalry between these two families is reinforced by a petition filed by a Charyton son-in-law, Manaszko Dubienski, complaining about the powerful people in the kahal and accusing members of the Zelmanowicz family, among others, of not paying their fair share of the taxes.[78]

An additional determinant of officeholding was connection to the Polish authorities. Wolf Abramowicz, Jankiel's son-in-law, appears as a rosh four times on the eight available lists—more than anyone else. In addition, he was a ne'eman at least once. Wolf was a merchant who served as factor to the noblemen administrators of Międzybóż and supplier to various army units. He was also on occasion the arrendator of the city.[79] Given the Polish administration's predilection to influence the composition of the kahal and its explicit prerogative to do so,[80] it may be that Wolf—and others—owed their offices to the direct or subtle pressure of the Poles.

Polish authority is also the explanation for the fact that every year the roshim included the general arrendator of Międzybóż. Maria Zofia Czartoryska, one of the owners of Międzybóż, once remarked, "According to ancient custom the arrendators have an important place among the elders of the kahal," and it is clear from the documents that this was already true during the tenure of her mother, Elżbieta Sieniawska. The 1741 instruction noting the administration's right to choose one of the roshim each year is apparently a reference to this practice.[81] The general arrendator was the single greatest local source of revenue for the lord, and the lord wanted to ensure that nothing was done to harm his efficiency. A seat among the roshim was an effective means of securing his—and the owners'—interests.

Another factor in determining an individual's political career was family. For some of the lower-economic-level officeholders, the key to their presence on the kahal seems to be not their personal wealth but their membership in wealthy families. Leybka Zelmanowicz, for example, paid only 30 zloty in excise tax in 1743. His three terms as gabbai were probably a function of his status as a younger member of the Zelmanowicz clan.[82]

Even more than wealth or family ties, the officeholders shared occupations. None of the officeholders named for Międzybóż can be definitely identified as an artisan, except for Michel the goldsmith (ne'eman in 1739 and 1740), whose highly skilled, expensive craft set him apart from the tailors, furriers, butchers, and bakers. All of the other officeholders whose occupation can be identified were either in commerce or held *arendy,* or both. The community's political class—the kahal and pospólstwo membership—was defined, then, by a combination of economic position, family, and occupation. While the pospólstwo was apparently composed of factions, such factions were closer to each other economically and occupationally than they were to the lowest taxpayers, who were excluded from officeholding and the political process.

The artisans lacked political franchise, but they were organized into guilds (Hebrew *havarot*), which afforded them a measure of economic protection, social status, and mutual aid in time of personal tragedy. As we shall see in the next chapter, the butchers' guild fought for the interests of its members against the oppressive tendencies of more powerful communal elements. The guilds established synagogues where their members could set the tone and need not see their socioeconomic inferiority mirrored in the seating arrangements and the distribution of honors in the main synagogue, which served symbolically to reinforce the status of the rich and prominent.[83]

From the fragmentary information available,[84] kahal expenses (totaling ca. 1740 approximately 8,000 zl. annually) can be classified into three broad categories: payments of many types to Polish authorities, officials, and army units; internal communal expenses; and debt service. The first category was by far the largest one, approximating one-half of the community's expenditures.

This relatively large proportion of kahal income devoted to payments to Poles might be seen as vindication of the Polish policy of supporting the institutions of Jewish autonomy. In Międzybóż, as elsewhere,[85] one could argue that the main purpose of the kahal was to provide revenues to Polish authorities. Even borrowing by the kahal was financially advantageous to Poles, because it provided useful investment opportunities for Church institutions and the nobility.[86] The importance of the financial health of the community to the Polish authorities is exemplified by the requirement that each rosh submit an itemized expense statement, in Polish, countersigned by two tuvim and two ne'emanim.[87]

The types of kahal business on which Jewish officials spent their time included conducting meetings of the kahal and tending to matters of legislation, negotiating with different levels and types of Polish officials over regulations, matters of security, and financial obligations. From the magnate to the local captain of the guard, the rosh had to cultivate cordial relations with all powerful Poles and respond to their financial demands. Internal communal business included arranging repairs of kahal property, tending to itinerant poor people and clergy, providing for the kahal's staff, and maintaining Międzybóż's links with the institutions of regional Jewish autonomy.

If the autonomous Jewish organization was charged with providing revenue to Polish agents and agencies, it also had a cardinal role to play in managing relations between Jews, on the one hand, and Polish officialdom and society, on the other. The price to the Poles of the monies provided by the Jews was an orderly arrangement of the conditions of Jewish life so that Jews could live in relative security, prosperity, and religious freedom.[88] Supplying income to the authorities also helped endow the kahal with the authority it needed to regulate internal communal affairs.

Such regulation was an important part of the kahal's functioning. Since, however, the vast majority of sources in the Czartoryski archive are in Polish, available documents do not reflect the full range of kahal responsibilities in this sphere. Most Polish documents relating to the kahal's activities are connected with financial matters or complaints to the Polish authorities. There are, however, a few Jewish communal regulations that were translated from Yiddish or Hebrew into Polish around 1745. In addition to the issues of political rights and honors in the synagogue, alluded to above, they include rules about giving donations to the synagogue (donations were to take effect immediately and were irrevocable; the wives of the gabbaim were in charge of the charity boxes), sumptuary regulations (limiting the number of guests and food courses at a circumcision or wedding feast), and relations with the clergy (visiting cantors were not to be paid more than 4 zloty for leading Sabbath services and the communal rabbi was to preach at the evening service, not the morning one).[89]

Międzybóż was a real place. It was an important Podolian town and a typical Jewish community. Living there, the Ba'al Shem Tov would have been subject to the authority of the kahal headed by people like the mercantile Zelmanowicz family, Wolf Abramowicz, factor to the noblemen, and the wealthy arrendators. He would have been expected to obey the rulings of the rabbi, Hersz Leybowicz Aptekarz. He would have had to contend with the economic influence of the great merchants like the Charytons and would have witnessed the social stratification across occupational lines. He would have noticed the many women who headed households.

On the basis of later legends told about the Ba'al Shem Tov, it is tempting to try to connect him with specific individuals. There are stories linking him with "a certain great merchant" whose "son used to go to Breslau to buy merchandise";[90] the affluent rabbi of Międzybóż in whose house "were a great many pieces of silverware";[91] and the bass singer who was assistant cantor in the synagogue.[92] The great merchant might have been Moszko Charyton or Haskiel Zelmanowicz. Rabbi Hersz Leybowicz Aptekarz does seem to have been well-off and able to afford fine tableware.[93] There was a *basista* who sang in the Międzybóż synagogue.[94]

The most persistent question is, how did the Ba'al Shem Tov fit into the socioeconomic structure of Międzybóż? The conventional image of the Besht as a poor, and poorly educated, populist figure suggests that he arrived as an itinerant preacher or wonder worker who made a place for himself on the margins of the established institutional framework of the community. As such, he might have been barely tolerated by the kahal but warmly welcomed by the artisans, identified with them, and perhaps taken in as a *sąsiędz* by one of them until he received official permission to reside permanently in the town.

We have already seen, however, that there are problems with such an image of the Ba'al Shem Tov. Being a ba'al shem and a hasidic type did not place him on the margins of respectability or make him into a populist figure. Moreover, with the highly institutionalized, entrenched establishment—which appears to have remained stable during the entire period of the Besht's residence in Międzybóż—it would have been difficult for him to attain any influence in the town in opposition to it. Speculation as to his position in the community and his links with various individuals and groups within it should be preceded by more understanding of the dynamics of intergroup relations in Jewish Międzybóż. This can aid in developing a clearer notion of who and what the Besht was.

CHAPTER FIVE

The Contentions of Life

Over the last generation, historians have reevaluated the place of the Jews in the Polish-Lithuanian Commonwealth as a whole and in their individual communities. From the view, popularized by Dubnow, of Jews largely as victims of an alien, hostile environment, desperately attempting various strategies of survival, historians of our generation have come to regard Jews as not only in Poland but of Poland and inextricably linked to the social, economic, and cultural processes of the country.

Hundert, a major proponent of the new approach, entitled a chapter "Jews and Other Poles" and insisted that to Polish Jews "Poland was as much theirs as their neighbors'."[1] This does not mean, however, that the Jews were perfectly integrated in an American ideal-type pluralist society. Hundert was quick to point out that while Jews felt at home in their communities, "there is no question that animus and tension were the governing qualities in relations between Jews and Christians. The historical issue is how this animus was expressed in relations between particular people and groups of people at particular times and in particular places."[2]

In Międzybóż, as in other privately owned towns, the Jews were promised physical safety, basic freedom of religion, the right to maintain autonomous institutions, and a broad field of economic enterprise. In return, they were obligated to pay taxes of various sorts, assume other obligations (such as guard duty, fire prevention, and participation in public works projects), and remain peaceable and law-abiding.[3] The owners, the Czartoryskis, would also go beyond this basic framework in an effort to ensure that the Jewish community—and with it the economic foundation of the town—remained financially viable and capable of supplying revenues.

An example of this occurred in 1739. In August of that year, Jan Swirski, the *podwojewoda* (deputy governor) of Podolia, informed August Aleksander Czartoryski that he had attended the recent meeting of the Jewish council of the district of Podolia where elections for Jewish district elders were held and the tax apportionment for the Jewish communities of Podolia was made. Swirski assured the magnate that he had been instrumental in the renewed election of the same—presumably acceptable to Czartoryski—elders as before and "did not allow the least increase in the taxes of the territories" belonging to Czartoryski.[4] In other words, Czartoryski had arranged for intervention with the district Jewish council to ensure that his Jews would not have to pay more taxes to the council, thus keeping more money in their pockets for his ultimate benefit.[5]

Most of the time there was no direct contact between the owners and the Jewish community. The Czartoryskis' Podolian lands were managed by an administrative hierarchy headed by a chief administrator based in Satanów and staffed with petty noblemen who served as local officials. It was these administrators who usually dealt with Międzybóż and its surrounding villages. Access to these men was a key to stability in the life of the community, and the leaders of the kahal invested both time and money in cultivating cordial relations with these officials. Frequently, this relationship was characterized by mutual support.[6] The need to expend considerable effort in the service of this goal points up the potential for tension that was inherent in the relationship between the officials and the Jews.

The clearest sign of such tensions is the contest between the Jews and the administrators over Jewish efforts to send direct appeals to the owners to intervene in matters of moment in Międzybóż. Such petitions were a common practice throughout the Commonwealth and were the right of anyone living on a private estate. The problem in Międzybóż—and probably elsewhere—was that the local administrators did not want the people under their jurisdiction circumventing their authority, complaining about them, and bringing down on them the wrath of the lord or lady.[7] The issues dividing Jews and administrators ranged from disagreements over the price or terms of arendy or over interpretations of the contract[8] to personal complaints over alleged unjust treatment at the hands of an administrator[9] to conflicts over demands made on the kahal[10] to accusations leveled by the *kahal* and others that the administrator was unfit, rapacious, corrupt, and violent.[11]

In 1730, the Międzybóż administrator Jan Dessier was charged with

> violating the rights of both Christians and Jews by diverting trials belonging to the jurisdiction of the municipality and Jewish community court to his own jurisdiction; by intervening in kahal elections, deposing the legitimately elected officials and appointing others of his own liking; by forbidding payment of the rabbi's salary; by allowing the factor, Ognisty, to start disputes and to influence judicial matters to his own profit; [and] in particular by expropriations: by confiscating land plots; by imposing tremendous fines; by forcing fish as well as cattle, sheep, and pigs—all from other latifundia—on the butchers compelled to take care of [his] pigs; by continually summoning the millers to [feudal] labor and forcing them to feed double the number of pigs required; and in many other ways: especially by punishing with imprisonment someone who out of distress went, or wanted to go, with a petition to Her Most Powerful and Gracious Lady [Maria Zofia Sieniawska Denhoffowa (not yet married to Czartoryski)].[12]

Such behavior on the part of the local man in charge made it difficult for the residents of Międzybóż to carry on life normally. In the case of Dessier, the owner realized this, intervened, and tried to put a stop to the oppression.[13]

Administrators were not the only sector of the Christian population with whom there could be tension. Frequently, it was the administrators who had to intervene when Jews were accused of detrimental actions. It was they who were responsible for protecting Jews against hostile interlocutors. A typical cause for complaint was that mercantile Jews were taking commercial advantage of the Christian public. In 1745, for example, Christians alleged that Jews were dumping bad fish on the market. Investigation by the Międzybóż administrator Wolinski revealed that the Jews' fish was "healthy and good" but that since the Jewish fishmongers stored their fish at their homes rather than in the marketplace, they left the impression of engaging in shady business.[14]

An important basis for intergroup antagonism was religion. In 1741, Catholic church officials filed a complaint with Wolinski concerning the "irreverence" of certain Jews who did not leave the street when the Corpus Christi procession came through the marketplace. They demanded that these Jews be criminally punished. The Jews involved countered that they had behaved no differently from Orthodox Ukrainians who also stayed in view when the procession passed by. Long-standing tradition was on the side of the complainants. In Europe generally, and in Poland as well, Jews were expected to disappear during Christian celebrations;

as infidels, their very presence constituted a provocation.[15] Wolinski sought a compromise. In lieu of specific punishment, the Jewish community was required to post a bond that would be forfeit if in the future the Jews did not go indoors when the procession passed.[16]

Sporadic violence across religious lines was, as noted in chapter 3, a constant problem in this period. In Podolia in general, Jews were often the targets of murder, rape, robbery, and beatings.[17] Typically, such violence occurred in the countryside or in smaller locales where administrative authority was weak. In strongly organized Międzybóż, major crimes and attacks against Jews were apparently rare. While the available sources are incomplete, the violence they do indicate is limited to insults and individual beatings. Sometimes Jews fought with other Jews and even with Christians. In the autumn of 1744, when two Jewish horse thieves were arrested in Mikołajów near Międzybóż, the Jews evidently staged a noisy protest and Wolinski feared a violent clash between Jews and Christians. By the end of February, a "tumult" and anti-Jewish violence did occur.[18]

The sources also indicate a modicum of cooperation between Jews and Christians. When Roman Skaminski was thrown into jail by Dessier, the money to secure his release was supplied through the combined efforts of his village council and the kahal. Christians and Jews petitioned together against the oppressive Dessier and Ognisty, and for receiving disaster aid after Muscovite invasions. When the rabbi of Międzybóż was faced with dismissal from his post, he enlisted the aid of a priest to put in a good word for him with the Polish authorities. In trials, witnesses from one group might testify on behalf of someone from the other.[19] In Międzybóż there was antagonism, not just between Jew and Christian but also between Jew and Jew and, more significant in the present context, between various groups within the Jewish community.

Discussions of social conflict in the Jewish communities of eighteenth-century Poland generally tend to consider the phenomenon in terms of the elite class versus the "common people." According to the usual construction, rich, politically powerful individuals—particularly those with close ties to Polish magnates—monopolized control over the institutional resources of the Jewish community in order to benefit themselves and exploit or oppress the poor and powerless.[20] There is evidence that, to some extent, this paradigm fits the circumstances of the Jews in Międzybóż during the time that the Besht resided there.[21]

The earliest clear example of this phenomenon in the available sources stems from circa 1730. A man by the name of Icko Ognisty, who worked as the factor of the aforementioned lessee-administrator of Międzybóż, Jan Dessier, was notorious for his rapacious activities—both in collaboration with Dessier and on his own behalf. He defrauded widows, expropriated merchandise from artisans, extorted payments from various people, accused people falsely in court, and generally harassed and intimidated the inhabitants of the town.[22] Ognisty was eventually punished by the Czartoryskis, but he was not the last of his ilk to try to lord it over Międzybóż.

In sources dating from the late 1730s, one of the most prominent people in Międzybóż was Wolf Abramowicz, a factor who served the noblemen administrators of the town and sold supplies to various army units. At times, he held office as one of the four elders (kwartalny or roshim) of the Jewish community,[23] possibly with the active support of the Polish administration.[24] In addition to supplying merchandise to powerful Poles, Wolf provided them with information about activities within the Jewish community that were of interest to them. He told about disputes between various factions and about complaints against the Polish administrators being sent directly to the Czartoryskis. For example, in 1745, the lower-level officials, Rapacki and Sinicki, used information supplied by Wolf to report to their superior, Walicki, the general administrator for Międzybóż. These reports concerned petitions being sent to the Czartoryskis with regard to a dispute between the arrendators and the kahal, in which the town rabbi was prepared to take the side of the kahal (see below on such disputes and on the rabbi's situation). Wolf had also reported that a Jewish woman named Manasterna had gone to petition the Czartoryskis, evidently with a complaint against Walicki. A different official, Rościszewski, told Walicki how Wolf (and the rabbi) had assured him that a certain petition did not originate in the official community institutions of Międzybóż but was the product of some malcontents who sent it from a neighboring locale.[25]

Wolf not only reported on disputes and petitions, he recommended specific responses by the Polish authorities. He advised allowing the arrendators to send their petition and insisted that Rabbi Hersz Leybowicz's contract for the rabbinate not be renewed.[26] He also was accused of taking advantage of his powerful position to advance his own interests and harm others. In a 1741 petition, the Jewish butchers' guild of Międzybóż complained that Wolf tried to extort a payoff from the guildmaster, Leyba, who sought permission from the kahal to build a barn near his home; attempted to force Leyba to sell him and his partners tallow and skins; apparently pocketed a fine levied against his brother-in-law for beating this same Leyba; and beat several butchers who ran afoul of him and had another (unjustly) placed in the stocks. For some of these acts Wolf claimed to be exercising his authority as "rosh of the month." In at least one of these instances, however, the petitioners pointed out how Wolf himself admitted that a different "rosh of the month," Chaskiel, would not have imposed the same punishment during his term of office.[27]

Assuming that this petition is credible, Wolf Abramowicz can be seen to have followed in the footsteps of Icko Ognisty. Like Ognisty, Wolf served the local Polish officials, gained a place of authority in the community, intimidated people, used strong-arm tactics to get his way, and specifically targeted the butchers' guild and its members as objects of his exploitation.

Other people with direct, though less entrenched, ties to the Polish officials were the arrendators who farmed taxes, tolls, customs duties, and other revenues and controlled mills, liquor manufacturing appliances, and other facilities—all by lease arrangement with the Czartoryskis.[28] The arrendators aimed to expand the range of enterprises they controlled and to maximize the revenues they collected. These objectives frequently conflicted with the interests of the town's small-scale merchants, artisans, and bartenders (not all of them Jewish). If prices and fees were raised, it was the latter group that would have to pay the increased rates; if a monopoly were expanded, their rights to do business freely would be curtailed.

In 1742, for example, the arrendators contracted with Czartoryski's representative to add to their liquor monopoly the exclusive right to serve liquor in the town on the Sabbath and Jewish holidays. This elicited a strong protest from the kahal on behalf of the poor bartenders, claiming that such a move would eliminate a major portion of their livelihood and do them incalculable damage. Eventually, the kahal agreed to buy back this particular feature of the lease.[29]

Merchants and artisans often tried to avoid paying duties and observed in the breach commercial rules designed as protectionist measures for the arrendators. Such practices are reflected in the 1745 complaint of the arrendators that customs evasion by those bringing merchandise to the market in the town was detrimental to the market and fairs. They also claimed that the artisan guilds' tariffs were so high as to discourage merchants from bringing outside merchandise for sale in Międzybóż, thereby reducing the duties that the arrendators could collect.[30] When, in 1746, there was a shortage of bread in Międzybóż, the head of the bakers' guild claimed that it was because his guild had been ruined by the "extortion of the arrendator" (*zdzierstwem arendarskim*), and one of the administrators confirmed that the arrendator had confiscated grain from the bakers.[31]

The arrendators held the upper hand because the Polish authorities gave them the right to confiscate contraband merchandise or even to arrange for the imprisonment or fining of anyone who violated their rights.[32] Such power lent itself to abuse, and the rabbi of Międzybóż may well have been on the mark when, in 1744, he denounced the arrendator, Leybka, as a "tyrant" and urged Czartoryski's commissioner, Walicki, to "liberate the poor people from his hand."[33]

This rabbi, Hersz Leybowicz Aptekarz,[34] apparently had a good working relationship with the magnate's men as well as with the local priest. He also can be considered in the category of those who derived influence from these ties. When the leaders of the Jewish community, including Wolf Abramowicz, decided not to renew his appointment as rabbi in 1744, he appealed to Walicki to force the community to retain him. He even asked the priest Losowski to write a letter of recommendation on his behalf.[35]

Direct ties to the Poles were not the only source of powerful position in Międzybóż. The *akcyzniki,* those who leased the right to collect the excise tax from the kahal, also wielded a significant degree of control in the community. Rather than remit the lease fee to the kahal in a lump sum, they paid the financial obligations of the kahal as these came due. This meant that it was the akcyzniki who effectively controlled the purse strings. Anyone owed money, such as the salaried employees of the kahal (rabbi, cantor, etc.), could be harmed if for any reason the akcyzniki decided to postpone payment.[36] The akcyzniki's tax-collecting authority also allowed them direct power over other people. As the arrangements had evolved by the late 1730s, every week on Thursday or Friday each merchant, storekeeper, bartender, and butcher had to report to the akcyzniki, under threat of the ban (*pod becheyrim*), what his turnover had been the previous week. The akcyzniki would then assess his tax. The exercise of their discretion in this matter could easily have been perceived as unfair by those who were dunned.[37] Also, this method was unwieldy and conducive to deceit. By 1744, the system was revamped and merchants, storekeepers, and artisans were assessed a predetermined sum set by officials of the kahal. (Bartenders—and apparently bakers—continued to be charged according to what they sold in practice, butchers according to what they butchered.)[38]

The kahal itself in Międzybóż constituted an elite interest group that at times was accused of disdaining the needs of those who did not belong to it. It controlled the granting of residence rights, the apportionment of the tax burden, and the distribution of seats in the community synagogue. These decisions were important determinants of economic status and social prestige for the people who lived in the community. Several documents imply that the poorer storekeepers and artisans were at a disadvantage in these matters.

In a petition to one of Czartoryski's senior officials, Manaszko Dubienski described himself as "a poor storekeeper here in Międzybóż who, having suffered much harm at the hands of the powerful members of the kahal, is appealing to the kindness of Your Most Powerful and Gracious Lord." Manaszko claimed that he, who did not even own his own home and made his living from a small store where he sold skins, boots, and "other small items," was assessed 90 zloty, the same amount as some international merchants who traveled several times a year to places in the Commonwealth and Germany, trading in imported luxury goods worth tens of thousands. The kahal members, according to Manaszko, played favorites with their colleagues and friends while they overburdened the poor.[39]

In 1741, the butchers' guild petitioned the Polish authorities concerning their synagogue.[40] They noted how they had refurbished the synagogue at their own expense and had even consented at one point to share it with the tailors' guild,[41] until the latter had arranged for their own place of worship. Once they did this, however, the kahal insisted that the butchers exchange their synagogue for the presumably plainer one that belonged to the tailors. The butchers refused, and for two years the kahal prohibited the use of their synagogue. Finally, after accepting a payment of five golden ducats[42] from the tailors, the kahal forcefully took possession of the butchers' building and gave it to the tailors, ordering the name of the butchers to be scratched off the sign in the front.[43] The butchers were now asking the Polish administration to restore their synagogue and allow them to appoint a rabbi who would judge them, a common device by which guilds and fraternities established their organizational status and weakened the kahal's hold on them.

The butchers were not the only group that wanted to set up its own congregation. On 24 November 1741, a Polish court document took note of the fact that Osior Moszkowicz and his companions had begun private prayer services. Like the butchers' synagogue, the establishment of this separate minyan was probably connected to the fact that the members of this group were not given ritual honors—or the social respect the conferring of such honors represented—in the main synagogue.[44]

It is apparent from the rules governing the distribution of honors in the synagogue, dating from about 1745, that these were at a (primarily financial) premium and that the kahal leaders might try to monopolize them.[45] More than honors were in short supply in the Międzybóż synagogue. Because of an influx of newcomers, the place was overcrowded and some new arrivals were taking the seats of established community members. Others were occupying temporarily free seats without paying for a "permanent place," as was customary.[46]

The overcrowding in the synagogue was just a reflection of a more basic problem. Many of the new settlers in Międzybóż were poor and did not pay taxes. This means that they also could not have paid the standard initiation fee that Jewish communities normally required of potential residents before granting them the right of residence (Herem Ha-Yishuv). These people were not only sitting in the synagogue contrary to accepted custom, they were unlawfully settled in the town. By 1743 the problem had become serious, and the Polish administrator, Wolinski, ordered the community to form a committee to straighten out the seating assignments in the synagogue and sell any remaining empty places. He further authorized the committee to make up a list of those who possessed the formal right of residence entitling them to settle in Międzybóż. Those "foreign and poor" Jews who were in the town illegally would be expelled. The kahal submitted a list of candidates for expulsion numbering over thirty persons, composed mainly of people in low-paying occupations.[47]

The material from Międzybóż not only presents examples of how elites bore down on the lower classes in the 1730s and 1740s but also indicates some of the ways in which those who were pressed by the establishment responded. The impression lent by the Polish sources, although they are obviously weighted in this direction, is that one of the most frequent forms of protest was petitioning the Polish authorities to step in and restrain the arrogant exercise of power by one of the sources of authority in the Jewish community.[48] Sometimes the protest was much more direct and took violent form. For example, in 1731 the butchers, in cooperation with the kahal, tried to poison Icko Ognisty.[49] There was also a tendency by those who viewed themselves as victims of discrimination to attempt to escape the control of the elite by setting up parallel institutions such as their own synagogue and their own rabbinic court.[50]

The Polish material would seem to confirm that the social situation in Międzybóż at the time of the Besht was congruent with what historians, working on the basis of Jewish sources, have taught us to expect. Powerful individuals in various roles took advantage of those low on the socioeconomic ladder. There was a social gap, and there were signs of enmity between ruler and ruled, rich and poor, elite and plebeians.

The elite groups I have singled out—factors who worked for the Polish administrators, arrendators of the magnate's rights, akcyzniki of the kahal's income, and the kahal itself—were not mutually exclusive. Icko Ognisty, Wolf Abramowicz, and the various types of lessees often served on the kahal in diverse capacities;[51] a lessee of the magnate one year could, in theory at least, become the lessee of the kahal the next. This overlapping makes it tempting to accept the paradigm with which we began—a monolithic establishment versus "the people"—as a sufficient description of the social situation in the Międzybóż community in this period. In reality, however, this relationship was not the only one at work.

I noted earlier that when Wolf wanted to punish a certain butcher, he said that he could not do it because Chaskiel and not he, Wolf, was currently the rosh.[52] Moreover, in protesting against Ognisty, the butchers tried to poison him in cooperation with the kahal. Similarly, there were appeals made by the kahal to the Polish owners of Międzybóż against Ognisty or the arrendators on behalf of those who were victimized.[53] The kahal, then, was capable, at least some of the time, of standing up for the interests of the common man. Resistance did not necessarily have to take the form of appeal to some outside authority or of overtly anti-establishment, violent behavior.

The body that was supposed to represent the best interests of the entire community—the kahal—sometimes did just that. There were apparently some safeguards to ensure that this would be the case. As noted in chapter 4, taxpaying members of the community, who were entitled to vote but who did not serve as members of the kahal, had influence on its actions through the pospólstwo, which seems to have exercised an advise and consent function. When the kahal acted against the general interest, the pospólstwo could protest and serve as a check on kahal power.[54]

By 1740, the power of the pospólstwo was institutionalized, with its representatives participating together with kahal leaders when deciding certain judicial, financial, and taxation matters. Important decisions were announced and conflicts were resolved by joint committees made up of an equal number of members from the kahal and pospólstwo.[55] In effect, there were two administrative bodies—kahal members and representatives of the pospólstwo—who had to cooperate in conducting the most important communal business.

This means that the pattern of exploitation of the weak by the strong was inconsistent, and the nonelite were not without representation and the means to resist.[56] Moreover, not only is the pattern of exploitation inconsistent, it is not the only paradigm of social conflict. The protest by the kahal against the arrendator's newly acquired monopoly over Sabbath liquor sales and its involvement in the machinations against Ognisty demonstrate that it might go against the factor or the arrendator. The interests of the various groups holding power did not necessarily coincide. The most common type of intraelite conflict was between the two classes of arrendators: those who leased the incomes of the magnate and those who leased the excise tax from the kahal. There are several sources that report one group protesting that the prerogatives of the other were infringing on their profits.[57] There were also conflicts between candidates competing for the same lease.[58]

The nonelite group was also not an undifferentiated, harmonious whole. This is demonstrated in two of the cases mentioned above: the confiscation of the butchers' synagogue and its cession to the tailors and the problem of people without formal residence rights overcrowding the synagogue. The tailors were obviously on better terms with the kahal than were the butchers, and they initiated, or at least cooperated with, the attempt to dispossess the butchers' guild of its synagogue. It was "the Jews of Międzybóż"—not just the elite—who complained about the overcrowding and usurpation of places in the synagogue. A joint committee of the kahal, the pospólstwo, and the rabbi drew up the list of those who were legitimate inhabitants of the town.[59] In other words, not surprisingly, many of the nonelite were also interested in expelling the "foreign and poor" Jews.

Thus in Międzybóż there were several rings in the vortex of social confrontation. In addition to conflicts of elite versus plebeians, there were different configurations of elite versus elite, as well as artisan versus artisan and poor versus poorer. The array of power relationships was not rigid, and alignments could shift.[60]

It is well to keep in mind the complex social structure and the intricacy of the patterns of social conflict in Jewish Międzybóż when attempting to characterize the Ba'al Shem Tov. Whether or not he was trying to found a movement, he had to function within this community. His ideas and behavior had to be expressed in relationship to the people and situations of this place. He could not foresee what would be made of his life generations after his death. He did have to respond to the life around him.

How did he do so? With so many issues and so many potential permutations of conflict and alliance, it seems simplistic to identify the Ba'al Shem Tov as allied with or opposed to "the establishment." If the rabbi and the kahal were at odds, whose side, if anyone's, did the Besht take? If the butchers were fighting the tailors, where did his sympathies lie? If those with residence rights wanted to expel those without them, what was his position? Was he in favor of Osior Moszkowicz's separate minyan or opposed to it? Choosing a position on any of these issues was not a simple matter of deciding who was in the moral right. Such choices entailed political judgments, economic realities, and social obligations. Perhaps the Besht avoided compromising political-social entanglements by refraining from participation in public controversies and remaining within the realm of ethereal spirituality, above the social fray.

To understand the nature of the Besht's involvement in his community, we must consider some more basic questions. What was the source of the Ba'al Shem Tov's power or influence? Which of the community's groups composed his constituency? What was his role or occupation in the town? These fundamental questions have been largely ignored by biographers who have seen their task to lie in describing the Besht as the founder of Hasidism and not as a citizen and functionary in the town in which he lived. Only by bringing the Besht down to earth will it be possible to evaluate his way in the service of heaven.

PART II

Texts

CHAPTER SIX

The Holy Epistle

The attempt to capture aspects of the Besht's life is dependent on the sources that are extant. As noted in the introduction, the sources connected to the Besht present difficult methodological challenges to scholars. Not only are they relatively few, but they actually grew in quantity and detail during the fifty years or so *following* the Besht's death. Most of the sources originate in oral traditions that constitute a rather weak historical foundation and lead scholars to decide unsystematically what information is reliable and what can be safely ignored. My aim here is to enumerate, characterize, and assess the historiographical weight of the various Besht sources.

Most of the material relating to the Ba'al Shem Tov is in Hebrew. Its ready accessibility has ensured that it would be the basis of representations of the historical Ba'al Shem Tov. In my opinion, the items in this group of sources should be placed on a scale of decreasing a priori reliability, based on their temporal proximity to the Besht's lifetime and the closeness of the relationship of a given author to the Ba'al Shem Tov.[1] This means beginning with things written during his lifetime by the Besht himself and then by his contemporaries, proceeding to descriptions by contemporaries after his death, and then evaluating hearsay depictions and citations.

This progression from the Besht's own writings to contemporary testimonies to later testimonies and finally to traditions about what he did and said is virtually the reverse of what has typically been done. Most

Besht descriptions begin with the traditions about the Besht's activities collected in *Shivhei Ha-Besht*, published more than fifty years after his death, and then employ other sources as illustrative or supplementary to the image they have derived from the traditional stories.[2]

This conventional approach builds the foundation of scholarly treatment on a very methodologically problematic category of sources and gives the post-Besht compilers and editors of these traditions a large, and largely unacknowledged, role in determining what have been seen as the basic motifs in the Besht's character and life story. As an example of this, I have already suggested that the *Shivhei Ha-Besht* view of the Besht's ba'al shemism as an obstacle to communication with establishment religious figures may reflect attitudes toward ba'alei shem in the late eighteenth century more than in the Besht's lifetime.[3]

A notable, if partial, exception to the "*Shivhei Ha-Besht* first" approach is Gershom Scholem's famous Hebrew article, "The Historical Image of R. Israel Ba'al Shem."[4] Scholem divided the sources into "independent, contemporary testimonies that could bear critical evaluation" and partisan sources, stemming from Hasidim or their opponents. Close inspection of Scholem's evidence, however, reveals that of the twenty pieces of information that he regarded as "independent [and] contemporary," only four are contained in sources actually written while the Besht was alive; a fifth is grouped with the partisan sources. Of the rest, some are testimonies or hearsay recorded decades later, which may reflect intervening factors. Some of these are passages in *Shivhei Ha-Besht* that, in Scholem's opinion, were "reliable and sufficiently substantiated," although he did not specify his criteria for making this determination. Some of the citations have been proven to be unconnected to the Besht.[5]

The thirty sources Scholem called "partisan" were almost all written down in the late eighteenth century. Twelve of them are statements quoted in the Besht's name many years after they were spoken, in books by the Besht's disciple Jacob Joseph of Polonne, the Besht's grandson, Moses Ephraim of Sudyłkow, or others who knew him personally. The others are oral traditions, hearsay, or posthumous evaluations, most of them from people who were deeply involved in the polemics surrounding Hasidism at that time. Some of these people had not had any personal contact with the Besht. In all, of the fifty citations—independent and partisan—that Scholem adduced, only five date from the Besht's lifetime. Despite Scholem's initial departure from the pattern of his predecessors, his account relies heavily on what he judged, without specifying systematic criteria, as authentic episodes in *Shivhei Ha-Besht* and authentic sayings recorded in the books of Jacob Joseph of Polonne.[6]

Two of the main themes of Scholem's article are that the Besht was truly a theurgic ba'al shem and that there was opposition and active resistance to the Besht during his lifetime, as the representative of a new religious approach. If Scholem was correct as to the second point, it would imply that the Besht indeed created a movement with a new ideology and new institutions. As we shall see, in his enthusiasm to substantiate these two theses, Scholem ignored some significant features of what are, in my opinion, basic sources: the Besht's letters. He also adduced sources that he interpreted as expressing opposition to the Besht but that have been shown to be either unreliable or, as noted, simply not related to him.[7]

Scholem's collection of Besht sources was, then, both eclectic and problematic in several ways. Moreover, in the more than thirty years since Scholem's article appeared, new sources and new versions of old sources have come to light. A reevaluation of the Hebrew Besht corpus that takes these into account seems only appropriate.

THE HOLY EPISTLE

The first document written by the Ba'al Shem Tov to be published is a letter he wrote circa 1752 to his brother-in-law, Gershon of Kutów, who had emigrated to the Land of Israel in 1747 (the letter is translated below). This is the most famous Ba'al Shem Tov source, yet the problem of the authenticity of the text is unsettled and requires consideration. Moreover, while the letter addressed family and personal matters, historical events occurring at the time, and mystical experiences, scholars utilized it primarily to arrive at an understanding of the Besht's mystical life, theological teachings, and messianic beliefs, paying scant attention to the Besht's purpose in writing it.[8]

This letter, termed by Hasidim the "Holy Epistle," was first published in 1781 in Koretz as an Appendix to *Ben Porat Yosef,* the second homiletic work of the Besht's disciple, Jacob Joseph of Polonne.[9] The printers, Solomon Lutzker and his partner (identified only as Simeon), introduced the letter as follows:

> The Holy Epistle Which Our Rabbi, Israel Ba'al Shem Tov, May His Merit Protect Us, Amen, Wrote to His Brother-In-Law The Holy Rabbi And Sage Rabbi Abraham Gershon From Kutów (The Memory of The Righteous is a Blessing) to the Holy Land.

This is the epistle which the rabbi, R. Israel Besht, his memory is for eternal life, gave to our rabbi, our teacher, the author Jacob Joseph the Kohen [i.e., of priestly descent], to be delivered to his brother-in-law R. Gershon Kutover who was in the Holy Land; but due to an obstacle placed by God, blessed be He, he did not travel to the Land of Israel and it remained in his possession in order to benefit our nation, the children of Israel.[10]

The authenticity of this letter has been based primarily on the assertion that Rabbi Jacob Joseph, who received it into his hand, was the person who published it.[11] However, anyone familiar with Jacob Joseph's four books knows that the situation is not so simple. To begin with, the preface to the letter at the end of *Ben Porat Yosef* is written in the third person: "This is the epistle which the Rabbi R. Israel Besht of blessed memory gave to the author, our teacher and rabbi, Jacob Joseph the Kohen . . ." It was not Jacob Joseph, then, who attached this letter to the manuscript of his book but rather the publisher or printer who decided to make it part of the book.

This is but one example of several phenomena[12] that imply that Jacob Joseph did not edit his books himself and raise the question of the degree of his involvement in their publication. Most telling are the very last lines in the first book, *Toldot Yaacov Yosef*. The two lines contain the apologia of the typesetter, Alexander Ziskind ben Mordecai: "Since this holy book was printed from several writings copied from the manuscript[s?][13] of the author, may he live, and it would require one search after another in the body of the books from the hand of the author in several places, therefore do not blame us . . ."

While the style is opaque, Ziskind seems to be saying that he had to base his work on several nonautograph copies of Jacob Joseph's manuscript[s?], without benefit of a master autograph copy. Since he could not refer as necessary to an autograph, he did not want to accept responsibility for errors. In essence, the printer also had to copyedit the text, which had already undergone structural and content editing.[14]

Based on this apologia and the generally disheveled state of the text, Nigal and Gries have argued convincingly that all of the material in Jacob Joseph's books was no more than notes he had written down throughout the years.[15] The publishers edited this material with little or no input from the aged author.[16] This explains such curious features as references at the beginning of the first book to passages that were to appear in later volumes as if they were written already, the seemingly contradictory double style of organization detectable in the first two books (both according to the Torah portion of the week and according to the order of the commandments), notes by the printer that certain words were illegible, much repetition, the absence of rhetorical devices one would expect to find in a homiletic presentation, and the lack of discrete, logically coherent units that develop some idea or thesis.

If Jacob Joseph's books are actually his notes, copied by others and edited by the publishers and printers, then the Holy Epistle must also be seen as a component of the raw material, which, like the books, may have been copied from the original source—perhaps more than once—before it was printed. As noted above, the preface to the printed letter indicates that it passed through the hands of the editors before becoming part of the book. Did the copyists or editors interfere in the text of the letter itself?

As early as 1923 it was evident that there was an alternate version of the Holy Epistle.[17] In 1971, Mordecai Bauminger published this alternate on the basis of a manuscript he held and claimed was an autograph (written by the Besht's son-in-law and signed by the Besht himself).[18] Its relationship to the *Ben Porat Yosef* text was not clear, for while there is much overlap between the two versions, each one contains passages not found in the other. Therefore, it is not that one is simply an abridgment of the other.

Most significant, the Bauminger text excludes the two most often cited passages of the Holy Epistle. These include the Besht's narrative about what happens to souls in heaven, his account of his meeting with the Messiah, and his prescription for bringing on the Redemption. Without these passages, the Holy Epistle is much less interesting and much less pregnant with theological meaning.

Once Bauminger's version of the letter was published, it gave rise to a spirited polemic concerning both its authenticity and its implications for the historical picture of the Besht.[19] If this text is the genuine one, then it limits what can be learned from the letter about the Besht and calls into question the reliability of transmitted Hasidic texts. It implies that Jacob Joseph or his editors interfered in the text that was published in *Ben Porat Yosef*, not only deleting passages but even adding some.

The situation was further complicated in 1980, when Yehoshua Mondshine published yet another version of the letter, included in a Rothschild manuscript (JNUL 8°5979), dated 1776, containing several early Hasidic texts.[20] This third version—in existence at least five years prior to the publication of *Ben Porat Yosef*—appears to be a different recension of the letter with a different structure. It is also missing the salutation and opening personal passage, beginning immediately with the

Besht's account of his ascent to Paradise. It ends abruptly with the Besht's reaction to the news that some Jews had been forced to convert and then killed, omitting the final third of the published letter as well as the closing greeting and signature.

Mondshine explained the discrepancy in the structure of the texts by assuming that the Rothschild manuscript is a copy of a different, pre-1752 letter of the Besht's to Gershon which the Besht knew had never reached its destination. The Besht attempted to rewrite this original, pre-1752 letter from memory. He gave the new, rewritten text to Jacob Joseph to deliver.[21] This second letter, written in 1752, is, according to Mondshine, the Bauminger text.

In 1781, the *Ben Porat Yosef* version was printed with the deletion of a sensitive passage (implying condemnation of those who submit to forced conversion)[22] from the 1752 letter (the Bauminger) and with additions from the pre-1752 letter (which was copied from the Rothschild manuscript or from a similar source).[23] According to Mondshine's construction, the Bauminger is the authentic version of the Besht's second letter to Gershon of Kutów, written in 1752. It was this that was in the possession of Jacob Joseph. The *Ben Porat Yosef* version is a conflation of the authentic text of the 1752 letter (the Bauminger) with the pre-1752 letter (the Rothschild). The editors of *Ben Porat Yosef* took the liberty of combining the two texts because they believed the Besht had addressed both the Rothschild and the Bauminger texts to Gershon of Kutów. With the same author and the same recipient, the two texts could be legitimately conflated—thus Mondshine.

In my view a different scenario is more likely. The 1776 Rothschild manuscript contains an original table of contents. The last two items it lists are "The Will of The Zaddik of Blessed Memory" and "The H[oly] Epistle." At the end of the manuscript, where these two items were to be written out, the following heading appears: "So as not to leave the paper blank I wrote a great deed of the Rivash[24] and the will of the Zaddik of Blessed Memory." Next comes the will; then the words "The Holy Epistle," and then the version of the Besht's letter.

The copyist was certain that his expected readers knew whose will (Rabbi Aaron the Great of Karlin, d. 1772) and which Holy Epistle these documents were. His headings provided the bare minimum of identifying information. The letter itself, as already noted, was missing its salutation, beginning, conclusion, and signature, which would have indicated that this document was indeed a letter and identified its author and recipient. A reader who had not previously heard about this epistle

and did not have some familiarity with its contents before reading it
would have had difficulty understanding the connection between this text
and the "great deed of the Rivash" in the heading. In the text as it stands
in the Rothschild manuscript, there is no overt indication linking it to
the Besht.

It is reasonable to conclude that this was not the first time a copy of
this epistle had appeared. It was already famous as *the* Holy Epistle. This
title and the contents sufficed to identify the text for the Hasidic reader
of the 1770s. In order for the letter to be so familiar, it must have been
copied at least several times between its being written in 1752 and its
appearance in the 1776 Rothschild manuscript and must have been
known to many people in oral versions.[25]

Another important point is that at the end of the zaddik's will the
copyist admitted that he had not transmitted the entire document: "Till
here the will of our teacher Aaron of Karlin was brought to us. Even
though it is not complete, still it should be studied." In other words, the
copyist believed that it was worthwhile to favor the public with an incomplete document. This would explain why he presented a version of
the Holy Epistle that begins and ends so abruptly. As with the will, so
with the Holy Epistle, the copyist set out only the parts available to him
or those he thought to be significant.

There is no need, therefore, to assume that the Rothschild manuscript
is a surviving copy of an additional, earlier letter of the Besht's.[26] Occam's
razor shaves such an additional document away and comes to rest on
the likelihood that the Rothschild manuscript is one of the steps in the
process of recopying—and in fact rewriting—the original 1752 letter. The
copyist of the Rothschild text in 1776 was probably reproducing a version of the already famous 1752 letter that he had seen or heard in one
or more forms circulating among the Hasidim.[27]

Moreover, the versions of the Holy Epistle that were known before
the appearance of the Rothschild text included material that was not in
the original letter but that was considered to consist of authentic words
of the Besht. This is demonstrated by the fact that a passage in the hanhagot (moral instructions) of Dov Ber, the Maggid of Mezerich, cited in
the Besht's name,[28] does not appear in the Bauminger but does show up
in the Rothschild and, as Gries was the first to note, in slightly different
form in the *Ben Porat Yosef* version. To my mind, since the 1776 Rothschild and the 1781 *Ben Porat Yosef* date from well after the Maggid's
death in 1772, we should conclude that they were influenced by the various oral and manuscript versions of the Maggid's hanhagot that were

in circulation, not that the Bauminger coincidentally deleted precisely that passage which was in the Maggid's hanhagot.[29]

I would claim, therefore, that the Bauminger version is the best representation of the 1752 text that the Besht wrote and handed over to Jacob Joseph. While it may not be an autograph,[30] the handwriting, ink, and paper do belong to mid-eighteenth-century eastern Europe, and it appears to be at least an early, authentic copy.[31] That later versions of the letter added material is not surprising. Ben-Zion Dinur, Gershom Scholem, Mendel Piekarz, Zev Gries, and Raya Haran have all demonstrated how Hasidic editors and publishers were not always careful about attributing texts and citations and did not always transmit texts accurately.[32]

Conversely, if we were to assume that either the *Ben Porat Yosef* version or the Rothschild manuscript version was the authentic letter, that would mean that the Bauminger version deleted, or the Besht forgot when rewriting the first letter, precisely the most interesting parts of the Holy Epistle, the parts revealing his ideas about the fate of souls in Paradise[33] and, especially, how to bring about Redemption.[34] What makes more sense? That these passages, relating to the foundations of Hasidic faith and doctrine, were deleted from the original letter or that they were added once these foundations were clarified? And a further question: If in 1776 there was a copy of the lost letter (the Rothschild manuscript), why—in 1752—was the Besht forced to rewrite it by heart, as he himself testified?[35]

Abraham Dov Urbach of Chmielnik, the *meivi le-veit ha-defus* (the person who shepherded the book through press, sort of a production editor) of *Ben Porat Yosef,* was Jacob Joseph's son-in-law and an adherent of both the Besht and the Maggid of Mezerich.[36] In all likelihood he viewed Hasidism as it had developed by 1780 as a whole cloth in which various traditions were woven into a harmonious whole. No wonder, then, that he or a similar, previous copyist of the Holy Epistle intervened in the text, deleting items that seemed to him unworthy or unnecessary and adding passages from the Rothschild manuscript or its models as well as other "authentic" Besht texts. He probably did this because, as Mondshine has suggested,[37] he believed it was right to bring together in one place the Besht's authentic writings, which had been scattered.

Rather than assert that a copy of the lost pre-1752 letter, unavailable to the Besht himself, suddenly surfaced as the Rothschild manuscript in 1776, it is preferable to hold that there was one surviving letter that was copied many times, perhaps sometimes by heart, gradually gaining accretions of other material attributed to the Besht. This process effectively ended once the printed version in *Ben Porat Yosef* was widely distributed. It can be compared to *Shivhei Ha-Besht,* where the printer declared that he was printing the book so as to put a stop to the process of error accretion that accompanied the successive copying of the manuscript.[38]

If I am correct that the Bauminger version is authentic and the additional passages in the *Ben Porat Yosef*—particularly the one dealing with bringing Redemption—were added later, then these passages cannot be utilized with confidence as historical sources, and a shadow is cast over the work that is based on them. The most prominent example of this problem is the extensive discussion with regard to the Besht's messianic posture.[39] A number of scholars have argued over whether the Besht, and early Hasidism in his wake, continued to believe in a theory of acute messianism or made a conscious effort to move messianism off the agenda of everyday Jewish life. The issue turns, to a large extent, on the interpretation of one of the sections of the Holy Epistle that appears in the *Ben Porat Yosef* version but is in a much abbreviated form in the Bauminger version. All of the scholars who have considered this question have regarded the *Ben Porat Yosef* version as the authentic one.[40] If, however, the longer version of the letter is, as argued above, a later pastiche, then the argument over the passage concerning the Messiah, which appears only in it and has been analyzed by so many scholars, is probably not an argument over the Besht's views but over those of the editors of the letter, circa 1780. Hasidic belief and practice, in general, at that time reflected the teachings of the man whom tradition has regarded as the Besht's successor, the Maggid of Mezerich.[41] Given the date of the letter's publication, the passage from the Maggid's hanhagot that appears in it, and the likelihood that it was edited by the publishers (who had links to both Jacob Joseph of Polonne and the Maggid of Mezerich) or the copy editor of *Ben Porat Yosef,* it is probable that the printed letter, too, reflects the legacy, not of the Besht, but of the Maggid.

What did the Besht believe about the Messiah? From the letter to his brother-in-law, it is difficult to say. Dubnow[42] called the letter a "manifesto of Hasidism," and it may be that the publishers of the *Ben Porat Yosef* version were trying to gain legitimacy for the evolving doctrines of the new movement by making sure that the Besht's letter reflected them.[43] In the form published in *Ben Porat Yosef,* this letter is not necessarily a presentation of the doctrines of the Besht. Scholarly efforts to make it so must be more convincing than heretofore. If the Bauminger version, translated below, is the authentic one, then this letter should serve primarily as a source of knowledge about the Besht's personal, as opposed to his intellectual, biography.[44]

[Heading:] Written [during the week of] the Torah Portion Terumah, 5512, here in the community of Raszkow.[45]

[A]. To my honored, beloved brother-in-law, my favorite, my friend in heart and soul, the great sage, the rabbinic paragon, the famous hasid in Torah and the fear of heaven, his honor, our teacher, Abraham Gershon, may his light shine, and peace to all who belong to him; and to his modest wife, Mrs. Bluma with all of her descendants. May all of them be granted the blessing of life. Amen. Selah.

[B]. I received the imprimatur of his holy hand at the Łuków fair in 5510,[46] which you sent with the emissary who traveled from Jerusalem, and it was written with great brevity and it said there that you had already written at length to each and every one[47] via a man who traveled to Egypt. However, those letters written at length did not reach me and I was much pained by this that I did not see the form of your holy hand which you wrote in detail. This[48] must have been because of the deterioration of the nations, due to our many sins, for the plague has spread to all the countries and even close to our region, having reached the community of Mohylów,[49] and the areas of Walachia and Kedar.[50] It also stated there[51] that the news[52] and the secrets which I wrote to you via the scribe, the Rabbi, the Preacher of Polonne,[53] did not reach you and I was also greatly pained by this; for you would have assuredly derived great satisfaction if these had reached you. At the present time I have, however, forgotten some of the things in them,[54] but details which I do remember I will write very briefly.

[C]. For on Rosh Hashana 5507[55] I performed an adjuration for the ascent of the soul,[56] as you know, and I saw wondrous things in a vision,[57] for the evil side[58] ascended to accuse with great, unparalleled joy and performed his acts—persecutions entailing forced conversion—on several souls so they would meet violent deaths. I was horrified and I literally put my life in jeopardy and asked my teacher and rabbi[59] to go with me because it is very dangerous to go and ascend to the upper worlds. For from the day I attained my position I did not ascend such lofty ascents. I went up step by step until I entered the palace[60] of the Messiah where the Messiah learns Torah with all of the Tannaim[61] and the righteous and also with the seven shepherds.[62] And there I saw exceedingly great joy and I don't know the reason for this joy. I thought this joy was—God forbid—over my departure from this world but they informed me afterward that I was not leaving yet because in the upper spheres they derive pleasure when I perform unifications[63] down below by the means of their holy teachings. The reason for the joy I still do not know. And I asked the Messiah, "When will the master come?" And he answered me, " 'Once your Torah will have spread throughout the world,' etc."[64] And I prayed there over why God did thus; wherefore that great wrath[65] that some souls of Israel were given over to the evil side for killing and of them several souls converted and afterward were killed and they gave me permission to ask the evil side himself directly, and I asked the evil side why he did this and how he viewed their converting and then being killed. And he replied to me that his intention was for the sake of heaven. For if they were to remain alive after apostasizing then when there would be some other persecution or libel they would not sanctify the name of heaven; rather everyone would just convert to save themselves. Therefore he acted; those who converted were later killed so that no son of Israel would convert and they would sanctify the name of heaven.[66] Thus it was afterwards, due to our many sins, in the community of Zasław there was a libel against several souls and two of them converted and later they killed them. The rest sanctified the name of heaven in great holiness and died violent deaths and then there were libels in the communities of Szepetówka and Dunajów and they didn't convert after they saw what happened in Zaslaw, but all of them gave their souls for the sanctification of God's Name and sanctified the name of heaven and withstood the test. And by virtue of this act our Messiah will come and take our vengeance. And God will conciliate his land and his people.[67]

[D]. And on Rosh Ha-Shanah 5510[68] I performed an ascent of the soul, as is known, and I saw a great accusation until the evil side almost received permission to completely destroy regions and communities. I put my life in jeopardy and I prayed: "Let us fall into the hand of God and not fall into the hands of man."[69] And they gave me permission that instead of this[70] there would be great epidemics and unprecedented plague in all of the regions of Poland and our neighboring areas, and so it was that the epidemic spread so much that it could not be measured, and likewise the plague in the other areas. And I arranged with my group[71] to say [Ketoret][72] upon arising to cancel this decree. And they[73] revealed to me in a night vision: "Did not you yourself choose 'Let us fall into God's hand,' etc.? Why do you want to cancel? Is it not accepted that 'the prosecutor cannot [become the defender]'?"[74] From then on I did not say Ketoret and I did not pray about this except by means of several adjurations due to great fear on Hoshannah Rabbah[75] when I went to the synagogue with the entire congregation. And I said Ketoret one time so that the plague would not spread to our environs. With the help of God we succeeded.

[E]. I would like to go on and meander at length but because of the tears when I recall your departure from me, I cannot speak. But my request of you is to review my words of moral instruction[76] which I said to you several times. They should always be in your consciousness; contemplate them and analyze them. You will certainly find in each and every statement several kinds of sweetness for what I said to you is not a vain thing because God knows that I do not despair of traveling to Eretz Yisrael, if it be God's will, to be together with you, but the times do not allow it.

[F]. Also don't be displeased that because of the treacherousness of the times I have not sent you money; there having been in our country plague and famine. Also several dependents from our family rely on me to support and feed them, in addition to the rest of the poor of Israel; and the money has run out. There is nothing left except our bodies. But, if God wills it, "when the

Lord enlarges [your territory, as he has promised you]" then, certainly, "[you will say, 'I will eat meat' because you will have the urge to eat meat.]"[77]

[G]. And also my grandson, the important young man, the honorable Ephraim, a great prodigy at the highest level of learning; certainly, if the time is propitious, it would be fitting for you to come here yourself and see and be seen with him face to face and to rejoice in our joy as you promised me.

[H]. Also my most urgent petition concerning my beloved, the famous rabbi, the hasid, our teacher Joseph Katz,[78] a servant of the Lord, to bring him close with two hands and with all sorts of favor because his deeds are pleasing before God and all of his deeds are for the sake of heaven. Also please write on his behalf to the wealthy people there with you to keep him well supplied and sustain him so that he "sits with support";[79] for you will surely derive satisfaction if he will be there together with you.

[I]. These are the words of your loving brother-in-law who expects to see you face to face and prays for long life for you, your wife and your progeny; and always seeking your welfare, all the days—including the nights—for good long life. Amen. Selah.

Israel Besht from Międzybóż

In this letter the Besht appears in the roles of extended family member, teacher of disciples, Kabbalist, and shaman who works to ensure the supernatural security of his community. This is first and foremost a personal letter from the Besht to his brother-in-law who was also his disciple. The conventional opening and closing greetings (paragraphs A and I) emphasize the family tie and close personal feelings. The first half of paragraph B takes note of Gershon's correspondence with family members and how sorry the Besht was that these letters did not arrive.

Paragraph F treats the perennial problem of support from the established main faction of the family for those who have ventured far away, specifically for a family member who has fulfilled the religious objective of immigration to the Land of Israel. The Besht implied that, in principle, he accepted responsibility for remitting funds to subsidize his brother-in-law in the Holy Land; however, this obligation was superseded by his commitment to support extended family members in Poland and other poor Jews there. His statement that "several dependents from our family rely on me to support and feed them" as well as the fact that the letters "written at length to each and every one" were actually sent to the Besht hint that he was the head of the clan. This perception is reinforced by Gershon's letter to him (see chap. 7).

The Besht also seems very much the family man when singing the praises of his grandson, Ephraim (paragraph G). The Besht was proud of his grandson's achievements in Torah and fervently desired that the scholarly great-uncle confirm in person how good the young man was.

Family matters, however, make up the periphery of this letter. At its heart is a different facet of Gershon's and the Besht's relationship—what the Besht had to teach Gershon. Previous analyses have emphasized that the Holy Epistle was intended to communicate the nature of the Ba'al Shem Tov's mystical experiences and how to bring the Redemption.[80] From the foregoing discussion it follows that while he did describe the experience of being in Paradise, the Besht's primary purpose in writing was to give a theologically meaningful interpretation to catastrophic events. He explained the fatal results of the libels in Zasław (1747), Szepetówka (1748), and Dunajów (1748) and the reason for the general epidemic in various regions of Poland in a way that made the suffering theologically rational.

After summarizing, in paragraph B, the vicissitudes of the correspondence between them, the Besht indicated his main reason for writing. In a previous letter he had imparted to Gershon "news and secrets." These had been lost, and now the Besht wanted to give satisfaction to Gershon by recapitulating, in briefer form, what he remembered of what he had written earlier. Then follow paragraphs C and D, which constitute the bulk of the Holy Epistle.

On the basis of what he communicated in these two paragraphs, it is apparent that the "news and secrets" the Besht had to tell Gershon related to what he found out during his "ascent of the soul" experiences. He recounted two occasions on which his soul rose up to Paradise. Both of these happened on Rosh Ha-Shanah, the Jewish New Year. A third ascent was later reported to have occurred on Yom Kippur, the Day of Atonement, in 5518 (24 September 1757).[81] Together, Rosh Ha-Shanah and Yom Kippur make up the "Days of Awe" or "High Holy Days." In Jewish tradition these are the most numinous days in the Jewish calendar, fraught with spiritual tension, when concentrated communication with the Divine is most possible and most likely to be efficacious. It does not seem coincidental that the three references to the Besht's ascents of the soul are associated with these days. The implication is that these ascents were not commonplace events but rare spiritual odysseys that could occur only when the Besht was at the peak of spiritual preparedness, as he would have been on the Days of Awe.

Taking place on these holy days when the synagogue was filled to capacity with people of both sexes and of all ages, these ascents were pub-

lic knowledge and probably represented the spiritual climax of the day
for those assembled. In the Holy Epistle the Besht confirmed that the fact
of the first ascent was already known at least to Gershon, while he mentioned that the second was known generally. The *Shivhei Ha-Besht* description of the 1757 ascent explicitly places it during the synagogue service while the Besht was conducting the *Ne'ilah* service, which leads into
the dramatic closing ceremony of Yom Kippur. As recorded there, the
purpose of this ascent was to combat an accusation lodged in heaven that
would lead to the loss of the Oral Law (i.e., the Talmud and other rabbinic teachings) to the Jewish people.[82] The story gives a vivid account
of how the Besht looked on earth when his soul was aloft in heaven.

> Before *Ne'ilah* he began to preach in harsh words and he cried. He leaned his
> head back on the lectern, and he sighed and he wept. . . . It was always his
> custom during the Days of Awe not to look at the holiday prayer book since
> the rabbi, Rabbi Yakil of Medzibozh,[83] used to prompt him from the holiday
> prayer book and he would repeat after him. When he reached the words
> "Open the gate for us" or "Open the gates of heaven," Rabbi Yakil spoke
> once and then twice, but did not hear the Besht repeating after him and he
> fell silent. The Besht began to make terrible gestures, and he bent backwards
> until his head came close to his knees, and everyone feared that he would fall
> down. . . . His eyes bulged and he sounded like a slaughtered bull. He kept
> this up for about two hours. Suddenly he stirred and straightened up. After-
> wards he began to pray the silent benedictions, and then the cantor's repeti-
> tion.

The ascents were no secret, and even their purpose, content, and outcome were evidently public knowledge. While not telling everything, the
Besht communicated the news and privileged information, revealed during these ecstasies, to close associates and even to the general public. In
all three cases known to us, the Besht played the role of shaman, ven-
turing into the spiritual realm to defend his community, or the people of
Israel in general. His report of what happened gave the etiology of events
that were occurring in real life, provided comfort to survivors, and guided
belief and behavior.

The first reported ascent confirmed that the contemporary persecutions in Zasław, Szepetówka, and Dunajów were indeed divine tests resulting from an accusation of Satan against the Jewish people; that those
who were executed despite their apostasy were intended as an object lesson; and that the proper behavior during religious persecution is to resist unto death and not to submit, even fictitiously. It is noteworthy that
the Besht's defense efforts failed in this case. His prayers and his attempts
to enlist the aid of his teacher, Ahijah the Shilonite, as well as the Mes-

siah himself, did not avert the decree. The most the Besht could achieve was a direct interview with Satan, where he was allowed to demand an explanation for what was destined to happen. The Besht's mission, however, was not a failure because he obtained the explanation. It was this that he brought back to earth. By ascending to Paradise, the Besht was able to ascertain that the suffering was both divine retribution and divine instruction. If this misfortune could not be avoided, the Besht helped people to make sense out of it as chastisement and punishment.

The Besht's 1749 ascent was marginally more effective in providing shamanesque defense, both for Jews in general and for those of his town. His importunings in Paradise changed the fated punishment from general violent destruction at the hands of an enemy (perhaps a reference to the Haidamak attacks then beginning to escalate)[84] to disease brought on by God. Back on earth, the Besht attempted to use a traditional theurgic technique for preventing death: the recitation of the Ketoret passage. For this he was rebuked for trying to force the heavenly powers to change their intent after he had agreed, when in Paradise, to the negotiated course of action of epidemic in place of persecution. The Besht then desisted from his attempt to forestall what had been decreed, although he did persist in staying God's hand from bringing the punishment to his own immediate environs. On this occasion, too, the most important facet of the Besht's divine activity was not the prevention of suffering but the placing of suffering in the proper perspective. After his ascent he could explain that the plague was a deserved punishment that could have been worse.

Although in these cases he was more messenger than protector, the Besht's powers as a shaman were taken for granted. He could report partial or even complete failure to protect the people from catastrophe without self-consciousness. He and his interlocutors were so convinced of his capabilities that a skeptical view of his efforts was not even entertained. If he failed, it was because God had refused him, not because he lacked access to the Divine realm. His ability to explain the theodicy of events was proof enough of his communication with God.[85]

The news of his ascents and the secrets he learned while in Paradise were not the only things the Besht had to teach Gershon. He also reminded his brother-in-law of the words of moral instruction he had said to him on several occasions (paragraph E). In other words, the Besht had offered Gershon instruction in ethical issues and daily behavior, and in the Holy Epistle he was reminding him to keep these teachings in his consciousness and make them his watchwords. In his ethical teachings, the

Besht apparently stressed the centrality of the Land of Israel in Judaism,
for by way of persuading Gershon as to the meaningfulness of his words,
the Besht assured him that he fully intended on traveling to Eretz Yisrael.

The final topic of the Holy Epistle, which may have been the immediate cause for its composition, is a recommendation for its bearer, Jacob
Joseph of Polonne. Jacob Joseph was on his way to settle in the Holy
Land, and the Besht asked his brother-in-law to take in the newcomer
and help him get established materially. The Besht was certain that Gershon would appreciate having Jacob Joseph with him.

Included in the news of the Besht from Paradise is the report of his
discussion with the Messiah. As Avraham Rubinstein pointed out,[86] the
Besht did not plan this interview. It was a by-product of his efforts to
avert the evil decree, not an attempt to forge a systematic eschatology.
Yet the exchange with the Messiah is revealing. On meeting the Messiah,
the Besht asked him the question that would occur to any traditional Jew:
"When are you coming?" The reply, "Once your Torah will have spread
throughout the world," puts the Besht in a category all his own. It implies that he had a central role to play in the process of Redemption and
that he was conscious of the novel and perhaps even revolutionary nature of his "Torah."

In general in this letter, the Besht displayed a highly developed sense
of himself and his own importance. There is none of the artificial modesty that often appears in rabbinic correspondence. Rather, the Besht
took it for granted that he was the person who could save the community from its fate. His group's recitation of the *Ketoret* prayer was a
match for the forces of heaven, which had to get him to stop if they were
to execute their plan. His moral instruction contains, in his opinion, "several kinds of sweetness." His relationship with Gershon was an unequal
one; the Besht was the one doing the edifying. He had the authority to
issue the request, which was really a demand, concerning the treatment
of Jacob Joseph. It was the Besht's Torah that would bring on the long-
awaited Redemption.

The letter also indicates that, in addition to heading his extended
family, the Besht was the head of a *havurah,* a group of mystics, of the
type described in chapter 2. They assisted him in performing the rituals
of practical Kabbalah, such as recitation of *Ketoret.* He probably guided
them similarly to the way he sought to instruct and guide Gershon in this
letter.

In the Holy Epistle the Besht expressed his fundamental confidence, demonstrated the use to which he put his spiritual virtuosity, revealed himself as a mentor, and disclosed some information about his basic reference groups: extended family and havurah. This text does not shed light on his early life, his relationship with various groups in the community, or the exact nature of his "Torah." These issues are raised by the other three Besht letters that are extant.

CHAPTER SEVEN

More Besht Correspondence

THE LETTERS PUBLISHED IN *SHIVHEI HA-BESHT*

In the collection of hagiographic stories about the Besht and his associates, *Shivhei Ha-Besht,* the compiler, Dov Ber of Ilintsy, included five citations from letters the Ba'al Shem Tov wrote. As noted in chapter 6, four of these citations are short excerpts that are actually Dov Ber's reports of hearsay quotations of what was in the letters: someone who had read the letter told Dov Ber what was in it; Dov Ber did not see a written text.[1] As such, these "citations" should properly be classified with traditions about the Besht. The fifth quotation, however, is introduced as follows: "There is in my possession a letter which the Besht sent to the Rabbi [Jacob Joseph], and this is the language of the copy." Unlike the other four cases, here Dov Ber indicated that he was copying, not what someone had told him, but what he saw in a manuscript copy of the letter.[2] The letter is translated as follows:

> (On the back of the letter is written:) From the community of Międzybóż to the great community of Niemirow, these words in a letter going about looking like a flash, the look of the Kohen,[3] the rabbi of the aforementioned holy community [Niemirow], a stronghold and tower, the wonderful rabbi who works wonders, the great sage, our teacher, Joseph the Kohen of the aforesaid holy community, the head of the court.[4] This is the content of the letter[5] to the hand of my beloved, the beloved of my soul, the rabbi, the great light, the righthand pillar, the powerful hammer, famous in hasidism, the complete

sage, the wondrous one who does wonders, who is attached to the walls of my heart closer than a brother, our teacher Joseph the Kohen; behold the form of his holy hand I received and I saw a sight in the two upper lines[6] and there it said that his highness says that it is supposedly mandatory to fast. My stomach was agitated by this declaration, and I hereby react:[7] by the decrees of the angels and together with the Holy One, Blessed be He, and His Presence, you should not put yourself in danger like this. For this is an act of melancholy and of sorrow, and God's Presence will not inspire out of sorrow, but only out of the joy of performing the commandments,[8] as his highness knows the things I taught several times; and these things should be on your heart. As for the subjects of your thoughts which bring you to this state, I will advise you: God is with you, mighty warrior; every single morning when you study, attach yourself to the letters with total devotion to the service of your Creator, blessed be He and blessed be His Name, and then they [the letters] will soften the verdicts with their root and lift the verdicts from you. And do not deny your flesh,[9] God forbid, to fast more than is required or is necessary. If you heed my voice, God will be with you. With this I will be brief and say *shalom* from myself, who seeks your welfare constantly. Signed, Israel Besht.[10]

This letter is not frequently cited by scholars. Neither Dubnow nor Scholem adduced it in their discussions of the Besht's views on asceticism.[11] Yet the letter to Jacob Joseph of Polonne seems to be a clear and reliable statement of the Besht's antiasceticism. Having been informed of Jacob Joseph's intention to fast, the Besht attempted to convince him not to do so and even ordered him to refrain from this unhealthy practice. Simultaneously, the Besht provided an alternative means—attachment to the letters of study texts—of attaining the same spiritual result that was to be achieved by fasting.[12] This letter probably represents the Besht's general position as to the futility of the ascetic practices associated with Jewish mysticism from at least the twelfth century.[13]

As a clear break with long-established hasidic practice, the Besht's antiasceticism was the most innovative element in his behavior. While he was not the first to speak against asceticism,[14] this trend became associated with his name and he apparently successfully substituted alternative means of mystic communion. His advice to Jacob Joseph to employ attachment to the letters in place of fasting was applied and developed by later Hasidic leaders.[15] However, it was not—as is often asserted—joy per se that the Ba'al Shem Tov advocated but the traditional concept of "the joy of performing the commandments," which as far back as the Talmud was contrasted with laughter and frivolity, among other things.[16] Such joy was not, then, a synonym for undisciplined pleasure seeking; but neither could it be attained through suffering.

THE HALAKHIC INQUIRY TO RABBI MEIR
OF KONSTANTYNÓW

In 1857 *Mayim Hayyim,* the responsa collection of Rabbi Hayyim ben
Dov Berish Rapoport, was published in Zhitomir. It contained a responsum addressed to Rabbi Meir, son of the famous Jacob Emden, who
was rabbi of the Konstantynów region.[17] The responsum begins with the
testimony of Mordecai ben Judah Leib, called ne'eman (lit. trustee) of
Międzybóż.[18] Mordecai testified how an adhesion could not be separated
from the lung of a freshly slaughtered cow and the butcher was sent to
bring the *moreh hora'ah* (assistant rabbi who dealt with questions of ritual law),[19] named R. Falk,[20] to examine the lung and decide whether the
animal was kosher for consumption or not. R. Falk came, hesitated, and
took the matter under advisement. (The continuation of the responsum
indicates that later he declared the animal kosher.) The passage following Mordecai's testimony reads:

> In our presence, the court signed below, our teacher, the aforementioned
> Mordecai, related all that is written above as testimony and then wrote all of
> this in his own handwriting and signed it with his very own signature. There-
> fore we have confirmed it and substantiated it as is proper. Signed, Israel Besh
> [Ba'al Shem] of Tłuste;[21] and signed, Moses Joseph Maggid Meisharim
> [preacher] of Międzybóż.[22]
>
> And behold regarding all of the foregoing we have requested from the
> rabbi, the great light, the light of Israel, the glory of the generation whose holy
> name we glorify, our teacher, Meir, may God protect and bless him, to in-
> form us as to his opinion in this matter. Did the *moreh* [*hora'ah*] do the right
> thing or not to permit the cow? And due to the size of the fire that became a
> torch because of this, etc., we therefore trust in him that he will consider our
> words so as to inform us as to what he thinks about this, and may there be
> therein peace from now and forever.

The "we" who were asking the question of Rabbi Meir and posing
the challenge to the Międzybóż assistant rabbi's decision were the two
signatories to the testimony, the Besht and the preacher who probably
was close to the Besht.[23] Rabbi Meir acknowledged the Besht as the chief
questioner by addressing the response directly to him.[24]

This source, then, is a question asked of Rabbi Meir of Konstantynów
by a group of people in Międzybóż, among whom the Besht was the most
prominent figure. The question posed a challenge to a controversial decision in the area of kashrut made by a clerical official of the Międzybóż
Jewish community. In his answer, Rabbi Meir agreed with the questioners that the decision was in error.[25] While there was some legal basis

for ruling that the adhesion did not render the meat unfit, the cow should have been declared nonkosher, in line with long-accepted Ashkenazic custom, sanctioned by Rabbi Moses Isserles in the sixteenth century.

The association of the Besht with the "trustee" and "preacher" of the Międzybóż community, attested to by this source, is striking. Since "trustee" was the title of a kahal officeholder and the preacher's title implies that he was employed by the kahal, it is apparent that the Besht was here in league with members of the communal establishment in opposition to a rabbinic decision.

The ramifications of this responsum went beyond the immediate issue of kashrut. The questioners themselves indicated that the question at hand had become a great controversy necessitating an urgent response that they hoped would reestablish peace. Near the end of his response Rabbi Meir implied that the assistant rabbi's position or even that of the community rabbi—Hersz Leybowicz Aptekarz—was hanging in the balance, writing that if "the rabbi"[26] admitted his mistake all should be well, but "if he is steadfast in his rebellion, as Maimonides decreed, his fate is decided. . . . He should not strike out on his own authority, destroying the words of the classic scholars by whose instruction we live and who are our guides."

If the rabbi who was threatened with dismissal was in fact Hersz Leybowicz Aptekarz, then this halakhic dispute was probably linked to the dispute between Wolf Abramowicz and the kahal, on one side, and the butchers' guild, on the other.[27] There, it will be recalled, Wolf was accused of persecuting Leyba, the head of the butchers, and other butchers as well. In what may have been related actions, the kahal dispossessed the butchers' guild of its synagogue and sought to dismiss the rabbi.[28] One of the points in this controversy was the accusation against Leyba the butcher that he had eaten nonkosher meat. He retorted that the rabbi had approved the meat. It may be that this was the lenient ruling under question in the responsum to Rabbi Meir. The "fire that became a torch" of which this halakhic dispute was a component appears to be a power struggle between the butchers' guild and the kahal, where Wolf and the arrendators were the powerbrokers behind the kahal and the rabbi had taken the side of the butchers.[29]

Whether "the rabbi" to be cashiered was Falk, the moreh hora'ah, or Rabbi Leybowicz, the Besht's position in the controversy is worth considering. If Falk was to be discharged for making a decision that contravened established tradition and was too lenient, then it was the Besht who was defending established precedent and advocating the stricter legal position. It should also be noted that leniency in kashrut decisions was bound to find favor with the poorer elements in the community; carcasses discarded or sold at a discount as nonkosher raised the price of kosher meat. If Rabbi Leybowicz was to be dismissed for siding with the butchers in a larger power struggle with the kahal, then, by opposing the kashrut ruling, the Besht was putting himself squarely in the kahal's (and the arrendators') camp.

In either case, this incident presents a dimension of the Besht not usually emphasized by the interpreters of the hagiographic stories about him in *Shivhei Ha-Besht*. It makes it difficult to portray him—as has often been done—as an unalloyed populist figure, alienated from the rabbinic or political establishment.[30] In this incident he seems to have more in common with the hasid who was the rabbi's assistant in Leipnik—the one who demanded the dismissal of the community shohet because he was not careful enough in matters of kashrut. There, it was the hasid who pressured the rabbi to adhere to a stricter application of the law.[31] Here, too, the Besht, a hasid, seems cast in the role of the rabbi's halakhic conscience. Similar to the Leipnik hasid who, in 1730, filed a formal complaint with Rabbi Pinhas Katznellenbogen, the Besht sought to reinforce his strict halakhic stance by way of appeal to a recognized rabbinic authority.

The difference between the Besht and the hasid of Leipnik is also instructive. While the Leipnik kahal refused to respond positively to the hasid's demands, in Międzybóż—so it appears from Rabbi Meir's comments concerning the rabbi's future—the Besht had significant influence in the question of whether the rabbi was to be retained or discharged. The Besht represented in this text—addressed with respect, complaining about a lenient kashrut ruling, seeking to unseat a rabbi via appeal to a higher rabbinic authority—seems to be ensconced among the elite of the town. If this incident is indeed connected with the affair of the butchers and the attempt to dismiss Rabbi Leybowicz, then the Besht's ties to the elite may have been close indeed. At the same time he identified himself as ba'al shem, and in greeting him in the responsum, R. Meir focused on his occupation as healer ("He provides balm and medicament to the person without strength").[32]

Scholem, in his determination to emphasize that the Besht was indeed a ba'al shem who employed the magical exercises of practical Kabbalah, considered this last point to be the most important aspect of the entire document. The Besht was essentially and unapologetically a faith healer.[33] Perhaps because he was convinced that the Besht was opposed by significant elements of the communal and rabbinic establishment, Scholem minimized the role and status of the Besht in the community as denoted by this text. Dinur saw the connection between the Besht and the establishment demonstrated here, but he claimed that the association with the establishment occurred at an early stage in the Besht's career and that later he aroused opposition.[34]

There is no proof for such an assertion. Polish sources imply that cordial relations were maintained between the Besht and the kahal of Międzybóż until his death.[35] Moreover, the main sources on which Scholem and, presumably, Dinur based their belief that there was establishment opposition to the Besht during his lifetime have proven to have no connection to the Besht.[36] This responsum, then, would seem to be an excellent starting point for attempting to gauge the Besht's position in his community and his relationship to the political and religious establishment. Combined with the Polish texts to be adduced in chapter 10, it indicates that the Ba'al Shem Tov had a defined, conventional, and respected role in the community.

THE LETTER TO MOSES OF KUTÓW

In 1885, Israel Ha-Levi Kutover published an edition of Sa'adia Gaon's classic treatise of medieval Jewish philosophy, *Ha-Emunot Ve-Dei'ot* (Beliefs and Ideas), together with his own commentary to the book, entitled *Shvil Ha-Emunah* (The Path of Faith) (Jozefow, 1878). Kutover was the great-great-great-grandson of Moses, the rabbi of Kutów (died 1738), who had also been a leading member of the circle of Kabbalistic pneumatics associated with this community.[37] Hasidic tradition reports that R. Moses was one of the first people to recognize the Besht's supernatural powers and that they had a good ongoing relationship.[38] It is therefore not altogether surprising to find that on the last page of *Shvil Ha-Emunah,* Israel Ha-Levi Kutover decided to publish a document that appears to have originated in the Kutover family archive. He wrote,

> I have decided to copy here a holy letter which the Besht, whose soul is in the heavenly treasure houses, sent to my great-grandfather Moses Kutover, may his memory be a blessing for eternal life, in reply to what he had written him: to travel to heal the child who had taken sick at his brother's, Rabbi Hayyim the preacher of Horodenka. On the back of the letter at the top it says as follows:
>
> 'These words come close and rest at the supreme member of the supreme council whom God has privileged, none other than the Rabbi, the great light, praise, strength and tower, the light of Israel, the glory of the generation, the

servant of God, the honored name of glory,[39] our teacher, Rabbi Moses, may he flourish[40] as the sun rising in its strength. From the Community of Tluste[41] to the Community of Kutów, may God protect it.'

And this is the Content of the Letter Itself:

'Blessed be God. May peace be increased for this great and dear man, a tree planted for the great trees, a lamp of light, a flow of rich olives, pomegranate syrup, none other than the rabbi, the great light, his teaching is clear and pure as the sun, his honored name of glory, our teacher, Rabbi Moses, may his light shine like the sun at noon.

'We have life and peace. May God grant and increase the same for you[42] with affection and kindness forever.

'Behold I descend and ascend[43] at master's will, and I set out [at master's command] to get up and act. I hastened to travel to the community of Horodenka and I made the matter right in accord with master's desire. Also, with regard to the question which you asked, as well as beyond it, I applied myself and searched out those vagabonds who travel at will[44] to reveal to the great honored sage, at the high place, the answer to the question, to understand what is to be understood. And now, at this time, I do not understand the reason for the grievance master has against me. Let him decide to reveal things which are in the heart and I will reply to his heart to examine well; and I will reply to his heart to understand the intensity of the matter. Let master follow [my prescription] and not be afraid of what comes from the tree. Let master take pieces of wood and finely pulverize them, put [the powder] in water and cook it, i.e., fry it well and put a tiny amount of sugar in it. This potion does not weaken or cause diarrhea, it only strengthens the brain and gladdens the heart for the service of God, blessed be He. This should be drunk every morning on an empty stomach.[45] All of this should be done to completion every morning. With this I shall close with "Grant Peace,"[46] these are the words of Israel the son of Eliezer from Tluste.'

This letter, although published some one hundred fifty years after it was written, is less problematic than the "Holy Epistle." Its provenance is clear: Rabbi Moses of Kutów received it and kept it until he died. It then passed into the possession of his daughter and son-in-law and stayed in the family, which remained in the region, for the next four generations.[47]

Internal evidence in the letter also strengthens its credibility. Before 1738, the year Rabbi Moses died, the Besht had not yet arrived in Międzybóż and was presumably in Tluste, as the signature says. Moses was an important rabbi and mystic who held a leadership position and could have commanded the loyalty of an aspiring mystic like the Besht, who did his bidding and wanted to be in his good graces.

The fact that Israel Kutover cited the address[48] and the salutation also implies that he was copying word for word from the document that was in his possession. Moreover, the picture of the Besht presented here is of a mere folk healer, subordinate to Rabbi Moses, with no leadership role or movement behind him, willing to learn from vagabonds, perhaps even Gypsies. Such a portrayal would hardly serve Hasidic internal pedagogical efforts, even less so propaganda projects directed at rabbinic and maskilic opponents. Its publication would not bring the edifying effects of the letters in *Ben Porat Yosef* or *Shivhei Ha-Besht*, which, while written after the letter to Rabbi Moses, were published generations earlier. From the Hasidic perspective, in its current form this letter was better left unpublished, as it was for so long.[49]

When he wrote this letter, the Besht was already known for his healing talents, even though he did not yet sign himself as "Besht"—perhaps an indication that his fame was still ahead of him. He had great respect for Rabbi Moses and was apparently within the orbit of the group of mystical hasidim who were based in Kutów and were one of many such groups throughout the Jewish world.[50] For his part, Rabbi Moses deferred to the Besht's superior knowledge in medical matters, which he had gained from various other sources, asking him to cure the boy in Horodenka and receiving a prescription for a potion from him. The Besht's demonstrated clinical abilities enhanced his status and provided the foundation, or at least a significant dimension, of his relationship with this important rabbi and mystic.[51]

This letter reveals some additional details about the Besht. The sophisticated use of Aramaic and Hebrew in the letter implies that the writer was far from being an ignoramus. The tone of the letter indicates that as important as it might have been to the Besht that he find favor with Rabbi Moses, he did not shrink from challenging the rabbi's anger—both reminding the rabbi of his devoted service and urging that they clear the air between them.

This letter, long left unpublished by Hasidim, has not, since its publication, received very much attention from scholars. The close attachment to a scholarly figure and to the Kutów hasidim, the high level of Torah knowledge displayed by the language, the concentration on healing physical ailments, the willingness to learn from non-Jews, or at least nonscholars—all of these clash with various standard conceptions concerning the Besht, based on traditions that served as the main sources of knowledge about him. Scholem, the one scholar who did refer to this letter—albeit based on a corrupt and incomplete copy of it—saw its significance merely as another confirmation that the Besht really did function as a ba'al shem.[52]

In my view, this letter is indicative of the Besht's personality, modus operandi as a ba'al shem, relationship to establishment figures, status in their eyes, and career development in the public arena. It implies that the Besht had the self-confidence, professional success, requisite apprenticeship in mysticism, level of learning, and public recognition that qualified him to be chosen as "mystic-in-residence" and head of the circle of mystics who were based in the bet midrash of Międzybóż.[53] This position gave him a forum to present his innovative ideas and to attract widespread attention.

PSEUDO-BESHT WRITINGS

THE COMMENTARY ON PSALM 107

Perush Al Hodu is an often-printed Hasidic commentary on Psalm 107. Hasidim traditionally attribute this commentary to the Besht, and Rivka Schatz-Uffenheimer, who accepted this attribution, devoted an academic study to it, attempting to utilize it in defining the Besht's theological stance.[54]

While Schatz-Uffenheimer's analysis of the commentary itself within the context of early Hasidism may be valid, the attribution to the Besht is not established. She herself recognized the many problems associated with the attribution of this text. The first person to mention that the Besht composed a commentary on Psalm 107 was apparently Rabbi Levi Yitzhak of Berdichev in the 1770s. Levi Yitzhak was a disciple of the Maggid, not the Besht, and by the 1770s could have been influenced by traditions that had grown up after the Besht's death. Conversely, one of the Besht's associates, Nahum of Chernobyl, observed that the Besht instituted the recitation of Psalm 107 on Friday evenings prior to the onset of the Sabbath, but he did not say that the Besht wrote a commentary, and Nahum's comments on the Psalm differ significantly from the written commentary that is attributed to the Besht. Both the Maggid and Jacob Joseph of Polonne paraphrased the commentary without attributing its ideas to the Besht.[55]

Moreover, the earliest copy of the Psalm 107 commentary attributing this text to the Besht is contained in a manuscript whose owner made a notation on it in 1789. Schatz-Uffenheimer assumes that this copy must have been written sometime before 1780 because it quotes from the writings of Jacob Joseph without mentioning the book the quotations came from, as was, she claimed, customary. Since the first book was published in 1780, Schatz-Uffenheimer believed that the manuscript must be earlier.[56] Perhaps it is, but that does not necessarily place the attribution within the Besht's lifetime.

More significant, there is a manuscript copy of this commentary that attributes it to Menahem Mendel of Bar, around 1760, the year of the Besht's death.[57] If this text had originated with the Besht, it would have been most unlikely that anyone would have dared, or wanted, to attribute it to someone of lesser stature. However, mistaken "promotion" of a document's holiness with time is a standard phenomenon.[58]

Claiming that the attribution to Menahem Mendel was ambiguous, Schatz-Uffenheimer rejected it, while Scholem accepted it.[59] Lacking compelling evidence linking the commentary to the Besht, Scholem's view must prevail. While the author of this text may have been influenced by the Besht's spoken ideas, it cannot be construed as an integrated presentation by the Besht of his theological views. In its written form this commentary probably tells us more about the ideas circulating within the circles of Hasidim in the 1760s (some of which were undoubtedly derived from the Besht) than it does about specific teachings of the Besht.

THE KHERSON LETTERS

In 1916, a bookseller named Naftali Zvi Shapiro offered to sell a scholar, Abraham Kahana, letters written by the Ba'al Shem Tov that had been stored in some *geniza* (cache of old documents).[60] By 1918, rumors about this cache were circulating throughout Jewish eastern Europe and appearing in the Jewish press. There was confusion as to where the geniza was, in St. Petersburg, Kiev, or Kharkov. Finally, in 1921, the letters appeared in Odessa, having originated (supposedly) in the government archive in Kherson. The story was that in the confusion following the Revolution of 1917, the letters were removed from the Kherson archive and brought to Odessa. There most of the letters were purchased by the Hasid Shmuel ben Shneur Zalman Gurary and given by him to the leader of the Habad Hasidim at the time, Rabbi Shalom Duber. After piecemeal publishing efforts, in the 1930s his successor, Rabbi Yosef Yitzhak, published some three hundred letters, purportedly from the pen of the Besht or his family members and associates, in the Habad journal, *Ha-Tamim*. Rabbi A. H. Glitzenstein republished the letters in one collection in his *Rabbi Israel Ba'al Shem Tov* (Kefar Habad, 1960).[61]

The discovery of the letters caused an initial rush of enthusiasm among Hasidim and academic scholars alike. It soon became apparent, however, that the excitement was misplaced. Close inspection of the contents, form, and paper of the letters cast serious doubt on their genuineness, and today, outside of the Habad Hasidic movement, there are virtually no authorities who consider these letters anything other than forgeries.[62]

In brief, the case against the letters rests on several categories of evidence. The first problem is provenance. The letters' sellers claimed they had been in the home of Rabbi Israel of Ruzhin and were confiscated from him when he was arrested around 1838 and held by the tsarist authorities for twenty-seven months. In fact, each of the letters is sealed and numbered and has a stamp indicating it was found in Rabbi Israel's home. The authorities then supposedly deposited the confiscated letters in the Kiev archive. At a later point the letters were transferred to Kherson, whence they were liberated in 1918 in the wake of the revolution, and arrived in Odessa.[63]

This scenario is most doubtful. Until the appearance of these letters there was no tradition that Israel of Ruzhin possessed such an archive or that papers such as these had been confiscated from him.[64] There is no one who saw these letters in Kherson or knew of their existence. Who liberated these documents from Kherson, and who brought them to Odessa? If they were liberated as a result of the revolution, why did Shapiro offer to sell them to Kahana as early as 1916? If they were kept in a Russian archive, why is there no Russian documentation concerning them?

Even if problems of provenance are overlooked, there are difficulties with the form. The Russian on the stamps is not idiomatic and seems to come from a nonnative speaker whose mother tongue was Yiddish. The Yiddish used in some of the letters is not Podolian in style, and the Hebrew contains several modernisms. The style of the language and the outward form of the letters are uniform despite the fact that some thirty people were supposed to have written them. The dates are all given in the same way: the year plus Torah portion of the week and the day of the week. The month and date are never given. David Z. Hillman assumed that this was a device to help the forger refrain from dating a letter on a Sabbath, when, of course, none of these correspondents would have written. Despite this sleight of hand, mistakes were made. In a few places the forger forgot that in certain years some portions were doubled on a given Sabbath. His system also allowed him to date letters on the last day of Passover, on Shemini Atzeret, and on the Ninth of Av—all days on which letter writing is prohibited to observant Jews.[65]

In addition, there are many anachronisms and inaccuracies; a few ex-

amples will illustrate the point. Rabbis who were famous for their association with a certain locale are assumed to have always lived in the same
place. Thus the Maggid of Mezerich is said to have come to the Besht
from Mezerich, when in reality at the time he met the Besht he lived in
Lukach. People who were not yet born or were small children when the
Besht was alive are assumed to have already attained maturity and greatness. People who died are made to participate in events occurring years
after their deaths. Certain details obviously stem directly or indirectly
from the discredited forgery *Ma'aseh Nora Be-Podolia* purporting to be
a report about the struggle of the Jewish community of Podolia against
the Frankists.[66]

Finally, a sample of the paper from some of these letters was tested
at a technical institute in Vienna, at the behest of Abraham Schwadron.
The scientists established that the paper on which these letters were written could not have been manufactured before 1846, some eight years
after Rabbi Israel of Ruzhin was arrested.[67] Any claim of credibility for
these documents is simply untenable.

The four sources—the Holy Epistle, the letter to Jacob Joseph of Polonne,
the passage in the responsum of Meir of Konstantynów, and the letter
to Rabbi Moses of Kutów—that can be reasonably considered as at least
reliable copies of documents originating from the Ba'al Shem Tov himself have been either ignored, underinterpreted, or demonstrably misin-
terpreted by scholars. The weight of these sources in constructing representations of the Besht should, on the face of it, be great.

This material implies that the Besht did not live or work in a vacuum.
He was connected both to the communal structure, as his participation
in the kashrut controversy shows, and to conventional hasidim like
Moses of Kutów. He did not arrive on the scene out of nowhere as an
upstart religious radical or social revolutionary. In the kashrut controversy he appears allied with the communal establishment, and he follows
conventional halakhic procedure by soliciting a ruling from Rabbi Meir,
a recognized rabbinic authority. The "trustee" and "preacher" of the
community were associated with the Besht, and his entire circle was
praised and blessed by Rabbi Meir. Moreover, the honorifics applied to
the Besht by Rabbi Meir, the scion of an important rabbinic family and
a leading rabbi of the time, indicate that the Besht was a person of some
fame and worthy of the respect of scholars.

There is no hint in any of these letters of a new movement surrounding the Besht, or of any institutions he founded. The only innovation that

emerges from these texts is his insistence that communion with the letters of study texts should become the functional substitute for radical asceticism.

The Besht of the letter to Rabbi Moses apprenticed as both a healer and a mystic. His healing work, which he may have learned in part from non-Jewish sources and in which he surpassed established mystics, was connected to, but separate from, his commitment to mysticism. As a mystic he came to maturity under the influence of the traditional mystical, hasidic groups and formed an attachment to a leading member of one of them, Moses of Kutów. Eventually, the Besht developed into a mystical leader in his own right, to whom others, such as Jacob Joseph, looked for guidance. Yet he did not turn his back on the minutiae of ritual observance or repudiate the acknowledged halakhic authorities. He certainly never belittled the importance of Torah erudition.[68]

From these sources, written by the Besht, it appears that neither his activity nor the circle of those close to him was repudiated by society or even actively opposed. On the contrary, he was known and respected by the three eminently reputable rabbis with whom he corresponded.[69]

Despite the historical ramifications of these letters, they have not occupied a central place in past representations of the Besht. The center of gravity of those representations has lain elsewhere, in sources that are less close to the Besht but more flexible in the interpretations they admit. This has made it easier for the Besht to be portrayed more in accord with later ideologies than with the views of himself by himself and by his contemporaries.

CHAPTER EIGHT

Testimonies

CONTEMPORARY TEXTS

Four Hebrew texts that mention the Ba'al Shem Tov were written during his lifetime by people who knew him personally. These sources prove that he actually did live and contain information about his role, activities, and character.[1]

The first of the testimonies is the responsum of Rabbi Meir of Konstantynow, referred to in chapter 7. This contains, in addition to the text signed by the Besht discussed there, remarks by Rabbi Meir addressed to the Besht.

> Champion in Judea and Israel! He who succeeds there at the small and the great. He provides balm and medicament to the person without strength. He is great in Babylonia and famous in Tiberias[2] and has prevailed in all things. The great sage, the eminent rabbi, famous for his good name, our teacher Israel, may God protect and bless him. And of all his colleagues, all of them beloved rabbis, the great and eminent sage, our teacher Gershon,[3] may God protect and bless him; and those whom I don't know [by name] I greet; may they all be granted the highest blessing.[4]

There can be no doubt that Israel from Międzybóż, addressed by Rabbi Meir, the man who "provides balm and medicament to the person without strength" and is associated with the sage Gershon (i.e., Gershon of Kutów, his brother-in-law), is the Besht. As noted in chapter 7, the tone of Rabbi Meir's remarks implies that the Besht was respected and famous.[5] Yet what Meir chose to single out in praise of the Besht were his healing abilities. It was, presumably, the Besht's activity as a ba'al shem that lay the basis for the fame to which Meir alluded twice.

Meir's remarks also indicate that the Besht stood at the head of a group. It was not, however, a very large one, for they were all "beloved rabbis," evidently meaning that they were part of the limited learned class, probably of its even more restricted Kabbalist ranks.[6] While the only other member famous enough for Meir to have heard of was Gershon, he knew that the group existed and deemed all of the Besht's associates as meriting his respect and worthy of the highest blessing. The Besht's occupation as a ba'al shem and his position at the head of a group of men who were scholars and, probably, mystical ascetics[7] posed no contradiction for Rabbi Meir. As we have seen, in the eighteenth century ba'al shem could be a respectable religious vocation that functioned alongside rabbis and was related to the realm of mystical-ascetic hasidism.[8]

A second, briefer, reference to the Besht in his lifetime was made by Rabbi Meir Teomim, an itinerant preacher, who made the rounds of towns in the Międzybóż region during the 1740s.[9] Teomim cited a passage from a letter, otherwise unknown, written by the Besht's brother-in-law, Gershon of Kutów, from Jerusalem to "his famous brother-in-law, the Ba'al Shem Tov, may he flourish."[10] The adjective "famous" carries weight because as the wish for his continued vitality indicates, this letter had already entered the public domain in the Besht's lifetime. If people were circulating and discussing the Besht's correspondence, then he must have been a public figure whose own words—or even the words of others written to him—were considered to be in the category of holy writ to be studied, discussed, and even committed to memory.[11]

The third text that mentioned the Besht while he was still alive is a second letter from Gershon, the Besht's brother-in-law, to the Besht, written from Hebron around 1748.[12] In this letter Gershon referred to the Besht once as "my brother-in-law, my soulmate," and later as "my beloved, my brother-in-law, my soulmate, closer to me than a brother."

The letter mentions the Besht in three contexts. First, Gershon asked the Besht, as well as the other members of his family, to write to him more often and at greater length, in order to dispel his loneliness. With regard to communications from the Besht, Gershon was particularly insistent.

> Inquire as to your brother's welfare; take up the tokens of our language as a seal upon your arm, because love is as fierce as death, [your love] was more wonderful than the love of women.[13] Do not stint your brother who thirstily

hungers to hear your pleasant words. Keep me informed from time to time with your words, so pleasant with you.

Gershon's attachment to the Besht appears even more intense than the feelings the Besht expressed for him in the Holy Epistle. While the Besht referred to Gershon with the standard "my beloved," Gershon used the combined biblical imagery of brotherly concern shown by David for his brothers, the love desire of the heroine of the Song of Songs, and the love of David for Jonathan to emphasize how close he felt to the Besht and how significant to him this relationship was.[14]

The second context is connected with Gershon's good fortune at succeeding in returning to Hebron in fall 1747 just as a plague set upon Jerusalem, killing hundreds of people there. After praising God for saving him, he addressed a request to the Besht: "How good it would be if you could send me a general amulet and there would be no need for a new one every year."

As Scholem emphasized, this is another in the series of statements from an array of sources attesting that the Besht was a theurgic ba'al shem. Like the rabbis Pinhas Katznellenbogen and Moses of Kutów, Gershon—hasid, Talmudist, and Kabbalist[15]—availed himself of the prophylactic services of the Ba'al Shem with no self-consciousness. He recognized that the Ba'al Shem's shamanesque field of expertise was a distinct one that required qualifications other than classical book study.

Moreover, Gershon made no qualitative distinction between the Besht's theurgic capabilities and his other mystical talents. As ba'alei shem (and shamans in general) defended against disease and misfortune, they also had mystical visions. While in the second context Gershon asked the Besht to provide him with a prophylactic amulet, in the third context Gershon addressed the Besht on the matter of a mystical vision.

> My beloved brother in-law, I wish to speak of something which happened in your holy dwelling. You once told me that you saw in a vision how a sage came to Jerusalem from the West[16] and he was a spark of the Messiah, except that he himself did not realize this and he was a sage great in both the exoteric and esoteric Torah and a great wailer.[17] Later you told me that you did not see him and it seemed to you that he died.
>
> When I came here I investigated the matter and they told me about a wondrous man, a wonder of wonders, whose name was R. Hayyim ben Attar,[18] a great hasid, sharp and erudite in both the exoteric and esoteric. Compared to him, all the sages of Israel were as a monkey compared to a man. . . . In short, he was a great hasid, ascetic, and holy person. Due to our many sins he did not live long in Jerusalem—only a year—and then died. This was about four years ago, around the time that you spoke with me.

I told the sages your words, what you said about him and they were stunned at the hearing. In short, your name is already known in the gates of Jerusalem and the sages here requested that I write you to urge you to come here and settle. They yearn to see you. But what can I do? I know your nature; you must pray in your *minyan*,[19] in addition to other things which make me despair of your ever coming to the Holy Land, unless the King Messiah comes, speedily in our days.

Here, too, Gershon reflects on the Besht's ba'al shem, shamanesque characteristics. In addition to effecting cures, he could see over the distance from Ukraine to the Land of Israel and observe the activities of the great sage from North Africa there. He also knew the metaphysics of the soul, discerning that the man possessed the spark of the Messiah and knowing when he had left the world.

Given the Besht's powers and his specific vision, Gershon was sure that the great sage who had appeared in the vision must have existed. After questioning the sages of the Jerusalem community he realized, and they agreed, that the Besht must have been talking about the Moroccan rabbi Hayyim ben Attar, who came to Jerusalem and died there around 1743.[20] The rabbis of Jerusalem, who on hearing of the Besht's vision might easily have dismissed Gershon's identification of Hayyim ben Attar as a coincidence and voiced skepticism about the Besht's long-distance sight and mystical talents, were eager to have the Besht join them and practice his form of mysticism among them.

This bespeaks a predisposition to believe in practical Kabbalah and its practitioners. The supernatural powers of someone like the Besht seemed to them entirely possible and expected. The spread of mystical-ascetic hasidim from Safed to Europe from the sixteenth century onward put the Moroccan, Hayyim ben Attar, the Ukrainians, Gershon of Kutów and the Besht, and the sages of Jerusalem in the same universe of discourse. Gershon's report elicited not skepticism but admiring amazement. The Besht was apparently one of the great mystics of the generation, and his place was in the capital of holiness.

In this passage in his letter, Gershon also disclosed some personal information about the Besht. Gershon himself complained earlier in the letter that in Jerusalem he was isolated: "the natures are not the same and the languages aren't the same."[21] For Gershon, the difference in language and mentalité between himself and the Sephardic—Ladino and Arabic-speaking—Jews constituted a wide cultural gap. Yet, though he would have to do it largely alone, Gershon was content to study and pray in the Holy Land. He emphasized how immersed in solitary study he was.[22]

Gershon knew, however, that for the Besht the most important religious act was prayer. Like many mystical-ascetic hasidim,[23] the Besht prayed in a minyan separate from the main community synagogue and was surrounded by like-minded individuals. For him, praying under optimal conditions—which included his relationship to the other worshipers—was even more essential than *aliyah* (migration) to Eretz Yisrael (the Land of Israel).[24]

In this connection it is noteworthy that later tradition made much of the Besht's attempted aliyah, and Dinur even tried to date the event. In his own letter the Besht had written to Gershon, "God knows that I do not despair of traveling to Eretz Yisrael, if it be God's will, to be together with you, but the times do not allow it."[25] In the present text Gershon was certain that for the Besht, aliyah was out of the question. He, like the Besht in his own letter, made no mention of the aborted trip that Dinur dated around 1744.[26] Is this because the trauma of the failed attempt was so strong and so evident that both men were chary of bringing it up? Or is it that the Besht was stating ambiguously what Gershon put more plainly, that the Besht never intended to go to Eretz Yisrael before the Messiah arrived, and, presumably, the conditions of prayer for him there would be perfected? Might it be that only later tradition made the Besht the subject of an actual journey that others of his stature had attempted?[27]

There is another letter that Gershon sent from Eretz Yisrael to Europe that has survived. This was written approximately eight years after the first one. It is addressed to the Besht and the rest of Gershon's family back in Podolia. Interestingly, the Besht comes first in the list of addressees and his name is preceded by flowery epithets, yet the body of the letter was directed to other family members. There is nothing particular that Gershon communicated to the Besht. This implies that the Besht was the acknowledged head of the extended family and when Gershon wrote home he showed due respect to the clan elder, even though there was no message specifically for him.[28]

Still, part of the florid opening does convey a smattering of information about the Besht, "who understands the secrets and the preeminence of the Supreme Mind, may he flourish, the right-hand pillar, the powerful hammer, hasid and ascetic, the divine Kabbalist, his honor, our teacher and rabbi, Israel Besht, his light will shine as the day and like the moon be established, and he will dwell in the heavens."

This text also indicates that in the eyes of his contemporaries the Besht's greatness lay in his Kabbalistic skills. He understood the esoteric holy elements and was capable of entering the heavenly realms. As late as 1756, only four years before the Besht's death, Gershon still referred to him as "hasid and ascetic," indicating that he still viewed the Besht, like Hayyim ben Attar, as attached to the tradition of mystical-ascetic hasidism.

POSTHUMOUS TEXTS

Another category of testimonies by the Besht's contemporaries is that of texts about him written only after he died. One group of these testimonies originates from the Besht's grandson, Moses Ephraim of Sudyłkow. In his book, first published posthumously in 1808,[29] Moses Ephraim recalled what might be termed the Besht's modus operandi. While Moses Ephraim attested that his grandfather placed great importance on Torah learning,[30] he knew that his grandfather did not teach in the formal mode of a Talmudist. He did not try to idealize the Besht into a scholar, or even someone with profound Torah knowledge gained in an unconventional way.[31] Rather, according to Moses Ephraim, the Besht, who did study and offered interpretations of various biblical verses and rabbinic passages,[32] could distill the essence of what wisdom teaches and serve God in truth through stories and common conversation.[33] As he put it, "I heard and saw from my master, my grandfather, his soul is in paradise, that he would tell stories and superficial things[34] and thereby worship God with the pure, clean wisdom with which he was endowed."[35]

In addition to his grandfather's unconventional approach to communicating divine teaching, Moses Ephraim remembered that the Besht saw himself bearing a tension that corresponds to that of the shaman who carries the responsibility for the cosmic fate of his people. While the Besht realized that he alone could not bring the Redemption, he understood his own importance in the process[36] and the crucial contribution of his prayers to the outcome. In the Holy Epistle the Besht noted the salutary effect in Heaven of his "unifying unifications," that is, unifying the disjointed parts of the Godhead and returning the divine sparks, dispersed at the moment of creation, to their source through prayer and other religious acts. Similarly, his grandson remembered him emphasizing the importance of the zaddik's task of unifying unifications and returning the sparks.[37] According to him, the Besht believed, "If there was another person to say *El Rahum Shemekhah* and *Aneinu*[38] as I do, then I could bring the Messiah."[39]

Aware of his responsibility for maintaining the spiritual welfare of the Jewish people, the Besht evidently feared that at any time he could be removed from his pivotal position.[40] As Moses Ephraim remembered him saying, "This I swear to you,[41] there is a person in the world who hears Torah from the mouth of the Holy One Blessed be He and His Shekhinah, not from an angel and not from a seraph, yet he does not believe that he will not be rejected by God, Heaven forbid, for he can easily be pushed into the depth of the great abyss."[42]

The Besht also expressed, according to his grandson, a clear idea of the division of labor between the "people of form and service" and "the people of materiality."[43] The former were like infantry soldiers who find themselves in the thick of the battle and must fight to the death for the honor of their king, while the latter are like cavalry solders who retreat easily from danger. Conversely, once the enemy is on the run, the cavalrymen surge forward and collect the booty, while the infantrymen must be content with leftovers and handouts from their mounted comrades. Thus, in religious terms,

> the people of form and service are the infantry, they always give their lives for the honor of the king, the King of the Universe, and they win the war to silence all of the accusers and detractors who rise up against them and want to keep abundance from the world; but they [the people of form and service] bring down the abundance to the world and the cavalrymen are the men of materiality who ride their big, fine horses—that is their good fortune; and when the war is won and the abundance comes to the world, they grab much of it, and the people of form are content with the supply of their daily needs, as is the way of Torah and security. They are satisfied that by winning the war the honor of the king is increased, and they assume that the people of materiality will certainly supply their needs, because they are the primary factor.[44]

If this metaphor accurately reflects the Besht's ideas, then he believed that the community consisted of two groups. The first was the spiritual elite whose task it was, primarily, to perform the religious acts that would ensure reward from God, silencing the heavenly accusers. The other was the regular people who went about their mundane lives, reaping the benefits from the spiritual victory of their religious leaders. Since the people of materiality owed their good fortune to the people of form and service, they also owed them financial support.[45]

Another allusion to the Besht, relating to both what he knew and how he was perceived, was originally published by Dubnow.[46] It is included in the foreword to the manuscript edition of the responsa of Rabbi Jacob

Halperin of Zwaniecz (d. 1738), written by Rabbi Jacob's son, Solomon Isaac.

> I remember when I was young that the famous rabbi, expert in the wisdom of the Divinity, our teacher Israel Ba'al Shem, the memory of the righteous is a blessing, made a dream inquiry and they showed him that the soul of my father, my teacher, of blessed memory, was the soul of Rabbi [Isaac] Alfasi.[47] Since Rabbi Alfasi did not write about the *Seder Kodashim*,[48] my master, my father came to complete [this work]. Thus he [the Besht] said explicitly.

Rabbi Solomon Isaac, born in 1727, was eleven when his father died. This memory, then, dates from his childhood. The Besht's identification of Rabbi Jacob's soul with Alfasi would normally have been done in private, so the son was probably recalling his father's recounting of the incident. However, Rabbi Solomon Isaac's childhood memory may include some direct experience of the Besht, such as seeing him pray or even hearing him speak. In any case, by the time he wrote down his comments, Rabbi Solomon Isaac's epitaph for the Besht singled out two elements: the Besht's fame and his expertise in the knowledge of God's divinity—not God's Torah, not Talmud, and not rabbinic codes.

This assessment does not strike me as a projection of the rabbi's later admiration for the Besht on the more distant past. If there were to be a change in Rabbi Solomon Isaac's evaluation of the Besht over time, one would expect it to be in the negative direction. According to Scholem, from the 1760s on this rabbi was an enemy of the organized Hasidic movement. If he saw a link between the movement and the Besht, he probably would have tempered his admiration of the great man. If there was no such connection in the rabbi's eyes, then the Besht's fame would have nothing to rest on except what he did during his lifetime. Remembering this, Rabbi Solomon Isaac succinctly echoed what we have seen the contemporary sources affirm: the Besht was well known in his lifetime, but not for his great knowledge of Torah. What he knew was considered to be of divine origin, but it was not the result of conventional Torah study.

A different recalling of the Besht by someone who knew him personally does seem to indicate a reassessment based on later reflection. In his 1798 book, Nahum of Chernobyl[49] sought to assure his audience: "But the Besht's curing was accomplished only via unifications of the Godhead which he would perform and thereby elevate the *Shekhinah*." This view of the Besht's curative powers as limited to prayer and the performance of commandments that "unify the Godhead" contrasts sharply with Rabbi Gershon of Kutów's request, cited above, that the Besht send him a theurgic amulet and the Besht's own testimony in his letter to Rabbi Moses of Kutów, where he specifically mentioned seeking after "vagabonds" and prescribed a proprietary potion.[50] If my assumption is correct that in the late eighteenth century there was a shift in attitude toward ba'alei shem and practical Kabbalah,[51] then Nahum's comment may be an attempt at refashioning the Besht's image to match current ideas about what constituted respectable Kabbalistic activity.[52]

Another contemporary of the Besht's who communicated an assessment of him only after his death was Moses ben Yokel of Międzybóż, who told the compiler of *Shivhei Ha-Besht* that[53] "once his father (Yokel) took him to the bet midrash. The Besht stood and prayed in front of the ark and his group prayed with him. Moses' father said to him in these words: 'My son, look and pay attention to this, because nothing like this will be seen in the world until the coming of our righteous Messiah. For the Besht is [the reincarnation of] Rabbi Simeon bar Yohai[54] and his coterie.' "

Yokel of Międzybóż was one of the Besht's closest associates.[55] It may very well be that his evaluation of the Besht was permanently emblazoned on his young son's consciousness. But whether Moses was reporting his father's or his own impression, here the greatness of the Besht is associated with prayer and the man conventionally viewed as the father of the Kabbalah. The Besht was great because he continued in the mystical tradition started by Rabbi Simeon bar Yohai, generally credited with being the author of the Zohar, the basic text of Jewish mysticism. The paramount expression of the Besht's participation in the mystical tradition was his mode of prayer.

An additional recollection of the Besht by someone who formed a youthful attachment to him is that of Rabbi Meir Margoliot (1707?–1790), rabbi beginning in 1767 of the important Ostróg region. In his book, *Sod Yakhin U-Boaz*,[56] Rabbi Margoliot discussed the way to enter on Torah study.

> Before studying one should think correct and pure thought and prepare himself to study for its own sake without any alien intention. As my great teachers in Torah and Hasidism—among them my friend, the rabbi, the Hasid, the sign of the generation, our teacher Rabbi Israel Besht, of blessed memory—admonished me: Is not the proper intention attained through study for its own sake? One should be in a state of adherence to the letters in holiness and purity, and work in speech and in thought to connect part of the various levels of the soul with the holiness of the candle of commandments and Torah, the letters which edify and produce abundant lights and true, eternal creatures.

And when he is privileged to understand and to adhere to the holy letters, he can understand from within the letters themselves, even the future, and therefore the Torah is called "enlightener of the eyes"[57] for it enlightens the eyes of he who adheres to its letters in holiness and purity like the letters of the Urim and Thummim.[58] From my childhood, from the day I recognized the communion of love with my teacher, my friend, the rabbi, our teacher, the aforementioned Rabbi Israel, may his soul be bound up in the bond of life, I knew for certain that this was his way in holiness and purity with great piety[59] and asceticism, and his wisdom—"the righteous man lives by his faith,"[60] for the secrets are revealed to him; the glory of God is that which is hidden.

The lesson that Margoliot took away from his childhood exposure to the Besht was the same one the Besht emphasized in his letter to his disciple, Jacob Joseph: the importance of adhering to the letters of the holy texts while studying.[61] The Besht, in Margoliot's mind, was great, not as an erudite scholar, but as someone who penetrated to the mystical significance of the text. The Besht taught how to learn, not the words that contained the exoteric meaning, but the letters that hold the deeper, mystical significance and theurgic power. One should employ his learning, not to gain the exoteric knowledge plain to all, but to transcend the exoteric and pierce the secrets. If one studied as the Besht did, he would utilize the text as an oracle that pointed the way to knowledge beyond the simple meaning. Like the Besht, he might even foretell the future.[62]

Similar to earlier testimonies we have reviewed, Margoliot remembered the Besht as pure in action and distinguished by his mystic Hasidism. Margoliot's family sent him to the Besht to learn the proper spiritual preparation for study, not for scholarly instruction per se. His singling out of the Besht as an ascetic seems to contradict the Besht's letter to Jacob Joseph of Polonne and other indications that the Besht was against asceticism. The implication is that the Besht's position on this matter changed. This would be consistent with the idea, put forth in chapter 2, that the Besht grew out of the mystical-ascetic hasidic tradition but eventually turned it in a new direction.[63]

Another frequently cited testimony is the view of the virulent anti-Hasid, David Makow, who did not actually know the Besht but remembered hearing about him while he was alive. Makow's testimony exists in two versions. In both of them he confirmed, grudgingly, the fact of the Besht's fame during his lifetime. Makow remembered that the Besht died in 1759 (actually it was 1760). According to him, at the time there was as yet no Hasidic movement to speak of; still, Makow, who did not live in Ukraine, heard about this death and even remembered its approximate date. This implies that the Besht was indeed a person of wide-ranging reputation, probably as a ba'al shem.[64] The same conclusion as to the fact of the Besht's fame and the reason for it is supported by another anti-Hasidic opinion, that of the Gaon's contemporary, Aryeh Leib Gunzburg (1695–1785), cited by Scholem. According to this source, "The Besht, whatever he knew was via dream adjurations every night."[65]

HEARSAY

The last two examples bring us to another kind of frequently adduced evidence concerning the Besht: hearsay reports by individuals who spoke with people who had had encounters and conversations with him. Many of these citations come from *Shivhei Ha-Besht*. Some of them appear quite plausible, particularly when seen in conjunction with the more direct evidence that exists. For example, it does seem entirely possible—probable for a ba'al shem—that the Besht once stopped his wagon in the forest, listened to the rustling of the leaves and the chirping of the birds, and was reminded that he had forgotten something back in the city.[66] It seems probable that a Mitnaged (opponent of Hasidism), living after the Besht's death, who wanted to maintain the Besht's lack of extraordinary holiness without completely delegitimizing him and calling his followers out-and-out liars, might, by way of compromise, say—as Rabbi Gunzburg is supposed to have declared—that the Besht reached his spiritual knowledge through adjurations and not ascents of the soul.[67]

However, the indirect transmission of such communications and their late recording dates make them problematic. How many factors of forgetfulness, later consciousness, and editorial interference have intervened between the happening and the telling? Was it Rabbi Gunzburg (or the Gaon) who wanted to find a way to offer limited recognition of the Besht, or was this an expression of the generation at the time the text was published, that of Hayyim Volozhin's disciples who were indeed attempting a rapprochement, or at least a moratorium, with the Hasidim?

Another term for hearsay reports is "tradition." Traditions about what the Besht did or said are much more abundant than writings by him or direct testimonies about him, and they grew in quantity with time.[68] The earliest and most important of these traditions are the reports of his apothegms and teachings collected in the four homiletic books that began appearing in 1780, written by the Besht's disciple, Jacob Joseph of Polonne.[69] The Besht died in 1760, which means that these sayings were not printed in their present form until at least twenty years after his death and up to forty years after they were pronounced. The sayings were originally said in Yiddish; the written versions are in Hebrew. Presumably the Besht did much of his teaching on the Sabbath, when it was forbidden to write down what he said. Even during the week, the occasions on which he would have spoken his wisdom were not, as Roman Foxbruner has pointed out, formal lectures but informal conversations and even inspirational settings that were ill-suited to note taking with quill and ink.[70] According to Hasidic tradition, the Besht had a strong aversion to disciples writing down his teachings, ever.[71]

There are only a few places where Jacob Joseph noted that the Besht was still alive when he recorded what was said, implying that most of his writing down of material in the name of the Besht was done after 1760. Moreover, in these books the vicissitudes of memory are evident, as some sayings are attributed to the Besht in one place and to someone else in another.[72] If attribution is faulty, can the text be more reliable?

It is also important to remember that Jacob Joseph of Polonne's four books were not written primarily to communicate the Besht's teachings. The several hundred short sayings he adduced are a small percentage of the material contained in the more than nine hundred pages these books comprise. The references to the Besht's sayings are only some of the departure texts, proof texts, and illustrations the author used to convince the reader to accept his interpretations of biblical texts.

That is what these books basically are: Jacob Joseph's biblical interpretations in service of his personal exposition of Judaism. The titles of these books are all biblically based allusions to Jacob Joseph's name; it is *his* teaching that is being transmitted here. He obviously incorporated what he had learned from the Besht into his personal creed, but the message had been taken out of its original context and embedded in a new one. Even if copied verbatim, the intertexts of the new synthesis would have transduced the sayings and transmuted their message.[73]

Nigal observed with perplexity that the differences in the interpretation and presentation of the Besht's ideas by his two chief disciples, Jacob Joseph of Polonne and Dov Ber the Maggid of Mezerich, are so marked.[74] If we understand that each man regarded the Besht's teachings as raw material to be selected, shaped, and utilized in the service of his own vision, then the differences between them cease to confound. But then we must also admit that their transmissions of the Besht's sayings are not simply that.[75]

There is an additional problem. In chapter 6 I reviewed the circumstances of the publication of Jacob Joseph's books and the likelihood that they are heavily edited versions of the author's unsystematic notebooks, representing many years of haphazard jottings. Consequently, even if we could be sure that Jacob Joseph had copied the Besht's sayings verbatim, there is no guarantee that what he actually wrote was printed in the texts we have. There was editorial interference.[76] What is more, unauthorized modification of manuscripts was not regarded as an ethical issue.

The practice of pseudepigraphy is an ancient one and in Jewish tradition goes back to late biblical texts. By Talmudic times it was evidently common for people to try to attract attention and acquire legitimacy for pronouncements by quoting them in the name of recognized authorities. While some authorities disapproved of this practice, others held that "if he heard a ruling and it seems to him that this should be the law, he may say it in the name of a great person as if he had received it from him."[77]

Gries has convincingly demonstrated that this is what Hasidic editors and publishers did with Hasidic doctrines from the beginning of Hasidic printing. In their case it was not only a generalized acceptance of well-intentioned misattribution. Hasidism was essentially an oral culture. The organization and conduct of Hasidic life was largely a matter of oral tradition. This tradition was passed on from father to son and veteran to novice. Spreading of the doctrines was done through personal encounter and face-to-face teaching. The oral *derashah* (homily) served an important social purpose in binding the group together; it was not initially viewed as a spiritual legacy to be carefully recorded. In general, early Hasidic books were sloppily edited and printed, and correct citation was not a supreme goal.[78]

There was no ideology of writing and publishing the master's teachings, outside of the Habad movement. Oral tradition was primary; published works were secondary. None of the early leaders took care to have their teachings written down, except as an afterthought. Few surviving manuscripts are authors' autographs. For most zaddikim, the manuscripts were written from memory by disciples and then in a less than careful fashion. There are usually multiple versions. Manuscripts were copied and recopied, often being combined in the process. Many extant Hasidic manuscripts are actually anthologies of teachings gleaned from several manuscripts without labeling the different pericopes. Many teachings appear in multiple sources attributed to different zaddikim. Furthermore, most writings had to be translated from Yiddish by the editor or publisher. It is no wonder that complaints by publishers and editors about the painstaking work that went into gathering the writings and correcting, editing, and translating them came to be standard in Hasidic books. The more translating, piecing together, and correcting that was done, the farther removed the finished product was from what the original zaddik taught.[79]

Even Hasidic authorities recognized how problematic recorded sayings might be. One of the earliest Hasidic publishers, Solomon Lutzker, disciple and publisher of the Maggid of Mezerich, said with regard to citations brought in the Maggid's name, "For I have seen that the writers of writings severely abridge the meaning of our master, teacher and rabbi. Sometimes they do not comprehend and write according to their own understanding," and he feared that he might do the same.[80]

The first leader of Habad Hasidism, Shneur Zalman of Ladi, was particularly sensitive to the problem posed by translation from Yiddish into Hebrew. He remarked several times that a slight change in formulation can lead to a drastic change in meaning.[81]

For all of these reasons, the possibility of connecting with the Besht the sayings cited in the Besht's name in Jacob Joseph of Polonne's books is very small. The books undoubtedly contain much authentic Besht material, but identifying it is a treacherous, and so far unaccomplished, scholarly task. In discussing these sayings, Dubnow already said that "the historian is obliged to utilize the material before him with utmost caution, distinguishing—to the extent possible—between the original creation of the author and what was added to it from the doctrine of his disciples."[82] He never explicated rules for making this distinction, and he left himself open to the following charge of Shai Ish Hurwitz: "Who gave [historians] the right to parse the material and to say this point suits me and this point doesn't suit me?"[83] Nigal, the modern editor and annotator of Jacob Joseph's books, remarked, "One of the serious questions which awaits the researcher is where does the thought of the Besht begin and end, and where does the thought of the disciple commence? To what extent did R. Jacob Joseph absorb [ideas] from his contemporaries, the pioneers of Hasidism? . . . These matters are not simple and require clarification."[84]

Scholem tried to solve this problem on stylistic grounds, claiming that the Besht's pithy, epigrammatic style made it possible to isolate his words from the context supplied by more erudite and more prolix disciples.[85] He did not, however, define the characteristics of this style or systematize a method for identifying what exactly the Besht said.

Foxbruner distinguished between Jacob Joseph as transmitter of what the Besht actually said (unlikely) and Jacob Joseph as conveyor of doctrines the Besht taught (probable). He cautioned, however, that only extensive and systematic comparison of the various versions of the Besht's statements cited throughout Hasidic literature offers the possibility of identifying the Besht's authentic ideas.[86] Whether this approach can overcome the problem of intertextuality between the citations in the name of the Besht and the texts in which they appear remains to be demonstrated. Convergence of attribution is not necessarily a guarantee of authenticity, while it is possible that only one witness, or none, preserved the original idea. So while the sayings quoted in the Besht's name might suggest directions for investigation, and perhaps be brought in secondary support of theses that rest on more reliable material, they cannot serve at this stage of our knowledge as a primary indicator of the Besht's ideas or way.

My admittedly unsatisfactory solution to this problem is to refrain from an intellectual biography of the Besht. This surrender is prompted by my agreement with Foxbruner: "Scrutinizing the language and terminology of Hasidic homilies, even those of Rabbi Jacob Joseph, can reveal much about the disciples who authored them, but little about the masters who delivered them."[87] Or, as Rahel Elior has pointed out in a short article on the life of the Besht, the recorded attributed sayings are important because "the development of the Hasidic movement was influenced to a great degree by the ideas formulated in the Besht's Torah, both those brought in his name and those presented as explications of his doctrine."[88] The sayings indicate how later tradition construed the Besht's teachings. As with the example of the accretions to the Besht's Holy Epistle analyzed in chapter 6, they illustrate how people in the maturing movement of the 1780s and later defined the Besht's legacy.

Research into oral tradition has shown that it mirrors the society it serves and is always up to date.[89] It reflects the current state of belief and practice, not necessarily that which obtained in the period being cited. Given this general rule and the lack of a reliable means of gauging the relationship of his interpreted legacy to what the Besht actually thought and taught orally in the 1740s and 1750s, it seems impossible to move beyond what tradition made of the Besht's teaching to arrive at an articulated and nuanced explication of what that teaching was.[90] The Besht's intellectual biography remains a desideratum.

Despite all these considerations, some persist in the attempt to extrapolate the Besht's teachings on the basis of the attributed sayings.[91] In practice, the high degree of arbitrariness in distinguishing between "authentic" and "inauthentic" statements of the Besht makes doing so a device for bending the source material to the purposes of one's own particular agenda.

This is even more true of stories about the Besht. Dubnow, for example, saw certain stories as metaphors for underlying historical events. Dinur thought that the stories about the Besht were essentially the "collective portrait" of the people in the early Hasidic movement. Scholem could use a story as historical evidence because "there is no doubt in my heart that the witnesses of the compiler of *Shivhei Ha-Besht* truly heard this story in its various versions from the mouth [of Leib the Preacher, who experienced the event]."[92]

The ease with which statements recalled in the Besht's name and events remembered in which he purportedly participated can be forced into the procrustean bed of one's preconceived notions about what the Besht was, what he stood for, and what he taught makes these sources difficult to utilize when attempting to portray the historical Ba'al Shem Tov. They have already undergone selection, reformulation, editing, shaping, and reinterpretation as part of the transition from oral tradition to print, and there are rarely reliable criteria for affirming their connection to the Besht. They are therefore doubly hazardous for the historian and should be used as heuristics and secondary supports only.

CHAPTER NINE

Life Stories

SHIVHEI HA-BESHT

Without question, the most fecund, interesting, intriguing, problematic, and most exploited source relating to the Ba'al Shem Tov is *Shivhei Ha-Besht*. The title in Hebrew means, literally, "Praises of the Ba'al Shem Tov," and the book is a collection of more than two hundred hagiographic stories concerning the Besht and some of the people associated with him.[1] A sample of the titles (added by twentieth-century editors) of some of the stories can lend an idea of the book's subject matter: The Birth of the Besht, The Besht's Marriage, The Besht and the Robbers, The Besht as Rabbi Gershon's Coachman, The Besht's Revelation, The Besht's Prayer, How the Rabbi of Polonne Drew Near to the Besht, The Besht Cures the Grandson of Rabbi David of Ostróg, The Incarnation of Sa'adiah Gaon, Traveling to Redeem Captives, The Priest Who Was a Magician, The Besht Has No Money, The Besht's Dream.

Virtually every writer on the Besht has made use of this collection in constructing a portrayal. The key questions they have considered are as follows: Given the methodological issues, what is the relationship of these stories to historical events? What is the historical kernel that underlies these stories or the historical reality to which they are pointing? Each scholar has picked and chosen among the stories, giving much more weight to some than to others. Some of the tales have been declared fantasies, some embellishments of historical events, and some "authentic," meaning that they are reliable reports of aspects of historical events that occurred.

Dubnow, and others following his example, apparently decided that the criterion for historicity was plausibility. Events that are consistent with rationality and sound as if they could have happened probably did. Yet since so many patently legendary details in *Shivhei Ha-Besht* get in the way of rationality, Dubnow, and others, relied more on the motifs and patterns of behavior repeated in the stories than on reported individual facts. Even if details were mistaken or legendary, the assumption of these scholars seems to have been that such details "reflect" the truth, while the aggregate portrait of the stories is fairly reliable.[2]

A good example is the way Dubnow handled the information in *Shivhei Ha-Besht* about the Besht's early life. The stories about the Besht's parents and his birth are among the most obviously legendary in the book. In attempting to fix the Besht's birthdate, however, Dubnow assumed that since the legend says that the Besht's father was taken captive in a war and the Besht was born after his safe return, "a time of turmoil preceded the birth of the founder of Hasidism and the child was born after peace returned. In fact the Turkish conquest of Podolia ended after the Treaty of Karlowitz in 1699 [and] therefore Israel ben Eliezer was born around this time."[3] Dubnow did not explain why it is necessary to assume that this legend has any link whatsoever with reality.

With regard to the Besht's childhood and adolescence, it would seem logical that knowledge about this period of his life would be the least well preserved. No one knew that he would become famous. Despite this truism, Dubnow and most scholars accepted these stories as a "more or less" accurate description of what the Besht did until he entered the public arena. Anything that did not appear to be "a strange fantasy" was accepted as at least "close to the truth." The possibility that these stories were designed to create a certain hero persona (miraculous birth, orphan, poor, humble, salt of the earth, part of a chain of tradition, innately wise, etc.) was not entertained. His humble origins, autodidacticism, and nature-loving, wise, but unconventional personality were taken for granted.[4]

Representative of how stories probably intended to create a persona were mistakenly subjected to historical exegesis is a cycle of stories recounting some of the exploits of one Rabbi Adam Ba'al Shem. In them Adam hosts a banquet for a king, exposes the Jew hatred of the king's minister, thus forcing his repentance, and teaches his own wife a lesson in modesty and inconspicuous consumption. Adam is also instructed in a dream to transmit the secret holy writings in his possession to the Besht—a mission accomplished through the offices of Rabbi Adam's anonymous son.[5]

Dubnow assumed that underlying these stories is the fact that the Besht really learned the secrets of mysticism from a certain man called, in the stories, Rabbi Adam. Scholem agreed and thought that this was a pseudonym for Heshel Zoref, the Sabbatean. Eliach claimed that this "Rabbi" Adam was actually a well-known Russian Orthodox priest.[6]

Shmeruk proved, however, that Rabbi Adam was a semilegendary ba'al shem, the stories about whom grew out of the milieu of Prague in the late sixteenth century. The historical kernel of these stories, if it exists, has nothing to do with the Besht or Poland. By the eighteenth century, Rabbi Adam was a familiar figure throughout Ashkenazic Jewry, but the Besht, living in the first half of the eighteenth century, could not have come into contact with Adam or his son.[7] The *Shivhei Ha-Besht* account seems designed to legitimize the Besht by placing him in a chain of mystical tradition. Trying to identify some person or event in the Ba'al Shem Tov's life embedded in the Rabbi Adam stories is a futile exercise.

In one place Dinur was somewhat more forthcoming than Dubnow in articulating his criteria for accepting stories as historical. These were two: (1) "continuity of tradition," which I take to mean provenance, that is, if the story was related by an eyewitness; and (2) "internal consistency of the details with the Besht and his ideas," or what the Besht did must be consistent with what one would have expected him to do on the basis of the sayings reliably reported in his name.[8] For Dinur, then, interpretation of the stories was dependent on interpretation of the sayings.

These criteria at least provide a rational approach to categorizing some of the stories. Legends about the early life preceding the Besht's career as an informal teacher might possibly be evaluated as a collective portrait of the movement; but they certainly do not refer to the Besht's personal life. Legends about the Besht's aborted trip to Eretz Yisrael or about his relationship to Frankism, however, might be interpreted on the basis of ideas that the Besht communicated in his sayings and letters. Still, Dinur himself pointed out the problems of the provenance of the sayings. In light of his hesitations as well as the considerations pertaining to Jacob Joseph of Polonne's citations (chap. 8), it seems to be a dubious proposition to make the stories dependent on one's understanding of the sayings.

Scholem also basically followed the *Shivhei Ha-Besht* stories in sketching the Besht's early life, but the real foundation of his description consists of nonpartisan reports and correspondence. Only after establishing the basic lines of his characterization on the basis of this material did he proceed to supplement it with carefully chosen passages from the stories and sayings. For example, having demonstrated through the independent statements and the letters that the Besht was both a professional practitioner of practical Kabbalah and more learned and respected than Dubnow and others supposed, Scholem added details to these basic facts, using the quoted sayings and Hasidic stories.[9] In the intervening years it has become evident that much of what Scholem regarded as reliable, independent, nonpartisan sources on the Besht were not such.[10] Moreover, in several places he pronounced himself satisfied that certain sayings or stories were "historical" without explaining his criteria for making this determination.[11] Scholem then proceeded to use the material he adjudged authentic to construct his core characterization. This, in turn, served as a guideline for adding details from the more historically equivocal stories.

Scholem did illustrate just what, to his mind, a legend with a "historical kernel" might be. He cited the following story told about the Besht by Pinhas of Koretz.

> There was someone who was writing down what he heard from [the Besht] and when the Besht found out about this he commanded the preacher to check these writings. The preacher saw that not one word of the Besht's was written. The Besht said that this man had not listened for the sake of heaven and therefore a *kelipah* [evil force] had taken hold of him and he had heard other things.[12]

Scholem called this story "realistic and perhaps authentic concerning an event that happened." He then cited a second version of the same story as it appears in *Shivhei Ha-Besht* in the name of Gedaliah of Ilintsy.

> There was a man who wrote down the *Torah* of the Besht that he heard from him. Once the Besht saw a demon walking and holding a book in his hand. He said to him: "What is the book that you hold in your hand?"
> He answered him: "This is the book that you have written."
> The Besht then understood that there was a person who was writing down his *Torah*. He gathered all his followers and asked them: "Who among you is writing down my *Torah*?" The man admitted it and he brought the manuscript to the Besht. The Besht examined it and said: "There is not even a single word here that is mine."[13]

In this way Scholem demonstrated how a verisimilar story could become legendary in the retelling within the space of one generation. He did not explain, however, how he knew that the first version of the story was authentic, or even "realistic." He implied that the teller's contemporaneity with the Besht and the simpler, plausible detail argued for authenticity. This tale and others concerned historical events that actually happened, and these stories were only one step removed from being chronicles.[14]

Judging by the standard criteria used to evaluate hagiography (e.g., contemporaneity of the source, simple, realistic detail, nondramatic tone, lack of direct quotation, absence of nonhuman actors), it is probable that Scholem successfully identified which version of the tale was the earlier one. Using the same criteria, however, there is no assurance that even the first version is "realistic and perhaps authentic."[15] Is it possible to isolate the historical elements?

Israel Yoffe first published *Shivhei Ha-Besht* in late 1814 in Kopys, White Russia. The book became very popular and was published twice more in Hebrew and three times in Yiddish within the next two years. The *maskil* (advocate of enlightenment), Josef Perl, reported that within roughly the same period it sold more than ten thousand copies.[16]

The text itself is problematic. The first Hebrew edition of 1814 was not based on an autograph manuscript. The one manuscript that does exist (and is also not an autograph) differs significantly from the printed text and from the manuscript employed by the printer.[17] Moreover, the printer informed his readers that he edited the manuscript he utilized. He changed the order of some of the stories, added material from other sources, enclosed sixteen passages in parentheses, and emended the text.[18]

The content of the stories is also troubling to the historian: there are stories that appear to be different versions of the same incident or parallels of stories told earlier about Rabbi Isaac Luria (the Ari) or other famous figures.[19] Even more problematic is the obviously legendary character of much of the material. Dan Ben-Amos and Jerome Mintz indexed the recognized folk motifs that appear in the stories. In their enumeration of 251 stories, only 44 do not contain any typical folktale motifs whereas 87 contain at least 5.[20] It may be true that life sometimes assumes stereotypical patterns and that the motifs were applied to a substratum of fact, but the sheer number of such motifs is a huge obstacle to internal historical analysis of these stories.

Even if it is assumed that the stories are "more or less" historical, they appear to be no more than collected anecdotes with no coherent connection. The events recounted are undated, and the surrounding circumstances are usually wholly lacking. In such a situation, trying to reconstruct the historical context is akin, in Dinur's words, "to solving an algebraic equation that consists almost solely of the variable."[21] All of this militates against threshing the historical kernel and might leave scholars close to despair.

However, after much arduous labor, some scholars have succeeded in demonstrating a "historical" layer at the base of these stories. Some of Scholem's academic descendants have made strides in crediting the kernel of truth approach. Rubinstein carried forward the attempt to isolate the historical elements of the stories via comparison of alternative versions of the stories themselves. In a series of articles,[22] he compared differing versions of some of the stories appearing in the various recensions of *Shivhei Ha-Besht*. By hypothesizing the biases of the respective editors[23] and explaining the discrepancies between the stories largely in this way, Rubinstein attempted to arrive at a determination of which details belonged to the "original" story, were not obviously mythic, and therefore could be considered factual.

Rubinstein made progress in tracing biographical information about some of the people mentioned in the collection and in showing some aspects of its structure and organizing principles. On the basis of his comparisons, he described the Besht as a double-sided personality: he was a ba'al shem–type miracle worker for the masses as well as an inspired religious leader who succeeded in gathering an elite group of disciples.[24]

While Rubinstein's interpretations are often ingenious, they depend almost exclusively on what amounts to internal analysis. One cannot be sure that the castle isn't hanging in air.[25] Moreover, a large part of Rubinstein's analysis was based on the assumption that the 1815 Yiddish translation represented an independent recension of the collection—an assumption that has since been disproved.[26]

Other scholars have tried to continue Scholem's effort to combine internal analysis with outside corroboration. Israel Bartal compared the stories in *Shivhei Ha-Besht* about the aliyah and death of Rabbi Elazar (Eliezer) Rokeah in Eretz Yisrael with various printed and manuscript sources about this rabbi, as well as with four letters written by him. Bartal concluded,

> Hasidic legend has preserved historical information, names and dates. It even hints at the messianic tension that anticipated the coming of the year 5500 [1739–1740]. Ideological tinkering and apologetic tendencies did not bring about significant changes in the "historical" layer of the story about the aliyah of R. Elazar from Amsterdam. The legend concerning the Besht's ability to see from a distance was woven around a real historical event, the dates of which can be confirmed. . . . It turns out that the historian can utilize the

legends in *Shivhei Ha-Besht* as a starting point for reconstructing historical events. If he is fortunate and discovers in his research parallel material that complements the information contained in the legend, then even what at first glance seems to be totally ahistorical may prove integrable into his historical work.[27]

For the student of *Shivhei Ha-Besht,* Bartal's assertions mean that after dismissing the legendary motifs of the stories, one may consider the details that remain to constitute a "historical layer" that is connected to a real historical event. The key expression is "starting point." The stories can alert the researcher that an event happened, yet not necessarily supply completely accurate information about it.

Another comparison of stories in *Shivhei Ha-Besht* with collateral sources was carried out by Jacob Barnai.[28] Using letters and other sources that originated in Eretz Yisrael and concerned figures and events mentioned in *Shivhei Ha-Besht,* he showed that there are many analogues between the stories and these letters. Barnai's opinion is that the stories in *Shivhei Ha-Besht* about events and people in Eretz Yisrael were probably written on the basis of the letters—many now lost or as yet undiscovered—that Hasidim who had settled in Eretz Yisrael sent back to Europe, combined with oral testimonies from those émigrés who returned to Europe for one reason or another. He summed up by saying that even if the publishers of the Hasidic stories colored them to suit certain ideological or propagandistic aims, these stories "contain real historical seeds [and] they can be considered an important historical source."[29] Barnai has placed some of the *Shivhei Ha-Besht* stories on a new footing. If he is correct that they are based, at least in part, on written primary sources, then their credibility is enhanced. Even if his supposition is mistaken, he—like Bartal—has demonstrated the heuristic value of the legendary tales.

The work of Bartal and Barnai and the Polish sources (see chap. 10) should cause us to take a renewed look at the stories of *Shivhei Ha-Besht* as historical sources. Where previously scholars like Scholem and Rubinstein relied primarily on internal analysis to isolate the historical elements of the hagiographic stories, the more recent approach has added the important element of collateral, independent sources. By using more collateral sources, it will continue on a more reasonable basis.

The search for the history underlying the text is not over, however, once realia have been defined and actual events and persons authenticated. Even assuming that a story that has plausibility, provenance, simplicity, and accurate detail is "historical," such a story is not necessarily a reliable guide to history. While analyzing individual stories, scholars should not lose sight of the book within which they are ordered.

Bartal's article demonstrated that while *Shivhei Ha-Besht* had preserved historical details of the events connected with Rabbi Elazar, they constituted just one of the layers of the story and not the most significant one. The real purpose of the story, according to Bartal, was to shape the figure of Elazar in such a way as to promote Hasidic and non-Hasidic cooperation and blunt the growing criticism from the maskilic camp at the time the story appeared. Rabbi Elazar's biography was recruited to service the ideological needs of the early nineteenth-century movement.

An example of the pitfalls of mistaking accurate historical details for a reliable evocation of a larger event is the story in *Shivhei Ha-Besht* about the Besht's reception in Międzybóż, alluded to in chapter 1.

> A story: When the Besht came to the community of Międzybóż, he was not important in the eyes of the hasidim, that is, R. Zev Kutzes and R. David Purkes,[30] because of the name which people called him, "Besht." This name is not fitting for a *zaddik*.[31]

The story then continues telling how the Besht was instrumental in getting a student of the two hasidim into Paradise and how the Besht taught Torah in the heavenly yeshiva. The dead student appeared to his earthbound teachers to inform them of the Besht's heavenly exploits.

> Immediately on that Sabbath they came to him[32] for the third meal and he said this Torah,[33] and when he asked the question, they told him the answer and he said to them, "I know that the dead man told you." From that day on they came close to him.

This story seems to have a strong historical kernel: it was told by the Besht's disciple,[34] Jacob Joseph from Polonne; there were hasidim before the Hasidim; in this period and geographic area, old-style hasidim did apparently sometimes criticize ba'alei shem for their utilization and publication of the divine names in order to perform wonders;[35] the names of the hasidim involved are specified, and we know from Polish sources that these two hasidim actually lived.[36]

However, this story is embedded as one of the strands in a larger theme in the book: how the Besht was opposed by most people who met him and how he proceeded to win them over one by one. This was necessary because, as the theme assumes and this story might imply, the Besht was known as a crude, popular ba'al shem and not a profound mystic. Once he demonstrated his profundity, or effectiveness, his opponents relented. This construction does not neatly match that yielded by at least one reasonable reading of the letters and testimonies examined in chapters 6, 7, and 8: that by the time of his arrival in Międzybóż, the Besht was not an unknown in mystical circles; he had served his mystical apprenticeship and established his reputation; and prominent scholars and others counted him as their respected friend and even teacher.

The story in *Shivhei Ha-Besht* also can be enlisted to perpetuate what was a main theme in Hasidic writing on the Besht and was adopted by scholars through at least Scholem: that every step of the way, the Besht—like his spiritual protégés in the late eighteenth century—met with entrenched and even organized opposition. As Scholem put it, "His path was not always strewn with roses."[37]

However, on closer inspection, this almost unanimous tradition is undermined. Again, the sources analyzed in chapters 6, 7, and 8 indicate that the Besht enjoyed a measure of respect and prestige. He was not regarded as other than a bona fide mystical adept, well within tradition and qualified to be an arbiter of what tradition requires, at least in certain areas. As least one hasid, Gershon of Kutów, consulted him as a ba'al shem. Moreover, as we shall see, the Polish sources show how the Besht was supported by the establishment of the Międzybóż Jewish community.

Evidence for opposition is weak. If the analysis in the last part of chapter 1 is correct, that ba'alei shem were not generally disrespected, and given the Besht's particular reputation, then the significance of the story in *Shivhei Ha-Besht* is limited. It and the other stories that mention opponents of the Besht talk about individuals who doubted his powers or methods as a ba'al shem or his claim to be a holy man. They were not portrayed as opponents of his spiritual way or religious message.[38] It was dislike for an individual, or distaste for his techniques, or refusal to recognize his spiritual powers that these people expressed. They were not representatives of an opposition faction that had doctrinal differences or political rivalry with the camp headed by the Besht. None of these scoffers can be construed as an organized opposing movement. The opposition to the Besht portrayed in these stories did not precipitate institutions.

Scholem attempted to prove that representatives of the conventional rabbinate found the Besht and his innovations objectionable by citing a book written in the early 1740s which criticized,

Newfangled people have appeared now who care about money, and God's word is a shameful thing to them. And a man goes around spouting hot air with parable stories and in a joking manner criticizes this people, but they don't speak frankly: "These are vanity; deceitful acts." They are ineffective in clearing the obstacle from my path that I might walk the straight and narrow.[39]

Scholem assumed that this was a critique of the Besht—the man spouting hot air—who was being accused of pandering to his audience so as to profit financially. Hayyim Liberman demonstrated, however, that Scholem had taken this passage out of context and that it actually was a critique of householders who, out of financial considerations, refused to support authentic scholars and invest in real Torah scholarship but rather made due with superficial moral instruction from popular preachers. The "newfangled people" are the stingy householders; the "man" referred to is a type—the popular preacher—and not a particular person.[40]

To be sure, later writers might have wanted to emphasize how much opposition the Besht faced. For the Hasidim at the turn of the nineteenth century, who were faced with institutional opposition, it was an assurance that they too could prevail. Just as their founder had doggedly and gradually convinced those whom he met that despite their prejudices he was great and his Torah was great, so would they ultimately win over their opponents and gain legitimacy.

For historians, opposition was a sign of the Besht's, and early Hasidism's, importance. If the Besht aroused institutional opposition, then he must have been challenging those institutions with new ones and must have actually founded a movement. If this movement was opposed, then it must have been numerically and doctrinally significant.

The evidence for the respect commanded by ba'alei shem, the status of the Besht at the time he arrived in Międzybóż, the lack of sources indicating institutional opposition, and even the descriptions of the kind of disapproval expressed toward the Besht in the relatively late stories of *Shivhei Ha-Besht* leave little basis for asserting that when the Besht came to Międzybóż he met with general opposition—despite the implication of the story in its setting in *Shivhei Ha-Besht*. He was a qualified mystic, and he did not represent some radical new path in the practice of Jewish religion. The story in *Shivhei Ha-Besht*, with its apparently bona fide historical kernel but lacking fuller contextualization, was presented by its tellers so as to convey a certain message: the Besht was scorned and confronted by entrenched, elitist opposition that he had to overcome. It does not accurately reflect the overall reception of the Besht in Międzybóż or his status in the community. The use of this particular historical kernel bereft of context can yield an incorrect perception of the place of the Besht in Międzybóż.[41]

Plausibility, realia, and even historicity are not sufficient criteria, then, for assessing authenticity. The first step in reading *Shivhei Ha-Besht* must be to accept that it is a work of hagiography, or sacred biography as the current academic lexicon terms it. This means that it was not written to record the biography of a great person in the past but to persuade people in the present to behave in a certain way or to accept a particular doctrine. Hagiography is primarily concerned with turning the exemplary life into a proof text for a position advocated in the present.[42]

Shivhei Ha-Besht is no exception. The stories it contains were written down and then published because both the compiler and the printer saw their potential for religious edification of the public. The compiler of the stories, Dov Ber ben Samuel, shohet of Ilintsy, stated in his preface,

> I wrote it down as a remembrance for my children and their children, so that it would be a reminder for them and for all who cling to God, blessed be He, and His Torah, to strengthen their faith in God and his Torah and in the zaddikim, and so they would see how His Torah purifies the souls of its students so that a person can reach higher levels.[43]

The printer of *Shivhei Ha-Besht,* Israel Yoffe, added in his preface,

> After I received these holy writings . . . I realized the many great benefits which would result from them, especially because it is written in the book that the Besht said that when a person relates the praises of the zaddikim it is as if he concentrates on the *Ma'asei Merkavah* [Mystical Secrets of the Divine].[44]

To make these stories religiously edifying, both the compiler and the printer ordered them in an anthology. This fact is of paramount importance for understanding the stories in the book and their relation to history. *Shivhei Ha-Besht* is an anthology edited at least twice, once by the compiler or "writer" (as he is identified in the text itself), Dov Ber of Ilintsy, and once by the printer, Israel Yoffe. The second redaction subsumed the first within it. One axiom of textual criticism is that an anthology, particularly an anthology of originally oral traditions, tells at least as much about the editors and their readers as it does about whatever the original material is supposed to represent.[45] In the case of *Shivhei Ha-Besht,* it must be made explicit that the material took its current form in the late eighteenth and early nineteenth century and reflects the concerns and the circumstances of the people who created it and for whom it was created at that time.

Whatever the Besht may have done during his lifetime, and whatever the content of these stories was during his lifetime or immediately after his death, what was preserved or altered or deleted or added was done so in the service of a vision that came along one or two generations later. Only after we assess how this book responded to the *sitz im leben* at the time of its redaction and publication can we successfully identify the raw material that went into it and that is most closely connected to the Besht of history.[46]

It is instructive, then, to pay close attention to the words of Dov Ber ben Samuel.

> Every day miracles dwindle and marvels go away. For in days gone by some-times . . . [Dov here gives examples of miraculous phenomena that used to occur with regularity] . . . Because of all of these things many would repent, and faith would be strengthened in the heart of every Jew. But now, due to our many sins, the *zaddikim* have decreased and those who see through the windows have dimmed; faith has greatly diminished and several heresies have been spread in the world. . . . I decided to write the awesome things which I heard from people of truth . . . and I wrote all of this as a remembrance . . . so that it should reinforce faith in God and His Torah and faith in the *zaddikim*, and the faith of everyone who draws near to God and His Torah.[47]

The point is that once miracles happened every day and served as a source for validating faith. Now miracles no longer occur and faith is rapidly weakening. Dov's solution was to tell (true) stories about mira-cles as a substitute for the miracles themselves in strengthening faith.[48]

In contrast, Israel Yoffe had other concerns. The compiler claimed that the number of zaddikim had decreased. The printer said, "There is no generation without famous zaddikim." The compiler regarded zaddikim as primarily miracle workers. The printer linked them with a leadership role, claiming that God never abandoned his people. In every generation He supplied zaddikim as leaders.[49]

The compiler's collection was designed to underscore the Besht's role as a miracle worker. The printer was interested in information about the Besht as a leader. In his editing of the text, the printer added the stories about the Besht's parents, his childhood, his gaining of esoteric knowl-edge, and his accession to leadership,[50] shaping the anthology so that the Besht could be viewed as an archetype of the nineteenth-century Hasidic *rebbe* at the head of his court. Rather than emphasize his importance as miracle worker, Yoffe detailed the process by which the Besht qualified to be a leader.[51]

For both compiler and printer, the historical details, however accurate, were but raw material to be used rhetorically to prove a theological or ideological point. Their first loyalty was to the spiritual needs of their audience, not to the task of reconstructing the historical milieu of the Besht's lifetime and writing the biography of the Besht.

Being an anthology, *Shivhei Ha-Besht* does not include all of the stories current about the Besht. The 1815 Yiddish translation, for example, contains four stories that were not in the original Hebrew recension (it also deletes many stories). There are also collections of Besht stories that apparently originated independently of *Shivhei Ha-Besht*. Such a collection, stemming from Habad circles, was apparently the source for most of what Yoffe added in the first section of the book.[52]

GEDOLIM MA'ASEH ZADDIKIM

Another example of alternative traditions is the collection *Gedolim Ma'aseh Zaddikim: Hasidic Tales* (Jerusalem, 1991), which Jacob Margoliot recorded, based on stories told about the Besht by Margoliot's own father and grandfather. These reflected personal incidents that occurred between the Besht and members of the author's family in the generation of his grandfather and great-grandfather, in the 1720s or 1730s.

This collection is much less problematic than *Shivhei Ha-Besht* in that the provenance of the stories is clear, the stories were redacted only once, and the textual problems are minor. It, too, is an anthology that the author declared he wrote in the last quarter of the nineteenth century in response to a request by the Rebbe of Sadigora.[53] Some of the traditions recounted in it are not only plausible in content and context but contain few folkloristic elements and supplement information from other sources. They merit examination as possibly containing historical reports.

For example, in contrast with *Shivhei Ha-Besht,* which purports to trace the Besht from his miraculous birth through his hero-conditioning childhood and young manhood, *Gedolim Ma'aseh Zaddikim* does not profess to know anything about the Besht prior to the contact established between him and Margoliot family members in Jazlowiec—an association also attested by Rabbi Meir Margoliot in his own book, *Sod Yakhin U-Boaz.*[54]

The first story in *Gedolim Ma'aseh Zaddikim* recounts how the brothers, Isaac and Meir Margoliot, sons of the rabbi of Jazlowiec, Zvi Margoliot, were attracted to the Besht.

> The Besht was then a ritual slaughterer in the village of Kaszelowiec near Jazlowiec. He kept to himself and nothing had yet been heard from him. He

was a slaughterer like the rest of the slaughterers. Suddenly, there arose in the hearts of each of the brothers a burning desire to go to the ritual slaughterer from Kaszelowiec. They did not know any reason for this, the why or the wherefore, only the overpowering desire in the heart of each one, burning without let-up. Each one spoke to his brother saying, "What has God done to us? Is this not a queer thing without explanation?" They could not reveal it to their father or to anyone, for they knew that it would appear weird, with everybody saying "What's this?" They themselves felt they could not conquer this burning desire. They had to sneak away from their father and their home, and the two of them went to the village in secret and came to his house. What they did there, what he spoke with them, how he dealt with them all the days they were in his house, they did not reveal to anyone—even their father—all their days.

They intended on staying in his house. Who knows how long they wanted to be detained before him? In their home there was a great noise and a tremendous commotion because these two great lights were lost. Many people spread out to every road junction to investigate and seek. Finally, after two weeks, someone said that on the road near the village he saw two people like these walking. They [the searchers] went to the village, from house to house, until they found them in the house of the ritual slaughterer and they were compelled to return home. Due to his great joy at their being found, their father did not ask them, "What about this terrible deed?" After a while he asked them: "My sons, please tell me what is the greatness of the slaughterer of Kaszelowiec that people such as yourselves would stay with him such a long time?" They replied: "I [sic] cannot describe for you the nature of this man because you have not seen him or dealt with him. But believe us in this: [in Yiddish] He is smarter than everyone else and more pious than everyone else." Afterward, when the Besht, of blessed memory, became famous they traveled to him every year.[55]

With regard to the Besht, the lack of elaborate plot and the few, simple details argue for the story being an early preserved tale about the holy man. In this case, "early" means close to the time of occurrence, since the story was related by those who were the subject of it, the Margoliot brothers, and repeated primarily within the family. As noted, the actual fact of close contact between the Besht and at least one of the brothers is confirmed by Meir himself. The focus of the story is actually on what the brothers did; the information about the Besht is almost incidental. Perhaps for that reason the teller apparently stuck to the few particulars he had received about the Besht and did not embellish.

Unlike *Shivhei Ha-Besht*, no claim is made here for the Besht's pedigree or his consciously hiding his true, miraculous or holy nature until some point of predestined revelation. No attempt is made to place him in a chain of legitimate mystical figures. His virtues are not the result of secret training but could plausibly turn up in any person: they are wisdom, not learning; and piety, not possession of age-old secret traditions. The Besht was a plain shohet about whom there was no reason that anyone should suspect anything extraordinary, even if they had been acquainted with his family and personal history. Some people began to recognize his extraordinary nature. They refrained from revealing their discovery, not because the holy man forbade it or because his time of revelation had not yet come,[56] but because they feared ridicule from conventional society. This attachment to the Besht could not have been formed later than 1737 when the lads' father, Rabbi Zvi, died. However, it could have occurred much earlier. If the Besht was born around 1700, then he could have been a shohet in a village as early as the 1720s.

This mode of revelation for a holy man—recognition by important individuals who came to spend time in his company and were so impressed that they did not want to leave—had precedents in Polish Jewish society. When Shabbetai Zvi was proclaimed the Messiah, two famous Polish rabbis spent several days with him and wanted to stay longer. In the end they announced that Shabbetai Zvi was indeed the Messiah.[57]

The goldsmith Heschel Zoref (1633–1700) was, until 1666, "a simple man without wisdom and engaged in goldsmithing. He always performed abnegations and would cry before the ark to gain wisdom and knowledge." From the late 1650s, he studied intensively on his own, and when the news of Shabbetai Zvi reached him he began to expound on the Zohar and to prophesy. People said that owing to his study of the Zohar and the spirit of wisdom that graced him, "he knew everything God would do in the upper spheres and what He was going to do until the coming of the Redeemer. His reputation as a man of the holy spirit spread throughout Poland and while he remained in seclusion several rabbis came to stay in his presence." He became one of the main continuators of Sabbateanism in Poland.[58]

In the generation after the Ba'al Shem Tov, when Solomon Maimon sought out the Maggid of Mezerich because he had heard of his spiritual reputation, he requested an interview with the holy man. But there were too many such people and the interview had to be a group affair, which ultimately led to Maimon's feeling that the rabbi's spiritual powers were superficial and even fake.[59]

Each of these descriptions is partially reminiscent of the meeting between the Margoliot brothers, of a distinguished rabbinic family, and the Besht, as described in *Gedolim Ma'aseh Zaddikim*. The Heshel Zoref story, in particular, illustrates how a seemingly simple man suddenly is believed to possess the divine spirit as a result of his newfound familiarity with the Zohar and Kabbalah in general.[60] This facility attracts bona fide rabbinic scholars to his home, where he lives in seclusion. As with the Besht in the *Gedolim Ma'aseh Zaddikim* story (and unlike the construction in *Shivhei Ha-Besht*), it is not pedigree or destiny or secretly granted esoteric knowledge that determines his sudden, newfound greatness but his piety and his wisdom.

This alternative explanation of how the Besht came to prominence, which corresponds to Meir Margoliot's own written description of how the Besht instructed him in piety and the proper preparation and method for study,[61] fits the circumstances of the eighteenth century with its non-scholarly, Kabbalistic holy men[62] better than the *Shivhei Ha-Besht* description. There, as noted, the Besht was made to resemble a nineteenth-century zaddik with a pedigree, an inherited body of esoteric knowledge, and a court. I think it much more likely that, as *Gedolim Ma'aseh Zaddikim* purports, the Besht turned from unknown shohet to respected Kabbalist as a result of his own efforts and because his behavior conformed to what was expected from a holy man type, like Heschel Zoref. As we have already seen with regard to his halakhic practices and his relationship to communal institutions, the Besht's style of spiritual leadership was not radically different from what was accepted in Jewish society of his time; rather, it evolved out of known models.

CHAPTER TEN

Light from the Archives

Jewish scholars have tended to view the Besht, Hasidism, and the relevant sources as quintessentially internal Jewish phenomena that grew out of a genuinely and exclusively Jewish tradition.[1] They also emphasized the Besht's thought and actions without much reference to the physical, social, and economic framework within which these had to have taken shape.

This approach lacks a dimension. Even if the Besht had been insulated from the human affairs around him, various facts of life in the towns where he lived would have conditioned many of the aspects of his life. It is evident, however, that the Besht was not isolated. By virtue of his being a ba'al shem, he had to be concerned with the personal problems of the people among whom he lived. His own letters and the traditions about him depict the Besht both as involved in issues on the public agenda and as active in helping individuals recover from illness, finance their marriages, exorcise demons, escape from danger, turn away from the path of sinfulness, and so on.[2] He intervened in the controversy over the rabbi's kashrut ruling in Międzybóż, took it upon himself to support the poor, and assumed responsibility to intercede in Heaven (and perhaps on earth) to avert evil decrees that threatened Jewish security in various places.[3] In his letter to his brother-in-law, Gershon of Kutów, the Besht exhibited awareness of the security situation and the vicissitudes of life in the Polish-Lithuanian Commonwealth, mentioning blood libels and the general treacherousness of the times.[4]

Moreover, the Besht did not relate only to Jews. He lived in a world where Jewish and non-Jewish strands were inextricably intertwined. Międzybóż society, like the heterogeneous Polish-Lithuanian Commonwealth in general, was made up of a number of sociocultural streams. Christians were aware of and reacted to Jewish communal and religious institutions,[5] while the Jews were expected to be respectful of Christian sensibilities.[6]

The geography and the economy of the town made it inevitable that Christians and Jews would have to come into contact. There was no ghetto in Międzybóż. In 1730, more than a third of the Jewish householders (75 out of 204) had at least one Christian neighbor.[7] Jews cooperated with Christians in defense of the town, and there were specific issues, such as the problem with Icko Ognisty, on which the Jewish kahal and the Christian municipality worked in tandem.[8] Jews, like non-Jews, considered the Polish administration to be responsible for their safety and welfare and submitted petitions to the administration requesting protection and special dispensations. The Jewish community, like the Christian municipality, had to account to the Polish administration for how it spent its budget. Jewish courts were an integral part of the overall court system in the town, and Jews were sometimes judged before non-Jewish courts.[9]

As for individual, person-to-person contacts, Międzybóż was no exception to the patterns of Polish Jewish life in this era. As was true elsewhere, it can be assumed that here, too, Jew and Gentile met within the matrices of many roles. Economically they were retailer-customer, wholesaler-supplier, agent-producer, employer-employee, debtor-lender, doctor-patient, partners, competitors, and disputants and litigants in court.[10] In the social sphere, there were many opportunities for unstructured everyday contacts: neighborliness, civic cooperation, crime, friendship, hostility and violence, casual contact in the street, marketplace, and inn—even the rare romance. Individual Jews would come into personal contact with Polish officials who judged them, registered them for tax purposes, and dealt with petitions and law enforcement.[11]

These matrices constitute a historical framework for stories in *Shivhei Ha-Besht* reporting that the Besht was in contact with Christians from many levels of society. According to the traditions, he engaged in theological disputes with priests, negotiated with—even made friends with and antagonized—various noblemen, employed a Christian servant, came into contact with robbers, and was patronized as a miracle worker and healer by some Christians.[12]

Shivhei Ha-Besht stories are not the only signs that non-Jews were a part of the Besht's everyday experiences and his universe of discourse. The sources that relate to the episode of the move to dismiss the rabbi from Międzybóż indicate that the Polish administrator, Walicki, was one of the parties in this controversy. If, as seems likely, the Besht was also involved, he may have had to deal with Walicki or his representatives.[13]

There are other possible venues of contact between the Besht and Gentiles. If my interpretation of the letter to Moses of Kutów is correct, the Besht gained herbal medical knowledge from non-Jews. His intervention in episodes of persecutions alluded to in his letter to Gershon of Kutów (and in *Shivhei Ha-Besht* stories) may have gone beyond prayer to attempts to influence potential non-Jewish protectors of the Jews to whom he had ties.[14]

The Besht was a well-known person, filled a public role in an important town, and maintained relationships of one kind or another with non-Jews. In light of this reality, non-Jewish sources might also have something to say about the life of the Besht. From World War II until the mid-1970s, Polish, Russian, and Ukrainian archives were, however, closed to Jewish scholars in the West and in Israel. As a result, with a few exceptions, those who tried to continue the tradition of the prewar Polish Jewish historians had to base their work on archival material that had come to light before the war. These were heavily weighted in the direction of documents originating from royal authorities and from the Sejm and legal documents in general. The treasure trove represented by the records of local authorities (*księgi grodzkie i ziemskie*) and the private archives of magnate owners of the vast latifundia had not been systematically reviewed.

Since the first cracks began to appear in the totalitarian regimes of Eastern Europe—as early as the late 1970s in Poland—foreign Jewish scholars have been visiting archives and microfilming archival material. The nature of research has gradually changed. Archival sources have become a more regular feature of the repertoire of Jewish historians researching Eastern Europe. Local and private archives, containing private correspondence, petitions, and much material of an economic nature, in addition to the more familiar court documents and declarations, are proving to be a mine of information.

This new material is particularly helpful in the case of a historical subject like the Besht. He was apparently a local figure who did not come to the attention of the royal authorities or the Sejm and does not seem to have been involved in any celebrated court cases.[15] The logical place to look for the Besht is not in records of the Sejm, the royal chancellery, or the royal courts. The search for the Ba'al Shem Tov should begin where he lived—in the towns of Podolia.

Many of the records of Międzybóż from the first half of the eighteenth century are preserved in the Czartoryski Library in Cracow. This material was the foundation of the attempt to sketch the environment for the Besht's activities presented in previous chapters. These records, from Międzybóż and elsewhere, also give many examples of circumstances that parallel situations known from *Shivhei Ha-Besht*. Dubnow tried to gauge what seemed plausible; Scholem intuited that some stories sounded "realistic." The Polish archival material reduces the need—and the temptation—to speculate. It makes it possible to demonstrate what were indeed typical situations and problems and to begin the process of threshing the historical kernel in accord with some documented knowledge.

The description of the matrices of daily relations between Jews and non-Jews and their echoes in *Shivhei Ha-Besht* is one illustration of this use of Polish material. There are others. To cite a few examples: Once, when the Besht served as a subarrendator, the arrendator who gave him the lease accused him of buying liquor "off the monopoly" and planned to have him beaten. Monopoly-busting and possible excesses committed by arrendators defending their rights were among the most common themes in the petitions that reached the Czartoryskis.[16] In two other stories the Besht was instrumental in preventing the apostasy of women who had established romantic relationships with Poles. In the Czartoryski material, there is a case of the daughter of a Jewish administrator who was either coaxed or coerced (depending on whose version of the story was correct) into conversion and rescued by her family.[17] According to *Shivhei Ha-Besht,* the Besht also became involved in a complaint about a rabbi that was directed to the Polish administration. The Czartoryski archives make it clear that final authority over the rabbi lay with the Polish nobleman under whose jurisdiction the rabbi's community lay.[18]

Paralleling the direction of Scholem, Bartal, and Barnai, the Polish material can also serve as the basis for confirming realia in the *Shivhei Ha-Besht* stories. In Międzybóż, as in other Polish towns, householders were required to pay an annual fee, called czynsz. This real estate tax was a leasehold fee charged by the owner of the town in consideration of his allowing the householder to reside on his land. Officials representing the Czartoryski family took inventory of the town virtually every year. They listed many of the public buildings and furnishings, the livestock, the agricultural accoutrements, crop yields, and other items relating to the revenues produced by the town and its surrounding villages—all of which were part of the Czartoryskis' vast latifundium. One of the main items in these annual reports was a street-by-street listing of each house in the town and who was subject to pay the czynsz by virtue of ownership of it or residence in it.[19]

Several of the individuals who appear in *Shivhei Ha-Besht* also are listed on these annual inventories, many of which have survived in the archives. They are also found on the copy of the 1764 census of Polish Jewry that includes the towns owned by the Czartoryskis.[20] The individuals named are Hersh, the Besht's son;[21] his daughter, Edel;[22] Yehiel, the Besht's son-in-law;[23] Hersh the scribe;[24] Yankiel, a person depicted in *Shivhei Ha-Besht* as one of the Besht's confidants;[25] Wolf Kuces[26] and David Purkes,[27] mystical-ascetic hasidim of the old type in Międzybóż, who according to the traditions in *Shivhei Ha-Besht* became the Besht's chief lieutenants.[28]

The Maggid Joseph who appears in both the *Shivhei Ha-Besht* stories and in the halakhic inquiry to Rabbi Meir of Konstantynow is probably Jos Jampolski, the preacher (also referred to as "seer") listed in the community in 1743.[29] The assistant cantor ("bass singer"; Polish *basista*) who accompanied the cantor in the synagogue in Międzybóż is likely the subject of the *Shivhei Ha-Besht* story concerning two demons who inhabited the synagogue because of the former bass singer who showed off his voice to the women of the town. This was apparently a regular position, because the existing inventories frequently list a person so identified and there was a budget to pay him. Interestingly, in the context of the *Shivhei Ha-Besht* story, the inventory for 1741 lists the house of Bun Basista as empty.[30]

The value of changing Polish monetary units is another source for evaluating the realia that appear in the stories and for sometimes roughly dating the events recounted. In one *Shivhei Ha-Besht* story,[31] Leib of Kremenets conveyed to the Besht the demand of a nobleman creditor that the Besht repay his 1,000 zloty debt incurred due to the ransom of arrendators who had been imprisoned for falling behind on their payments. The Besht sent Leib back to the nobleman with an order to pay, but without any money. Leib asked the nobleman to review his calculations, and it turned out that the Besht did not owe any money but rather that the nobleman had to return 200 zloty that the Besht had overpaid. The nobleman gave Leib 11 *czerwony zloty* (golden ducats) to cover the 200 zloty (copper coins). Then Leib said, "You are still short two zloty," and the nobleman paid the remainder. The implication of this story is that 11 czerwony zloty equal 200 − 2, or 198 zloty. In fact, from 1702 until at least the mid-1740s, the official rate of exchange of golden ducats to copper coins was 18:1.[32] Since 18 × 11 = 198, the story accurately preserved the money value and the event probably occurred in the 1740s before inflation eroded the rate of exchange.

In contrast, in another story,[33] the Besht asked a man to take a czerwony zloty and donate it as follows: "Give twelve zloty to the members of the kloyz.[34] . . . the remaining twelve zloty you should distribute among the poor." This sets a ratio of 24 zloty to 1 czerwony zloty, a value that probably reflects the late eighteenth-century circumstances when the story was retold. Notably, in the one extant manuscript of *Shivhei Ha-Besht,* the text of the same story reads: "and six zloty you should distribute to the other poor," probably preserving the original version.[35]

A third example is the story about a merchant who had been instructed by the Besht to stay away from his home for a year and was in dire need of a customer in order to earn his livelihood.[36] He fortuitously met a man who turned out to be the biblical prophet Jonah ben Amitai, to whom he sold his wagon-load of merchandise for 160,000 czerwony zloty, equaling 2,880,000 zloty. Such a sum would be much more than double the total head tax paid by the 750,000 Jews of the Commonwealth in 1765. Whatever historical kernel this story may have had, the story was reworked into a miraculous tale emphasizing the Besht's ability to perform wonders.

In connection with the Ba'al Shem Tov, Polish sources sometimes introduce information that for some reason was excluded from the Jewish sources or obscured in them. The Polish tax and census lists through the 1760s refer to someone named Szmoyło, or Samuel, as the "stepson" (*pasierb*) of the Besht.[37] This is a person who is not explicitly mentioned in *Shivhei Ha-Besht* or in any of the standard sources. According to a little-known, modern Hasidic tradition, one of the Besht's disciples was called *horeg* (stepson).[38]

There are several possible explanations as to who this person was and how he became attached to the Besht. A story in *Gedolim Ma'aseh Zaddikim*[39] tells that Rabbi Isaac Duber Margoliot sent his sixteen-year-old sick son to live with the Besht for a year in order to be cured. The Besht promised, "Know that he will be a veritable son to me. I will take him with me wherever I go." The young man's name was Samuel. However, the fact that the story emphasizes that he stayed with the Besht for only a year and was very closely attached to his father militates against identifying Samuel Margoliot as the pasierb.

In one story in *Shivhei Ha-Besht,* the Besht and Wolf Kuces were said to have taken in an orphan boy and girl and arranged for their marriage to each other.[40] No identifying signs are given, so it is impossible to say if Szmoyło was the boy in question. A different tradition preserved in *Shivhei Ha-Besht* noted that the Besht's wife Hanna was a divorcée when she married him;[41] perhaps this boy was her son.

The Polish material, then, can aid in separating the legendary from the historical, identifying and describing individuals, and even lead to putting the stories into rough chronological order. All of this, together with a better understanding of the anthology as a whole work, contributes to a more informed perspective from which to engage in historical analysis of the stories. Some sources from Międzybóż relate directly to the Besht and those close to him. They offer new insights into his role in the town and his place in history.

The real estate tax rolls that contain information on individuals connected to the Besht do not usually include the buildings belonging to the kahal, which were exempt from the czynsz tax, but a few times they do. These are the occasions when the Besht makes his appearance in Polish sources. One of the tax-exempt buildings in Międzybóż was a house near the synagogue. In the extant tax registers for the period that concerns us, the tax-exempt occupant of this house was listed as follows:

1739: *Dom kahalski wnim Moszko duchowny* (Kahal house in which is Moszko the clergyman).

1740: *Dom kahalski seu kantorski wnim kabalista* (Kahal or cantor's house in which there is the Kabbalist).

1742: *Balsem w domu kahalskim* (The Ba'al Shem in the kahal house).

1758: *Balsam* (The Ba'al Shem).

1760: *Balszam Doktor liber* (The Ba'al Shem, the doctor, exempt).

1763: *Herszko w domie kahalnym* (Herszko in the kahal house).[42]

Another record that has relevance for the biography of the Besht is the Polish summary of the annual expenses of the Międzybóż Jewish community, to be paid by the akcyza (excise) tax arrendators for the year 1743. This document is in essence the budget of the community approved by the Polish administrator, Wolinski. It was these expenses, and not any others, that the arrendators were allowed to cover. By issuing this compendium, Wolinski exercised control over Jewish community finances and ensured that obligations he considered to be important, such as debt payment and tax levies, were met. He also gained a large measure of control over communal activity. Only activities that met with his approval could be funded.[43] One line of this official budget reads as follows: "To the poor Jews living in Międzybóż who are recognized by the kahal here and are approved by me [Wolinski] for the current year only."[44] There follows a list of five men, two of whom—Wolf Kucego (Yiddish Kuces [pronounced Kitzes]) and Dawid Purkow (Yiddish Purkes)—received 2 zloty weekly; the other three received 1 zloty per week each.

What is the implication of these entries for the biography of the Ba'al Shem Tov? Five people in the tax lists (and later in the 1764 census) were identified by virtue of their relationship to "the Ba'al Shem": either "of the Ba'al Shem" (balszema, balszemów), or more explicitly "son of the Ba'al Shem" (balszemowicz), "son-in-law of the Ba'al Shem" (zięc balszema), "stepson of the Ba'al Shem" (pasierb balszemów), "scribe of the Ba'al Shem" (pisarz balszema). With the exception of Szmoyło, the stepson, each of these people is known from Shivhei Ha-Besht.[45] It stretches credulity to imagine that in Międzybóż of the 1740s and 1750s people known by tradition to be associated with Israel Ba'al Shem Tov lived near or in the house of another person called the Ba'al Shem. It cannot, therefore, be reasonably disputed that the Ba'al Shem spoken of in these documents is in fact the Ba'al Shem Tov of Hasidic fame, Israel ben Eliezer.[46]

The Polish tax official regarded the most efficient identification for these people to be their relationship to the Ba'al Shem Tov and not, as was customary, their patronymic, occupational tag, place of origin, or some physical characteristic. This is probably a reliable indicator of the Besht's prominence in the town and the fact that the Christians, as well as the Jews, realized he was a central figure. Furthermore, Wolf Kuces and David Purkes, the Besht's close associates in Międzybóż, according to Shivhei Ha-Besht, were not identified in this way. This may reflect their presence in Międzybóż before the Besht arrived there (as Shivhei Ha-Besht implies);[47] they were already known to the Polish officials by their patronymics. Wolf definitely owned his own home, next door to the town rabbi's official residence on the street leading from the castle to the marketplace—probably the town's main thoroughfare. This was a prominent address, and his house was large enough that he was able to take in poor people, including some of those designated for expulsion in 1743. His own son, Faybisz, owned a store in the Międzybóż marketplace.[48]

At least four of the five who were identified as "of the Ba'al Shem"— his son, stepson, son-in-law, and scribe—could be considered as belonging to the Besht's extended household. This might also be true of the fifth, Jankiel Ayzykowicz. He was, perhaps, the Besht's servant or personal assistant, as implied by a story in *Shivhei Ha-Besht* in which he prompted from the prayer book when the Besht led the congregation in prayer with his eyes closed.[49] Since it is only these most intimate associates of the Besht who "belong" to him, the use of the appellation "of the Ba'al Shem" does not signify the members of his "movement"; conversely, the absence of this identification does not necessarily denote the lack of any connection to the great man.

Returning to the five people listed as receiving a weekly stipend, two of them—Wolf Kuces and David Purkes—are among the main characters in the stories in *Shivhei Ha-Besht*. Wolf Kuces is depicted as a traditional type, a Talmudic-oriented scholar who also knew astronomy. Initially he was described as skeptical about the Besht's powers. After the Besht was established in Międzybóż, however, *Shivhei Ha-Besht* indicates that Wolf (or Zev) Kuces was extremely close to him, often dining with him. When the Besht was engaged in a Torah knowledge contest with a Rabbi Mikhel, he relied on Wolf to bring off the victory. Three times in the stories when the Besht cannot communicate because he is in some sort of trance, it is Wolf whom the people consult to ascertain whether there is something wrong with the holy man. Wolf explains the Besht's behavior and at such times mediates between him and the public.[50]

Wolf was an educated, articulate, and respected figure in Międzybóż. Moreover, although listed as one of the poor stipend recipients, he was not poor. The location and size of his home and the fact that his son owned a store in the marketplace indicate that he was among the more affluent people in the town. His appearance on the "poor list" may indicate that this list was something other than its budgetary classification indicates.

David Purkes, originally portrayed as skeptical about the Besht, is represented in *Shivhei Ha-Besht* as becoming one of his most devoted followers, traveling with him and being used by him for theurgic purposes. On one occasion he maintains a stricter standard of kashrut than the Besht. David is described as both a preacher and a cantor. According to *Shivhei Ha-Besht*, he also had contacts with the Maggid.[51]

Shivhei Ha-Besht makes the point that Wolf Kuces and David Purkes were known to be hasidim of the old style before the Besht's arrival and resisted accepting him as leader of the hasidim there. Leaving aside the question of whether they actually resisted his leadership and why,[52] the structure of the situation seems to have been that, as in Kutów, Brody, and other places, there was a recognized group of hasidim in Międzybóż, probably consisting of the five people who received the stipends. Since these people were supported by the community, their institution would have been a bet midrash.[53] This group had a leader whose role would have paralleled that of Moses of Kutów in the kloyz there.[54]

As demonstrated by Wolf Kuces's circumstances, the members of this group were not necessarily poor. The fact that the Polish expense summary refers to them as such may reflect disingenuousness on the part of the Jewish community in order to get Wolinski to approve this budget item. He may have been willing to allow resources to be devoted to supporting the poor but remained unconvinced that the Międzybóż Jewish community needed a group of elitist, ivory tower, mystical scholars.

This brings us to the occupant of the tax-exempt "kahal house." In 1739, the person listed as residing in this house was Moszko Duchowny, which translates as "Moses the clergyman." This is a generic term applied to a Jewish religious or communal functionary. Usually in these lists Jewish holy men and public servants were tagged with their function: *rabin* (rabbi), *kantor* (cantor), *bakalarz* or *introligator* (teacher), *kaznodzieija* (preacher), and *szkolnik* (bailiff or beadle). Moszko was given a nonspecific title.

The 1740 entry clarifies the significance of the term "duchowny" in this context. In that year the resident of the house was called *kabalista*, Kabbalist. In other words, the resident of this house was neither rabbi, nor cantor, nor preacher, nor teacher; he was a mystic. It is reasonable to assume, given the situation in other towns,[55] that this person was the town's mystic-in-residence, expected to spend his time in Kabbalistic contemplation and practice and to serve as the head of the community's officially sponsored circle of mystical-ascetic Hasidim, its bet midrash.[56]

Moszko left the house, and perhaps the town, within the year after the 1739 registration; in 1740, the registrar no longer knew the name of the person in the house. He was now called by his occupation, kabalista. By 1742, the Polish officials knew what the Jews called the occupant of the kahal house; he was the Ba'al Shem. The Besht stayed in this house through the 1750s, and by 1760 the Polish registrar added the term "doktor" as a gloss on Ba'al Shem, perhaps reflecting the role in which Christians in the town commonly came into contact with him.[57] By 1763, the Besht no longer lived in his house and the occupant was named Herszko.

My construction of this information is that the position of mystic-in-residence and head of the bet midrash in Międzybóż was filled by Moszko for the period ending in 1739. In 1740, as we would expect on the basis of Hasidic traditions,[58] a new Kabbalist took up the post. This was the Besht. He remained in the position until 1760, when, according to Jewish sources, he died. The Herszko (Yiddish, Hersh) living in the house in 1763 was probably the Besht's son of that name, who out of respect for his father was allowed to stay in the house after his death. The practice of identifying descendants and associates of the Besht in the tax lists as "of the Ba'al Shem" continued through at least the 1760s.

The Polish sources on the Besht do reflect a non-Jewish point of view, determined both by non-Jewish concerns (tax collection) and non-Jewish perceptions (Besht as doctor, bet midrash members as welfare recipients). Their terse, technical nature also opens them up to a range of interpretation that may be broader than that of some narrative-type sources. The Polish sources on the Besht are, however, the least problematic in terms of provenance and authenticity. There are no doubts concerning what copyists may have deleted or added or how later partisans may have shaped the material. The tax lists are what they purport to be: genuine archival records written in a given year by a scribe mandated to do so by people responsible for recording potential taxpayers. They have been preserved for over two hundred years as part of the Czartoryski archive, and there is no evidence that anyone has tampered with them.[59] Being so technical, these lists are also the least tendentious of sources about the Besht. There is no question of an author attempting to use details of a story to prove some polemical point.

The methodological strength of the Polish sources make them a powerful tool that can guide interpretation of the more difficult material. Their ramifications should be incorporated into any new assessment of the Besht's life. The fundamental point they indicate is that during his entire tenure in Międzybóż, the Besht lived tax-free in a house belonging to the kahal that was reserved for public religious figures. He had a recognized, publicly supported role to play in the community and fit comfortably into the existing institutional structure. Those who were closest to him as disciples—Wolf Kuces and David Purkes—were also part of an established communal institution, the bet midrash, while the members of his extended household were identified, and presumably viewed in a positive light, by virtue of their association with him.

There is no trace of separate, novel institutions that the Besht founded, or of a particular group within the town's population that was regarded as his special supporters. The only group he apparently headed was the small elitist circle of the bet midrash.

This information, combined with the findings developed on the basis of the Hebrew sources and our knowledge of the various contexts of his life, calls for a reevaluation of the traditional image of the Besht. He seems to be less innovative, and more tied to conventional patterns, than any of the standard portrayals have intimated.

PART III

Images

CHAPTER ELEVEN

A Person of His Time

Until recently, the Polish sources were not available to biographers of the Ba'al Shem Tov. They emphasized hearsay and traditional Hebrew material that is full of colorful detail. They paid little attention to, or ignored altogether, some of the written sources from the Besht, as well as some of the testimonies. The largely prosaic nature, limited scope, and sparse detail of these sources seem to have relegated them to second place. Furthermore, the unsystematic, even arbitrary, way in which many scholars set about interpreting the Hebrew sources they were willing to use led to an often-confusing portrayal of the Besht. Scholars have been preoccupied with the Besht's "message" and "way," to the exclusion of serious consideration of the physical, social, economic, and cultural parameters of his existence. As a result of this unbalanced and unsystematic use of the sources, the points scholars most commonly agreed on were largely based on the most legendary sources. Moreover, there remain fundamental contradictions with regard to the nature of the Besht's character and activities.[1]

Within these limitations, however, some specialized scholarship on Hasidism over the past two generations has seen the gestation of a tendency to regard early Hasidism as evolving out of the past, rather than rebelling against it. In the late 1960s, Shmuel Ettinger, basing his findings in part on the work of Israel Halpern and Yishai Shahar, declared that early Hasidism was not a movement of social radicalism but that it actually worked to strengthen traditional social structures.[2] A decade later, Mendel Piekarz demonstrated that Hasidism was not theologically innovative; virtually all of its religious doctrines were anticipated or expounded by non-Hasidim.[3] As elaborated in chapters 1 and 2, other scholars found earlier precedents for such essentials of Hasidism as the use of the title "Ba'al Shem Tov" and the existence of organized, Kabbalistically inclined groups. With regard to the Besht himself, Gershom Scholem, Avraham Rubinstein, Immanuel Etkes, and Ada Rapoport-Albert all showed various aspects of his connection to traditional concepts and institutions.[4]

In essence, the preceding ten chapters have articulated and consummated this trend, at least insofar as it applies to Israel Ba'al Shem Tov. The primary thesis of this book is that the Besht was much more a representative and perpetuator of existing religious, social, political, and even economic realities than he was an innovator. He certainly was no rebel against the establishment, whether religious or social. He fit into the institutions of his time and conformed to behavior patterns expected of the type of holy man he was.

As to the history of Hasidism, the Besht did not inaugurate new, fully developed forms that became the hallmarks of the movement. Rather, he appears to have made some moderate changes in existing forms that were eventually transformed into the mature institutions of Hasidism. The Besht did not create a movement; he modified some conventions.

More than that, he embodied the conditions of the society he lived in. This is evident, first of all, in the pattern of his residential history. In his progression from the pioneer outpost of Okóp Góry Swięty Trojcy through small towns like Tłuste, to the important city of Międzybóż, the Besht mirrored the development and flourishing of Podolia in general. His childhood hometown was established as part of the Polish recolonizing effort in the wake of the Turkish occupation. He subsequently moved to towns that were borne on the rising tide of early eighteenth-century reconstruction. His coming to Międzybóż in what might be termed a nonessential religious role is one indication that the town was thriving. That the Jewish community of Międzybóż could afford to support—in addition to the basic clerical complement of rabbi, cantor, and preacher—a Kabbalist and the circle around him (the bet midrash) is a function of the growth and prosperity of the town and a sign that its middle and upper class were well established.[5]

While there is no evidence for a mass movement surrounding the Besht, the sources do indicate that he functioned as the head of a small group. In his 1752 letter he spoke of his group (havurah) saying the *Ke-*

toret prayer to avert plague. Meir of Konstantynów greeted the members of the Besht's group, and the hasidim of Międzybóż with whom he was associated were, as implied by the Polish sources, organized as a group. I have assumed that this was the bet midrash of Międzybóż—a group of old-style hasidim, supported by the community, engaged in study and elitist, Kabbalah-mandated, religious practices.[6]

The Ba'al Shem Tov's role in the town as resident Kabbalist, healer, and leader of the bet midrash reflects the religious structure of the Międzybóż Jewish community and Ashkenazic Jewish society in general at this time. The Ba'al Shem Tov and his mode of spirituality required no special dispensation. They were taken for granted in the religious and cultural milieu of eighteenth-century Poland.[7] This was the age of popular mysticism in Poland. Holy men whose vocation was magical security were an accepted, normative type in both Jewish and Christian culture. Such a person could attain a respected place and even share in the religious leadership of the community, functioning parallel to the rabbi, who handled ritual and legal matters. The Besht did not need to prove that he was in the tradition of the great halakhists like Rabbeinu Asher or Moses Isserles; he did need to be perceived as advancing the mystical tradition of Simeon bar Yohai and Isaac Luria. His being "expert in the wisdom of the Divinity," or "smart and pious,"[8] was a functional substitute for being scholarly and erudite. To attract attention and gain legitimacy in this major town, the Besht did not need to dispel any embarrassing connotations of his title; he had to show that he could fulfill its promise.

There was not only one hierarchy of deference in the Jewish community. In his classic work, *Tradition and Crisis,* Jacob Katz stressed how the plutocratic tendencies of the kahal structure were tempered by "treating a certain level of scholarship as a substitute for wealth."[9] Leaving aside the a priori nexus between wealth and learning, what Katz proposed was that there were two ideal types in Jewish society, the rich person and the scholar. Anyone adjudged to have attained either status was worthy of respect and could command authority. The existence of people like the Ba'al Shem Tov and other influential ba'alei shem suggests that a third category of deference must be added: mystical adepts who communicated directly with the Divine spheres. These specialists in Divine communication had their own claim to respect and influence. Both the rich and the learned might come to them for help.[10]

A sort of division of spiritual labor was implied in the Besht's 1752 letter to his brother-in-law. Rabbi Gershon of Kutów was an accomplished scholar, but he needed the Besht to inform him as to the occurrences in Paradise. He could have taught the Besht Talmud and legal codes, yet the Besht was still his teacher: "But my request to you is to review my words of moral instruction which I said to you several times. They should always be in your consciousness."[11]

The Besht was the master of the unseen and unexplained. An individual's disease, a community's persecution, or a general epidemic was only a symptom of disruptions or irregularities in the harmonious relationship between the Divine and the human. The Ba'al Shem Tov understood the genesis of these symptoms, and it was his job either to restore harmony or to explain the reason for the disharmony while it ran its course in physical manifestations.[12] A rabbi could only urge people to observe the halakhah as a means of preventing punishment and then merely speculate on the etiology of suffering when it came. The Ba'al Shem Tov could positively identify the cause of suffering and then prescribe or engage in behavior that would limit or end it.

There was also another type of division of labor—between the "people of form and service" and the "people of materiality." According to his grandson, Moses Ephraim, the Besht saw himself as part of the former who were spiritual commandos fighting to "bring down the abundance to the world." For their willingness to "give their lives for the honor of the King" and the protection they provided against supernatural "accusers and detractors," these righteous people deserved to be financially supported by the "people of materiality."[13]

For its part, the community was interested in sponsoring a class of mystics whose praiseworthy activities and lifestyle added vicarious merit to the people as a whole. Some of the members of the bet midrash, like Zev Kuces, inclined more to scholarship; some, like the Besht, were less learned and more spiritually oriented. All of them derived from the medieval tradition of mystical-ascetic hasidism.[14] By supporting them, the community was reinforcing its relationship with God and retaining representatives who, when necessary, could communicate directly with the Divine.

Understanding that the communal institutions were structured to include people like the Besht, we can return to the questions raised at the end of chapters 4 and 5. There is no trace of the Besht's formative influence on the organization or power alignments of his community. While the kahal and pospólstwo were faction oriented, none of the factions seems to have been closely associated with the Besht. He appeared neither as leader nor as opponent, but as supporter. It is he who was evidently on the side of the kahal leadership against Rabbi Hersz Leybowicz

Aptekarz and the butchers in the early 1740s.[15] The explanation for this is that he was co-opted by the establishment immediately on his arrival in the town.

The Besht settled in Międzybóż in the kahal-owned house. This means that he was already known when he came and was invited to take up a recognized, institutionally defined role. He did not arrive as a scorned, itinerant wonder worker who had to fight to make his mark on the community. His constituency was not limited to the ignorant, poor, and disenfranchised. He was to minister as ba'al shem to everyone in the community, and whatever vicarious spiritual credit derived from his mystical activities accrued to the benefit of all. His role and potential contribution were conventional and therefore understood and encouraged from the outset.

This is not to say that all groups in the community were equally attracted to him. The Ba'al Shem Tov obviously had much closer relations with the mystical bet midrash members than with most other people. At the other end of the scale, there are traditions in *Shivhei Ha-Besht* that may accurately reflect the fact that some of the wealthy merchants, perhaps the Charytons or the Zelmanowiczes, had their doubts about the Ba'al Shem Tov's capabilities and resisted associating with him.[16]

Intriguing with regard to the Besht's connections to various groups is David Makow's comment in the late eighteenth century concerning the Besht's supposed special relationship with the town's women.[17] Given that women were typically in charge of matters relating to illness and commonly dealt with the occult side of life—both spheres that were within the Besht's purview—this would not be surprising. Also, relegated to a minor role in the rabbinic-sanctioned institutions of kahal and synagogue, women may have found in the Besht's mystical activity a direct form of legitimate inspiration. Unfortunately, the relative invisibility of women in the available sources makes it difficult to go beyond conjecture in this matter.

The conventionality of the Besht's position was the key to his influence in the community. As spiritual protector he had the right to voice his opinions on matters impinging on the community's spiritual health. Such phenomena as his intervention in the kashrut controversy, his conduct of his own prayer minyan, and his offering of moral instruction are all consistent with his defined role. For the Christians of Międzybóż, too, it was normal for the Jews to employ a professional "Kabalista." They understood and, according to *Shivhei Ha-Besht,* took advantage of his talents.

The Ba'al Shem Tov's activity in Międzybóż is often depicted as fraught with historical drama. As one very popular account put it,

> But the message of the Ba'al Shem Tov and his followers went far beyond an expression of resentment at the domination of the rabbis and their Talmudic academies. It was also an effort to combat the mood of despair which had fallen on the East European Jewish world after the year Tach, 1648. According to Kabbalistic dreamers, that was the year when the Messiah would come; instead, bands of Cossacks, under Hetman Chmielnicki, decimated hundreds of Jewish communities.
>
> Exhausted by the struggle to keep alive in poverty-stricken circumstances, chastised by their leaders for not devoting time to the study of the sacred books, and bleeding from pogroms, the East European Jewish world was beset by a mood of black bitterness—*mora shkhora*. It was this mass melancholia the Ba'al Shem undertook to change.[18]

The Ba'al Shem Tov of the sources examined in this study is much different from the one described in the preceding citation. He expressed no resentment at the role and power of the rabbis. If he was at odds with the rabbi of his own community, it was due to the latter's leniency in a kashrut ruling, and probably as part of a larger political struggle in which the Besht was aligned with the establishment. Moreover, as we have seen, the Besht did not believe in slighting the sacred books, consulted Rabbi Meir Margoliot, tried to find favor with Rabbi Moses of Kutów, and counted distinguished rabbis like the Margoliots, Jacob Joseph of Polonne, and Gershon of Kutów as his disciples.

If a mood of despair had descended on the Jewish world as a result of the depredations of the mid-seventeenth century, its manifestations were mitigated by the mid-eighteenth century. As demonstrated in chapters 3 and 4, the Jews of Międzybóż and Podolia in general were suffering neither mass poverty nor mass melancholia. The effects of the Chmielnicki Revolt had been long since diffused. Even in the *Shivhei Ha-Besht* stories, while there is tension between the Ba'al Shem Tov and Shabbetai Zvi, Chmielnicki is absent. Shabbetai Zvi's spiritual descendants, as Frankists and in other guises, still posed a live issue for the eighteenth-century Jewish community; Chmielnicki was by now only a bad memory.

The Besht, as would be expected from an accomplished ba'al shem, came to Międzybóż to fight against threats from the supernatural realm in his own day, not expressly to defend the honor of the nonlearned classes, or to uplift downtrodden spirits, or to ameliorate a century-old devastation. He did not offer a spiritual refuge from historic suffering but rather the hope of successfully confronting potential sources of contemporary trouble. He was occupied with robbers, noblemen, priests, sinners, and satanic accusers in the here and now.

How did Israel ben Eliezer become the Ba'al Shem Tov? The stories at the beginning of *Shivhei Ha-Besht* describing his hero-conditioning childhood must, at least until further evidence surfaces, be taken with a grain of salt. Likewise, the tradition that he received the mystical writings teaching him the Kabbalistic secrets from Rabbi Adam Ba'al Shem, who lived in the sixteenth century, seems to be an obvious attempt to legitimate the Besht to a potentially doubting public by placing him under the aegis of a famous, established predecessor.[19]

Much less tendentious is the offhand mention in both *Shivhei Ha-Besht* and the Margoliot tradition that the Besht was a shohet, or ritual slaughterer,[20] and, as the original compilation of *Shivhei Ha-Besht* by Dov Ber of Ilintsy noted, he may have been a melamed, petty arrendator, and *mohel* (circumciser) as well.[21] While there is no independent confirmation of his engaging in these occupations, this pattern of multiple employment is certainly typical for the era.[22] Also, the three ritual occupations would have afforded him the opportunity for a modicum of text study that might lead him to gain Kabbalistic knowledge and adopt Kabbalistic rituals without becoming a bona fide rabbinic scholar. It is interesting that his grandson ascribed to the Besht study of the book *Brit Menuhah,* subtitled "a profound book of Kabbalah concerning the vocalization of the words," as well as the Zohar and various Lurianic works.[23]

In addition to his study of these and other books,[24] the language and allusions in the Besht's letters imply that he had a good command of Hebrew and knew at least some Aramaic. He was able to employ some standard phrases and clichés based on rabbinic usage. He was not steeped in Talmud and codes, but he was conversant with basic sources of biblical commentary and Kabbalistic doctrine. In light of this, J. G. Weiss's claim as to the Besht's "relative illiteracy" is exaggerated. Scholem was closer to the mark, but perhaps still too circumspect, when he observed that the Besht's knowledge of traditional sources "was not insignificant."[25] While the Besht had no interest in matching erudition with rabbis, he had to be familiar with the terms of rabbinic—particularly Kabbalistic[26]—discourse to engage the rabbis and those who respected them.

With regard to knowledge of folk medicine techniques, village arenda holding would have made it possible for the Besht to get close to nature and learn peasant herbal medicine traditions. He could also have practiced the mystical hasidic custom of isolation, while his wife ran the tavern, as mentioned in *Shivhei Ha-Besht*.[27] His Kabbalistic training was probably rounded out through his association with Rabbi Moses of Kutów, as hinted at both in the letter he sent this rabbi and the traditions recorded in *Shivhei Ha-Besht*.[28]

Adding Israel ben Eliezer's personality to these possible venues for his preparation as ba'al shem, we can begin to see how he came to be the impressive figure that so captivated those who met him. The Besht of the writings and testimonies was, from young adulthood, a confident type with a clever mind[29] who believed in his own powers and his own importance, whether prescribing medicine for Rabbi Moses of Kutów,[30] instructing his protégés in the proper method of attaching themselves to the letters of the texts they studied,[31] reminding his scholarly brother-in-law to review his moral instructions, or explaining his own importance to the process of Redemption to his grandson. The Besht's charisma was the product of a combination of his Kabbalistic initiation, healing techniques, quick mind, and radiant confidence.

By the time he reached Międzybóż and took up his official residence there, the Besht was famous. His fame during his lifetime was noted by Meir Teomim,[32] implied by the greeting to him from Meir of Konstantynów[33] and by the recollections of the anti-Hasid, David Makow.[34] The unknown but inspiring shohet who enchanted the Margoliot brothers sometime in the 1720s or 1730s had become a recognized public figure by 1740. He was probably known throughout Podolia and perhaps beyond, not as the founder of a new movement, but as a prodigiously talented ba'al shem.

What did the Besht have to offer the Jewish public? What did the community of Międzybóż, the members of the bet midrash, Gershon of Kutów, Jacob Joseph of Polonne, and Meir Margoliot (all of whom received instruction from him), or anyone who came into close contact with him gain from the Besht? What was it that made him *the* Ba'al Shem Tov and not just another ba'al shem tov?

"Balszem Doktor," as the Polish tax registrar called him,[35] must have been an effective healer. He testified that he cured Rabbi Moses of Kutów's nephew and prescribed a stomach potion for the rabbi himself.[36] Meir of Konstantynów spoke of how "he provides balm and medicament to the person without strength."[37] Various stories in *Shivhei Ha-Besht* portray him curing sick people and competing successfully with doctors.[38] But the Besht did not just administer medicaments; he was expert in amulets, exorcisms, and other techniques of shamanesque magical defense. He described his travel between cosmic realms, bringing the concerns of one sphere to the attention of the other. While the stories emphasize how successful he was as the human intermediary before the Divine power, his own report makes it clear that when he faced major disasters he might have been able to influence their course, but he could not necessarily avert them.[39]

Perhaps his very willingness to tackle such great dangers as Haidamak attacks, religious persecution, and epidemics contributed to his mystique and his reputation. Bringing the privileged information he gained during his soul's ascents to the attention of those who did not have such experiences was a means of involving them in the secrets of the supernatural realm. It could also reinforce faith and sustain hope in the future. Even if the Besht could not cancel the evil decrees, he could explain them and offer instruction for coping with them. The Ba'al Shem Tov was a ba'al shem par excellence, offering the promise of collective security for the entire House of Israel and not just magical defense for individuals or his own community.[40]

The Besht also distinguished himself as a religious model and guide. He emphasized prayer in general and evidently perpetuated the custom of prayer *kavvanot* (preparatory mystical prayers). It is interesting to observe that in connection with prayer—the most popular religious activity—the Besht continued and intensified the accepted modes of communion, perhaps even composing his own kavvanot.[41] As Kabbalah-based rituals, especially in prayer, became more and more accepted, he could serve as an accessible model of piety. In this regard, Moses ben Yokel of Międzybóż recalled his father saying, "For the Besht is [the reincarnation of] Rabbi Simeon bar Yohai and his coterie."[42]

The Besht was also a teacher. In his letters and in the eyewitness reports, he is explicitly portrayed as teaching his disciples moral instruction, techniques of spiritual concentration and Divine communion, explanations of the ways of Divine decision making, and even magical skills. In the citation from Nahman of Horodenka (quoted in chap. 2), it was the Besht who finally taught him the proper method for ridding himself of "wayward thoughts" (Hebrew, *mahshavot zarot*), by confronting and mastering them, rather than attempting to hold them at bay by steeling himself through daily cold immersions.[43]

In the stories, the Besht is shown to teach more common people by example and through object lessons. J. H. Chajes has suggested that in this second type of teaching the Besht resembled the Christian friars of the early modern period who employed popular methods to communicate the doctrines of high religion to unsophisticated audiences.[44] As Peter Burke put it, they were "men of the university as well as men of the marketplace."[45] Similarly, the Besht was a man of the bet midrash as well as a man of the marketplace.

The Besht's most intensive teaching was of members of the learned elite like the Margoliots, his brother-in-law, Gershon, Jacob Joseph of Polonne, and, presumably, the members of the Międzybóż bet midrash (*Shivhei Ha-Besht* broadens this circle somewhat). To them he appears to have emphasized some novel doctrines. To spiritualize the elite's favorite activity, study, he revived the Cordoveran custom of attachment to the letters as a means of communion with the Divine. It was this technique that he stressed in his letter to Jacob Joseph of Polonne and that Meir Margoliot chose to recall as the Besht's main lesson to him.[46] It may be that the Besht established a hierarchy of mystical techniques that he introduced to initiates according to their level, with novices concentrating on his prayer mode, including kavvanot, while more advanced individuals learned from him the proper form of study, utilizing letter attachment.[47] This may be connected to the later Hasidic tradition that kavvanot were intended for the rank and file Hasidim but not the zaddikim, who were on a higher plane.[48]

Another novel, if not entirely original,[49] direction the Besht apparently promoted among the hasidim of his day was antiasceticism. While early in his career he is reported as having engaged in isolation and other ascetic practices,[50] the letter to Jacob Joseph of Polonne, probably dating from the late 1740s or early 1750s, indicates that he was against excessive fasting and self-flagellation. Not suffering, but the "joy of performing mitzvot" was to inform the religious life.[51] As noted near the end of chapter 2, this tendency eventually became one of the hallmarks of the new Hasidism.

A further aspect of the Besht that emerges from the sources I have considered is his identification with his family. The impression gained from the correspondence with Gershon and the Polish tax lists is that the Besht was the head of a large extended family and an expanded household. While he had only two children of his own, his responsibilities and close relationships expanded to include in-laws, grandchildren, stepson, and nonrelatives, such as his scribe and members of the bet midrash, like Zev Kuces and David Purkes.

Conversely, the Besht did not have a Hasidic court as was typical in the nineteenth century. There is no evidence for large numbers of Hasidim who considered themselves to be devoted followers of the Ba'al

Shem Tov and would come to spend long periods with him. However, in searching for the roots of the later Hasidic rebbe's court, the Besht's arrangement might be one precedent. The numbers were much smaller, but the notion of the Besht as a paternal figure to all those connected with him—even a few nonrelatives—responsible for their well-being, financial and otherwise, and viewed as the central authority in their lives adumbrates the role of a rebbe in his court among his Hasidim.[52]

The possible link between the Besht's household and the later Hasidic court leads us to the question of the connection between the Ba'al Shem Tov and Hasidism. In characterizing the history of Hasidism, Etkes wrote,

> The transition from an elitist mystical-hasidic group which crystallized around the Besht to a broad movement, including in it also common people, did not happen all at once. There was a gradual process with every stage displaying its own character and particular spiritual and social dynamic.[53]

As suggested in chapter 2, it is useful to think of the Besht as a transitional figure in the differentiation of Hasidism from hasidism. As the head of one group of elitist mystical-ascetic hasidim that had a history predating his arrival in Międzybóż, he was loyal to both the mystical doctrines and communal institutions within which he reached maturity. He did not establish new institutions; he did not rebel against the establishment; he did not start a new religious or social movement.

Based on the sources analyzed in this study, what he appears to have done is to make some changes in old-style hasidism. These include attachment to the letters of the texts as an alternative technique for spiritualizing study and the rejection of asceticism as a tool of communion. These innovations had important ramifications for the popularization of Hasidism as an approach to life. By eschewing asceticism, the Ba'al Shem Tov removed a most daunting obstacle facing the potential Hasid. Without the physical commitment required to carry out fasts and flagellations, the Kabbalistic doctrines and rituals were much more accessible.

Second, if the significant component of the study texts is the letters rather than the words, then one need not be a sage to have access to the import of these texts. With mystical contemplation, rather than content mastery, as the key to meaningful utilization of the holy texts, the scholar loses his unique status. Moreover, if the letters were the essence, then one might substitute the more familiar prayer texts for the study ones. Traditional erudition, while not overtly denigrated, became by implication only one alternative path to communion with the Divine.[54]

It is highly doubtful that the Besht was aware of the potential effects of these innovations. He directed them at the mystical-ascetic hasidim to improve their chances for Divine communion and never advocated the expansion of this group or the neglect of study. However, in the late eighteenth century, the Mitnagdim complained bitterly about the denigration of scholars and scholarship by the new Hasidim and the adoption of Kabbalistic practices by those who were unqualified. While the Besht was hardly responsible for this state of affairs, it is possible to see how his activity was a contributing factor in its development. By extension, this might explain why in the popular imagination the Besht has often been portrayed as giving preference to prayer over study and making it possible for the unlearned person to attain a spiritual level equal to that of a scholar.

The Ba'al Shem Tov, as an outstanding ba'al shem, who commanded respect and achieved a large measure of influence within his community, also represented a precedent for religious leadership not based primarily on halakhic erudition. He stood at the top of the third alternative hierarchy of deference—based on Divine communication—noted above. His position apparently played a role in the development of the concept and function of the Hasidic zaddik whose authority, as Arthur Green has pointed out, had to be grounded in something other than book learning.[55]

The Ba'al Shem Tov also contributed to the new Hasidic movement the aura of his charisma, mediated by those who had learned from him and saw their activities as somehow continuing his. Jacob Joseph of Polonne, Nahum of Chernobyl, the Maggid of Mezerich, Moses Ephraim of Sudyłków, and other catalysts of the new Hasidism credited him with originating many of the doctrines they promulgated, and his reputation as the founder of Hasidism grew.

In this context it is interesting to note once again the original compilation of *Shivhei Ha-Besht* with its stories as retold by Dov Ber ben Samuel of Ilintsy, around 1795. As indicated in chapter 9, Dov Ber ben Samuel intended to emphasize the Besht as a miracle worker and showed no sensitivity to his lack of Hasidic institutional trappings and dissimilarity from the style of the later zaddikim. The versions of the stories in this recension naively portray the Besht as someone who has connections to various old-style hasidic figures but never attains a central leadership position. He establishes no institutions. At most he is surrounded by a small group consisting of his scribe and close associates, such as Zev Kuces and David Purkes, who travel with him.

Thus it is significant that until recently, most scholarship on Hasidism dealt with eighteenth-century figures as representing the true Hasidic movement, while what followed in the nineteenth century was regarded as a distortion, even perversion, of the pristine ways of the Besht and therefore scarcely worthy of scholarly treatment. Actually, something close to the opposite is the case; it was in the nineteenth century that the movement matured and its institutions took on their permanent character. That academic scholars found this developed Hasidic movement to be a poor match with its presumed founder and that Habad tradition had to revise sources (see chap. 12) in order to document a solid connection between the two are measures of the difficulty in tracing the direct influence of the Besht on the movement with which historical memory associated him.[56]

The Besht's relationship to Hasidism is analogous to Jesus' relationship to Christianity. Neither consciously founded a new religious movement. The ideals they exemplified in their teachings and by their behavior were adopted, developed, and made into institutions by later figures. Only when the differentiation of Hasidism from hasidism was in an advanced stage was the role of "founder" filled. It was long after the Besht's death that Hasidim and Mitnagdim alike pronounced him to be the founder of the new Hasidic movement. The Besht probably would have described himself as a hasid of the old style who introduced limited changes based on existing precedents.

This does not mean that the Ba'al Shem Tov was an insignificant figure during his lifetime. In his special fields of supernatural defense and Divine communication, the Besht had a firm base in an important community, was active beyond its confines, and enjoyed fame that outlived him. While probably not as well known outside his own region[57] in his lifetime as the Vilna Gaon was in his, he did have a following of associates who felt they were promulgating and elaborating his teachings after his death, much as the Gaon's (and Jesus' and the Ari's) disciples did for their master's legacy. In the case of the Besht, this intellectual legacy was unwritten and inchoate. Together with personal contact between the Besht and his associates, this legacy inspired profound religious creativity in his name. Those who built the new Hasidic movement as a mass movement utilized both the ramifications of his innovations and his reputation as the foundation of their efforts. Their success transformed the Ba'al Shem Tov from a person who was important in his time and place to a figure of surpassing historical significance.

The new movement began with people like Jacob Joseph of Polonne and the Maggid of Mezerich citing the Besht as the authority for their ideas and practices. Reading later Hasidism into the Besht's biography and teachings was a continual concern and an important method for legitimating developments within the movement. The final chapter is an attempt to understand one example of this process.

CHAPTER TWELVE

From the Historical Besht to the Usable Besht

The Image of the Ba'al Shem Tov in Early Habad

The image I have proffered of the Besht as a man who fit in with the institutions, doctrines, and practices of his time, helped to perpetuate them, yet also developed them, contrasts with the common denominator of most Besht portrayals. Whether they saw the Besht positively or negatively, as a religious or a social activist, as a near-ignoramus or a profound thinker, nearly all the standard accounts made the Besht into a religious revolutionary who established something new and virtually unprecedented—doctrinal and institutional constellations that quickly coalesced into the new Hasidic movement.

This insistence on the Besht as organizational pioneer entails a fair measure of projection onto him of later beliefs and institutions. A good example of this is the image of the Besht that emerged around the Lubavitch, or Habad, Hasidic court at the time of its transition from the generation of its first zaddik, Shneur Zalman of Ladi, to its second, his son, Dov Ber of Lubavitch.

As can be seen in the history of Christianity or Islam, when religious movements develop, institutionalize, expand, and diversify, a host of internal conflicts—personal, political, and doctrinal—arise. Controversies over leadership, power, and belief beset successful religious movements and often result in violent internal conflicts or schisms.

In its early stages in the late eighteenth century, the Hasidic movement appeared to have successfully avoided these types of conficts. There seemed to be room for a multiplicity of leaders, leadership styles, and doctrines. Many Hasidic zaddikim or rebbes and the groups surrounding them coexisted peacefully, and leadership struggles were few.

Rapoport-Albert has shown that this was true mainly because the movement was not yet fully institutionalized. Groupings around one zaddik or another were temporary and fluid. Once the zaddik leading a group died, the group typically broke up and its members gravitated to other zaddikim, not necessarily en masse.[1] The principle seems to have been that a Hasid should choose some zaddik to guide him to holiness. The choice was, however, of a person, not a "school," a court, or a dynasty. A zaddik's appeal derived from his personal charisma and not from some institutionalized devolution of authority to him. The idea of a "zaddikate" with its own characteristic theology and style, passed on in institutionalized form, dynastically or otherwise, did not take hold until the second decade of the nineteenth century.[2]

One of the first examples of a group of Hasidim becoming a permanent institution is the Bratslav Hasidim, who were associated with Rabbi Nahman of Bratslav. The usual presentation of the situation that ensued on Nahman's death in 1810 is that his Hasidim could not imagine anyone taking his place and therefore decided to refrain from choosing a new zaddik.[3]

Until that time, however, only a few groups of Hasidim had chosen a formal successor, much less a hereditary one, to a departed rebbe. There is no evidence of the Besht passing on the reins of leadership to the Maggid of Mezerich, or of the Besht's followers continuing as a group under the Maggid's leadership. Neither the Besht's nor the Maggid's sons became zaddikim.[4]

The instance of Rabbi Shneur Zalman (also known by his Hebrew acronym, Rashaz) of Ladi assuming leadership of Hasidim in White Russia also illustrates the noninstitutionalized nature of leadership succession. The Hasidim there were originally led by Menahem Mendel of Vitebsk. When he emigrated to the Land of Israel in 1777, he planned to continue to guide his Hasidim by letter. This did not prove to be an effective method, and his followers began to drift apart. Eventually the vacuum was filled by Shneur Zalman of Ladi, a disciple of Menahem Mendel but also of the Maggid of Mezerich. He was certainly not Menahem Mendel's declared successor either institutionally or doctrinally. It was only with great reluctance that Menahem Mendel agreed to Shneur Zalman's assumption of authority, and, in theory at least, Shneur Zalman was to be his deputy and not his successor. Menahem Mendel was still alive and still interested in leading his group.[5] Shneur Zalman's leadership was not the result of a mechanism of succession but rather of the right person being in the right place at the right time. The membership of his group differed from that of Mendel's, and there was no doctrinal or even stylistic continuity.[6]

Nahman of Bratslav's followers were faced with their leader's death in October 1810. Their immediate innovation was not their failure to choose a successor to the departed rebbe but their decision to keep the group together, despite the leader's death. From now on, the group would have an identity transcending its particular leader. It would be a permanent institution. The question of leadership and its succession, however, was not yet resolved.

THE QUESTION OF SUCCESSION

When Rabbi Shneur Zalman of Ladi died some two years after Nahman, in December 1812, while enduring the hardships of the Napoleonic War in Russia, his followers were in a quandary. Not only had their venerable and revered leader died but there was also no clear direction for the group's future. Even Habad tradition, which understandably emphasized the continuity and harmony of succession in the movement, implies that on Rashaz's death the continuation of the group was not taken for granted. Some said that "just as with the Besht and the Maggid—may their rest be in Paradise—after their deaths the rabbinate was divided among their great disciples, so should it be now."[7] Other Rashaz followers said, "After our great master, there is no other rabbi who can fill his place, and they went around the towns crying: 'Oy! Oy! We have no rabbi and Hasidism has died.'"[8] In other words, they expected the group to split up and the individual Hasidim to attach themselves to new rebbes. This implies continuation of a decentralized model of small groups continually forming and splitting, based on the charismatic appeal of a particular leader.

If this was the situation, then anyone who tried to keep the group together as an institutionalized entity and establish a legitimate claim to leadership was setting a precedent. He would have to convince the Hasidim that despite the leader's death the group should stay together under a single new leader who had legitimate claim on Rashaz's authority and power. Whatever loyalty and obedience had been shown to Rashaz should now be directed to the new man. There were three candidates who were willing to attempt to set this precedent.[9]

One of the candidates for the leadership of Habad Hasidism was

Rabbi Aaron ben Moses Ha-Levi Horowitz, better known as Aaron of Staroszele. Rabbi Aaron was born in the town of Ursha in 1766 and was a direct descendant of the great Talmudist and Kabbalist, Rabbi Isaiah Horowitz. Aaron himself was a bona fide scholar, well known for his mastery of both mysticism and halakhah. He also was a gifted preacher considered until today to be one of the primary exponents of the doctrines of Habad Hasidism. Aaron spent some thirty years as a close associate of Rashaz and was considered to be his "chief disciple" (*talmid muvhak*). He also served as tutor-companion to Rashaz's eldest son, Dov Ber, six years his junior.[10]

According to Habad sources, late in Rashaz's life an accusation was made to him about Aaron. As a result, Aaron was made to feel unwelcome among the Habad Hasidim and his relationship with Rashaz deteriorated. He sold his home near Rashaz in Ladi and moved back to his birthplace, Ursha.[11]

Aaron did not resign himself to his banishment from the inner circle of Habad, and when Rashaz died he claimed the leadership. His claim had a theoretical basis. According to Aaron, Hasidism was continuous with and based on the secret teachings of the great sixteenth-century Kabbalistic sage Rabbi Isaac Luria, the Ari. These teachings were revealed and explained in a progressive, evolutionary manner. In each successive generation there was a central figure who was the chief teacher of the era and, by implication, the leader of the Hasidim.[12] The primary qualifications of this chief teacher were his divinely inspired spirit and his association with his predecessor in the previous generation. It was the predecessor who passed on the Ari's teachings to the new chief teacher.

The first person in this chain of holy reception was the Besht, whose late birth precluded his sitting at the feet of the Ari. He merited an even more exalted teacher, Elijah the Prophet, who "revealed [to the Besht] the mysteries of this wisdom." From the Besht on, the holy knowledge passed through chief disciples: from the Besht to the Maggid and from the Maggid to Rashaz. By this logic, the next in line for the teaching, and the authority that went with it, was Rashaz's chief disciple, Aaron of Staroszele. His thirty years of devoted discipleship had prepared him to inherit the leadership by virtue of his profound and unrivaled comprehension of the teaching communicated by Rashaz.[13]

Aaron's intimate familiarity with the teachings of Rashaz, his teacher, and his ability to penetrate to the inner meaning of these teachings gave him license to decide to publicize what had been secret. Together with his claims on the leadership, Aaron formulated his own philosophy of Hasidism, based on what he claimed was the proper understanding of Rashaz's legacy.[14] Two of the central points of this philosophy were the proper style of prayer and the need for a hierarchical structure in teaching and organizing Hasidism.

With regard to prayer, Aaron's watchword was that the soul and the flesh must strive together. One way of achieving this was to conduct prayer with physical exertions that induce ecstasy: jumping, clapping, shouting, and falling down. The physical dimension could bring the soul to a state of religious wonder and prepare it to communicate and commune with the Divine.[15]

As to the requisite hierarchy, Aaron believed that people stand on differential levels of wisdom and spirituality. Not everyone is capable of absorbing all types of religious knowledge. There are certain things that "are not meet for every person, but rather for the enlightened only," while other knowledge is intended for "those who don't understand." Common working people cannot understand, and will probably misunderstand, the most lofty teachings. These are reserved for those who have reached the highest level.[16]

The second candidate to succeed Rashaz was apparently his youngest son, Moses. According to the later testimony of two Maskilim, Pesah Ruderman, a Habad Hasid in his youth, and Ephraim Deinard, Moses, a great Torah scholar, "thought that he was the one to inherit his father's place."[17] Little is known about his bid and how it failed. In a letter requesting support from the Hasidim, written around the spring of 1813, R. Dov Ber mentioned his younger brother, Hayyim Abraham, but not Moses. However, Moses did sign, together with his two brothers, the forewords to the editions of Rashaz's books, the *Tanya* and the *Shulhan Arukh*, which were published in 1814, a little over a year following the great zaddik's death. Future editions were signed by the eldest brother, Dov Ber, alone.[18] This implies that the contest for the leadership was joined in 1813 but still not decided when the first editions were published in 1814. Two years later, when the second editions of the books were published, Dov Ber had already established his spiritual primogeniture.

There are various reports about Moses subsequent to the contest over the leadership of Habad, all indicating that he left the orbit of Hasidism and probably even of Judaism. In 1821, the Jewish Englightenment figure Isaac Ber Levinsohn related that he had learned from Hasidic informants that Moses had converted of his own free will and had been interviewed by the tsar. In 1843, Bonaventura Mayer, a convert to Christianity, wrote that in the course of his travels in Russia he had met Moses serving as a Russian bureaucrat, something a nonconverted Jew would not have been able to do. According to Habad tradition, Moses caused much grief to his family but at the end of his life repented.[19]

The third and successful candidate to inherit Rashaz's place was the firstborn son, Dov Ber. To succeed, Dov Ber had to prove not only that the leadership of the group should be inherited, and inherited by only one person, but also that he was the right person. He had to show that he was the one destined to interpret and propagate the teachings and take the lead. Since the dynastic principle had not yet been firmly established, Dov Ber could not simply assert that as the firstborn he was the presumptive heir. He had to demonstrate that his personal talents qualified him to take the position.

That was the problem. The same Maskilim who testified as to Moses' Torah scholarship and his ambition to take over from his father expressed their opinions as to Dov Ber's ability as a master of Talmudic study. According to Ruderman, in contrast to Moses who "was adept in Talmud and codes," Dov Ber "knew almost nothing in the exoteric Torah, but his power was great in mysticism and hypocrisy." Deinard asserted that "Dov Ber was an ignoramous and a man of conspiracies."[20]

Not only dyspeptic Maskilim expressed doubts as to Dov Ber's proficiency in Torah. Even Habad sources hint that he was not initially regarded as a scholar, or even as expert in the doctrines of Hasidism. As Naftali Loewenthal, himself a loyal Habad Hasid, gingerly put it, for some of the important Hasidim, Dov Ber "did not represent the ideal Hasidic leader."[21] H. M. Hielman reported that one Hasid advised Dov Ber to set up his court in Ukraine because there he would find an audience, whereas in White Russia, where the Hasidim were familiar with his father's teachings, he would have nothing new to say. Even Dov Ber's own schoolfellow, Rabbi Nahman of Oshatz, was reportedly skeptical about his friend's ability to master great amounts of Torah in a short time.[22]

Moreover, in the collection of Hasidic stories edited by Ya'acov Kaidaner, *Sippurim Noraim* (Lemberg, 1875), Kaidaner goes to great lengths to include stories emphasizing Dov Ber's erudition and intellectual acumen and to show "that it is not as the cacklers and loudmouths assert against His Honorable Holiness [Dov Ber], that in the study of the exoteric Torah he was not one of the greats of the land."[23] Letters written by some of Dov Ber's supporters to justify his ascension to the leadership emphasize how close he was to Rashaz, how much Torah he learned from his father, and how his father allowed him to teach in public. They appear to be attempting to counteract popular opinion.[24]

Dov Ber himself implied that he recognized his weakness in the realm of scholarship and teaching by insisting that such attainments were not of paramount importance. In an open letter that he sent to Rashaz's Hasidim in 1814, he several times denigrated the importance and questioned the efficacy of public teaching and preaching. Casuistic virtuosity was not of the essence.

> For from my youth I have been accustomed to examine myself with a sharp eye concerning this. I know very well all of the afflictions and pain of our people[25] and how to focus in on the essence of the soul of each and every one, from the smallest of the small until the great. This was an obligation and a commandment for me, to speak in private with each one, and in this way the life of his soul was put on the path of truth and honesty in the manner appropriate for him. This is worth more than a hundred homilies which he hears, but not even one reaches him.[26]

Aaron of Staroszele may have known how to dazzle his listeners with his prodigious learning and his homiletic techniques. Dov Ber claimed that he was willing to forego such virtuosity in favor of knowing how to change people's souls and behavior as a result of individual contact.

In addition to meeting criticism of his lack of scholarly qualifications, Dov Ber had to respond to Aaron's version of Hasidic doctrine, which sharply conflicted with his own. Others have explored this point in depth.[27] In the present context, it is important to concentrate, once again, on the issues of the style of prayer and the hierarchy of the Hasidim.

Dov Ber opposed artificial actions that were supposed to induce ecstasy in prayer and lead to wonder and communion. Physical exertions affected only the outer heart of flesh. They boiled the blood, resulting in an "alien enthusiasm" from which the Divine element was completely absent. When people made a conscious decision to yell during prayer, they were yelling merely to hear their own voices, not to speak to God. The various types of falls that people took during prayer brought on an alien fire. The way of falling diverted people from the ways of truth.[28]

In Dov Ber's opinion, the precondition to communion with God was not artificial ecstasy but negation of the material self and heartbreak; what he called "nothingness" or "brokenness." If the worshiper has negated his material self, broken his heart, communicated with the Divine, been suffused with spiritual inspirations, and *then* lets out a spontaneous scream or makes a spontaneous physical gesture, that is fine.

Physical expressions of ecstasy—screams, falls, and so on—must not be the starting point of prayer. They cannot serve as the basis of a calculated attempt to reach communication and communion with God.[29]

On the question of hierarchical status among the Hasidim, Dov Ber believed that the inner circle should be as wide as possible. Anyone able to read should be permitted to know and to feel close to the zaddik and the essence of Hasidism. It was wrong that those who traveled to visit the rebbe bragged and lorded it over those who could not afford to do so.

> Only a tenth come and nine-tenths stay home, bereft. They are the people, the people of truth, whose hearts have been more affected by the fear of God than the travelers who boast about hearing homilies and preachers when they come.[30]

Dov Ber protested against the custom of traveling to the zaddik in small groups of two or three instead of en masse. This also created divisions and invidious distinctions among the faithful. Much of Dov Ber's activity was aimed at reaching out to the 90 percent who could not come to his court and at preventing the creation of a hierarchy based on physical proximity to the rebbe. He did not want a small "in-group" to dominate the majority.[31]

Another obstacle to Dov Ber's claims on the leadership was Aaron's assertion that the rightful heir was the chief disciple, not the son. In the absence of an established succession principle in Hasidic circles, Aaron's construction of Hasidic history that in each generation one disciple—the Besht, the Maggid, Rashaz—was anointed as chief teacher, while not precise, certainly fit what was known in 1814 much better than a dynastic explanation. Everyone knew that the sons of the Besht and the Maggid did not approach the greatness of their fathers. Dov Ber, then, had to undermine Aaron's claims of closeness to Rashaz and of possessing unique understanding of his teaching. Dov Ber also had to demonstrate the fallacy of Aaron's model of leadership transfer.

The sources available do not reveal a precise chronology of Dov Ber's climb to the head of Habad; but some of his significant moves are plain. After Rashaz's death in December 1812, Dov Ber's circumstances were not propitious. At the time he was on an errand for his father in Kremenchug. There were no Hasidim with him. The houses belonging to Rashaz's family in Ladi had been destroyed by fire, making return there impossible. Rashaz had not left "any will from him, neither verbally or in writing." Dov Ber had no visible means of support. Rashaz had issued the "Liozna Regulations" to control the stream of Hasidim to him, had enjoyed abundant contributions from the visiting faithful, and had been generously supported during the Napoleonic War by one of his Hasidim.[32] In contrast, Dov Ber had to write an open letter to his father's Hasidim with a supplicatory tone.

> Please remember to credit the sons on account of the graciousness of the fathers; comfort them and refresh their soul in their time of trouble. . . . [L]et each person send his regular contribution and God forbid that he give less. As you, our people, have taken upon yourselves in writing your strong connection to my father, my teacher, may I be atonement for him, may great mercy be aroused on my behalf that I not have to make the rounds collecting money for my family in Ukraine and Poland.[33]

This was not the command of a zaddik to his Hasidim. It was an appeal by someone who had to convince and motivate his intended audience. The embarrassment entailed in the spectacle of Rashaz's son roaming like a beggar in search of handouts was offered as a prod to his father's Hasidim to deal kindly with him.

There was apparently some response to this appeal, for on 13 September 1813, Dov Ber settled in the town of Lubavici (Lubavitch) after its Polish nobleman owner gave him permission to reside there.[34] This gave Dov Ber a base from which to begin to realize his ambition to take over his father's place and gain the loyalty and obedience of the Habad Hasidim. Few details about his activities during the crucial 1813–1816 period are known, but some of Dov Ber's efforts and claims are clear from his writings and from the book publications he sponsored.

Dov Ber attempted to confront the obstacles in his path: (1) the absence of an established precedent for Hasidic groups to remain together after the zaddik's death under a new institutionalized leadership; (2) the doubts as to Dov Ber's personal qualifications to be such a leader; (3) the opposition to his doctrines and his interpretation of Hasidism; and (4) the claim that leadership should be passed on through a chain of tradition from teacher to chief disciple, that is, Aaron of Staroszele. The task was further complicated because Rashaz had not expressed an opinion on any of these matters, in public at least, and Dov Ber himself wrote that the great man had left no will. Dov Ber proceeded to confront the challenge with a multitrack strategy.

It appears that one track was gathering recommendations from important personages, such as the two letters that are excerpted in the semi-official Habad history of the lives of the rebbes.[35] In both of these letters, the claim was made that in his lifetime Rashaz had given authority to Dov Ber. Rabbi Pinhas Schick even told how he witnessed a private meeting between the father and son during which Rashaz explicitly appointed Dov Ber his successor.

Such endorsements were not sufficient, and by late 1813 Dov Ber was already taking additional steps. In the course of 1813–1814 he wrote three long open letters to "our people." The three were written as a series, copied over many times, circulated by hand, and printed only years later.[36] These tracts are essays that can be called Dov Ber's spiritual platform. In them he detailed his ideas about the various levels of ecstasy and reflection that a Hasid must pass through to arrive at communication and communion with the Divine.

Dov Ber wrote much about the correct way to pray. He noted the importance of fulfilling the various religious commandments with the proper intent. He emphasized the need to reach the mystical roots of the letters of the Hebrew alphabet. He called for balance between negation and abnegation, on the one hand, and joy, on the other. He confronted the potential conflict between the quest for spirituality and the need to earn a livelihood. He championed the Jews who were not considered to be part of the elite, insisting that they too were entitled to know the doctrines of Hasidism.[37]

Between the theology and philosophy, Dov Ber also put in some comments on the proper behavior for a zaddik. As a response to the need to communicate with the 90 percent who did not make it to the rebbe's court, Dov Ber made an original proposal: if the Hasidim could not come to him, he would go to them. Dov Ber proposed that every year he would travel to several regional gatherings of his Hasidim for a month at a time.[38] This differed from the style of Rashaz and went against the hierarchical theory of Aaron.

In several places in these essays, Dov Ber criticized the style of prayer advocated by Aaron. At some points it appears that the criticism was being leveled at Aaron himself. For example, Aaron was a great preacher and claimed to have unique insight into the teachings of Rashaz. Dov Ber said, "Thus they received from the great preachers who say to them, 'I have the secret,' and this is an egregious error."[39] Elsewhere, he seemed to be referring to Aaron, who had appeared to be an intimate of Rashaz and a great authority on Hasidism but ultimately was estranged and rejected. Dov Ber wrote, "Also with regard to him who in the eyes of man is dressed in the beautiful garments of Hasidism, but God sees to the heart and a person's end indicates his beginning . . . as is clearly demonstrated with several people who rose and then descended to the very depths . . . and a wise person can take the hint."[40]

At the end of his first essay, Dov Ber indicated what he took to be the basis of his authority, the reason the Hasidim should accept his doctrines and leadership. He understood that he had to defend himself against "the slander of people who want to be haughty and make a name for themselves saying, 'I have a secret that not everyone knows' " (evidently a reference to Aaron). Those who claimed secret knowledge believed that they understood what was not explicit in the teachings of Rashaz and that the explanations of Dov Ber reflected not his father's teachings but his own thoughts.[41]

Dov Ber's retort to this accusation was, first, that he taught nothing that had not been placed in his heart by his father, with whom he had studied daily for twenty years. These teachings became a part of him and he was merely reproducing them, not inventing them. Second, Dov Ber averred that "all of the teachings are available and can be understood by anyone who has tasted the taste of Hasidic doctrine from his youth." Nothing was a priori secret; there was no inner knowledge that only a "chief disciple" might be able to fathom, or was authorized to reveal and then only to an elite inner circle. Finally, Dov Ber stated, "I was very accustomed for more than twenty years to be in the holy sanctuary of my master, father, teacher and rabbi of blessed memory, and I knew from him all of the particulars of the afflictions of our people and I checked by myself the heart of each one." He had learned from his father not only the theoretical doctrines of Hasidism but also the proper manner of relating to the individual Hasid.[42] The truth of these claims was demonstrated by still another direction in Dov Ber's activity: publication of his father's books.

Three of Rashaz's works appeared in his lifetime: the *Tanya, The Laws of Torah Study,* and *The Table of Blessings.* In 1814, after the new court had been established in Lubavitch, Rashaz's three sons sponsored the publication of what were expanded and completed editions of the *Tanya* and the *Laws.* In the spring they published *Iggeret Ha-Kodesh* (The Holy Epistle), which was the *Tanya* supplemented by two appendixes. Shortly afterward, the sons published three volumes of Rashaz's *Shulhan Arukh,* a full-scale code of Jewish law.[43]

The sons all signed the forewords to these two books, explaining why they had decided to publish them. They cited their intention that the books serve as a monument to their father and that writings that he did not have the opportunity to publish be printed. They also wrote, in the introduction to *Iggeret Ha-Kodesh,* that it was necessary to add the two appendixes to complete the *Tanya.* Nahum Karlinsky has suggested that these supplements were added to introduce a new, spiritualistic dimension to the writings of Rashaz, which in their first edition had appeared opposed to the spiritualism of the Maggid. According to Karlinsky, Rashaz did not dwell on the spiritualistic in his lifetime, and it was his sons and disciples in their editions who brought the material that reflected this side of his teachings, a side that was emphasized and developed to a great degree in Dov Ber's writings.[44] This new edition of the *Tanya* could reinforce and put the imprimatur of Rashaz on many of the ideas Dov Ber presented in his three essays written in the same year.

In their long introduction to their edition of Rashaz's *Shulhan Arukh,* the sons emphasized their father's expertise in halakhah. They told how the Maggid of Mezerich himself chose Rashaz to write this new code of Jewish law and urged him to carry out the project in order

> to publicize in sevenfold refined form the essence and inner meaning of the reasons for the laws given by all of the earlier and later halakhic scholars, each explanation in its own terms without confusion and muddling, together with the legal decisions which are clarified and set according to all of the authorities up until our day.[45]

The sons were also careful to point out that the famous and respected rabbinic brothers, Shmelke and Pinhas Horowitz, saw the first results of Rashaz's efforts when they visited the Maggid. "They praised him and hailed him very very much" and blessed the work itself.[46]

The long and detailed birth certificate for the *Shulhan Arukh* was necessary because, as reactions to previous codes of Jewish law had demonstrated, any attempt to summarize and simplify Jewish law was liable to elicit severe criticism.[47] In the absence of Rashaz, the sons were even more exposed to criticism for their impudence in publishing a book that the great man himself obviously did not rush to publish and that had the declared purpose of making the law accessible to every person without intermediation of halakhic experts, by implication diminishing the value of Talmudic casuistry.[48]

If, however, outside criticism was expected, publication was worth the risk, because it could help bring about a much desired internal goal: consolidation of the post-Rashaz Hasidic group. In the absence of the great leader and his unifying personality, his halakhah could both give the group an identity and maintain their unity through the propagation of uniform halakhic practice. Uniform behavior in the fulfillment of religious obligations could concretize the ties binding the Hasidim and serve as a focus for their identity. This would be an important step in the in-

stitutionalization of a group that had been based on the charisma of a
single leader.

In addition, one of the basic tenets of Dov Ber in his essays, and later
in his books, was the idea of equality among all members of the group
and democratization of the knowledge of the doctrines of Hasidism. He
was interested in reaching the 90 percent who could not come to him.
Presenting the everyday obligations of a Jew in an accessible form was
a good way to promote these goals. If everyone could read the law for
himself and know it, then each individual might feel that he understood
what the rebbe demanded of him, even without a personal interview or
listening to the rebbe's sermons. This undermined part of the basis of hierarchy and invidious distinctions among the Hasidim.

The publication of *Iggeret Ha-Kodesh* and the *Shulhan Arukh* in
1814 was congruent with several of the tendencies expressed in the essays of Dov Ber at around the same time. It also reinforced the basis for
the continuation of the Habad group as a united, institutionalized movement under new leadership. The identity of that new leadership in Dov
Ber's mind was evident in his three tracts of 1813–1814, although he still
had to convince the Hasidim that his style of leadership and practice was
the correct one. He apparently also still needed the added strength of an
alliance with his two brothers to legitimize the publication of the books
and the new ideas they contained, as well as to hold off Aaron's bid for
the leadership. The multisignatured 1813–1814 forewords thus hint at
the instability of Dov Ber's position at that stage.

These forewords contained a notice that implied a significant weakness in Dov Ber's basic claim against Aaron. At first glance, the publication of Rashaz's books by his sons gave the impression that they enjoyed a special status as transmitters of his doctrines and strengthened
their title, as sons, to the presumptive right to inherit his leadership. Their
own words in the forewords, however, weakened this claim. At the beginning of *Iggeret Ha-Kodesh,* they wrote,

> The manuscripts written by the holy hand itself, which were extremely punc-
> tilious with not one letter superfluous or missing, are no more. All that is left
> is a remnant from what was abundant, pieced together from copies scattered
> among the disciples. If there is any error—"Mistakes who can fathom?"—it
> will be seen to be a scribal error and the intent should be clear.[49]

The foreword to the *Shulhan Arukh* contains a similar passage.

> Due to the many troubles, turns and events which passed over our heads, and
> in particular the multiple burning of our houses, the manuscripts of the holy

hand of our honored master, father, teacher and rabbi of blessed memory, himself, are no more. What has survived are only the copies scattered among the disciples, one here and one there. As they come into our hands we bring them to the printing house and they become units in the hand of the creator, until they are pieced together, God willing. . . .

In this connection we have come to issue an awesome warning to anyone who holds any holy writings from our master, father, teacher and rabbi of blessed memory, whether of exoteric Torah or esoteric Torah, that they may not be brought to the printing house, but only to us.[50]

In these two passages the sons admit that they have not published autograph manuscripts of their father's work but rather formed a whole text out of copies made by various students of Rashaz. As Gries has shown, this is typical of Hasidic books published in the late eighteenth and early nineteenth century.[51]

In the context of the contest for leadership, Rashaz's sons' repeated admission, in print, that they did not have any autographs of their father's writings is significant. They were dependent on others to publish their father's literary legacy. They could not prove that the writings that were published were word for word what Rashaz taught. The sons themselves acknowledged that in the process of copying mistakes crept in. We can add that the editing they had to do would of necessity have entailed, at a minimum, deciding between textual variants and adding transitional passages.

In this light, Dov Ber's defense at the end of the *Essay on Ecstasy* in 1814, adduced above, is understandable. There might well have been skepticism as to whether his words came from the interior of his heart, where his father had placed them, or from his own mind. Since Dov Ber did not have writings to prove that his doctrines were those of his father, he had to argue on the basis of his personal credibility: the fact that he had spent twenty years at his father's side.

This was a weak claim. How was Dov Ber, the son, essentially different from any other disciple? The chief disciple, Aaron, who served the master, not twenty, but thirty years protested that Dov Ber misunderstood the teachings. It was he—Aaron—who properly understood what Rashaz had taught, and his interpretation was the correct one. Doubts as to Dov Ber's expertise in Torah and his father's esteem for his abilities would have reinforced such an assertion. It was also true that Aaron had been the young Dov Ber's teacher. Relying only on his own reputation and proffered familiarity with his father's teachings, Dov Ber was at a considerable disadvantage in a contest with Aaron of Staroszele.

After 1814, Dov Ber continued publishing his father's books—without the co-signatures of his brothers—in addition to books of his own, more than a dozen titles in all. In retrospect, it is apparent that Dov Ber embarked on a publishing campaign designed to spread his own version of Hasidism to the widest possible public. This was one way to establish and strengthen his leadership.[52]

Dov Ber's rival, Aaron, did not attach importance to book publishing as a means of gaining acceptance for his ideas and his leadership. He did not start publishing until 1820, in an effort that proved to be too little, too late.

Dov Ber probably realized that he had to change his treatment of the issue of the source of his authority to present and interpret the teachings of Rashaz if he was to be convincing. After 1814, there was an obvious shift in his argument. The 1816 edition of the *Shulhan Arukh* appeared with a new foreword signed only by Dov Ber and without any mention of the lack of autograph manuscripts. This new text emphasized the closeness of Dov Ber to his father. In a similar vein, Dov Ber changed his explanation of the relationship between himself and his father's writings. In the introduction to the prayer book (Kopys, 1816), he wrote,

> For more than thirty years his pure words, sparks of fire from the light of Israel, were spoken in pleasant speech to the desirous public . . . and especially these excellent words concerning the mysteries and sweet secrets of Torah, the wellspring flowing from the overflowing well every Sabbath to us his sons in private and to a few chosen ones with us. There was nothing, even a fragment, which we did not review several times with the deepest deliberation possible. In particular to bring it into writing and colloquial language that would be understood by the great and the small . . . in several notebooks which have been scattered in different copies which people copied from the manuscript, as is known to all those who possess them. Of course not every person is privileged to be able to determine by himself the truth of the light stemming from the text without a tradition contained in a listening heart and a seeing eye . . . and I have anthologized from several notebooks, from copies I possess which many copied from the manuscripts and also many notebooks from my very own handwriting.

The claims here are much different from what was put forth in 1814. According to this new construction, the sons were part of a very select group that was privileged to hear Torah from Rashaz each Sabbath. It was the members of this group who undertook to write down what Rashaz had to say. The manuscripts in circulation were copies of Rashaz's teachings as they appeared in the original manuscripts written by Dov Ber, by himself, or as part of the writing group. Dov Ber heard what most disciples could not hear, and the only written form of Rashaz's words are what his brothers and colleagues wrote down together.

Israel Yoffe, who printed several of the books Dov Ber initiated or wrote and was himself a follower of Habad and particularly close to Dov Ber and Rashaz,[53] expatiated on the theme of Dov Ber's involvement in writing down his father's teachings. On the title page of Rashaz's commentary to the Zohar (Kopys, 1816) he wrote,

> Our teacher and rabbi, Shneur Zalman, may his soul be in the upper spheres, used to preach before his sons—may they live—every Friday night, and chose [Dov Ber] to be the one to write all of the things he heard from [Rashaz's] holy mouth, because he knew in his soul that [Dov Ber] would not stray from his intent. . . . Most of these holy writings went before the honored, holy Admor,[54] may his rest be in Paradise, and they were very good in his eyes.

In other words, Rashaz chose Dov Ber to write down his words and even managed to check most of what was written and give it his stamp of approval. According to this depiction, there were no disciples, not even any brothers. The single legitimate source for the words of Rashaz was Dov Ber and his writings.

With this new history of transmission, Dov Ber and his partisans could point out qualitative differences between himself and Aaron. Until the end of Rashaz's life, Dov Ber belonged to the coterie of closest disciples. Aaron had become estranged and moved away from Rashaz before he died. Early in the leadership contest, Dov Ber expressed his opinion as to what happens to a disciple who leaves his teacher: "When he leaves his teacher for a long time, even if the teacher is still alive, then the connecting cord of great love is cut and he falls from his station of great love in Divine service, as this has befallen several people, as is known."[55]

By contrast, Dov Ber could claim that not only had he remained attached to Rashaz in the closest possible way, both as son and as disciple, but also that it was he who had written his father's words directly as they were heard. He was now in a position to spread his father's legacy, not only via interpretation of works published in his father's lifetime but also, perhaps primarily, by publishing hitherto unknown words of the great man.

In reply to this, Aaron could merely say that he remembered what he had learned and his learning authorized him to interpret the true meaning of the Tanya. In his writings, Aaron emphasized how close he had been to Rashaz and how thoroughly he had comprehended the rebbe's words. Aaron held that there was a hidden dimension to Rashaz's teachings that only a chief disciple could discern. With regard to publishing Rashaz's supposed words, Aaron took the position that what was primary was not what was written but what was heard.

> For now after the light has gone up and his holy teachings—heard from his holy mouth, may his rest be in Paradise—remain in writing on paper since whoever heard his holy words wrote down his words in written words, each one according to his understanding . . . to warn those who look into and consult the holy writings of the teaching of our holy rabbi, may his rest be in Paradise, to be careful and to be on guard concerning this; especially those who did not hear themselves from his holy mouth. And there is also he who heard but did not understand properly.[56]

For Aaron, the writings per se were not the crucial factor, because everyone wrote according to his own understanding. The question was, did the transmitter understand properly? Understanding is a function of the character of the individual and of his relationship with the zaddik when the words were spoken. Written records were not the essence; correct exposition of the teaching was. This is what Aaron set out to do in his two books, *Sha'ar Ha-Yihud Ve-Ha-Emunah* and *Sha'arei Avodah*.

THE BESHT AS A MODEL

In his struggle against Aaron, Dov Ber took several tacks. He assembled recommendations and testimonials. He disseminated his spiritual platform in the three tracts he circulated in 1813–1814. He published books that would reinforce his ideas and style and at the same time clearly demonstrate that he was authorized to disseminate and interpret his father's teachings.

There was apparently an additional aspect to the contest. It only supplemented the main activities, and on the basis of available sources its existence can only be surmised from circumstantial evidence. It was imperfectly done and may not have had the desired impact. It is important, however, as an illustration of how the Besht's image could be shaped in the service of ideological or political objectives.

Israel Yoffe printed two additional books that were not written by either Rashaz or Dov Ber but that could serve as independent proof texts for Dov Ber's ideas, leadership claims, and religious style. The first book, which came out in the summer or fall of 1814, was *Peri Ha-Aretz*.[57] It included a selection of homilies and letters, mainly from Menahem Mendel of Vitebsk, who had been living in Tiberias in the Land of Israel.

Some of the texts were attributed to Abraham of Kalisk,[58] also in
Tiberias, and Abraham, the Angel, son of the Maggid of Mezerich.[59] Karlinsky has demonstrated that the body of letters in this anthology tends
to reinforce the doctrines and leadership claims of Dov Ber (which ca.
1814 were shared by his brothers).[60] Some of the homilies in the book
also seem to support positions expressed by Dov Ber; for example, that
every generation requires a zaddik, and just one, as its focal point; that
the way to communicate with God is through wonder, deliberation, and
negation of the material; that the leaders must draw close to the common people bogged down in earning their livelihood; that despite the
availability of a famous zaddik, with various honorable qualities, to be
the leader of the group, it is better to remain with a leader who has been
involved with the people from his youth and understands the heart of
each and every one.[61] One passage in particular seems calculated to
make any reader familiar with the history of the relations among Rashaz, Aaron, and Dov Ber sit up and take notice.

> Like the way of a slave who controls all of the wealth of his master and flees
> from his master through all the places in the realm. Wherever he sets his foot
> his master rules. When he says that he is fleeing they torment him and put
> him on trial to determine what is in his heart, whether he will return to his
> evil ways.
>
> But the way of a slave who is the son of his master's maidservant, a slave
> born in his master's house, he certainly will not run away from his master
> and will be his slave forever because he is his slave from the day he was born
> and also his ancestors' way is his own, for his mother was his master's maid-
> servant. This kind of slave will certainly not run away and does not need to
> be tested and tried.[62]

A reader who knew that Aaron was a great scholar who indeed was
at the nerve center of Rashaz's court in Ladi but had come under suspicion and had run away and now sought to take over the leadership
could be expected to think of him as the slave who, once having betrayed
his master, could never again be trusted. Dov Ber, however, was a disciple who was born in his master's house. His father's doctrine was his
birthright, and he would never rebel. If a home-born slave could be
trusted implicitly forever, how much more so a true son?

Peri Ha-Aretz utilized the words of famous zaddikim to support Dov
Ber's doctrines and claims to leadership. The publication of *Shivhei Ha-
Besht*, in my opinion, marked an oblique attempt to use the biography
of the Besht to legitimate Dov Ber's style of leadership and religious behavior. I stress "publication," because as I attempted to demonstrate in

chapter 9, *Shivhei Ha-Besht* was *written* under one set of circumstances and for one set of purposes; it was *printed* in a wholly different context.

The writer's compilation of *Shivhei Ha-Besht* had great polemical potential for the cause of Dov Ber of Lubavitch. Fortuitously, the Besht portrayed in the manuscript of the writer behaved in ways reminiscent of Dov Ber in many respects. Both men began their leadership careers in small villages, far from the mass of Hasidim and in difficult economic circumstances. Both met with initial skepticism from potential followers. Both concentrated more on forming individual relationships with people and helping them solve their problems than on delivering public sermons or developing Talmudic virtuosity. Both traveled to their followers, rather than holding court for a limited elite. Both limited ascetic behavior among their followers and stressed genuine joy as a mode of divine service.

Perhaps the critical parallel between Dov Ber and the Besht of the writer's manuscript was in the area of prayer. In the conflict between Dov Ber and Aaron of Staroszele, one of the key issues was the style of prayer. Was it proper, as Aaron allowed, for prayer to begin with a priori ecstasy induced by artificial techniques of shouting, falling down, making gestures, and so on? Or should prayer be "normal," with ecstasy emerging organically out of the process of establishing a connection with the Divine? Prayer is one of the most common subjects in the original *Shivhei Ha-Besht* compilation, and the material there tends to support Dov Ber's style of prayer.

From the manuscript one could claim that the congregation that prayed with the Besht did not pray in an ecstatic state. For example, one story quotes the Besht as saying, "Anyone who wants his prayer to ascend to heaven should pray word for word with me."[63] It is difficult to imagine that people jumping, yelling, and falling down could pray word by word in a disciplined fashion. The writer, Dov of Ilintsy, claimed that he observed how the Besht's disciple, Jacob Joseph of Polonne, "would always look inside the prayer book and listen to the cantor during the repetition of the Amidah prayer."[64] Once when Abraham Abba, the father of Pinhas of Koretz, prayed in the same synagogue as the Besht, "the Besht was praying in front of the holy ark and [Abraham Abba] was praying in a loud voice; and R. Pinhas was afraid lest, God forbid, [his father] might confuse the Besht and the Besht would scold him."[65] The Besht himself did sometimes cry out, tremble, and pray in ecstasy. But *Shivhei Ha-Besht* always depicts his ecstatic behavior as involuntary rather than calculated and conscious. The compiler cited no less an authority than the

Maggid of Mezerich as saying that the Besht behaved this way when he had attained Divine inspiration and was not in this world.[66]

Moreover, there was one action that the Besht of the manuscript never performed, even at the height of Divine communion: falling down. Dov Ber severely criticized this practice,[67] and the Besht's behavior seems to have backed him up. There is an often-cited story in *Shivhei Ha-Besht* describing how the Besht looked while he was engaged in an "ascent of the soul" to Paradise: "The Besht began to make terrible gestures, and he bent backwards until his head came close to his knees, and everyone feared that he would fall down. . . . He kept this up for about two hours," but never fell.[68]

Another characteristic of prayer in the *Shivhei Ha-Besht* manuscript that seems to echo Dov Ber's style is the need to pray with a broken heart. The Besht publicly humiliated David Purkes on Yom Kippur for this purpose. "I broke your heart so that you would not have any wayward thoughts in your heart and then I ordered you to pray."[69]

The idea that the Besht could serve as a model for spiritual behavior advocated by Dov Ber is not mere speculation. When Dov Ber described the highest state of spirituality that one is to aim for during prayer, he wrote, "Like the Besht when he was engaged in an ascent of the soul, etc., he was stripped of all corporality, like one who faints, and was as if in a trance . . . not feeling any pain or blow."[70] Dov Ber was interested in the Besht as a precedent setter and guide. The manuscript of *Shivhei Ha-Besht* offered an opportunity for developing this interest and utilizing the stories about the Besht as a source of legitimacy. This may explain why *Shivhei Ha-Besht* was published by a Habad Hasid, in 1814, and in White Russia. All three of these facts are rather curious given the origins of the stories.

As Gries has shown, early Hasidism preferred oral tradition, reinforced by manuscripts in the hands of members of the elite, to printed texts.[71] When learning is from storytellers or teachers rather than from books, control over the content of what is learned remains largely with the authoritative elite. The transmitters can easily modify the content to fit changes in doctrine and shape the message to be sure that the audience understands it as deemed desirable. Once content—especially of stories intended to be told orally—is printed, readers gain independence to interpret by their own lights, not always in accord with what the elite wants them to think.[72]

For Israel Yoffe to print these stories, then, was a significant cultural precedent. It meant giving a modicum of power over the content of beliefs to the anonymous reader as well as sacrificing the ability of the leadership to update the stories to match new developments. There must have been a compelling reason, in addition to any commercial incentive, that made this precedent seem worth the concessions it entailed, particularly when we consider that Yoffe was printing stories that had been crystallized some thirty years previously and grew out of a Podolian, not a White Russian, milieu.[73]

Given Yoffe's close ties to Dov Ber, it is reasonable to assume that he (and perhaps Dov Ber himself) understood the value of *Shivhei Ha-Besht* with its potential for legitimation of Dov Ber and many of his ideas. Printing it might affect the climate of opinion during the leadership struggle that was at its height in late 1814 when the book appeared. We should recall that for Yoffe the printer, as opposed to Dov Ber of Ilintsy the writer, the subject of this book was the Besht as leader.[74] In 1814, fifty-four years after the Besht's death, the legitimacy of his leadership and the process by which he rose to it was not a problem. It was not necessary to prove that the Besht was a "faithful shepherd" in his generation. What was necessary to prove was that in the current generation—even after the departure of the great Rashaz—there was no need to despair. If in the past a man like the Besht—even less a priori qualified than Dov Ber of Lubavitch and even more scoffed at by the elite—could arise, it could happen now, too. From the changes that Yoffe introduced into the text of *Shivhei Ha-Besht,* it is apparent that the issue that was on his mind was the legitimacy of Dov Ber as leader of the Hasidim.[75]

The coincidental analogy between Dov Ber and the Ba'al Shem Tov could not be a perfect one. Since the stories and the manuscript took shape long before Dov Ber was a candidate to become the leader of Habad, the original manuscript compilation contained elements that contradicted or ignored essential features of Dov Ber's assertions. Yoffe rearranged some of the stories, added other traditions, and in some places emended the text. The overall result, while not completely consistent, created the general impression that the Besht provided a precedent for Dov Ber's style and ideas. For example, there is one passage concerning the prayer of the Besht and his group that reads in manuscript: "At the morning service the Besht was the cantor and they prayed with great enthusiasm . . . because he would raise them all up and they would all pray with a great shout."[76] This implies that the Besht's followers did pray with shouting and induced ecstasy, something Dov Ber opposed. It is interesting, then, that Yoffe's printed text eliminates the references to the entire congregation shouting "The Besht would pray as the cantor with great enthusiasm . . . because he would raise them all up and he would pray with a great shout."[77]

Another important point in Dov Ber's argument was that he deserved the leadership because he was the son of a great man. In Dov Ber of Ilintsy's manuscript, however, the words "Israel ben [son of] Eliezer" appear in one story only.[78] The only description of the Besht's father in the original collection is a brief mythic story telling how as a sailor he once, by virtue of knowledge revealed to him in a dream, successfully advised his king on how to capture a certain fortress.[79] What was his relationship to the Besht? Did he teach him and prepare him for leadership?

In Yoffe's printed version of *Shivhei Ha-Besht,* Eliezer, the Besht's father, gets much more detailed treatment. Although he was not famous, and certainly not the leader of any recognized group, in Yoffe's version he is at least called "a great zaddik." Like Rashaz, who according to Habad tradition advised Russian officers during the Napoleonic War, Eliezer is presented as a royal adviser. He "set the words in the heart" of his son, just as Dov Ber had claimed his own father had done. The Besht was truly tied to him and remembered his advice. After Eliezer died, people dealt kindly with the young Besht out of respect for his father.[80]

Moreover, while in the two-hundred-odd stories of the writer's manuscript the question of a father bequeathing to a son is raised only once, in the first seventeen stories, added or reedited in the printed edition, the question of a father passing on his spiritual legacy to a son comes up three times. The three father-son pairs introduced by the printer were Eliezer and the Besht, Abraham and Gershon of Kutów, and Rabbi Adam Ba'al Shem and his anonymous son.[81] In the printed version the father-son relationship is a crucial determinant in spiritual training and destiny.

Another point emphasized by Dov Ber, not satisfactorily treated in the manuscript, was the process of acquiring authoritative instruction by which the Besht ascended to leadership. The Besht's father was not a famous zaddik and not generally believed to possess ancient esoteric knowledge. While he may have been the source of the Besht's righteous character, he could not be the source of his knowledge. Thus Yoffe introduced Rabbi Adam Ba'al Shem, whose own son was not worthy of inheriting his writings. Instead, Rabbi Adam passed them on to the Besht. Dov Ber's claim to leadership was based on his close association with his righteous father and the possession of his father's writings. The Besht of the printed version, raised by a righteous father, also rose to greatness on the basis of his possession of the writings and not, as Aaron of Staroszele had claimed, by virtue of what he learned at the feet of Elijah the Prophet.[82]

A fourth problem with the writer's manuscript, from the perspective of a supporter of Dov Ber, was that it gave no clear indication that the Besht was chosen as the leader of the Hasidim of his generation. Nowhere do they anoint him as their leader or even accept him into their group.[83] This would leave Dov Ber without a precedent. In the printed version, however, it states clearly that after the Besht had revealed himself to an important Hasid, "when all the Hasidim and the rabbi heard these things . . . all of them went to his village to invite him to come to town. . . . When they encountered each other they all went to a place in the forest where they made a chair out of the branches of trees. They placed him on the chair and they accepted him as their rabbi. And the Besht taught Torah to them."[84]

God ordains leaders according to the needs of the time; from *Shivhei Ha-Besht* it is possible to understand what a leader of the generation should be like. Reading this book, especially after Yoffe edited it, it was possible for a sympathetic reader to conclude that the background, experiences, and behavior of the Besht were very similar to those of Dov Ber. To the extent that they resembled each other, Dov Ber could be seen not as attempting to initiate a new succession principle but as continuing in the same path as the founder of the movement. The Besht of the printed *Shivhei Ha-Besht* turns out to be a nineteenth-century-style Hasidic leader with a court, whose father was in some sense a zaddik; who possessed authoritative, esoteric writings; who successfully overcame the skepticism of the Hasidim and was accepted as their leader; who did not subscribe to a theory of induced ecstatic prayer for the masses; who believed in the centrality of the individual relationship between rebbe and Hasid; and who eschewed excessive asceticism.

Israel Yoffe edited, modified, and printed *Shivhei Ha-Besht* in such a way that it could be adduced in support of Dov Ber's effort to secure the Habad leadership.[85] It set forth an image of the Besht that was reminiscent of Dov Ber in many ways. This image does not fit the historical data analyzed in previous chapters. It does make the Besht a suitable forerunner for Dov Ber of Lubavitch and nineteenth-century Hasidic zaddikim in general.

THE BESHT AS IDEOLOGICAL EMBLEM

The relative ease with which Yoffe could rework *Shivhei Ha-Besht* to portray the Besht in the style of a nineteenth-century zaddik illustrates the point of departure in the introduction. The historical image of the

Besht has been exceptionally malleable in the service of ideology. With so little in the way of written sources, traditions could be interpreted, shaped, and rewritten to make the Besht conform to the perceived needs of contemporary reality.

As primarily ideological reifications, most descriptions of the Ba'al Shem Tov over the past two hundred years or so tell relatively little about him but very much about the issues confronting Jewish culture in the Western world beginning at the end of the eighteenth century. The Besht has served as a Rorschach test for proponents and opponents of modern Jewish cultural movements, among them Hasidism, Haskalah, liberal Judaism, and Jewish nationalism. They have held him up as a model to be emulated or scorned. In addition, his person has served as a vehicle for non-Jews to express their conceptions of Jews and Judaism. The Besht's life and attributed apothegms have served as proof texts for various ideologies. The hollow left by the lack of sources or by their highly equivocal nature has been filled and shaped by polemicists. They have made available, in the convenient form of a famous personage, a historical precedent for the cultural style they happen to advocate. With continual reinvention, the Ba'al Shem Tov can authoritatively epitomize or serve as a counterpoint to one cultural trend or another.

For example, to the advocate of Enlightenment and rational renewal of Jewish culture, Heinrich Graetz, the Besht embodied the response of the benighted, superstitious eastern European masses to the arid scholasticism of the rabbis. The Besht was an ironic confirmation of the demoralization of traditional rabbinic Judaism that Graetz's hero, Moses Mendelssohn, came to rectify.[86] To the Marxist-nationalist historian Rafael Mahler, the Besht was the defender of the masses against the establishment—just what a popular socialist leader in the Jewish communities of pre–World War II Eastern Europe was supposed to be.[87] For the Conservative (i.e., liberal) rabbi Harold Stern, the Besht was concerned with the best method for bringing the masses close to the service of God and therefore chose as his successor, not the " 'orthodox' but unbending" Jacob Joseph of Polonne, but the Maggid of Mezerich "who was willing to compromise in order to win souls"; one apt description of the ideal Conservative rabbi.[88] For the Habad Hasidic movement, the Besht has continued to serve at various times as a precedent for the legitimacy, activities, and leadership style of the regnant zaddik.[89]

I challenge all of these—and other—images of the Ba'al Shem Tov. By analyzing relatively neglected sources and placing the Besht in context, the boundaries of interpretation have been narrowed. If the description proposed here—of the historical Ba'al Shem Tov as someone who filled a conventional role in an unconventional and impressive manner—is valid, the Besht cannot be considered to be the founder of a populist movement, an opponent of the establishment, a democratic nationalist, a tribune of liberal Judaism, an inventor of a mysticism that was acceptable to the intelligentsia, an archetypical Hasidic zaddik with a court, a rejector of magic and superstition, a symbol of degenerate rabbinic Judaism, or any of a host of other labels that have been applied to him.

The fact that there have been so many attempts to appropriate the Ba'al Shem Tov in the service of ideology and politics is testimony to the power of his image in Jewish collective memory. Perception of Israel Ba'al Shem Tov resonates through the ages and across the Jewish spectrum. The historian's Besht is but one component of the people's Besht—and not necessarily the most interesting one. The historian's Besht is essential, however, for understanding the history of Polish Jewry, Hasidism, and the process by which memory transmutes history to serve culture and society.

Notes

ABBREVIATIONS

AGAD   Archiwum Głowny Akt Dawnych (Central Historical Archive),
            Warsaw

AL   Aaron Horowitz. *Avodat Ha-Levi* (The Levite's Service). Lvov,
            1842–1861

BC   Biblioteka Czartoryskich (Czartoryski Library), Cracow

CSHAU   Central State Historical Archive of Ukraine, Kiev

DME   Moses Ephraim of Sudyłkow. *Degel Mahane Ephraim* (The Flag
            of Ephraim's Camp). Koretz, 1810

EJ   *Encyclopaedia Judaica*. Jerusalem, 1972

EP   G. D. Hundert, ed. *Essential Papers on Hasidism*. New York,
            1991

EW   BC Ewidencja

H   Hebrew

HUS   *Harvard Ukrainian Studies*

JNUL F, R   Jewish National and University Library, Jerusalem: microfilm,
            rare book

KH   Yehoshua Mondshine. "Shnei Ma'asarav Shel Rabeinu Ha-
            Zaken" (The Two Incarcerations of Our Old Master in Light of
            New Documents). *Kerem Habad* 4a (1992): 17–108

l.   letter

LB   Dov Ber Schneersohn. *Likutei Beiurim*. Warsaw, 1868

LJ	M. J. Rosman. *The Lords' Jews*. Cambridge, Mass., 1990
P	Polish
R	Russian
RDSG	*Roczniki dziejów społecznych i gospodarczych* (Journal of Social and Economic History)
RM	Rewizya Miasta (Town Census)
SA	Aaron Horowitz. *Sha'arei Avodah* (Gates of Service). Shklov, 1821
SB	Dov Ber ben Samuel. *Shivhei Ha-Besht* (In Praise of the Ba'al Shem Tov). Trans. and ed. Dan Ben-Amos and Jerome Mintz. Bloomington, Ind., 1970
SBF	*Shivhei Ha-Besht*. Ed. Yehoshua Mondshine. Jerusalem, 1982
SBH	*Shivhei Ha-Besht*. Ed. Avraham Rubinstein. Jerusalem, 1991
SG	*Słownik Polski Geograficzny Królestwa Polskiego* (Geographic Dictionary of the Polish Kingdom). Warsaw, 1880–1902
SH	Hillel Ba'al Shem. *Sefer Ha-Heshek*. Vernadsky Library, Jewish Division, ms. Or 178
SYE	Aaron Horowitz. *Sha'ar Ha-Yihud Ve-Ha-Emunah* (The Gate of Unity and Faith). Shklov, 1820
TB	Babylonian Talmud
U	Ukrainian
Y	Yiddish
YM	Pinhas Katznellenbogen. *Yesh Manhilin* (There are Those Who Bequeath). Ed. I. D. Feld. Jerusalem, 1986

INTRODUCTION

1. M. J. Rosman, "The Quest for the Historical Ba'al Shem Tov," in *Tradition and Crisis Revisited*, ed. B. D. Cooperman (Cambridge, Mass., in press).

2. Ibid. The fame of the Besht has probably outstripped that of any other eighteenth-century Jew. During 1992, "the Ba'al Shem Tov" was mentioned in episodes of two American, popular, commercial television series, *L. A. Law* and *Civil Wars*.

3. See A. Schweitzer, *The Quest of the Historical Jesus* (London, 1956); other examples are Shaka Zulu (D. Golan, "Construction and Reconstruction of Zulu History," Ph.D. dissertation, Hebrew University, Jerusalem, 1988), Saint Martin (C. Stancliffe, *St. Martin and His Hagiographer: History and Miracle in Sulpicius Severus* [Oxford, 1983], and S. Farmer, *Communities of Saint Martin: Legend and Ritual in Medieval Tours* [Ithaca, 1991]), Yohanan ben Zakkai (J. Neusner, *Development of a Legend: Studies on the Traditions Concerning*

Yohanan ben Zakkai [Leiden, 1970], and *A Life of Yohanan ben Zakkai* [Leiden, 1970]). The list could be extended at great length; see chapter 11.

4. E. Bickerman, "Das Messiasgeheimnis und die Komposition des Markusevangeliums," in *Studies in Jewish and Christian History* 3, ed. A. I. Baumgarten, 34–52 (Leiden, 1986); M. Smith, "Prolegomena to a Discussion of Aretalogies, Divine Men, The Gospels and Jesus," *Journal of Biblical Literature* 90 (1971): 174–199; and the bibliographical and methodological discussion in E. P. Sanders, *Jesus and Judaism* (Philadelphia, 1985), 1–58. On parallels between the development of the images of Jesus and those of the Besht, see Rosman, "Quest." On the development of *Shivhei Ha-Besht,* see M. J. Rosman, "The History of a Historical Source" [H], *Zion* 58 (1993): 175–214, and below, chapter 9. Citations from *Shivhei Ha-Besht* will, unless otherwise noted, follow the English translation by D. Ben-Amos and J. Mintz, *In Praise of the Baal Shem Tov* (Bloomington, Ind., 1970), hereafter abbreviated *SB.*

5. With this statement I acknowledge the realm of postmodern, rhetorically self-conscious criticism. Within the limitations of the introduction, this bare mention must suffice. For a summary of the implications of rhetorically self-conscious criticism for historiography, see P. Novick, *That Noble Dream* (Cambridge, 1988), the chapters "The Center Does Not Hold" and "There Was No King in Israel." On the genre of biography and postmodern criticism, see I. B. Nadel, *Biography: Fiction, Fact and Form* (London, 1984), and D. Novarr, *The Lines of Life: Theories of Biography, 1880–1970* (West Lafayette, Ind., 1986), 138–154. For responses by historians to the rhetorical critique, see G. M. Spiegel, "History, Historicism and the Social Logic of the Text," *Speculum* 65 (1990): 59–86; M. Ermath, "Mindful Matters: The Empire's New Codes and the Plight of Modern European Intellectual History," *Journal of Modern History* 57 (1985): 506–527; T. L. Haskell, "The Curious Persistence of Rights Talk in the 'Age of Interpretation,' " *Journal of American History* 74 (1987/1988): 984–1012; T. L. Haskell, "Objectivity Is Not Neutrality: Rhetoric vs. Practice in Peter Novick's *That Noble Dream,*" *History and Theory* 29 (1990): 129–157; J. T. Kloppenberg, "Objectivity and Historicism: A Century of American Historical Writing," *American Historical Review* 94 (1989): 1011–1030; P. Zagorin, "Historiography and Postmodernism: Reconsiderations," *History and Theory* 29 (1990): 263–274. Carlo Ginzburg presented a series of lectures entitled "History, Rhetoric and Proof" in Jerusalem in December 1993. These are scheduled for publication in book form by Mercaz Shazar.

6. See n. 3.

7. Rosman, "Quest."

8. For a critique of contextual explanation, see H. White, *Tropics of Discourse* (Baltimore, 1978), 65–71, and *Metahistory* (Baltimore, 1973), 17–21.

9. Nicholas Zurbrugg, "Samuel Beckett, Deirdre Blair, *Company* and the Art of Bad Biography," in *Reading Life Histories: Griffith Papers on Biography,* ed. James Walter (Canberra, 1981), 8.

10. For example, J. Weiss, "The Beginnings of Hasidism" [H], *Zion* 16 (1951): 46–106; B.-Z. Dinur, *Historical Writings* [H], vol. 1 (Jerusalem, 1954), 181–227; A. Rapoport-Albert, "God and the Zaddik as the Two Focal Points

of Hasidic Worship," in *EP*, 301–314; M. Idel, "Jewish Magic From the Renaissance Period to Early Hasidism," in *Religion, Science and Magic in Concert and in Conflict*, ed. J. Neusner et al. (New York, 1989), 100–106, and, according to the index, "Ba'al Shem Tov" in Idel's *Kabbalah: New Perspectives* (New Haven, 1988); and works in progress by M. Idel, R. Elior, and I. Etkes.

CHAPTER ONE. BA'AL SHEM TOV

1. For summary and analysis of various biographical syntheses of the Besht, see M. J. Rosman, "The Quest for the Historical Ba'al Shem Tov," in *Tradition and Crisis Revisited*, ed. B. D. Cooperman (Cambridge, Mass., in press); on ba'alei shem, see G. Nigal, *Magic, Mysticism and Hasidism* (Northvale, N.J., 1994), 1–31; M. Hillel, *Ba'alei Shem* [H] (Jerusalem, 1993); and below.

2. There are dissenters from this consensus; some, such as A. Z. Aescoly-Weintraub and Y. Schiper, who believed that the Besht was a mythological character; others, like E. Z. Zweifel, who deemphasized his faith healing; see Rosman, "Quest." A. Marcus, *Hasidism* [H] (Benai Berak, 1980), 13, thought he was born in 1690. The 1700 birthdate appears to be a conjecture based on S. M. Dubnow's misreading of the first story in *Shivhei Ha-Besht* ("The Beginnings: The Ba'al Shem Tov [Besht] and the Center in Podolia," in *EP*, 26–27, 51n.4). The "humble origins" postulate is likewise based on uncritical acceptance of *Shivhei Ha-Besht*.

3. Rosman, "Quest."

4. On the proponents of the various answers, see Rosman, "Quest."

5. See n. 9.

6. *Pirkei Avot* 4:17; see also Prov. 23:1 and Eccles. 7:1.

7. See the pioneering nineteenth-century study of Hasidism, E. Z. Zweifel, *Peace Unto Israel* [H], pt. 1, ed. A. Rubinstein (Jerusalem: 1972), 147; and the perennial textbooks, M. L. Margolis and A. Marx, *A History of the Jewish People* (New York, [1927] 1969), 582, and S. Grayzel, *A History of the Jews* (Philadelphia, [1947] 1984), 525. Even the recent M. Mansoor, *Jewish History and Thought: An Introduction* (Hoboken, N.J., 1991), stated "The title *Ba'al Shem Tov* . . . which is given to a person of good reputation who performs miracles and helps others in their hour of need" (p. 340). Other authors translated Ba'al Shem Tov literally but refrained from informing their readers as to the precise meaning of the term, leaving the interpretation ambiguous; see S. Ettinger's section in H. H. Ben Sasson, *History of the Jewish People* (Cambridge, Mass., 1976), 768. See also the popular works M. Aron, *Ideas and Ideals of the Hasidim* (Secaucus, N.J., 1980), 30–31; the widely selling H. Weiner, *9 ½ Mystics: The Kabbala Today* (New York, 1992), 124; and A. Eban, *Heritage: Civilization and the Jews* (Tel Aviv, 1984), 218. A more candid approach was taken by R. M. Seltzer, *Jewish People, Jewish Thought: The Jewish Experience in History* (New York, 1980), 487; and C. Potok, *Wanderings* (New York, 1986), 350.

8. Men and not women. Women with mystical powers were often regarded as witches or possessed. See, for example, *YM*, 97; *SB*, 34–35.

9. Apparently the earliest use of the term "ba'al shem" is in *Sifrei Zuta*: see H. Liberman, *Ohel Rahe"l* (Brooklyn, 1980), 5. On ba'alei shem and ba'al shemism, see Nigal, *Magic*, 1–31; G. Scholem, *EJ* 4:5–7; G. Scholem, "The De-

bate over Hasidism in the Book *Nezed Ha-Dema*" [H], *Zion* 20 (1955): 80; G. Scholem, "The Historical Image of Israel Ba'al Shem Tov" [H], *Molad* 18 (1960): 338; I. Etkes, "The Role of Magic and Ba'alei Shem in Ashkenazic Society in the Late Seventeenth and Early Eighteenth Centuries" [H], *Zion* 60 (1995): 69–104. In the eighteenth century, Jacob Emden spoke of "the art of practical Kabbalah," *Iggeret Purim*, Oxford-Bodleiana MS 2190 (JNUL F 20473), 7a. On the history of Jewish use of divine names for magical and other purposes, see M. Idel, *The Mystical Experience in Abraham Abulafia* (Albany, N.Y., 1988), 14–19.

10. Mircea Eliade, *Shamanism: Archaic Techniques of Ecstasy* (New York, 1964), 4–8, 134–144, 181, 215–216, 259, 297–299; see also P. Brown, "The Rise and Function of the Holy Man in Late Antiquity," in P. Brown, *Society and the Holy in Late Antiquity* (Binghamton, N.Y., 1982), 120–126, 143–147; P. Brown, "The Saint as Exemplar in Late Antiquity," *Representations* 1 (1983): 10, 19; B. M. Bokser, "Wonder-Working and the Rabbinic Tradition: The Case of Hanina Ben Dosa," *Journal for the Study of Judaism* 16 (1985): 42–92.

11. Eliade, *Shamanism*, 5, 8, 140–141, 143, 145–179, 299, 331.

12. Many, but not all. For example, ba'alei shem did not wear a special costume. This is not surprising, because Eliade was creating an ideal type, and he himself spoke of the independent nature of the the various manifestations of shamanism. In modern Europe he described the "vestiges" of shamanism in non-shamanistic religions (ibid., 376–377). This would seem to describe accurately the situation in early modern Judaism.

13. Hebrew: *kefitzot ha-derekh*, i.e., travel from one place to another in a fraction of the time normally required; see Nigal, *Magic*, 33–49.

14. Found among Jewish mystics in the sixteenth century: see Nigal, *Magic*, 18–19, 24; L. Fine, "The Art of Metoposcopy: A Study in Isaac Luria's Charismatic Knowledge," *Association for Jewish Studies Review* 11 (1986): 79–101, esp. 82–83. This accretion of elements illustrates Eliade's principle that shamanism is often combined with other magical techniques (*Shamanism*, 5).

15. YM, 96.

16. The report (Nachricht) of the authorities describing the circumstances of Rabbi Frankel's accusation and incarceration has been published by G. Nigal, together with a Hebrew introduction, *A Ba'al Shem Condemned to Life Sentence: The Tragedy of R. Hirsch Frankel* [H] (Ramat Gan, 1993).

17. Ibid., introduction, 18–19; Nachricht text, 12, 14. See also ba'alei shem stories collected by Hillel, *Ba'alei Shem*.

18. J. Emden, *Beit Yehonatan Sofer, Sifrei Pulmus*, vol. 2, ed. B. Agorek (New York, n.d.), 7b, 9b; see also Nigal, *Magic*, 17–19; on Eybeschuetz's biography and importance, see G. Scholem, *EJ* 6:1074–1076.

19. See *Encyclopaedia Judaica* in German (Berlin, 1928–1932), series of articles on various ba'alei shem, 3:828–841; Nigal, *Magic*, 11–24; C. Roth, "The King and the Cabalist," in C. Roth, *Essays and Portraits in Anglo-Jewish History* (Philadelphia, 1962), 139–164. While preparing this book for publication in Kiev, I was made aware of a handbook for ba'alei shem called *Sefer Ha-Heshek*, written by Hillel Ba'al Shem, a Polish Jew, after 1739 (hereafter abbreviated *SH*). This 300-page manuscript (Or 178) was discovered by Yohanan Petrovsky several years ago in the Vernadsky Library. It is the most extensive

exposition of ba'al shem techniques and experiences that I know of. My thanks to Dr. Petrovsky and his assistant Natan Hazine for sharing their find with me.

20. Dubnow, "Beginnings," 31–32; I. Zinberg, *A History of Jewish Literature*, vol. 9 (Cincinnati, 1976), 34; R. Mahler, *A History of Modern Jewry* (London, 1971), 456; E. Wiesel, *Souls on Fire* (New York, 1972), 16; Liberman, *Ohel Rahe"l* , 17.

21. Eliade, *Shamanism*, 297.

22. Nigal, *Life Sentence*, introduction, 15; Nachricht text, 12.

23. Nigal, *Magic*, 12–13; Scholem, "Image," 338; M. Piekarz, *The Beginning of Hasidism* [H] (Jerusalem, 1978), 137.

24. See the texts of these letters in chapters 6 and 7. Polish sources also refer to him simply as Ba'al Shem; see chapter 10.

25. See chapters 6 through 10; see also M. Idel, "Jewish Magic from the Renaissance Period to Early Hasidism," in *Religion, Science, and Magic: In Concert and In Conflict*, ed. J. Neusner et al. (New York, 1989), 100–108.

26. Dubnow, "Beginnings," 31–32; J. Weiss, *Studies in Eastern European Jewish Mysticism* (Oxford, 1985), 10–14; J. Weiss, "The Beginnings of Hasidism" [H], *Zion* 16 (1951): 54–56. See also Liberman, *Ohel Rahe"l*, 3–5.

27. Dubnow, "Beginnings," 32; Zweifel, *Peace Unto Israel*, 147. This view also apparently was the organizing principle for the stories in *SB* that loosely trace the pattern of the Besht's gradual acceptance as he proves that he is not merely a ba'al shem; see discussion below.

28. B.-Z. Dinur, "The Origins of Hasidism and Its Social and Messianic Foundations," in *EP*, 125–159; Weiss, "Beginnings," 56–58; K. Shmeruk, "The Hasidic Movement and the 'Arendars' " [H], *Zion* 35 (1970): 185–192.

29. *SB*, 173–174.

30. These names are vocalized according to the way they appear in the Polish documents, EW 41 (see chap. 10) and not as they appear in the *SB* English translation; see *SB*, 173.

31. See Eliade's inclusion of psychopomp among the features of the shaman's role (*Shamanism*, 4).

32. Piekarz, *Hasidism*, 136–137.

33. Nigal, *Magic*, 13–16, and *Life Sentence*. Hillel, *Ba'alei Shem*, collected stories about three additional ba'alei shem: Elijah of Worms, the aforementioned Joel of Zamość, and Adam of Ropshitz. Hillel Ba'al Shem also singled out Joel and Elijah as well as Heschel, Peretz, Jacob, and Naphtali Katz—all called "Ba'al Shem"; see *SH* 154b, 277a.

34. Nigal, *Magic*, 15–22.

35. See A. Rubinstein, "On the Status of Ba'alei Shem" [H], *Alei Sefer* 6–7 (1979): 184–186, whose contentions fall away in light of Nigal's and Hillel's findings; see also chapter 7, the Besht's letter to Moses of Kutów, which shows that the Besht's healing abilities lay the foundation for his relationship with this distinguished rabbi and mystic. Hillel Ba'al Shem, although itinerant, also had good relations with various rabbis and communal leaders, including Dr. Isaac Fortis, head of the Council of Four Lands, who taught him medical knowledge. See *SH* 11b, 27b, 42b, 84a, 98b, 126a, and passim.

36. Z. Gries, *Conduct Literature: Its History and Place in the Life of Besht-*

ian Hasidism [H] (Jerusalem, 1989), introduction and pp. 45, 82–83, 90–92, 98–102.

37. Ibid.; see also T. Kohn, *Ma'aseh Tuviah* (Venice, 1707), 110d. Thomas Hubka's work in progress on the architecture, design, and decoration of eighteenth-century wooden synagogues implies that these buildings gave the general public access to the more popular aspects of mysticism; see M. Idel, "Perceptions of Kabbalah in the Second Half of the Eighteenth Century," *Journal of Jewish Thought and Philosophy* 1 (1991): 76–79.

38. J. Elbaum, *Openness and Insularity* [H] (Jerusalem, 1990), 184, 219, 353, and passim.

39. See S. Maimon, *Autobiography,* trans. J. C. Murray (London, 1954), 71–80, for a description of how he took up Kabbalistic studies under the tutelage of the preacher—not the rabbi—of his community.

40. Unfortunately, this manuscript, *Imrei Binah* (Sayings of Understanding), has been missing from the JNUL since 1984; we are dependent on a brief summary by A. Y. Brawer, "A New Hebrew Source on the History of the Frankists" [H], *Ha-Shiloah* 33 (1918): 152.

41. Printed in Izmir in 1731–1732, it was apparently a crypto-Sabbatean text. See A. Ya'ari, *The Mystery of a Book* [H] (Jerusalem, 1954); I. Tishbi, "Sources of *Hemdat Ha-Yamim*" [H], *Tarbiz* 25 (1955): 66–92; I. Tishbi, "Early Eighteenth-Century Sources in *Hemdat Yamim*" [H], *Tarbiz* 25 (1956): 202–230; Y. Liebes, "New Light on the Matter of the Besht and Shabbetai Zvi" [H], *Jerusalem Studies in Jewish Thought* 2 (1983): 568–569; see also *SB,* 85, where Jacob Joseph purchases this book and the Besht considers it to be contaminated, evidently because of its Sabbateanism.

42. *YM,* 74. Rovigo made at least three trips to Germany; see G. Scholem, *EJ* 14:356. Pinhas stated that he was 12 or 13 at the time of this incident. Perhaps his memory was not accurate and he was only 11.

43. E. Reiner, "Wealth, Social Position, and the Study of Torah: The Status of the Kloyz in Eastern European Jewish Society in the Early Modern Period" [H], *Zion* 58 (1993): 298–299, 309n.51, 323–326.

44. *YM,* 74; see also G. Scholem, *The Dreams of Mordecai Ashkenazi the Sabbatean* [H] (Jerusalem, 1938).

45. *YM,* 392.

46. See Eliade, *Shamanism,* 110, and *SB,* which has the Besht learning the secrets, indirectly, from various sources, some human, some supernatural. See my analysis in M. J. Rosman, "The History of a Historical Source: On the Editing of *Shivhei Ha-Besht*" [H], *Zion* 58 (1993): 200–201, and Nigal, *Magic,* 27–28. Hillel Ba'al Shem learned his skills mainly from esoteric manuscripts and from Zvi Hirsh ben Abraham of Mezerich; *SH* 117b–118b, 119b, and passim

47. R. Michael, *EJ* 10:828; *YM,* 15–16.

48. *YM,* 88–89, 95–99, 107–108. Another example of a prominent person using a ba'al shem is documented in Emden, *Iggeret Purim* (JNUL F 20473), 7b: "a wealthy person among men, the intimate of the nobleman, Moses Kadainer"; see also *SB,* 48–49.

49. Nigal, *Magic,* 11, 223n.61.

50. Earlier Katznellenbogen had called him "a great ba'al shem."

51. *YM*, 107–108; Katznellenbogen reported that he never actually used this remedy but substituted a different one involving placing names on the woman's forehead, which turned out to be effective. *SH* contains a huge number of techniques for ensuring an easy birth, e.g., 10a–b, 11a, 32a, 46a.

52. *YM*, 11.

53. In fact, what he felt he had to explain was his grandfather's admonition *not* to deal in the holy names. It was the refraining from practical Kabbalah that must be justified, not its use; see below.

54. See Eliade, *Shamanism*, 297, on the discreteness of the shaman category as distinct from other religious figures: priest, sorcerer. Rabbi and ba'al shem, while often combined in one person, were two separate roles. With regard to the rabbi consulting the ba'al shem, Emden, *Iggeret Purim* (JNUL F 20473), 7b, claimed that his enemy Eybeschuetz encouraged people to believe in and consult ba'alei shem. The question of Eybeschuetz's crypto-Sabbateanism aside, this would seem to be another example of peaceful coexistence and even symbiosis between rabbis and ba'alei shem. See also chapter 7, near n. 51.

55. It is noteworthy that Rabbi Katznellenbogen accorded both Benjamin Beinish of Krotoshin and Joel Halpern great respect. These men were singled out by Scholem ("Image," 338) as "ba'alei shem of the magical, 'scorned' type." Scholem was of the opinion that there were two types of ba'alei shem, spiritualist (respectable) and magical (disreputable). He brought no proof for this distinction. Rabbi Katznellenbogen's respect for the very two men that Scholem brought as examples of the disreputable type of ba'alei shem indicates that Scholem's distinction does not hold. He may have been influenced by later, rationalistically tinged ideas about ba'alei shem, similar to Nahum of Chernobyl's 1798 comment that the Besht used only Kabbalistic prayers and not theurgic formulas or tools to effect his cures (Scholem, "Image," 341) and Shneur Zalman of Ladi's opinion, expressed in 1798, that the magical practices employed in an earlier generation are mistakenly called Kabbalah (*KH*, 50). While this may have been considered a mistake in 1798 or in 1960, there was obviously a time when practitioners of practical Kabbalah were considered by at least some as bona fide Kabbalists (see, however, A. Green, "Typologies of Leadership and the Hasidic Zaddiq," in *Jewish Spirituality*, vol. 2, ed. A. Green [New York, 1987], 154n.7). If Rabbi Katznellenbogen is representative of such "believers" in the early eighteenth century then it is difficult to claim that the elite would have nothing to do with magical ba'alei shem.

56. Piekarz, *Hasidism*, 137. Hillel Ba'al Shem also complained about ba'al shem imposters; *SH* 94b, 155, 171a, and passim.

57. See sources adduced by Nigal, *Magic*, 2–4, 10; on Shneur Zalman of Habad, see *KH*, 50, 88.

58. Nigal, *Magic*, 29–31, 230–231.

59. Ibid., 225n.84.

60. *Iggeret Purim* (JNUL F 20473), 7a–b. Emden's critique here seems to parallel that of Dov of Bolechow in the second half of the eighteenth century, when he called ba'alei shem "swindlers who defraud people and threaten them with demons and gremlins," cited by Brawer, "Frankists," 152.

61. On the controversy that raged between these two men, see J. J. Schacter, "Rabbi Jacob Emden," Ph.D. dissertation, Harvard University, 1988, 370–498.

62. *Iggeret Purim* (JNUL F 20473), 7b.

63. Ibid., 7b; on the relationship between the Ba'al Shem of London, Samuel Hayyim Falk, and the pretender to the Corsican throne, Theodore de Neuhoff, see Roth, "The King and the Cabalist," 139–164.

64. Y. Liebes, " 'Two Young Roes of a Doe': The Secret Sermon of Isaac Luria Before His Death" [H], *Jerusalem Studies in Jewish Thought* 10 (1992): 129. For defense by a ba'al shem against his critics, see *Mifalot Elokim* (Zolkiew, 1725), endorsement of Joel Ba'al Shem and introduction of the anonymous compiler. This source and its interpretation were raised by H. Pedaya, "On the Development of the Social-Cultural-Economic Model of Hasidism: The *Pidyon*, the *Havurah* and the Pilgrimage" [H], in *Religion and Economics*, ed. M. Ben Sasson (Jerusalem, 1994), near nn. 77–80.

65. Nigal, *Magic*, 4, 10, 230n.150.

66. J. Wistinetzki and J. Freimann, eds., *Sefer Hasidim* (Jerusalem, 1969), 76.

67. *YM*, 89.

68. Ibid., 87–95.

69. Ibid., 96–99.

70. Ibid., 101.

71. For another example of a seventeenth- to eighteenth-century Ashkenazic family (in Poland) in which the interest in Kabbalah apparently increased with the generations, see the chronicle of Judah ben Nisan Katz, Y. Jacobson Collection MS microfilm JNULF 31652. Judah's father downplayed the prophetic significance of dreams, while he and his sister took dreams very seriously. Rachel's request is in *YM*, p. 101. In Podolia, too, it seems that by the 1740s physicians were in demand; see BC 5965 l.42850 Szumanczowski to Szuwalski 4/9/1745, where the writer praises Dr. Karol Fryzon's activities in Husiatyn and wants to arrange for him to visit Satanów to treat patients there as well. *SB* portrays the Besht in competition with doctors. On the purpose of the stories that do so in the collection itself, see Rosman, "Source," 213–214.

Hillel Ba'al Shem, writing in the mid-eighteenth century, showed respect for doctors and medicine and combined medical cures he learned from doctors with his magical practices. *SH* 6a, 11b, 12a, 13b, 21a, and passim.

72. See Hillel Ba'al Shem's story about the hesitations on the part of some people in Ostróg to employ him. In the end the kahal issued a formal request that he conduct an exorcism. *SH* 126a–b.

CHAPTER TWO. HASIDISM BEFORE HASIDISM

1. See Pinhas Katznellenbogen's description of how the "hasidim" in Fürth received Abraham Rovigo in 1701: *YM*, 74, and chap. 1, near n. 42.

2. Heinrich Graetz, *History of the Jews*, vol. 5 (Philadelphia, 1967), 374–375; S. M. Dubnow, *History of Hasidism* [H] (Tel Aviv, 1975), 1–8; see, for the newer view, G. Scholem, *Major Trends in Jewish Mysticism* (New York, 1961), 345–346, and I. Etkes, *From Esoteric Circle to Mass Movement: The Emergence of*

Early Hasidism, vols. 9–10 of *Polin—The Jews of Eastern Europe: History and Culture* [H] (Tel Aviv, 1991), 42–44.

3. For etymological history of the word *hasid*, see E. Ben-Yehuda, *Dictionary of the Old and New Hebrew Language* [H], vol. 3 (Tel Aviv, 1948), 1666–1668; see also L. Jacobs, "The Concept of *Hasid* in the Biblical and Rabbinic Literatures," *Journal of Jewish Studies* 7 (1957): 143–154.

4. 1 Maccabees 2:42; see V. Tcherikover, *Hellenistic Civilization and the Jews*, trans. S. Applebaum (Philadelphia, 1966), 196–198.

5. I. Marcus, *Piety and Society: The Jewish Pietists of Medieval Germany* (Leiden, 1981).

6. S. Schechter, *Studies in Judaism* (New York, 1958), 259–260; R. J. Z. Werblowsky, *Joseph Karo: Lawyer and Mystic* (Oxford, 1962), 38–83; R. J. Z. Werblowsky, "The Safed Revival and Its Aftermath," in *Jewish Spirituality II: From the Sixteenth-Century Revival to the Present*, ed. A. Green (New York, 1987), 7–33; D. Tamar, *Studies on the History of the Jews in the Land of Israel and in Italy* [H] (Jerusalem, 1973), 95–100; L. Fine, *Safed Spirituality* (New York, 1984), 10–16, 27–80; A. J. Heschel, *The Circle of the Ba'al Shem Tov*, ed. and trans. S. H. Dresner (Chicago, 1985), 83–87.

7. S. Assaf, "Letters from Safed" [H], *Kovetz Al Yad* 3(13), pt. 1 (1939): 122–133; cf. Z. Gries, "From Mythos to Ethos: An Outline of the Image of R. Abraham of Kalisk" [H], in *Uma Ve-Toldoteha*, ed. S. Ettinger, vol. 2 (Jerusalem, 1984), 122–125; E. Reiner, "Wealth, Social Position, and the Study of Torah: The Status of the Kloyz in Eastern European Jewish Society in the Early Modern Period" [H], *Zion* 58 (1993): 291–294.

8. M. Idel, *Studies in Ecstatic Kabbalah* (Binghamton, N.Y., 1988), 103–106, 141n.5; Marcus, *Pietists*, 15–16; J. Katz, *Halakha and Kabbalah* [H] (Jerusalem, 1984), 197–198; Reiner, "Wealth," 323; J. G. Weiss, "A Circle of Pneumatics in Pre-Hasidism," in J. G. Weiss, *Studies in Eastern European Jewish Mysticism*, ed. D. Goldstein (Oxford, 1985), 27–42; Heschel, *Circle of the Ba'al Shem Tov*, 113–117. Y. Liebes, "How Was the Zohar Written?" [H], *Jerusalem Studies in Jewish Thought* 8 (1989): 5–8, has posited that it was a group of mystics who produced the Zohar; see also M. Idel, *Kabbalah: New Perspectives* (New Haven, 1988), 215, 380.

9. J. Elbaum, *Repentence and Self-Flagellation in the Writings of the Sages of Germany and Poland, 1348–1648* [H] (Jerusalem, 1993), 40–53, 80–93, 172–176, 231; I. Abrahams, *Hebrew Ethical Wills* (Philadelphia, 1976), 289–294; Reiner, "Wealth," 323; I. Zinberg, *A History of Jewish Literature*, vol. 6 (Cincinnati, 1975), 155–158.

10. This difference had far-reaching ramifications for the different organization, membership, function, and status of the two institutions; see Reiner, "Wealth," 285–328.

11. Ibid., 312–313, 323–326; Weiss, *Studies*, 27–42; B.-Z. Dinur, "The Origins of Hasidism and Its Social and Messianic Foundations," in *EP*, 159–172; M. J. Rosman, "Międzybóż and Rabbi Israel Ba'al Shem Tov," in *EP*, 219. (In light of Reiner's work, it is clear that what is being described is the bet midrash, not the kloyz, of Międzybóż; see Reiner, "Wealth," 304).

12. *YM*, 85. From Talmudic times, a twenty-four-hour waiting period was considered to be the strict standard; for most people the practice was to wait six hours between meat and milk and half an hour or even less between milk and meat; see TB *Hullin* 105a.

13. On the various penitential techniques, see Elbaum, *Repentence,* according to the index.

14. See Reiner, "Wealth," 324, on how in groups in outlying small towns the enthusiastic pietism often outstripped the erudition; also compare the behavior of Ber of Bolechow and his fellows in Tysmienica: A. Y. Brawer, "A New Hebrew Source on the History of the Frankists" [H], *Ha-Shiloah* 33 (1918): 152, and chap. 1, near nn. 40–41.

15. S. Maimon, *Autobiography,* trans. J. C. Murray (London, 1954), 81–83.

16. For descriptions of these groups and the behavior of their members in Poland, see sources in nn. 9 and 11, and *KH,* 46, 95; and Y. Hisdai, " 'Eved Ha-Shem' (Servant of the Lord) in Early Hasidism" [H], *Zion* 47 (1982): 258–266, 290–292.

17. Reiner, "Wealth," 320–326; G. Scholem, "Two Testimonies about Hasidic Groups and the Besht" [H], *Tarbiz* 20 (1949): 231–238.

18. *YM,* 75–78.

19. As moreh zedek, he would have had a say in shehita, but only when asked by either the patron or the ritual slaughterer, and his decision could always be appealed to the rabbi.

20. K. Shmeruk, "The Social Significance of Hasidic Ritual Slaughtering" [H], *Zion* 20 (1955): 47–72; I. Kuperstein, "Inquiry at Polaniec: A Case Study of a Hasidic Controversy in Eighteenth-Century Galicia," *Bar Ilan* 24–25 (1989): 27–38; see also *SB* stories involving shohetim, s.v. Index, "shohetim."

21. *YM,* 75–78.

22. *Toldot Ya'acov Yosef* (Koretz, 1780), Parshat Naso, 123a; Y. Hisdai, "The Emergence of Hasidim and Mitnagdim in the Light of the Homiletic Literature" [H], Ph.D. dissertation, Hebrew University, Jerusalem, 1984, 149–157.

23. *Toldot Ya'acov Yosef,* 123a.

24. S. H. Dresner, *The Zaddik* (New York, 1960), 56; G. Nigal, *Leader and Followers* [H] (Jerusalem, 1962), 14–15.

25. Hisdai, "Emergence"; see also M. Piekarz, *The Beginning of Hasidism* [H] (Jerusalem, 1978), 391–392.

26. *SB,* 173–174; see chap. 1, near nn. 29–30.

27. See chapter 7 for the analysis of the Besht's letter to him.

28. *SB,* 156.

29. On the development of the eighteenth-century hasidic havurot, see H. Pedaya, "On the Development of the Social-Religious-Economic Model of Hasidism: The *Pidyon,* the *Havurah* and the Pilgrimage" [H], in *Religion and Economics,* ed. M. Ben Sasson (Jerusalem, 1994), near nn. 42–60; Gries, "From Mythos to Ethos," 117–146.

30. Maimon was born in Lithuania into a traditional Polish Jewish family and went through the conventional stages of life: intensive Talmudic-style education, arranged marriage, fatherhood as an adolescent. In his teenage years,

however, he lost his faith and rebelled, abandoning his wife and child and traveling to Germany. There he attached himself to Enlightenment circles, studied philosophy, did some writing, and died at the age of 46. He wrote his autobiography, which included several chapters on his life in Poland. While reflecting the bias of a renegade and written for the non-Jewish German reader, it is a valuable description of eighteenth-century Jewish life in Poland-Lithuania.

31. S. Maimon, "On a Secret Society," in *EP*, 11–12.

32. On the contemporaneity of new- and old-style hasidic groups and the conflicts between them, see Dinur, "Origins," 159–172; I. Etkes, "Hasidism as a Movement—The First Stage," in *Hasidism: Continuity or Innovation?* ed. B. Safran (Cambridge, Mass., 1988), 5–6; I. Etkes, "The Gaon of Vilna and Early Opposition to Hasidism," in *Transition and Change in Modern Jewish History: Essays Presented in Honor of Shmuel Ettinger* [H], ed. S. Almog et al. (Jerusalem, 1987), 457. An example of the weakness of the opposition to the Hasidim among the nonhasidic component of a mainstream community is Pinsk. M. Nadav, *Pinsk* [H] (Tel Aviv, 1973), 187–193, concludes that opposition to the Hasidim in Pinsk came about mainly as a result of pressure from the Gaon and his associates in Vilna.

33. *KH*, 17–18, 21–23; Dubnow, *Hasidism*, 269–275.

34. For the first interrogation the original Hebrew is available, including facsimile; for the second, the existing text is mostly the Russian translation of the zaddik's Hebrew answer, retranslated into Hebrew; see *KH*, 42–60, 79–100.

35. *KH*, 43, question 3.

36. Ibid., 46–47, 95, 98–99.

37. At one point, Shneur Zalman did seem to praise asceticism, but his definition of asceticism for his age was that the foundation of a person's feelings of fear or joy should be his relationship to God and not the mundane experiences or instinct that normally give rise to these feelings; ibid., 90.

38. Etkes, "Gaon of Vilna," 439–458; see also Dubnow, *Hasidism*, 108–110, 114–115, 243–254; *KH*, 162–221. Etkes, basing himself on contemporary evidence originating from the opposition camp as well as on letters written years later by Shneur Zalman, takes the view that the Gaon was the initiator and orchestrater of the opposition to the Hasidim in Vilna and throughout the Polish-Lithuanian Commonwealth. Mondshine, arguing that many of the Mitnagdic sources are demonstrably false and therefore all are suspect, primarily uses Hasidic sources to contend that while the Gaon was clearly opposed to the Hasidim, his opposition (1) was relatively moderate and (2) was due to his being misled by others who brought him false reports about the group. Since he led such a reclusive lifestyle, he was in no position to investigate the truth for himself. Moreover, being financially dependent on the kahal, he would have followed their lead. In my view, Mondshine fails to provide a convincing reason for why the kahal would want to persecute the Hasidim. His hypothesis is that in the Polish partition period, with the kahal rapidly losing power, it had to strike out in unconventional ways at any threat to its authority. However, there is no evidence that it struck out in conventional ways before the 1770s or that the Hasidim were ever perceived as a political threat. All of the accusations leveled at them concern observance and ritual—the purview of the rabbis—not questions of taxa-

tion or order, the purview of the kahal. Even Shneur Zalman associated opposition to the prayers of the Hasidim with the rabbis who were appointed by the Polish noblemen, not with the *kehalim*, or lay leadership. Moreover, none of the sources adduced by Mondshine indicates that the kahal was primarily responsible for the persecution. Those who supposedly presented the "false" evidence to the Gaon were those close to him, not kahal officials. As to the intensity of the Gaon's opposition, Mondshine's Hasidic sources may have been interpreting the Gaon's gestures in a manner common to persecuted minority groups, which tend to assume that the supreme authority would support them if only he was not led astray by his evil advisers. (Before the Gaon's death the Hasidim were spreading rumors that he had indeed changed his opinion about them; see B. D. Weinryb, *The Jews of Poland: A Social and Economic History of the Jewish Community in Poland from 1100 to 1800* [Philadelphia, 1973], 289–290.) It seems more likely that Etkes, who in addition to the Mitnagdic sources that Mondshine disqualifies, reinforces his thesis with citations from Shneur Zalman, is correct. It makes sense that the opposition to the Hasidim, who were fundamentally a religious phenomenon, stemmed from religious authorities who disapproved of them. We need to know more about the relationship of the Gaon to the kahal and the nature of his public role and activities. It should be emphasized that Mondshine agrees that the Gaon was opposed to the Hasidim (even if his opposition was misguided) and admits that "the persecutions of the Hasidim could not have continued if the Gaon had published his opinion that they should be stopped" (*KH*, 197). These concessions reduce his argument with Etkes to the issue of whether the Gaon naively allowed himself to be exploited by the kahal authorities. Given the evidence for the Gaon's intelligence, independence of mind, and stubbornness, this seems most unlikely.

39. For this and similar stories, see B. Landau, *The Gaon and Hasid of Vilna* [H] (Jerusalem, 1968), 18–19 and passim. On the Gaon's devotion to study and the reasons for it, see I. Etkes, *Rabbi Israel Salanter and the Mussar Movement* (Philadelphia, 1993), 17–18, 23–27.

40. Only late sources assign a comment about the Besht to the Gaon, which others attribute to Hayyim of Volozhin's other teacher, Aryeh Leib ben Asher; see *KH*, 183, and G. Scholem, "The Historical Image of Israel Ba'al Shem Tov" [H], *Molad* 18 (1960): 343.

41. For this type of contrast, see, e.g., S. Grayzel, *A History of the Jews* (Philadelphia: [1947] 1984), 521–533; M. L. Margolis and A. Marx, *A History of the Jewish People* (New York, 1969), 582–583, 586–588; or compare I. Zinberg's description of the Gaon as a "fanatical zealot who bowed down before every dead letter of the written law," with his assessment of the "real form" of the Besht, "remarkably beautiful in its harmonious integrity and glorious simplicity" (*A History of Jewish Literature*, vol. 6 [Cincinnati, 1975], 229; vol. 9 [Cincinnati, 1976], 34).

42. I. Klausner, *Vilna: Jerusalem of Lithuania, Generations from 1495 to 1881* [H] (Kibbutz Lohamei Ha-Gettaot, Israel, 1988), 75–77, has a general summary; Landau, *Gaon*, brings citations and references; see also H. H. Ben Sasson, "The Personality of the Vilna Gaon and His Historical Influence" [H], *Zion* 31 (1966): 39–86, and Etkes, *Salanter*, 17–29.

43. *SB*, 50–51.

44. Eulogy by the Gaon's son Abraham, *Sa'arat Eliyahu* (The Storm of Elijah) (Warsaw, 1877), 7b–8a.

45. Introduction by the Gaon's sons to *Bei'ur Orah Hayyim* (Commentary to Orah Hayyim) (Shklov, 1803).

46. On the differences and similarities between a bet midrash and a kloyz, see above, near and in n. 10.

47. Etkes, *Salanter*, 17–20; Landau, *Gaon*, chap. 4.

48. A. J. Heschel, *The Circle of the Ba'al Shem Tov*, ed. and trans. S. H. Dresner (Chicago, 1985), 11.

49. Etkes, *Salanter*, 23–29.

50. Ibid., 27–29; see also Ben Sasson, "Gaon"; Klausner, *Gaon*.

51. Karlin was a suburb of Pinsk and an important early center of Hasidism. It was from there that Hasidim came to Vilna; see W. Z. Rabinowitsch, *Lithuanian Hasidism* (New York, 1971), 107–120; Nadav, *Pinsk*, 187–193, 206–209. For critiques of Hasidim by Mitnagdim, see M. Wilensky, *Hasidim and Mitnagdim* [H], 2 vols. (Jerusalem, 1970).

52. *KH*, 47–48n.23.

53. See, for examples of crisis and response analysis, Graetz, *History*, 5:374–375, 394; Dubnow, *Hasidism*, 35–36; Scholem, *Major Trends*, 327–334; Dinur, "Origins," 95–98; but see S. Ettinger, "The Hasidic Movement—Reality and Ideals," in *EP*, 229–230; Etkes, "Stage," 2–5.

54. See chap. 1, near n. 36.

55. M. Buber, *The Origin and Meaning of Hasidism*, trans. and ed. M. Friedman (Atlantic Highlands, N.J., 1988), 24; Scholem, *Major Trends*, 337–344; Scholem, *The Messianic Idea in Judaism* (New York, 1971), 208–209, 231; Gries, "From Mythos to Ethos"; N. Loewenthal, *Communicating the Infinite* (Chicago, 1990), 1–6; see also Ettinger, "Reality and Ideals," 231. Interestingly, Hubka (in an article entitled "The Eighteenth-Century Interior Domed Wooden Synagogues of Eastern Europe: The Art and Architecture of a Pre-Hasidic Culture," scheduled for publication in *Polin*) finds that by the nineteenth century, when Hasidism had taken root, the elaborate and mythological-style decoration of Polish synagogues fell into desuetude. Could this be because the aural-oral approach had replaced the visual? Had the zaddik's promise of direct access to the esoteric made the art, which is only a reminder of the mystical profundities, obsolete as a spiritual tool? See M. Idel, "Perceptions of Kabbalah in the Second Half of the Eighteenth Century," *Journal of Jewish Thought and Philosophy* 1 (1991): 97–103.

56. During his incarceration, Shneur Zalman was interrogated concerning his activities. In his testimony he was attempting to avoid further punishment, so it can be expected that his answers were pitched to the message that he assumed his interlocutors wanted to hear. Still, his answers contained the raw material of truth as he understood it. Careful reading and analysis can penetrate to what he, a leading exponent of Hasidism in his day, regarded as the key features of the movement.

57. *KH*, 48–50, 62, 74, 81, 95.

58. Ibid., 81. In several other passages of his testimonies, Shneur Zalman alluded to his use of Kabbalah when preaching to general audiences. He also was

liberal in allowing formal study of Kabbalah: "He knows one famous book of one of the great Kabbalists, printed now (evidently Moses Cordovero, *Or Ne'erav* [Koretz, 1786]) which he permits people to begin studying from the age of twenty" (*KH*, 81n.3).

59. Ibid., 95.

60. Ibid., 49–50.

61. Ibid., 89.

62. Ibid., 50; see also what Shneur Zalman had to say about the practical Kabbalah of the Besht, ibid., 88.

63. Ibid., 88.

64. See n. 61.

65. Scholem, *Major Trends*, 342, 346; Scholem, "*Devekut*, or Communion with God," in *EP*, 275–298; K. Shmeruk, "The Hasidic Movement and the 'Arendars' " [H], *Zion* 35 (1970): 185–186. See also A. Rapoport-Albert, "God and the Zaddik as the Two Focal Points of Hasidic Worship," in *EP*, 299–329; I. Etkes, "Trends in the Study of the Hasidic Movement" [H], *Jewish Studies* 31 (1991): 18.

CHAPTER THREE. A COUNTRY IN DECLINE?

1. This is the thrust of Martin Buber's portrayal, which despite his disclaimer—"But the life about which we shall learn here is not what one ordinarily calls the real life"—has had tremendous influence on the popular perception of the Besht's biography; see M. Buber, *The Legend of the Ba'al Shem* (New York, 1969). The quote is on p. 9.

2. B. D. Weinryb, *The Jews of Poland: A Social and Economic History of the Jewish Community in Poland from 1100 to 1800* (Philadelphia, 1972), 262–269, concentrated on a questionable comparison of the Besht and Hasidism with Jacob Frank and Frankism, rather than relating the Besht and his activities to the socioeconomic context. S. M. Dubnow, *History of Hasidism* [H] (Tel Aviv, 1975), 8–18, depicted "the social situation in Poland" in general without attempting to isolate local factors.

3. For general surveys of the history of the Commonwealth in English, see A. Gieysztor et al., *History of Poland* (Warsaw, 1979); N. Davies, *God's Playground: A History of Poland* (New York, 1982); and J. K. Fedorowicz, ed., *A Republic of Nobles* (Cambridge, 1982). For background to the period discussed here, see F. E. Sysyn, *Between Poland and the Ukraine: The Dilemma of Adam Kysil* (Cambridge, Mass., 1985), 5–20; J. A. Gierowski and A. Kaminski, "The Eclipse of Poland," in *New Cambridge Modern History*, vol. 6., ed. J. S. Bromley (Cambridge, 1970), 681–715; J. Lukowski, *Liberty's Folly: The Polish-Lithuanian Commonwealth in the Eighteenth Century, 1697–1795* (London, 1991).

4. O. Balzer, *The Armenian Court System in Medieval Lwów* [P] (Lwów, 1910); M. Oles, *The Armenian Law in the Polish Kingdom* (Rome, 1966); G. D. Hundert, "On The Jewish Community in Poland During the Seventeenth Century: Some Comparative Perspectives," *Révue des etudes juives* 142 (1983): 362; E. Nadel-Golobic, "Armenians and Jews in Medieval Lvov: Their Role in Oriental trade, 1400–1600," *Cahiers du monde russe et sovietique* 20 (1979): 353.

5. The number of Jews in the Commonwealth at various periods has been the subject of much scholarly debate. Weinryb, *Poland,* 316–318, estimated 170,000 in 1648, but his flawed method yielded a number that is obviously too low. S. W. Baron, *A Social and Religious History of the Jews,* vol. 16 (New York, 1976), 192–207, ventured a figure of 450,000 (out of a total population in the country of 10,000,000), which seems high. Most researchers now accept the estimate of 750,000 in 1764 offered by R. Mahler, *The Jews of Old Poland in Light of Numbers* [Y], vols. 1–2 (Warsaw, 1958). See M. Rosman, *Polin: The Jewish Community in Poland—Geographic, Demographic, and Legal Foundations* [H] (Tel Aviv, 1991), 40–55; S. Stampfer, "The 1764 Census of Polish Jewry," *Bar Ilan* 24–25 (1989): 41–147.

6. Baron, *Social and Religious History,* 146–161; Weinryb, *Poland,* 71–78; Hundert, "Community," 349–354; G. D. Hundert, *The Jews in a Polish Private Town: The Case of Opatów in the Eighteenth Century* (Baltimore, 1992), 85–115.

7. M. J. Rosman, "Jewish Perceptions of Insecurity and Powerlessness in 16th- to 18th-Century Poland," *Polin* 1 (1986): 19–27.

8. On the revolt, see Sysyn, *Kysil,* 141–174, and his extensive bibliographic note, pp. 319–320; M. Nadav, "The Jewish Community of Nemyriv: Their Massacre and Loyalty Oath to the Cossacks," *HUS* 8 (1984): 376–395; Weinryb, *Poland,* 179–190.

9. E. Barwinski, "Zygmunt III and the Dissidents" [P], *Reformacja w Polsce* 1 (1921): 50–57; J. Tazbir, "The Fate of Polish Protestantism in the Seventeenth Century," in *A Republic of Nobles,* ed. J. K. Fedorowicz (Cambridge, 1982), 198–217.

10. Davies, *Playground,* 177; O. Subtelny, *Ukraine: A History* (Toronto, 1988), 89, 94–96; J. A. Gierowski, "Centralization and Autonomy in the Polish-Saxon Union," *HUS* 3–4 (1979–1980): 274; Sysyn, *Kysil,* 32–36.

11. Davies, *Playground,* 172–176; O. Halecki, *From Florence to Brest* (New York, 1959); N. L. Fr.-Chirovsky, ed., *The Millennium of Ukrainian Christianity* (New York, 1988), 52–55; Subtelny, *Ukraine,* 99–101; D. Doroshenko and O. W. Gerus, *A Survey of Ukrainian History* (Winnipeg, 1975), 152–161; Sysyn, *Kysil,* 30, and especially the literature in his notes, pp. 251–252.

12. Gierowski and Kaminski, "Eclipse," 681–686; J. A. Gierowski, "The International Position of Poland in the Seventeenth and Eighteenth Centuries," in *A Republic of Nobles,* ed. J. K. Fedorowicz (Cambridge, 1982), 227–231.

13. Lukowski, *Folly;* Gierowski and Kaminski, "Eclipse," 691–715.

14. Lukowski, *Folly,* 62–72; J. Rutkowski, *Economic History of Poland* [P] (Warsaw, 1953), 187–197; J. Gierowski, "Crisis of the Manorial-Feudal Economy," and K. Piwarski, "The Economic Decline of the Towns" [P], both in *Historia Polski,* vol. 1, pt. 2, ed. H. Lowmianski (Warsaw, 1958), 616–665; Gierowski, "Autonomy," 273–274; M. Bogucka and H. Samsonowicz, *History of Towns and Townspeople in Pre-Partition Poland* [P] (Wrocław, 1986), 339–346; A. Homecki, *Grain Production and Trade in the Lubomirski Latifundium in the Second Half of the Seventeenth and First Half of the Eighteenth Century* [P] (Wrocław, 1970), esp. 16–18.

15. Davies, *Playground,* 339–348, 462–469; Piwarski, "Economic Decline," 675–718.

16. Gierowski, "Crisis," 702–705; Gierowski and Kaminski, "Eclipse," 686–688; Davies, *Playground*, 492–510; Lukowski, *Folly*, 121–123.

17. Gierowski and Kaminski, "Eclipse," 697–715; Lukowski, *Folly*, 130–131, 151–163; Davies, *Playground*, 495–497, 505–508.

18. This is the title of a book in Polish by J. A. Gierowski (Wrocław, 1971).

19. Lukowski, *Folly*, 129–146; Gierowski, "Crisis," 718–745; Davies, *Playground*, 497–508.

20. Lukowski, *Folly*, 146–151; Gierowski and Kaminski, "Eclipse," 703–715; Gieysztor, *Poland*, 239–251; Davies, *Playground*, 492–510.

21. L. R. Lewitter, "Intolerance and Foreign Intervention in Early Eighteenth-Century Poland-Lithuania," *HUS* 5 (1981): 290–303.

22. Gierowski, "Crisis," 746–763; Lukowski, *Folly*, 14–16, 28–35, 149–150; *LJ*, 7–22.

23. Davies, *Playground*, 502.

24. On the magnates and their role, see *LJ*, 1–22 and references there.

25. For a discussion of the nomenclature for Ukraine, see W. A. Serczyk, *History of Ukraine* [P] (Wrocław, 1979), 7–8, and Doroshenko and Gerus, *Survey*, v–vi.

26. On early Podolia, see N. Molchanovskii, *Outline of Information about the Podolian Territory before 1434* [U] (Kiev, 1885); A. Jabłonowski, "Volhynia and Podolia at the End of the Sixteenth Century" [P], *Pisma* 4 (1911): 144–233; Sysyn, *Kysil*, 20–32. On the colonization and its Jewish aspects, see Subtelny, *Ukraine*, 72–91; Doroshenko and Gerus, *Survey*, 114–124; S. Ettinger, "The Legal and Social Position of the Jews in the Ukraine in the Fifteenth through Seventeenth Centuries," *Zion* 20 (1955): 128–152, and "Jewish Participation in the Colonization of the Ukraine," *Zion* 21 (1956): 107–142.

27. *LJ*, 106–142 and references.

28. Subtelny, *Ukraine*, 80–102; Doroshenko and Gerus, *Survey*, 119–124, 154–161; Sysyn, *Kysil*, 20–36; *LJ*, 52–73.

29. Subtelny, *Ukraine*, 103–122; Doroshenko and Gerus, *Survey*, 125–139, 161–181; Sysyn, *Kysil*, 22–26, 78–89; Lukowski, *Folly*, 57–60; J. Burszta, "Desertion of Peasants from the San Region in the First Quarter of the Eighteenth Century" [P], *RDSG* 34 (1973): 56–57, 61–69.

30. A. Bruckner, *History of Polish Culture* [P], vol. 2 (Warsaw, 1958), 647–652; Sysyn, *Kysil*, 20–22.

31. Sysyn, *Kysil*, 141–174; N. N. Hannover, *Abyss of Despair*, trans. and ed. A. Mesch (New York, 1950).

32. J. Perdenia, *The State of the Nobles' Republic with Regard to Ukrainian Affairs at the Turn of the Eighteenth Century* [P] (Wrocław, 1963), 13–59; D. Kołodziejczyk, *The Kamieniec Province: Podolia Under Ottoman Rule* [P] (Warsaw, 1994), pts. 2–3. He shows that "the ruin" began with the 1648 war and was well advanced by the time the Turks took over; see pp. 133, 137–140.

33. Kołodziejczyk, *Podolia*, 132, 148; W. A. Serczyk, *Magnate Economy in Podolia in the Second Half of the Eighteenth Century* [P] (Wrocław, 1965), 24; Serczyk, *Ukraine*, 186; M. Karasia and A. Podrazy, *Ukraine: Past and Present* [P] (Cracow, 1970), 274; A. I. Baranovich, *Magnate Economy in Southern Volhynia in the Eighteenth Century* [R] (Moscow, 1955), 10–35; Subtelny, *Ukraine*,

153–154, 161–163; N. L. Chirovsky, *An Introduction to Ukrainian History,* vol. 2 (New York, 1984), 198–200; Doroshenko and Gerus, *Survey,* 309–310, 486–488; M. Hrushevsky, *A History of Ukraine* (New York, 1941), 433–434.

34. Perdenia, *Ukrainian Affairs,* 143–224; Serczyk, *Ukraine,* 170; Karasia and Podrazy, *Ukraine,* 274; Subtelny, *Ukraine,* 161–163; Chirovsky, *Ukrainian History,* 198–200.

35. *LJ,* 1–22; Lukowski, *Folly,* 129, 149.

36. Z. Guldon, *Commercial Ties between Magnate Latifundia in Right Bank Ukraine and Gdańsk in the Eighteenth Century* [P] (Torun, 1966), 12–46, 136–137; Serczyk, *Magnate Economy,* 155–159; Davies, *Playground,* 265; Lukowski, *Folly,* 30; Kołodziejczyk, *Podolia,* 45–47.

37. J. Baszanowski, *On the History of Polish Commerce in the Sixteenth and Seventeenth Centuries: The Cattle Trade* [P] (Gdansk, 1977), 58–113.

38. Doroshenko and Gerus, *Survey,* 503–505; Hrushevsky, *Ukraine,* 425–427; J. Kłoczowski, *The Church in Poland* [P], vol. 2 (Cracow, 1969), 932–940, 1003–1025; J.-P. Himka, "The Conflict between the Secular and the Religious Clergy in Eighteenth-Century Western Ukraine," *HUS* 15 (1991): 35–47; Lewitter, "Intolerance," 285–290.

39. Serczyk, *Ukraine,* 186.

40. Subtelny, *Ukraine,* 191–192; Doroshenko and Gerus, *Survey,* 485–486; Hrushevsky, *Ukraine,* 436.

41. Z. E. Kohut, "Myths Old and New: The Hajdamak Movement and the Koliivshchyna (1768) in Recent Historiography," *HUS* 1 (1977): 359–378; Serczyk, *Ukraine,* 187–188, 190–193; Karasia and Podrazy, *Ukraine,* 275–276; Subtelny, *Ukraine,* 191–193; Chirovsky, *Ukrainian History,* 216–220; Doroshenko and Gerus, *Survey,* 488–501; Hrushevsky, *Ukraine,* 436–441; S. Velychenko, *National History as Cultural Process* (Edmonton, 1992), 65–75, 207–208.

42. See sources in previous note and W. A. Serczyk, *Koliszczyzna* (Cracow, 1968); S. M. Dubnow, *History of the Jews in Russia and Poland,* vol. 1 (Philadelphia, 1916), 183–186.

43. For the impact of Haidamak uprisings on Jewish consciousness, see *SB,* 53, 59, 67, 186, 210. On the apparent links between the Besht and the Haidamaks, see *SB,* 124, 210.

44. The exact relationship and differences among Haidamaks, Opryshky, and other such groups are not completely clarified. While the Haidamaks are usually regarded as an at least semiorganized movement with nationalist, religious, and social aspects and a political program, the others are conventionally classed as bandits. This distinction does not always hold. See Serczyk, *Ukraine,* 189; Kohut, "Myths," 369; Hrushevsky, *Ukraine,* 436.

45. Subtelny, *Ukraine,* 192; S. Vincenz, *On the High Uplands: Sagas, Songs, Tales and Legends of the Carpathians,* trans. H. C. Stevens (New York, 1956), 69–95.

46. Serczyk, *Ukraine,* 189.

47. Ber of Bolechow, *The Memoirs of Ber of Bolechow,* trans. and ed. M. Vishnitzer (London, 1922), 96–101.

48. Ibid., 101.

49. Dubnow, *Jews,* 172–180; Hundert, *Opatow,* 40–41; J. Goldberg, "Poles

and Jews in the 17th and 18th Centuries: Rejection or Acceptance," *Jahrbücher für Geschichte Osteuropas* 22 (1974): 275; Z. Guldon and J. Wijacka, "Ritual Murder Trials in Red Russia, Podolia and Ukraine in the Sixteenth–Eighteenth Centuries" [P], *Nasza Przeszłość* 81 (1994): 51–84; Weinryb, *Poland,* 150–155. Weinryb (p. 151) and Hundert (p. 176) point out that there were a large number of witchcraft trials, indicating a general climate of superstitious accusations against social groups perceived as threatening; see also H. Levine, *Economic Origins of Antisemitism* (New Haven, 1991), 83–88, for an imaginative discussion of the blood libel issue—roundly criticized by G. D. Hundert in his review, *American Historical Review* 97 (1992): 1246.

50. See S. Maimon, *Autobiography,* trans. J. C. Murray (London, 1954), 20–22; *SB,* 78–80, 161, 217–218, 242.

51. For examples of these, see D. Cyzevs'kyj, *A History of Ukrainian Literature,* trans. D. Ferguson et al. (Littleton, Colo., 1975); C. Miłosz, *The History of Polish Literature* (New York, 1969); M. A. Shulvass, *Jewish Culture in Eastern Europe: The Classical Period* (New York, 1975).

52. Davies, *Playground,* 160, 199–200.

53. See, e.g., BC 5905 l.28027 4/19/1744, l.28032 5/20/1744; BC 5811 l.11073–l.11170 1740–1746, letters of administrators from Tarnoruda and Satanów which frequently refer to Jewish practices; for negative remarks, see BC 5782 l.5892 1/30/1715; BC 5905 l.28027 4/19/1744, l.28032 5/20/1744; BC 5935 l.34888 5/29/1726. Knowledge of Jewish customs could even be profitable; e.g., BC 5939 l.35795 11/6/1744, in which an administrator observed how certain Jews celebrated Shabbas (Sabbath) in style and were willing to bear the expense of the higher-quality fish, thus providing a market for fish from latifundium fish ponds; see also BC 5987 l.48287 3/26/1744; BC 5939 l.35786.

54. Lewitter, "Intolerance," 290–303; BC 5987 l.48331 5/17/1745.

55. *Ma'aseh Tuviah* (Venice, 1707), 110d.

56. M. Bałaban, "Sabbateanism in Poland" [P], *Księga jubileuszowa ku czci Prof. dr. Mojżesza Schorra* (Warsaw, 1935), 49–56; I. Zinberg, *A History of Jewish Literature,* vol. 6 (Cincinnati, 1975), 160–170.

57. Vincenz, *Plateau,* 51.

58. V. Kubijovyc, ed., *Ukraine: A Concise Encyclopedia* (Toronto, 1963), 1: 341–348; Vincenz, *Plateau,* 47–65; for examples of Jews consulting non-Jewish sorcerers, see Vincenz, 54–55; *SB,* 180, 201; *SH* 6b–7a, 99b; CSHAU fond 254|1269, p. 16.

59. See chap. 9.

60. *SB,* 149; see also pp. 13, 123, 248; *SH* 120b.

61. See E. Horowitz's studies, such as "The Way We Were: Jewish Life in the Middle Ages," *Jewish History* 1 (1986): 78–83; "Eve of Circumcision: A Chapter in the History of Jewish Nightlife," *Journal of Social History* 23 (1989): 45–46, 51, 53–54; also D. Ruderman, *Kabbalah, Magic and Science: The Cultural Universe of a Sixteenth-Century Jewish Physician* (Cambridge, Mass., 1988), 1–2.

62. For examples of Jews and Christians together in various social situations, see Ber of Bolechow, *Memoirs,* 65, 75, 94, 102, and passim; *SB,* 44, 100–101, 129, 241–242, 248, and passim; N. E. Shulman, *Authority and Community* (New

York, 1986), 26–37 and references; see also Hundert, *Opatów*, 37–45; *LJ*, 42–48, 59–60, 71–74, 81–85, 242, and passim. War is at both ends of the suggested spectrum because war sometimes served as a catalyst for turning on one's neighbors (Hannover, *Abyss of Despair*) and sometimes as an opportunity for close cooperation and solidarity (B. Pendzich, "The Jewish Community of Sluck after the Polish-Muscovite War of 1654–1667," in *Proceedings of the XI Congress of Jewish Studies*, vol. B2 [Jerusalem, 1994], 173–180). This spectrum must eventually be refined to allow for such phenomena as the complex relationship between the landlord and the arrendator (*LJ*, 134–142) and marginal intergroup sexual contact (*SB*, 163, 246–247).

63. J. Katz, *Tradition and Crisis* (New York, 1971), 18–42.

64. *SB*, 114–116, 242; see also M. J. Rosman, "A Minority Views the Majority," *Polin* 4 (1989): 37.

65. O. Pritsak, "Ukraine as the Setting for the Emergence of Hasidism," in *Israel and the Nations: Essays Presented in Honor of Shmuel Ettinger*, ed. S. Almog et al. (Jerusalem, 1987), lxxxi–lxxxii and references. See also G. Scholem, "The Historical Image of Israel Ba'al Shem Tov" [H], *Molad* 18 (1960): 339; Y. Eliach, "The Russian Dissenting Sects and Their Influence on Israel Baal Shem Tov, Founder of Hassidism," *Proceedings of the American Academy for Jewish Research* 36 (1968): 59–61.

66. G. Scholem, "Redemption through Sin," in G. Scholem, *The Messianic Idea in Judaism* (New York, 1971), 78–141.

67. Scholem, "Image," 339; Weinryb, *Poland*, 261–262, 271–273; M. Idel, *Kabbalah: New Perspectives* (New Haven, 1988), 321n.137. This region did, however, have subdivisions. M. K. Silber in an unpublished paper, "On the Relationship between Hasidism and Sabbàteanism: A Geographic Exploration," asserted on the basis of a geographic comparison of the centers of Sabbateanism and Frankism with the localities visited by the Besht: "It would seem as if the Besht were avoiding in almost conscious fashion precisely those areas where he had begun his career and which now had become Sabbatean centers."

68. Eliach, "Russian Dissenting Sects."

69. K. Shmeruk, *Yiddish Literature in Poland: Historical Studies and Perspectives* (Jerusalem, 1981), 139n.49; B. D. Weinryb, "Reappraisals in Jewish History," in *Salo W. Baron Jubilee Volume*, ed. S. Lieberman, vol. 2 (New York, 1974), 971–974.

70. Eliach, "Russian Dissenting Sects," 82.

71. O. Pritsak, "Emergence," lxxxi, summed it up: "The history of Ukrainian religious sects, especially mystical ones, has yet to be written." See also T. Ysander, *Studien zum B'estschen Hasidismus in seiner religionsgeschichtlichen Sonderart* (Uppsala, 1933).

72. G. D. Hundert, "The Conditions in Jewish Society in the Polish-Lithuanian Commonwealth in the Middle Decades of the Eighteenth Century," *Hasidism Reappraised*, ed. Ada Rapoport-Albert (London, 1996), 45–46.

73. M. J. Rosman, "The History of a Historical Source: On the Editing of *Shivhei Ha-Besht*" [H], *Zion* 58 (1993): 201–203.

74. Weinryb, "Reappraisals," 973.

75. Eliach, *Russian Dissenting Sects*, 67–68; Shmeruk, *Studies*, 119–139, originally published in *Zion* 28 (1963): 86–105; Weinryb, "Reappraisals," 972,

adds that Zernikov had nothing to do with the schismatics and wrote in Russian, a language the Besht did not know.

76. Dubnow, *Hasidism*, 8–18; much of this also appeared in English in his *Jews*, vol. 1, 167–187.

77. Dubnow, *Hasidism*, 17–18.

78. See *LJ*, 8–31.

79. Stampfer, "Census," 147. For an example of recolonization leading to Jewish resettlement, see I. Halpern, *The Records of the Council of Four Lands* [H], ed. I Bartal (Jerusalem, 1990), 80.

80. N. Loewenthal, *Communicating the Infinite* (Chicago, 1990), 1–6.

81. M. Nadav, *Pinsk* (Tel Aviv, 1973), 99–103; G. D. Hundert, "Security and Dependence," Ph.D. dissertation, Columbia University, 1978, introduction. This process can be observed in the magistrate court records from Dubno in 1648–1651. See CSHAU fond 3316.

CHAPTER FOUR. MIĘDZYBÓŻ

1. *SB*, 15, a story that, according to my analysis of the book (see M. J. Rosman, "The History of a Historical Source: On the Editing of *Shivhei Ha-Besht*" [H], *Zion* 58 [1993]: 192–194, 202–203), stems from the original collection compiled around 1790 by Dov Ber of Ilintsy, stating that the Besht was "from the city of Okop." A later tradition added by the printer (ca. 1814) notes that the Besht was living there at the age of 14. These traditions have never been confirmed by other evidence. It does strike me as implausible that Dov Ber would have invented a spurious geographic connection, especially one that has no apparent polemical purpose, within the period of living memory of the Besht. S. M. Dubnow, "The Beginnings: The Ba'al Shem Tov (Besht) and the Center in Podolia," in *EP*, 26–27, 51n.4; M. Balaban, *On the History of the Frankist Movement* [H], vol. 1 (Tel Aviv, 1934), 23, and most other scholars also accepted the tradition as historical and assumed, for lack of any information to the contrary, that the Besht had been living in Okopy since his birth.

2. In his letters to Meir of Konstantynów and Moses of Kutów (see chap. 7, near nn. 21, 46), the Besht signed himself as being from there; see also *SB*, 36, 211.

3. In the Holy Epistle (see chap. 6), the Besht identified himself as living in Międzybóż, and this is confirmed by the Polish sources (see chap. 9) and the stories in *SB*. There are also traditions that the Besht resided at various times in Jazlowiec and in Kolomiya and Kutów.

4. This identification is likely because of its location in Podolia and its development around the time of the Besht's birth; see *SG*, vol. 7 (Warsaw, 1892), 432–433. However, there is no conclusive proof; see *SBH*, 44n.36.

5. *SG*, vol. 7, 432–433.

6. S. Stampfer, "The 1764 Census of Polish Jewry," *Bar Ilan* 24–25 (1989): 134.

7. Dubnow, "Beginnings," 26–27, 51n.4, interpreted the first story of *SB* recounting the birth of the Besht as reflecting the end of the Turkish-Polish war in 1699. He also asserted, *ex silentio*, that there was no organized Jewish

community in Okopy. While it is clear from the census list that an official community existed there by 1764, if the Besht's family settled in the town during the first period of its development (ca. 1700), there may not have been enough people to qualify as an independent *kehilla* (community) with its own kahal. Okopy could have been a satellite of a nearby kahal—perhaps Zwaniecz, as Dubnow suggested. When the transition was made to full-fledged kehilla is not known.

8. *SG*, vol. 12, 353; Stampfer, "Census," 135; BC 5825 l.13556 4/22/1741 regarding damage assessment.

9. Pronounced in Polish, Miendzibuzh (sometimes Miedzyborz = Miendzibozh); in Ukrainian, Medzhybezh; in Russian, Mezhybozh; in Yiddish and in Hebrew, Mezibozh or Mezibzh.

10. See *SB* stories and Dubnow's and Dinur's accounts in *EP*.

11. That is, the lands belonging to Poland before the 1569 Union of Lublin. Podolia was the southeasternmost region of Crown Poland.

12. *SG*, vol. 6, 367; on Międzybóż as a refuge from those who "plunder, rob and murder" Jews and others, see BC 5825 l.13517, l.13539 9/1739; BC 5987 l.48200 7/19/1739. The Jewish community in Międzybóż dates from before 1547. In May of that year the community was granted a customs privilege, subsequently renewed by later kings; AGAD Księgi Kancellarskie 115, 6 November 1577. My thanks to Prof. Jacob Goldberg for bringing this source to my attention.

13. *SG*, vol. 6, 368–369; Jan Pasek, *The Memoirs of Jan Chryzostom z Gosławic Pasek*, trans. and ed. M. A. J. Święcicka (Warsaw, 1978), 454; D. Kołodziejczyk, *Podolia Under Ottoman Rule* [P] (Warsaw, 1994), 83–85, 92–96.

14. Kołodziejczyk, *Podolia,* 112; EW 40 Arenda contract.

15. The earliest evidence for Sieniawski's control over the town are arenda contracts he let to Joseph ben Israel, apparently as representative of the kahal, in 1691 and 1692. The contracts are in EW 41 and EW 40, respectively. According to Turkish sources, in 1681 there were approximately 1,500 people in Międzybóż. See Kołodziejczyk, *Podolia,* 142–146. Skaminski made his observation in a petition he submitted around 1735, contained in EW 87.

16. See chap. 3; *SG*, vol. 6, 369; *Volumina Legum,* VI 454, p. 232b.

17. BC 4078 1740; M. J. Rosman, "Międzybóż and Rabbi Israel Ba'al Shem Tov," in *EP*, 212–213. Jan Dessier, the administrator of Międzybóż in the early 1730s, took pride in the population growth and new construction in the town: BC 5796 l.8495 12/30/1730, l.8556 1/29/1731. The 5,000 figure should be seen as a minimum estimate. It is based on the list of pieces of property subject to taxation in the town. In some of these homes, as the register indicates, there was more than one household. Later, in 1764, there were 2,039 Jews in Międzybóż, according to the official census (Stampfer, "Census," 135). In 1760 (BC Gospodarcze 306), there were at least 282 Jewish property tax–paying households. Allowing for the fact that poor households may not have been recorded, that the number of households probably increased slightly in the intervening four years, but that the census takers probably undercounted the Jews, the average number of Jews per household was between 7 and 8. Demographic historians generally agree that in this period the number of Christians per household was smaller than that for Jews. I. Gieysztorowa, *Introduction to the Demography of Old Poland*

[P] (Warsaw, 1976), 161–162, put the Christian average at 6. These rough indexes lead to my estimate. At this time the population of Cracow was approximately 5,000 (J. Lukowski, *Liberty's Folly* [London, 1991], 62), Warsaw, about 30,000, including approximately 1,200 permanent Jewish residents (see W. T. Bartoszewski and A. Polonsky, *The Jews in Warsaw* [Oxford, 1991], 4, 9, 95 ff.).

18. On Międzybóż as an administrative center, see, e.g., BC 5881 l.23400 5/13/1744, l.23412 2/14/1745, re: bringing revenues collected in Zinków to Międzybóż; in general, see correspondence of Międzybóż-based administrators Grętkowski (BC 5825), Obrębski (BC 5905), Pęsky (BC 5913), Rościszewski (BC 5931), Rynkiewicz (BC 5939), Sinicki (BC 5948), and Wolinski (BC 5987). From the correspondence it appears that the commissioner for the Czartoryskis' holdings in Podolia and Ukraine was based in Satanów, but see W. A. Serczyk, *Magnate Economy in Podolia in the Second Half of the Eighteenth Century* [P] (Wrocław, 1965), 157, who stated that Międzybóż was the Czartoryskis' main Ukrainian headquarters. On Międzybóż as a regional commercial center: BC 5758 l.481 11/12/1745 and BC 5881 l.23412 2/14/1745, merchants travel to fair in Międzybóż; BC 5939 l.35790 6/29/1744, Kałusz Jews bring salt to Międzybóż; BC 5939 l.35806 3/10/1745, on Międzybóż fair, which was to begin on Sunday, 14 March 1745; BC 5929 l.33438 4/12/1745, on Międzybóż merchants making the village rounds; on caravans: BC 5796 l.8515 5/10/1709; on garrison: BC 2532 1764–1765 Accounts of the Międzybóż Garrison; on Międzybóż merchants elsewhere: BC 5825 l.13527 n.d.; BC 5939 l.35803 2/27/1745; BC 5948 l.38546 6/11/1744; BC 5987 l.48194 6/23/1739; EW 87 Manaszko Dubienski petition, Moszkowicz and Morduchowicz petition; G. D. Hundert, *The Jews in a Polish Private Town: The Case of Opatów in the Eighteenth Century* (Baltimore, 1992), 58.

19. BC 5987 l.48158 10/31/1738, l.48164 12/10/1738.

20. BC 5775 l.4816 4/11/1737, l.4818 1/11/1738, *Tygodnik Illustrowany,* Warsaw Tom XV nr 382 1/19/1867, p. 31; BC 5788 l.7170–7173 4/22/1744 12/15/1745 1/3/1746 12/12/1745; in the neighboring town of Mikołajów, also part of the Międzybóż administrative complex, a new tavern was built in 1744, BC 5987 l.48304 9/30/1744.

21. EW 40 1/1/1743 Arenda contract.

22. See arenda contracts in EW 40 and EW 41.

23. The price for sheep in the Międzybóż area also rose by 12% from 1743 to 1744, BC 5939 l.35785 4/14/1744; see also *LJ,* 125–128.

24. BC 5939 l.35804 3/8/1745; Rynkiewicz evidently did not consider the drop in arenda prices to be of great significance—or did not want Walicki, the main administrator of the latifundium, to think so.

25. BC 5951 l.39368 2/15/1745.

26. BC 5905 l.28027 4/19/1744, forced sale of cattle; BC 5939 l.35790 6/29/1744, l.35806–35807 3/10/1745–3/15/1745, forced sale of fish; on the phenomenon of forced sales in general, see Z. Guldon, *Commercial Ties between Magnate Latifundia in Right Bank Ukraine and Gdańsk in the Eighteenth Century* [P] (Toruń, 1966), 123–124, 179n.18; *LJ,* 87.

27. BC 5905 l.28044 7/3/1745, flood; BC 5987 l.48180 3/20/1739, l.48200 7/19/1739, l.48201 8/2/1739; Serczyk, *Magnate Economy,* 25. On Muscovite

incursions in 1734 and 1735, see BC 2465, a detailed register of damages caused to the people in Międzybóż and Stara Sieniawa by the Muscovite army; EW 87 Petition of 30 (26 Jews, 4 Christians), raid victims seeking relief.

28. BC 5987 l.48304 9/30/1744, BC 5905 l.28032 5/20/1744, l.28035 7/19/1744, l.28037 11/30/1744, l.28040 3/13/1745, l.28044 7/3/1745, arrendator financial problems; BC 5905 l.28022 12/30/1743; BC 5905 l.28025 4/9/1744, BC 5939 l.35801 1/3/1745, low competition.

29. BC 5939 l.35801 n.d.

30. BC 5948 l.38548 6/18/1744, contract cancellation; BC 5905 l.28023 1/11/1744, l.28039 3/6/1745, l.28043 6/26/1745, l.28053 1/21/46, city arrendator financial difficulties.

31. EW 41 Regestr Taxy . . . 1744.

32. See next chapter. Other indicators of economic problems are the difficulty in selling latifundium honey and the apparent expectation that Jews would begin defaulting on loans, BC 5987 l.48291 4/29/1744.

33. CSHAU fond 40I2, 104, 108–109. A significant proportion of the Jews must have been granted tax exemptions because in 1667 there were only four taxpaying Jewish households. See AGAD Archiwum Skarbu Koronnego (ASK) Rejestr poboru podymnego wojewodztwa podolskiego 71/13 (1662), 65/46 (1667).

34. Kołodziejczyk, Podolia, 142–146. See also I. Halpern, The Records of the Council of Four Lands [H], ed. I. Bartal (Jerusalem, 1990), 79–80. With a recorded history going back to 1547, Międzybóż was an important community prior to 1648. One of the most famous rabbis in history, Joel Sirkes, was rabbi there ca. 1605–1612 (E. J. Schochet, Bach: Rabbi Joel Sirkes, His Life, Works and Times [Jerusalem, 1971], 24, 28).

35. Rosman, "Międzybóż," 212–213; LJ, 42–49; see also Stampfer, "Census," passim.

36. EW 41 Specifikatia Żydów Międzyboskich.

37. On single women servants, see Hundert, Opatów, 71–75; H. H. Ben Sasson, Theory and Practice [H] (Jerusalem, 1959), 156–157; S. M. Dubnow, ed., Pinkas Ha-Medina (Berlin, 1925), 32; AGAD Archiwum Potockich z Łancuta 168 (HM 366), 1764 census of Międzybóż and other Czartoryski-owned towns which identifies servants in some homes.

38. See LJ, 45–46, on boarders in Staszów and Sieniawa.

39. BC 4085 1742.

40. M. Adler, Jews of Medieval England (London, 1939), 17–18, 37–42; M. Calmann, The Carrière of Carpentras (Oxford, 1984), 83–84, 105, 116–117; R. Emery, The Jews of Perpignan in the Thirteenth Century (New York, 1959), 26; C. Tallan, "Medieval Jewish Widows: Their Control of Resources," Jewish History 5 (1991): 63–74. See also B. Hanawalt, "Introduction," in Women and Work in Preindustrial Europe, ed. B. Hanawalt (Bloomington, Ind., 1986), xi, xiv; K. L. Reyerson, "Women in Business in Medieval Montpellier," in Women and Work in Preindustrial Europe, ed. B. Hanawalt (Bloomington, Ind., 1986), 118–119; M. Kowaleski, "Women's Work in a Market Town: Exeter in the Late Fourteenth Century," in Women and Work in Preindustrial Europe, ed. B. Hanawalt (Bloomington, Ind., 1986), 156.

41. *The Life of Gluckel of Hameln*, trans. and ed. B. Z. Abrahams (New York, 1963). For the widow to take over most or all of her husband's assets in payment of the financial obligations to her which he had assumed at the time of the marriage was typical in medieval Europe; see Tallan, "Medieval Jewish Widows," 63–74, esp. 66–67. See also K. L. Reyerson, "Women in Business in Medieval Montpellier," in *Women and Work in Preindustrial Europe*, ed. B. Hanawalt (Bloomington, Ind., 1986), 118–119.

42. See information on widows in *Women and Work in Preindustrial Europe*, ed. B. Hanawalt (Bloomington, Ind., 1986), according to index.

43. *SB*, 34–35, 48, 164; Dubnow, "Beginnings," 57n.57.

44. EW 41 Regestr Taxy . . . 1744.

45. Problems in linking records across lists means that some identifications are doubtful, while some people who appear on both lists under different names are counted separately; see M. J. Rosman, "The Polish Magnates and the Jews: Jews in the Sieniawski-Czartoryski Territories," Ph.D. dissertation, Jewish Theological Seminary of America, 1982, 475–483.

46. See EW 41 Akcyza contracts; see also Hundert, *Opatów*, 90.

47. EW 41.

48. Ibid.

49. We do not know how many dropped into the exempt group.

50. BC 4075 1740; EW 41 1740.

51. The sources in EW 41 use the term *kupiec* (merchant) to describe Charyton, while others are called *kramarz* (storekeeper); also see EW 87 Manaszko Dubienski petition mentioning other international merchants of Międzybóż; and Hundert, *Opatów*, 58.

52. G. D. Hundert, "The Role of the Jews in Commerce in Early Modern Poland-Lithuania," *Journal of European Economic History* 16 (1987): 268–275; M. J. Rosman, "Les rôles des Juifs dans l'économie polonaise du XVIe au XVIII siècle," *La société juive à travers l'histoire*, vol. 3, ed. S. Trigano (Paris, 1993), 275–278.

53. Hundert, *Opatów*, 95; *LJ*, 49–51, 153, 199.

54. See Kowaleski, "Women's Work," 151–153, 155.

55. In addition to the information on the tax rolls, a Jewish copper worker and kettle maker were mentioned in BC 5931 l.33969 1/1740.

56. M. Rosman, "An Exploitative Regime and the Opposition to It in Międzybóż, Ca. 1730," in *Transition and Change in Modern Jewish History: Essays Presented in Honor of Shmuel Ettinger*, ed. S. Almog et al. (Jerusalem, 1987), xxv–xxvi; Rosman, "Międzybóż," 215; EW 41 Akcyza contracts and "Punkta Cechu Rzeźników"; and see below.

57. This was probably the job of the arrendator's helper; Polish: Mirocznik.

58. *LJ*, 51; EW 87 1742 Kahal and pospólstwo petition; see also Maimon, *Autobiography*, 23–24; Hanawalt, "Introduction," xi; Kowaleski, "Women's Work," 151; I. Pinchbeck, *Women Workers and the Industrial Revolution, 1750–1850* (London, 1969), 296.

59. These positions are mentioned in the akcyza contracts in EW 41 or as last names in the various inventories. The rabbi, cantor, sexton, and one duchowny were exempt from paying tax. The weekly salaries paid by the excise tax ar-

rendator were as follows: "Old Rabbi": 1 zl. Rabbi: 12 zl. Kantor: 6 zl. Bass Singer: 2 or 3 zl. Sexton: 2 zl. 15 gr. Preacher: 4 zl. Butcher: 4 zl. Bath Attendant: 2 zl. By way of comparison, the administrator (*gubernator*) of Międzybóż in 1741 earned 800 zloty per year, plus payments in kind (EW 256 Międzybóż expenses); see also Hundert, *Opatów*, 89–91. On the Kabbalist, see chapter 10.

60. EW 41 Regestr Taxy . . . 1744 and inventories; see also BC 5939 l.35783 1/12/1744.

61. Identified on the tax roll as Wolf "the storekeeper," he may be identical with Wolf Abramowicz the factor; see below.

62. He may be identical with Szmoyło Woloszyn, whose son Szlomo was also a successful storekeeper.

63. Their names appear both in the arenda contracts in EW 40 and EW 41, on various reports of money paid out by the arrendators in EW 41, and on the taxpayer inventories, e.g., EW 41 1742; for Moszko Charyton as store owner and arrendator, see EW 41 Pretensje 10/28/1726 point 17.

64. See *LJ*, 49–51.

65. For descriptions of the structure and functioning of the kahal and other institutions of this type of community, especially their interaction with the Polish authorities, see *LJ*, 185–205; Hundert, *Opatów*, 85–155.

66. EW 41 "Kopia Punktów" translation of communal regulations into Polish, ca. 1745.

67. See EW 41 Lists of the elected officeholders certified by the electors, "Kopia Punktów" ca. 1745, and the "Regestr Taxy tak utożyli *Elektorowie* . . . 1744"; the more usual term for tax assessor was *censor* in Polish and *shamai* in Hebrew. The total number of officeholders—23—is the same as the number of members of local courts (Sanhedrin) in ancient Palestine and may reflect long-standing tradition.

68. 1726 EW 40 Arenda contract for 1727–1728; 1737(?) EW 86 Undated petition from kahal and pospólstwo to Czartoryski; 1738 EW 40 List of expenses paid by *Akcyza Żydowska* arrendators; 1739 EW 41 Register of Jewish communal officials, 26 April 1739; 1740 EW 41 Register of Jewish communal officials, 14 April 1740; 1742 EW 41 Register of Jewish communal officials, 14 April 1742; 1743 EW 41 Akcyza contract 1744; 174? EW 80/1 Copy of decision made by Rabbi and kahal of Międzybóż, which lists the four roshim (since it includes the Rabbi, Hersz Leybowicz Aptekarz, this document must date from the 1740s).

69. See M. Bałaban, *History of the Jews in Cracow and Kazimierz, 1304–1868* [P], vol. 1 (Cracow, [1931] 1991), 544–545; I. Halpern, *Eastern European Jewry: Historical Studies* [H] (Jerusalem, 1968), 56–58.

70. The other roshim were Yekutiel Zelman Aronowicz, Shmuel ben Pinhas, Zvi Hirsh ben Shelomo, Major Tarnopolski, Izrael Niemierzynski, Scharya Lachowiec, Moszko Charyton, Abramko Gabrielowicz, Chaim Illowicz, Judka Gierszonowicz, Leyba, Dereżenski's son-in-law, and Morduch Sopsajowicz.

71. Bałaban, *Cracow*, 544–545; and see R. Mahler, *History of the Jews in Poland* [H] (Merhavia, 1946), 366, on other places with similar patterns. Adding together Aron's terms with those of his father, Yekutiel Zelman Aronowicz, and his brother-in-law, Chaim Rabinowicz from Rzeszów, raises the Międzybóż

ratio to 1.71:1, but still well below that for Cracow. For the entire twenty years documented by Bałaban, 1622–1648, the ratio was much more lopsided, 6.2:1; once the steady officeholders make their appearance in the sources, they stay there. The same may have happened in Międzybóż, although only Baruch Czarny appears in both 1726 and 1738–1742. Also the more auspicious beginning in eighteenth-century Międzybóż implies that the ratio would remain more balanced; see Hundert, *Opatów*, 86–87, and D. Tollet, *Histoire des Juifs en Pologne du XVIe siècle à nos jours* (Paris, 1992), 44.

72. Since it can be difficult to link records, the ratio may actually be somewhat higher.

73. Rosman, "Międzybóż," 213–215; Hundert, *Opatów*, 131–132; M. Nadav, *Pinsk* (Tel Aviv, 1973), 77–78.

74. BC 4080 1741, p. 15b; EW 41 "Z dóbr podolskich" 1740; 11/6/1739 Akcyza arenda contract; 10/12/1741, 3/28/1743 Wolinski orders; 1740 *Taxa* contract; 1744 Akcyza arenda contract; EW 86 undated and EW 87 1742 Kahal and pospólstwo petition; see also EW 179 Satanów petition.

75. Pospólstwo petitions: EW 41 11/17/1714, 3/8/1716, EW 87 8/23/1715; EW 41 1726 Instructions of Elżbieta Sieniawska, reconfirmed 4/25/1737.

76. EW 41 "Kopia Punkta" ca. 1745; see also J. Katz, *Tradition and Crisis* (New York, 1971), 180–181.

77. BC 4080 1741, p. 15b, EW 41 11/6/1739 Akcyza arenda contract; seven representatives of the pospólstwo signed. Of these, five served on the kahal in other years, three as roshim. On the undated EW 86 petition, assuming the last four names to be representatives of the pospólstwo, two served on the kahal in other years, one as rosh; see also Bałaban, *Cracow*, 544, pospólstwo representation in Cracow in 1609. There is no indication that scholarship could serve as a substitute for financial qualifications in determining membership in the pospólstwo and candidacy for office, as apparently was true elsewhere; see Katz, *Tradition and Crisis*, 108–109.

78. EW 87 Petition from Dubienski to Wolinski; see the organization of elections in the Grodno Jewish community by Queen Bona Sforza according to factions, ca. 1553 (S. A. Bershadskii, *Russko-Evreiskii Arkhiv*, vol. 2 [St. Petersburg, 1903], 31, nr. 35).

79. BC 4114 1753.

80. BC 4080 1741, p. 15b. In general, the trend in this period was for owners to interfere more and more with the choice of kahal members and the activities of the kahal; see *LJ*, 185–205.

81. BC 2702 6/6/1730; EW 41 1726 Instructions of Elżbieta Sieniawska, reconfirmed 4/25/1737; EW 41 Międzybóż general arenda contract; BC 4080 1741 15b; EW 41 "Kopia Punkta" ca. 1745. This was also the case in other communities; see Mahler, *Poland*, 366.

82. EW 41 "Regestr Taxy . . . 1744"; EW 41 Registers of elected officials 1739, 1740, 1742.

83. Weinryb, *Texts and Studies*, 100–102 (English section), 225–229 (Hebrew section); B.-Z. Dinur, "The Origins of Hasidism and Its Social and Messianic Foundations," in *EP*, 130–132; Katz, *Tradition and Crisis*, 157–167.

84. EW 40 List of expenses paid by Akcyza Żydowska arrendators, 1738–1739; EW 41 Miscellaneous summaries of Międzybóż kahal expenses, 1732, 1733, 1737, 1739–1744, and undated.

85. See the examples analyzed by B. D. Weinryb, "Beiträge zur Finanzgeschichte der jüdischen Gemeinden in Polen," *Hebrew Union College Annual* 16 (1941): 187–214; Weinryb, *Texts and Studies*, 31 (English section); and Hundert, *Opatów*, 98–104.

86. Rosman, "Les rôles," 273–274.

87. The requirement appears in EW 41 Election register 4/14/1740; EW 41 includes several such statements for 1732, 1733, 1737, and 1739–1744. In the early 1740s, members of the pospólstwo were added to the expense validation process.

88. See *LJ*, 206–212; Hundert, *Opatów*, 156–158, and his doctoral dissertation, "Security and Dependence: Perspectives on Seventeenth-Century Polish-Jewish Society Gained Through a Study of Jewish Merchants in Little Poland," Columbia University, 1978.

89. EW 41 "Kopia Punkta" ca. 1745.

90. *SB*, 48.

91. Ibid., 179.

92. Ibid., 108.

93. See chap. 5, n. 34.

94. See chap. 10, near n. 30.

CHAPTER FIVE. THE CONTENTIONS OF LIFE

1. G. D. Hundert, *The Jews in a Polish Private Town: The Case of Opatów in the Eighteenth Century* (Baltimore, 1992), 36–39; see also B. D. Weinryb, *The Jews of Poland: A Social and Economic History of the Jewish Community in Poland from 1100 to 1800* (Philadelphia, 1972), 156–176; A. Kaminski, "Poland-Lithuania as a Host Country for the Jews," in *Poles and Jews: Myth and Reality in the Historical Context*, ed. H. B. Segel (New York, 1986), 16–31; M. J. Rosman, "Jewish Perceptions of Insecurity and Powerlessness in 16th–18th Century Poland," *Polin* 1 (1986): 19–27.

2. Hundert, *Opatów*, 38; see also M. Stanislawski, *Tsar Nicholas I and the Jews: The Transformation of Jewish Society in Russia, 1825–1855* (Philadelphia, 1983), 4–5.

3. *LJ*, 53–54.

4. BC 5957 l.40898 8/29/1739. In the same year the administrator of Granów asked Czartoryski to intercede with the Jewish Council of the Lwów district to reduce taxes on the Granów Jews, BC 5987 l.48188 5/27/1739. Other examples of the magnate or administrators supporting Jews' interests are BC 5939 l.35789 6/10/1744, l.35790 6/29/1744, on the need to repair equipment used by arrendators and on their unforeseen losses due to bad market conditions for salt; BC 5939 l.35801 1/3/1745, a priest who beats a Jew daily must be punished, or no one will take the lease again. Arrendators also appealed to the lord against local administrators; e.g., Obrębski correspondence BC 5905; for discussion of status and power or powerlessness of arrendators, see *LJ*, 124–141.

5. See *LJ*, 64–70.

6. See chap. 4, near nn. 84–87, regarding payments of various types to Polish officials; for examples of administrators helping Jews, see BC 5931 l.33997 2/21/1746; BC 5939 l.35790 6/29/1744, l.35801 1/3/1745; and Obrębski's efforts on behalf of arrendators, chap. 4, near n. 30.

7. On such petitions and attempts to prevent or intercept them, see BC 3822 nr. 76, p. 335; BC 5948 l.38548 6/18/1744, l.38568 6/25/1745; BC 5929 l.33449 6/26/1745. On the phenomenon of petitions to the owners, see J. Leśkiewiczowa and J. Michalski, eds., *Peasant Petitions of the Eighteenth Century from the Archive of Michal Poniatowski* [P] (Warsaw, 1954).

8. BC 5905 Obrębski correspondence and various petitions in EW 87 contain many references to these kinds of disputes; see also BC 5905 l.28027 4/19/1744; BC 5939 l.35786 4/18/1744; BC 5929 l.33449 6/26/1745.

9. BC 5929 l.33449 6/26/1745; petitions in EW 87.

10. BC 5825 l.13609 6/25/1745, on kahal refusal to purchase wax, which the administration was forcing on it; BC 5905 l.28022 12/30/1743, Jewish refusal to purchase surplus latifundium vegetables and fowl; BC 5905 l.28055 2/21/1746, on a threat to force the kahal to pay off a debt owed Pan Miecznik; BC 5987 l.48331 5/17/1745, where the administrator Wolinski claimed that he had been prevented from carrying out a certain order because the regulations required the presence of a rabbi in such a case.

11. M. J. Rosman, "An Exploitative Regime and the Opposition to It in Międzybóż, Ca. 1730," in *Transition and Change in Modern Jewish History: Essays Presented in Honor of Shmuel Ettinger,* ed. S. Almog et al. (Jerusalem, 1987), xix–xxix.

12. BC 3822 nr. 76, p. 335; see also EW 87 Petition of Roman Skaminski.

13. Rosman, "Regime," xix–xxv.

14. BC 5987 l.48322 3/20/1745; on general charges of exploitation by Jews, see *LJ*, 72, 169; Hundert, *Opatów*, 47–48.

15. B. D. Weinryb, *Texts and Studies in the Communal History of Polish Jewry* (= *Proceedings of the American Academy for Jewish Research* 19) (New York, 1950), 69n.152 (English section), 173 (Hebrew section).

16. EW 80/1 *Dekret* 11/24/1741; BC 5987 l.48265 7/6/1741, l.48283 8/4/1742.

17. BC 5843 l.16655 9/21/1737 Jezierski to Siedliski: "Last Wednesday farmhands killed four Jews, horrendously, in our forest"; BC 5871 l.21584 1745, on the rape of a Jewish young woman; BC 5987 l.48180 3/20/1739, on Jews leaving town when the army came to be quartered; BC 5939 l.35801 1/3/1745, on an Orthodox priest who beat a Jewish arrendator daily and violated the liquor monopoly.

18. BC Gospodarcze 1566 1732; BC 5987 l.48305 10/25/1744, l.48307 11/15/1744, l.48318–48319, 2/28/1745–3/5/1745, l.48327 4/21/1745; *LJ*, 59–61.

19. EW 87 Skaminski and a group of thirty petitioners; Rosman, "Regime," xix; BC 5987 l.48294 5/19/1744; on the rabbi and priest, see below.

20. B.-Z. Dinur, "The Origins of Hasidism and Its Social and Messianic Foundations," in *EP*, 102–113, 125–134; R. Mahler, *History of the Jews in Poland* (Merhavia, 1946), 415; Weinryb, *Jews of Poland*, 282.

21. The Besht lived in Międzybóż from approximately 1740 until his death in 1760; see S. M. Dubnow, "The Beginnings: The Baal Shem Tov (Besht) and the Center in Podolia," in *EP*, 35, 44; G. Scholem, "The Historical Image of Israel Ba'al Shem Tov" [H], *Molad* 18 (1960): 337, 342; and M. J. Rosman, "Międzybóż and Rabbi Israel Ba'al Shem Tov," in *EP*, 217–218.

22. Rosman, "Regime," xix–xxix; see also Hundert, *Opatów*, 43–47.

23. The election rosters list him as rosh four times, more than anyone else (see chap. 4, near n. 70). His commercial and factoring activities are mentioned in various documents in EW 40 and EW 41.

24. BC 4080 1741, p. 15b, notes that the latifundium owner's administrator has the right to choose one of the four elders. Wolf's membership in the kahal's ruling group might, then, have resulted directly from his close relationship with the administrators (see chap. 4, near nn. 80–81).

25. BC 5948 l.38568 6/25/1745; BC 5929 l.33449 6/26/1745; BC 5931 l.33988 7/10/1745.

26. BC 5948 l.38568 6/25/1745; BC 5929 l.33449 6/26/1745.

27. In EW 41, this petition is entitled "Punkta Cechu Rzeźników Żydowskich Międzyboskiego przeciwko Judce, Leybce Niesmacznemu, Jankielowi Arendarzom, y Wolfowi Abramowiczowi . . . October 14, 1741" (Points of the Międzybóż Jewish butcher's guild against Judah, Leyba Niesmaczny, Jankiel Arrendator, and Wolf Abramowicz). It also contains a protest against the kahal's confiscation of the butchers' synagogue (see below), which was probably related to the complaints against Wolf.

28. For details, see EW 40 1743 Międzybóż general arenda contract; *LJ*, 106–120.

29. EW 87 1742 Petition from kahal and pospólstwo; EW 41 Settlement in Hebrew and Polish, dated 20 Tevet 5403 and 31 March 1743. See also BC 5825 l.13594 3/30/1745, BC 5931 l.33965 11/27/1739, on "szynk szabaszowy," Sabbath liquor sales. For background on the problem of Jews serving liquor on the Sabbath when work is prohibited, see H. H. Ben Sasson, "Statutes for the Enforcement of the Observance of the Sabbath in Poland and Their Social and Economic Significance" [H], *Zion* 21 (1956): 188–190, 199–200.

30. EW 41 1745 Summary of petitions and the responses to them (see points 3–5).

31. BC 5913 l.29489 2/17/1746. According to the EW 40 1743 Międzybóż general arenda contract, the bakers had to buy all of their wheat from the arrendators for more than the market price.

32. EW 40 1743 Międzybóż general arenda contract; EW 41 Summary of petitions (point 3); BC 5931 l.33997 2/21/1746, l.33999 2/21/1746. On powerful arrendators, see M. J. Rosman, "The Relationship between the Jewish Arrendator and the Polish Nobleman: The Other Side" [H], in *Jews in Economic Life*, ed. N. Gross (Jerusalem, 1985), 237–243.

33. BC 5870 l.21169 12/21/1744.

34. He signed his correspondence "Hersz Leybowicz" (see BC 5870 l.21169 12/21/1744). In BC 4085 1742 Międzybóż inventory, p. 12r, "Hyrszko Aptekarz" is called "the current rabbi" (*rabin teraźnieyszy*). The same document indicates that Hersz Aptekarz owned two stores on the marketplace (BC 4085

p. 15v, stores nos. 10 and 14). In his December 1744 letter, Rabbi Hersz Leybowicz mentioned that he owned two stores. In AGAD Archiwum Potockich z
Lancuta 168, p. 122a 1764 no. 64, he was listed as Herszko Aptykarz Leybowicz. There is no doubt, therefore, that Hersz Aptekarz and Rabbi Hersz Leybowicz are the same person. It is also clear that the rabbi had several sources of
income. In addition to his rabbinical salary and his stores, he manufactured and
sold liquor (EW 87 Undated general arrendators' petition answering petition of
Akcyzniki). His last name, Aptekarz (apothecary), may have been inherited from
his father and the stores may have been leased to others. For examples of other
rabbis who derived income from real estate and business while serving in the active rabbinate, see Jacob Josue Falk (D. Wachstein, "Fragments from the Account
Book of Rabbi Jacob Josue, Author of *Penai Yehoshua*" [H], in *Studies in Jewish Bibliography in Honor of A. S. Freidus*, ed. A. Freimann [New York, 1929],
15–31: moneylending) and Samuel ben Avigdor rabbi of Vilna (I. Klausner,
Vilna at the Time of the Gaon [Jerusalem, 1942], 53–54 and passim: moneylending, real estate, commerce).

35. BC 5870 l.21168 12/21/1744, l.21169 12/21/1744; BC 5929 l.33449
6/26/1745; BC 5931 l.33988 7/10/1745; see also BC 5891 l.25463 11/29/1739,
on a Przemyśl rabbi who tried to retain his post, and BC 5987 l.48326 4/15/1745,
on the dispute between the rabbi and the kahal of Mikołajów. By June 1745,
while Wolf persisted in his opposition, the kahal had resigned itself to the fact
that the rabbi would stay on and enlisted him in its petition to the owner; see
BC 5929 l.33449 6/26/1745. Father Losowski was the parish priest of Międzybóż; see BC 5880 l.23255 12/3/1732, l.23269 11/8/1745, l.23270 2/4/1746. The
attempt to unseat the rabbi was apparently connected to the controversy, alluded
to above, between the butchers and Leyba, on the one hand, and Wolf Abramowicz and his coterie, on the other; see chapter 7 for analysis of the Besht's letter
to Rabbi Meir of Konstantynów and the Besht's possible involvement in this
episode.

36. EW 41 contains several lists of payments made by akcyzniki. On the payment order system in general, see *LJ*, 128–130.

37. EW 41 1739 Akcyza contract; EW 41 1740 *Taxy* contract; BC 5778
l.5250 3/28/1745. For a case of alleged trumped-up tax on the part of the akcyzniki, see EW 41 10/14/1741 Butchers' petition.

38. EW 41 1744 Akcyza contract; bakers do not appear on the akcyza tax
lists for 1743 and 1744.

39. EW 87 Petition of Dubienski to Wolinski. Being a son-in-law of someone in the wealthy Charyton family, Manaszko's protestations may have been
somewhat disingenuous; see chapter 4, nn.18, 61.

40. EW 41 10/14/1741 Butchers' petition.

41. The arrangement was that on alternate Sabbaths members of one of the
guilds would receive all of the honors distributed during the service.

42. This equals 90 zloty. In this period, a small wooden house cost 50 to 80
zloty in the town of Brzeżany (M. Maciszewski, *Brzeżany* [Brody, 1910], 121–
122). If this is a reliable guide, then 5 ducats seems like a reasonable price to pay
for a one-room small wooden synagogue (which this building probably was).

43. Another case where it is specified that the kahal has the power to pro-

hibit the use of a a guild's synagogue by its members as a result of a conflict between the guild and the kahal is preserved in the minute book of Włodawa; see
Weinryb, *Texts and Studies*, Włodawa Hebrew section, p. 225, doc. no. 10.

44. EW 80/1 *Dekret* 11/24/1741. The identity of this group is not clear, but
it is unlikely that this was a separate group of hasidim or Kabbalists because
such a group was already apparently supported by the kahal; see Rosman,
"Międzybóż," 219; and Jacob Katz, *Tradition and Crisis* (New York, 1971),
180–182, 207–208.

45. EW 41 "Kopia punktów"; see discussion of these rules near the end of
chapter 4.

46. EW 41 Wolinski order 3/28/1743 and "Specifikatia Żydów Międzyboskich" (list of potential expellees from the community). A seat in the synagogue
was viewed as real estate that could be bought, sold, and inherited; see Katz, *Tradition and Crisis*, 180.

47. EW 41 Wolinski order 3/28/1743 and "Specifikatia Żydów Międzyboskich" (there is no indication of whether the expulsion was executed); see Rosman, "Międzybóż," 215, 219–220; chap. 4, near n. 36; on Herem Ha-Yishuv,
see Katz, *Tradition and Crisis*, 103–106. "Foreign" Jews might suffer from other
types of discrimination as well. In 1745, when a certain Leyba from Stanisławów
died while visiting Międzybóż, his widow, Ruchl, was charged an exorbitant 100
zloty by the rabbi and burial society to bury him; BC 5865 l.20331 7/25/1745;
see also Hundert, *Opatów*, 76–77.

48. EW 41 and EW 87 include petitions of this type.

49. Rosman, "Regime," xxv. See also G. D. Hundert, "The Decline of Deference in the Jewish Communities of the Polish-Lithuanian Commonwealth" [H],
Bar Ilan 24–25 (1989): 43–44.

50. The request of the butchers and the private prayer services in the house
of Osior, cited above, nn. 40, 44, are relevant examples.

51. In chap. 4, near nn. 80–81, I cited both the 1741 rule granting the magnate's administrator the right to appoint one of the four kahal elders and the custom that the arrendator of the town would automatically become one of the elders. It is not clear whether these two provisions were in force at the same time;
and if they were, whether they were just different ways of stating the same thing.

52. EW 41 1741 Butchers' petition.

53. EW 87 1742 Petition of kahal and pospólstwo; BC 3822 nr. 76, pp.
335–336, petition of the kahal vs. Ognisty; EW 80/1 *Dekret* of the rabbi and kahal.

54. See chap. 4, near n. 74 and passim; see also Hundert, *Opatów*, 86–88,
131–132, 142–143.

55. Rosman, "Międzybóż," 213–215; BC 4080 1741, p. 15b; see also chap. 4,
n. 75.

56. See Rosman, "Regime," xxvii–xxix.

57. EW 87 Petition of general arrendators answering petition of the ak-
cyzniki; EW 41 Petition to *WImP* Woyskiego Rawskiego; EW 41 "Punkta do
WWPana" ca. 1744, pts. 7–9; BC 5931 l.33994 12/31/1745; BC 5948 l.38562a
6/9/1745. Other types of arrendators also fought with each other, e.g., EW 41
"Punkta do WWPana" ca. 1744, pt. 5; EW 87 2/16/1739 Petition of Leyba
Jankielowicz et al.

58. EW 87 Petition of akcyzniki, Leyzor Charyton et al., to Wolinski; BC 5758 l.483 11/25/1745. Apparently part of the reason for Wolf and his brother harming poor Leyba the butcher (see above) was because doing so would lower the income of their rivals, the "current akcyzniki"; EW 41 1741 Butchers' petition; see also *SB,* 128, 200–201.

59. EW 41 Wolinski order 3/28/1743 and "Specifikatia Żydów Międzyboskich."

60. See S. Ettinger, "The Hasidic Movement—Reality and Ideals," in *EP,* 230: "among the rabbis and the ritual slaughterers and the wandering preachers, some are connected with the ruling group and some are against it."

CHAPTER SIX. THE HOLY EPISTLE

1. A. Green, "Typologies of Leadership and the Hasidic Zaddiq," in *Jewish Spirituality,* ed. A. Green, vol. 2 (New York, 1987), 153–154n.7, proposed a similar approach, although I disagree as to the details. By a priori reliability, I mean that this proposed hierarchy of sources is no more than a heuristic device. Once engaged, each source must be evaluated on its own merits. The testimony of a supporter, for example, would be analyzed differently from the testimony of an opponent. A source that appears in print later might, under certain circumstances, preserve an early version of events.

2. See, for example, the standard accounts by S. M. Dubnow, "The Beginnings: The Baal Shem Tov (Besht) and the Center in Podolia," in *EP,* 25–48; R. Mahler, *A History of Modern Jewry* (London, 1971), 455–467; I. Zinberg, *A History of Jewish Literature,* vol. 9 (Cincinnati, 1976), 27–61.

3. Chap. 1, near n. 58 and at the end; for more on *SB,* see chaps. 9 and 12.

4. *Molad* 10 (1960): 335–356.

5. H. Liberman, *Ohel Rahe"l* (Brooklyn, 1980), 38–49; M. Piekarz, *The Beginning of Hasidism* [H] (Jerusalem, 1978), 131–141, 306–321; Z. Gries, *The Book in Early Hasidism* [H] (Tel Aviv, 1992), 18.

6. The five really contemporary records Scholem cited are short quotations from three of the four known Besht letters (the full texts are analyzed in this chapter and the next), a brief passage from one of the two known letters written to the Besht by his brother-in-law, Gershon of Kutów, and a comment about the Besht made by Meir Teomim. As to the historical utility of the later citations and traditions, see this chapter and the next three. For criticism of Scholem's and others' judgment as to what was authentic in the sayings and stories, see Piekarz, *Hasidism,* 21–22, 39–40, 136–138.

7. Scholem, "Image," 344–345, himself expressed doubt as to the reliability of the letter from Rabbi Hayyim Ha-Kohen Rapoport; as to the other sources, see n. 5, and the Polish sources adduced in chapter 10, which also indicate a lack of established opposition.

8. The most detailed analysis of the printed version of the letter's contents is by A. Rubinstein, "The Letter of the Besht to R. Gershon of Kutów" [H], *Sinai* 67 (1970): 120–139. Other important treatments are Scholem, "Image," 348; G. Scholem, "The Neutralization of the Messianic Element in Early Hasidism," in G. Scholem, *The Messianic Idea in Judaism* (New York, 1971), 178–184; I.

Tishby, "The Messianic Idea and Messianic Trends in the Growth of Hasidism" [H], *Zion* 32 (1967): 1–45, esp. pp. 29–32; Dubnow, "Beginnings," 37–39; B.-Z. Dinur, *Historical Writings* [H], vol. 1 (Jerusalem, 1954), 181–183, 192. I. Etkes, "Hasidism as a Movement—The First Stage," in *Hasidism: Continuity or Innovation?* ed. B. Safran (Cambridge Mass., 1988), 18–19, and Rubinstein, "Letter," recognized the value of the letter for describing the Besht's activities.

9. Four books by Jacob Joseph of Polonne were published. They are, in addition to *Ben Porat Yosef, Toldot Yaakov Yosef* (Koretz, 1780), *Zofnat Pa'anei'ah* (Koretz, 1782), and *Ketonet Pasim* (Lwów, 1866). On the precise relationship of Jacob Joseph to his published books, see discussion in the text below. G. Nigal is in the process of publishing modern, annotated editions of these books. So far, the latter two have appeared.

10. Colophon to *Ben Porat Yosef;* for information on Lutzker and the process of publishing this book, see Gries, *Book,* 54–56.

11. Rubinstein, "Letter," 120; Rubinstein, "On a Manuscript of the Letter of the Besht to R. Gershon of Kutów" [H], *Sinai* 72 (1972): 196.

12. Piekarz, *Hasidism,* 20, 27–31; G. Nigal's introduction to *Zofnat Pa'anei'ah* (Jerusalem, 1989), 10–12; Gries, *Book,* 54–56.

13. The abbreviation *k"y* could be plural or singular.

14. See Gries, *Book,* 54.

15. Nigal, *Zofnat Pa'anei'ah,* 10–12; Gries, *Book,* 54–56.

16. This is Gries's conclusion; Nigal seems to think otherwise, but does not explain why.

17. Published by D. Frankel, *Letters of the Besht and His Disciples* [H] (Lwów, 1923), but not widely credited because it appeared together with many documents from the Kherson Genizah (see chap. 7), which most scholars consider to be forgeries.

18. "Letters of Our Rabbi Israel Ba'al Shem Tov and His Son-in-Law Rabbi Yehiel Mikhl to Rabbi Abraham Gershon of Kutów" [H], *Sinai* 71 (1971): 248–269.

19. See the articles by Rubinstein and Bauminger in *Sinai,* vols. 72 and 73. The manuscript is not in the public domain.

20. *Migdal Oz* (Kefar Habad, 1980), 119–126, and expanded version of his discussion with parallel versions of the text side by side in his facsimile edition *SBF* (Jerusalem, 1982), 229–239.

21. There is a hint to this effect at the beginning of the letter (see translation below, passage beginning: "It also stated there that the news . . ."). There is no way of knowing, however, if the 1776 text is indeed the one to which the Besht was referring.

22. See translation: "the name of heaven . . ."

23. *SBF,* 229–231. Mondshine did not solve the puzzle of how the pre-1752 letter, which was lost to its writer and recipient, managed to show up in a manuscript written more than 25 years later, except to speculate that a copy remained with the scribe, Judah Leib of Polonne.

24. Like Besht, an acronym (= Rabbi Israel Ba'al Shem) signifying the Ba'al Shem Tov.

25. It is apparent that already during the Besht's lifetime his correspondence

was circulated (presumably after having been recopied). Thus, sometime in the 1750s, Rabbi Meir Teomim could refer to the contents of a letter that Gershon of Kutów, the Besht's brother-in-law, wrote to the Besht in 1748; Ar J. Heschel, *The Circle of the Ba'al Shem Tov*, ed. and trans. S. H. Dresner (Chicago, 1985), 98–99; see chap. 8, near n. 10.

26. This is not to deny that the Besht wrote other letters, including some to his brother-in-law. He says so himself in the Bauminger version of the Holy Epistle, as Mondshine pointed out. What should not be assumed is that this letter, which did not reach its destination and was not available to the Besht, nevertheless survived.

27. In this connection it should be recalled that in *Shivhei Ha-Besht* there are four examples of reproducing parts of the Besht's letters by heart; SB, 41, 75, 78, 213.

28. *Zava'at ha-Rivash*, ed. J. E. Shohat (Brooklyn, 1975), par. 75, p. 23.

29. On the book, *Zava'at Ha-Rivash*, its sources and ideas, see Z. Gries, *Conduct Literature: Its History and Place in the Life of Beshtian Hasidism* [H] (Jerusalem, 1989), 149–230. The remark about the parallel passage was made at a conference entitled, "Tradition and Crisis Revisited," sponsored by the Center for Jewish Studies at Harvard University, October 1988.

30. Rubinstein, "Manuscript," 198–202, critique of the text; also, the passage about the fate of souls in heaven, which appears in the *Ben Porat Yosef* but not in the Bauminger (it begins and ends with the Hebrew word, *bemar'eh* ["in a vision"]—see translation), may have been deleted from the Bauminger version because of a homoteleuten, i.e., a copyist's error. To a large extent the argument over whether this text is an autograph or copy turns on the question of the Besht's signature. Bauminger ("Letters," 268) claimed that the signature here was independently confirmed; Rubinstein ("Manuscript," 201) disagreed. With no means of checking either the letter itself or Bauminger's suggested model for the signature, the problem remains unsolved.

31. See Bauminger, "Letters," 254–255, and Rubinstein, "More on the Matter of the Letters of the Besht," *Sinai* 73 (1973): 180. In 1984, Professor Shmuel Ettinger related to me that he had seen the Bauminger manuscript at the British Museum where it was being tested to determine its date and provenance, in preparation for sale at auction. He was assured by the expert in charge that the ink and paper came from eastern Europe in the mid-eighteenth century.

32. Dinur, *Historical Studies*, 195n.13, 198n.31, 203–204n.64; G. Scholem, *The Messianic Idea in Judaism* (New York, 1971), 189; Piekarz, *Hasidism*, 16–21; Gries, *Conduct*, 106, 111–117, 292–313; Gries, *Book*, 24–27, 56–59; R. Haran, "On the Copying and Transmission of Hasidic Letters" [H], *Zion* 56 (1991): 299–320. For a lively exchange on this subject, see R. Haran, "In Praise of the Rav: On the Reliability of Hasidic Letters from The Land of Israel" [H], *Katedra* 55 (1990): 22–58; challenge by Y. Mondshine, "The Reliability of Hasidic Letters from The Land of Israel" [H], *Katedra* 63 (1992): 65–97 and 64 (1992): 79–97; rejoinder by Haran [H], *Katedra* 64 (1992): 98–102. Note that by claiming that the *Ben Porat Yosef* version is a conflation of two authentic letters, even Mondshine admits that editors could and did doctor the Holy Epistle's text.

33. If the Bauminger text is not an autograph (see above, n. 30), then this

passage, which appears in the *Ben Porat Yosef,* may have also appeared in the original letter and may have been eliminated by the copyist of the Bauminger as a homoteleuten.

34. Here, too, if the Bauminger version is not an autograph, then the "etc." with which the Messiah citation ends (see trans. par. C) may denote elision of part of the quote. There is no basis, however, for claiming that the later versions preserve the original text. The fact that the answer of the Messiah begins differently in the Bauminger version than in the later version implies that the later documents represent paraphrases and expansions based on recopyings and retellings.

35. See translation: "I have however forgotten . . ."

36. Y. Alfasi, *Encyclopedia of Hasidism: Personalities,* vol. 1 (Jerusalem, 1986), 67–68.

37. *SBF,* 231.

38. *SB,* 2; M. J. Rosman, "The History of a Historical Source: On the Editing of *Shivhei Ha-Besht*" [H], *Zion* 58 (1993): 194–196. See also W. J. Ong, *Orality and Literacy* (London, 1982), 96, 119, 132–133, 157–158.

39. See n. 8 above.

40. The only scholar to accept the Bauminger (Frankel) text without reservation was Heschel, *Circle,* 45 and passim; see also Scholem, "Image," 348nn.33,34.

41. Gries, *Conduct,* 106–124, 146–148.

42. *EP,* 36.

43. Solomon Lutzker, the printer, was a follower of the Maggid and editor and publisher of the most important collection of his teachings, *Maggid Devarav Le-Ya'akov;* see Gries, *Book,* 56–59.

44. For translation of the *Ben Porat Yosef* version, see L. Jacobs, *Jewish Mystical Testimonies* (New York, 1977), 148–155.

45. This is an introductory colophon. The corresponding Gregorian date is the week of 13 February 1752.

46. The Besht received a letter from Gershon at the Lukow fair held either on the Sunday before Good Friday or on 8 September 1750.

47. Probably referring to each member of the family; see Gershon's letter in next chapter.

48. The failure of the letters to reach their destination.

49. On the Turkish border.

50. "Kedar" denotes Tatar-controlled areas.

51. In Gershon's brief letter, which did arrive in 1750.

52. The word in the text is *hiddushim* (sing. *hiddush*), literally "new things." It is usually employed to denote new interpretations of Torah literature or, more generally, new discoveries. I have translated it here as "news" because what the Besht was doing was telling Gershon about events he experienced.

53. This is apparently Judah Leib the Preacher; see *SB,* s.v. Index "Preacher of Polonnoye"; *SBF,* 231.

54. He had forgotten some of the news and secrets.

55. 15–16 September 1746.

56. On this mystical technique, see M. Idel, *Kabbalah: New Perspectives* (New Haven, 1988), 88–96.

57. This is the location of the possible homoteleuten (see n. 30 above). If there was a homoteleuten, then the following passage, which occurs in the *Ben Porat Yosef* version, should appear here as well: "which I had not seen from the day I became conscious until now. And what I saw and learned when ascending there is impossible to tell about and to speak of even face to face, but when I returned to lower paradise and saw certain souls of the living and the dead, both familiar and unfamiliar to me, without measure or number, running back and forth to ascend from world to world via the pillar [see Idel, *Kabbalah,* 321n.133] known to mystical initiates with abundant, great joy which the mouth cannot tell about and the fleshly ear cannot hear of. Also wicked ones repented and were forgiven for their sins because it was a time of great favor. Also in my eyes it was most wondrous that so many were received as penitents whom you also knew and they too were exceedingly happy and also ascended the aforementioned ascents and all of them as one asked me and insisted for a long time saying, 'To Your Honored Torah Highness, God has graced you with super understanding to apperceive and to know about these matters. Go up with us to be a help and support to us.' And because of the great joy which I saw among them, I intended to ascend with them, and I saw in a vision . . ."

58. *Sitra mesa'avuta* = Satan.

59. This was the biblical prophet Ahijah the Shilonite (I Kings 11:19–29 and TB *Bava Batra* 121b) who in mystical lore was believed to be a mystical adept and the sixth of seven people whose consecutive life spans cover all of historical time (the others are Adam, Methusaleh, Shem, Jacob, Serah or Amram, and Elijah). He was the Besht's heavenly guide; see Jacob Joseph of Polonne, *Toldot Ya'akov Yosef, Parshat Balak,* 156a; G. Nigal, "The Teacher and Master of R. Israel Ba'al Shem Tov," *Sinai* 71 (1972): 150–159. See also Y. Liebes, "The Messiah of the Zohar" [H], in *The Messianic Idea,* ed. S. Re'em (Jerusalem, 1982), 113n.114.

60. Hebrew *heikhal.*

61. These are the rabbis whose statements make up the content of the Mishna, edited ca. 225 C.E.

62. Adam, Seth, Methusaleh, Abraham, Jacob, Moses, and David; see Mic. 5:4, TB *Sukkah* 52b.

63. Hebrew *yihudim;* theurgic acts that have the mystical effect of unifying the Godhead; see L. Fine, "The Contemplative Practice of Yihudim in Lurianic Kabbalah," in *Jewish Spirituality,* ed. A. Green, vol. 2 (New York, 1987), 64–98, esp. 78–87.

64. The "etc." means that there was more to the Messiah's answer that either the Besht or the copyist deleted. It is this gap that was filled in by the later versions of the letter (see nn. 30, 34). The *Ben Porat Yosef* version inserts here a long passage that begins "And he answered me, 'Thus you should know, when your teaching will be famous and be revealed in the world and your springs will flow outward [Proverbs 5:16. Gershon Bacon has suggested interpreting this phrase in light of TB *Ta'anit* 7a], what I have taught you and you have attained, and they also will be able to perform unifications and ascents like you and then all the *kelipot* [forces of evil] will expire and it will be a time of favor and salvation.' " The passage continues with further comments of the Besht to Gershon and includes the section from *Zava'at Ha-Rivash,* par. 75 (see n. 29).

65. A variation on Deut. 29:23.

66. "Sanctify the name of heaven" means to martyr oneself. The words after the first occurrence of "the name of heaven" (Hebrew *shem shamayim*) through the second occurrence of "the name of heaven" are deleted in the *Ben Porat Yosef*. This might also be a homoteleuten but more likely is due to the later editors' decision to drop this reference to such a delicate topic—apostasy under duress and its consequences—around which there was traditionally much controversy.

67. Translation based on Rashi's interpretation of the verse Deut. 32:43, the accepted interpretation among traditional Jews like the Besht.

68. 13–14 September 1749.

69. A variation on II Sam. 24:14, which is also included in the daily liturgy.

70. Instead of the wholesale destruction.

71. Hebrew *havurah*.

72. A Talmudic passage (TB *Keritot* 6a) recited as part of the standard liturgy. According to the Zohar (*Parshat Pinhas* 224a; see *Gershom Scholem's Annotated Zohar*, ed. Y. Liebes, vol. 6 [Jerusalem, 1992], notes on pp. 3062–3063), whoever recites this prayer, recounting the various species of incense offered in the Temple in Jerusalem, will be spared death. On p. 84b of the Lurianic prayer book written by Moses of Lubomla in 1750 (see chap. 8, n. 91), there is a section entitled "*Pitom Ha-Ketoret* for Times of Plague."

73. The representatives of heaven.

74. A common proverb that appears in TB *Berakhot* 59a and in many other places.

75. The last day of the Sukkot (Tabernacles) holiday, considered a time for repentence.

76. Hebrew *musar*.

77. Deut. 12:20; the Besht's use of this verse reflects Rashi's comment that this verse comes to teach that affluence is a prerequisite to meat eating; the Besht is telling Gershon that when God decides to grant us wealth, then we will be able to spend it on material things.

78. That is, Jacob Joseph of Polonne, who was to deliver this letter.

79. Based on TB *Ketubot* 111b, meaning someone is in a comfortable position.

80. See above, n. 8.

81. *SB*, 54–58; Rubinstein, "Letter," 130–132.

82. *SB*, 54–58.

83. In Polish, Yankiel; see chap. 10, near n. 25.

84. See chap. 3.

85. See Pinhas Katznellenbogen's unquestioning belief in Benjamin Beinish Ba'al Shem, despite the failure of his published remedies; chap. 1, near n. 55.

86. Rubinstein, "Letter," 134.

CHAPTER SEVEN. MORE BESHT CORRESPONDENCE

1. *SB*, 41, 65, 75, 78, 213. G. Scholem, "The Historical Image of Israel Ba'al Shem Tov" [H], *Molad* 18 (1960): 342, said that one of these letters (*SB*, 41)

was "copied into *Shivhei Ha-Besht*" and that "it is very possible that it is authentic." Scholem did not apparently pay attention to the note in the story that the citation from the letter was told orally to Dov Ber of Ilintsy by the son of a man who had seen it.

2. My translation follows the text of the manuscript of *Shivhei Ha-Besht*; see *SBF*, 160. Habad has a copy of the letter that they claim is an autograph and is slightly different from the printed version; see *SBF*, 160–161, 280.

3. This is a play on words. According to tradition, the look on the face of the Kohen Gadol (High Priest) when he emerged from the Holy of Holies on Yom Kippur was to be compared to various beautiful sights (see Yom Kippur Prayer Book, Avodah Service), some of which involved lighting effects. Here the Besht is evidently comparing the flash of the letter speeding to its destination to the brightness of the countenance of Jacob Joseph, who was a kohen.

4. This is the literal translation of Av Beit Din, which two lines above was translated idiomatically as "rabbi of the . . . community."

5. The Hebrew, *iggrot*, literally means "letters" in the plural.

6. That is, near the beginning of the letter; an expression based on Mishna *Pesahim* 1:1.

7. Hebrew *mosif*, lit. "add."

8. Evidently based on TB *Berakhot* 31a: One should not stand up to pray while immersed in sorrow, or idleness, or laughter, or chatter, or frivolity, or idle talk, but only while rejoicing in the performance of a commandment."

9. Wordplay based on Isa. 58:7, where this phrase appears as part of a critique of fasting unaccompanied by sincere penitence. Isaiah admonishes his audience not to fast and then turn a blind eye to needy relatives (one's flesh and blood). The Besht seems to be saying, you will not achieve your spiritual goals by denying your flesh.

10. The letter is followed by a corrupt passage that is evidently a greeting to Jacob Joseph's son, Shimshon; see *SBH*, 105–106nn.43–44.

11. S. M. Dubnow, *History of Hasidism* [H] (Tel Aviv, 1975), 56, for example, in discussing the Besht's views on asceticism cited the *Zava'at Ha-Rivash*, which was not written by the Besht and is essentially a collection of the Maggid's hanhagot (see Z. Gries, *Conduct Literature: Its History and Place in the Life of Beshtian Hasidism* [H] [Jerusalem, 1989], 149–230); Scholem also did not adduce this letter in his article on the historical image of the Besht and emphasized instead a hearsay citation from a different letter (see above, n. 1); G. Nigal, *Leader and Followers* [H] (Jerusalem, 1962), 17, mentioned this letter in passing; S. H. Dresner, *The Zaddik* (New York, 1974), 51–52, incorporated this letter into his discussion of Jacob Joseph's ascetic tendencies.

12. According to the collection of Besht teachings published in 1794–1795, called *Keter Shem Tov* (Jerusalem, 1968), 22, the Besht called for attachment to prayer texts as well as study ones. On the problems of relying on the statements reported in this book, see chap. 8, n. 69.

13. See chap. 2, on hasidism before Hasidism.

14. G. Scholem, "The Two First Testimonies Concerning the Hasidic Groups and the Besht" [H], *Tarbiz* 20 (1949): 235.

15. J. G. Weiss, "The Kavvanoth of Prayer in Early Hasidism," in Weiss,

Studies in Eastern European Jewish Mysticism, ed. D. Goldstein (Oxford, 1985), 103–107.

16. See n. 8 above.

17. Sec. *Yoreh Dei'ah,* no. 27. The first writer on the Besht to notice this text was Eliezer Zwiefel, *Peace Unto Israel* [H] (Zhitomir, 1868) (see the edition published by A. Rubinstein [Jerusalem: 1972], 87–88). Some eighty years, later Dinur once more cited this text; see his *Historical Studies* [H], vol. 1 (Jerusalem, 1954), 205–206. Scholem also briefly cited this text in his "Image," 337.

18. The title ne'eman denotes a kahal official, often a treasurer; here, in view of the context, perhaps it means the official in charge of collecting the money people paid for slaughtering in the communal abattoir.

19. This term is synonymous with the term "moreh zedek" used in other communities and employed by Pinhas Katznellenbogen; see chap. 2, near n. 19.

20. In BC 4085 1742 Inventory of Międzybóż, 12b, "Falk Duchowny" appears. "Duchowny" is a generic term for clergyman and is consistent with Falk's serving as assistant rabbi.

21. The town where the Besht lived before moving to Międzybóż; see chap. 4, near n. 8.

22. The first signatory is obviously the Besht, who had moved from Tłuste to Międzybóż. As to the second one, according to Polish sources (BC 4080 no. 86; EW 41 1743 Akcyznik expenses), in the early 1740s the preacher in Między-bóż was one Jos Jampolski (Joseph from Jampol; see *SB,* 125, 206–207, where the preacher of Międzybóż is also called Joseph). Dropping the first name in certain usage was common. For example, the Besht's brother-in-law, Abraham Gershon, was usually referred to as just Gershon. Jacob Joseph of Polonne was usually called Joseph; so Moses Joseph the Preacher is probably identical with Joseph the Preacher. Moses Joseph is probably the person referred to as Joseph Maggid Meisharim in both Polish and Jewish sources; see M. J. Rosman, "Międzybóż and Rabbi Israel Ba'al Shem Tov," in *EP,* 209–210nn.4–5.

23. From traditions in *Shivhei Ha-Besht,* 125–126, 206–207, it is evident that the Besht had great respect for Joseph the Preacher.

24. *Mayim Hayyim,* Yoreh Dei'ah, no. 27.

25. See chap. 8.

26. While the questioners referred to the moreh hora'ah as the decisor in this matter, Rabbi Meir, in his answer, termed the protagonist "the rabbi." This might be just another way of signifying Falk, who must have had rabbinic ordination, or it might be an indication that *the* rabbi of the community, Hersz Leybowicz Aptekarz, had become involved in this very controversial matter, which seems to have been connected to a larger dispute (see below).

27. See chap. 5, near n. 27.

28. Chap. 5, near nn. 35, 40.

29. Leyba purportedly ate meat that was *nieżylowane* (lit. meat from which the veins had not been removed, a description of the hindquarter meat that was always sold as nonkosher; by extension, this word can be a general Polish term for nonkosher meat, parallel to the Yiddish term *treif* [lit. torn, rather than ritually slaughtered in the prescribed manner]); see the butchers' petition EW 41 10/14/1741; and BC 5870 l.21169 12/21/1744, where the rabbi called one of

the arrendators a "tyrant." Dinur, *Historical Studies,* vol. 1, 206, conjectured that the responsum of Rabbi Meir dates from ca. 1744; its *terminus ad quem* is ca. 1747, the year when Gershon of Kutów—addressed by Rabbi Meir as present in Międzybóż—emigrated to the Land of Israel. Since the Polish documents, concerning the rabbi's possible dismissal, date from 1744 and 1745 (BC 5870 l.21168 4/2/1744, l.21169 12/21/1744; BC 5929 l.33449 6/26/1745; BC 5931 l.33988 7/10/1745), the time frame is further circumstantial evidence for postulating that the Polish and Hebrew sources relate to the same incident.

30. Such a portrayal can be found, for example, in S. M. Dubnow, "The Beginnings: The Baal Shem Tov (Besht) and the Center in Podolia," in *EP,* 39–41; R. Mahler, *A History of Modern Jewry* (London, 1971), 456–458; B.-Z. Dinur, "The Origins of Hasidism and Its Social and Messianic Foundations," in *EP,* 134–139; I. Zinberg, *A History of Jewish Literature,* vol. 9 (Cincinnati, 1976), 30, 44–51. This view has percolated into more popular works as well: P. Johnson, *A History of the Jews* (London, 1988), 295–296; C. Potok, *Wanderings* (New York, 1986), 351–352; H. Weiner, 9½ *Mystics: The Kabbala Today* (New York, 1992), 124; E. Wiesel, *Souls on Fire* (New York, 1972), 17–21, 25–27. By contrast, there are stories in *SB* that depict the Besht as rather strict in ritual matters; e.g., *SB,* 90–91, 195, 254–255, cf. p. 192. In one story, p. 202, the Besht sides with an apparently powerful community member from Bar against the rabbi, but then it is shown that the rabbi was right after all. This case does not seem to be an echo of the butchers/Rabbi Hersz Leybowicz Aptekarz episode; the place, issue, and people involved all are different.

31. See chap. 2, near nn. 18–21.

32. Rabbi Meir's response will be discussed in chapter 8.

33. Scholem, "Image," 337; see also p. 341. Cf. the issue of the status of ba'alei shem, chap. 1, near nn. 32–35.

34. Dinur, *Historical Studies,* vol. 1, 206.

35. Rosman, "Międzybóż," 217–219, and chap. 10.

36. See chap. 6, n. 5.

37. J. G. Weiss, "Some Notes on the Social Background of Early Hasidism," 6; "A Circle of Pneumatics in Pre-Hasidism," 31–40, both in his *Studies in Eastern European Jewish Mysticism,* ed. D. Goldstein (Oxford, 1985); A. J. Heschel, *The Circle of the Ba'al Shem Tov,* ed. and trans. S. H. Dresner (Chicago, 1985), 113–117, 148–149 (the translation states that Israel Ha-Levi was the great grandson of R. Moses, but the introduction to his book—and Heschel's original Hebrew text—indicates clearly that he lived two generations later); *SBH,* 64.

38. *SB,* 28, 34, 42, 180–181, 209; this relationship was further embellished in oral traditions appearing in H. Gelernter, *Oneg Hayyim Le-Shabbat* (Life Joy for the Sabbath) (Munkacz, 1908), introduction.

39. These adjectives appear in the form of acronyms and some are open to other interpretations; e.g., "none other than" may be read as "the great sage," "servant of God" may be read as "the eye of the people."

40. Lit. "may his light shine."

41. Tłuste is the town the Besht lived in before he settled in Międzybóż; see above, his signature to the question asked of Rabbi Meir of Konstantynów.

42. Here and elsewhere in the letter, "you" appears in the plural as a sign of

respect. The alternate form of second-person address is to use the word *mar*, translated here as "master."

43. See Targum Onkelos on Gen. 28:12; the implication being that as the angels are messengers of God, the Besht is a messenger of Rabbi Moses.

44. Slight emendation of the Hebrew text as suggested to me by Elhanan Reiner yields the common cliché: "who travel from here to there." In any case, this may be a description of Gypsies, who were believed to possess magical and medical knowledge. (As Avraham Holtz pointed out to me, the Hebrew term for vagabonds, *arhi-parhi*, can be a synonym for Gypsies; see N. Stuchkoff, *Lexicon of the Yiddish Language* [Y] [New York, 1950], sec. 120, p. 112.)

45. See TB *Shabbat* 109b.

46. The opening words of the final paragraph of the Amidah prayer said every day.

47. M. Bauminger, "Letters of Our Rabbi Israel Ba'al Shem Tov and His Son-in-Law Rabbi Yehiel Mikhl to Rabbi Abraham Gershon of Kutów" [H], *Sinai* 71 (1972): 251, announced that this letter was in his possession and partially described it.

48. Kutower stated that the address he copied was "on the reverse of the letter at the top [*u-mei-eiver ha-mikhtav mi-le-ma'alah*]," while Bauminger, "Letters," 251, mentioned that an address, perhaps an additional one, was written on a second piece of paper that served as a wrapping or envelope for the letter itself.

49. The letter was also published in shortened, emended form in late 1878 in the book attributed to R. Barukh of Międzybóż, *Butzina De-Nehora* (Lamp of Light) (Lemberg), edited by Nahman Liebman of Bar, apparently after Liebman had seen Kutover's book in either manuscript or printed form. This would be consistent with the fact that all of Liebman's book was copied from published sources; see A. Shisha-Halevi, "On the book *Butzina De-Nehora*" [H], *Alei Sefer* 8 (1980): 155–157. The changes in the *Butzina De-Nehora* version of the letter seem to be attempts by Liebman to improve difficult readings. Scholem, "Image," 341, referred only to the *Butzina De-Nehora* version of this letter and asserted that "there is no doubt as to its authenticity" on the grounds that it had remained among R. Barukh's papers. However, the origin of all of the material in *Butzina De-Nehora* is questionable and its relationship to R. Barukh doubtful (see Shisha-Halevi). Liebman himself did not claim that this or any of the other letters he published (as opposed to the teachings in the book) came from R. Barukh's personal archive.

50. On "pre-hasidic" Hasidism, see Weiss, "Circle," 27–42; Heschel, *Circle*, 113–117; Dinur, "Origins," 159–172; and chap. 2.

51. See chapter 1 in connection with the controversy over the status of ba'alei shem. Rabbi Moses' availing himself of ba'al shem services, as this letter demonstrates, supports the position that ba'alei shem could be well respected and part of the normative leadership.

52. Scholem, "Image," 341–342, referred only to the *Butzina De-Nehora* version, which as observed (n. 45 above) is late and unreliable.

53. On the institution of bet midrash in general, see chap. 2, near n. 10; on the Besht and the bet midrash in Międzybóż, see chapter 10.

54. R. Schatz-Uffenheimer, "The Besht's Commentary to Psalm 107," *Hasidism as Mysticism* (Princeton, 1993), 342–382.

55. Schatz-Uffenheimer, "Commentary," 342–347, 370.

56. Ibid., 351–353.

57. Ibid., 353; see also G. Scholem, *Explications and Implications* [H] (Tel Aviv, 1975), 344n.3; G. Scholem, *The Messianic Idea in Judaism* (New York, 1971), 189.

58. Common examples with regard to the Ba'al Shem Tov are reading of *Zava'at Ha-Rivash* as the Besht's will rather than a collection of the Maggid's *hanhagot*, some of which are attributed to the Besht; use of the portrait of Samuel Hayyim Falk, the Ba'al Shem of London, by John Singleton Copley, as if it were a portrait of the Besht.

59. Schatz-Uffenheimer, "Commentary," 353, 370–371n.50; see also A. Green, "Typologies of Leadership and the Hasidic Zaddiq," in *Jewish Spirituality,* vol. 2, ed. A. Green (New York, 1987), 154n.7, who evidently agreed with Schatz-Uffenheimer.

60. See Kahana's account, "On Manuscript Letters of the Besht and his Disciples" [H], *Ha-Yishuv* 24 (Adar 5685[= 1925]): pt. 3, p. 425.

61. Y. Rafael, "The Geniza of Kherson," *Sinai* 81 (1977): 129–150. The documents themselves are housed in the Habad archive in Brooklyn and are not accessible to non-Habad scholars.

62. See M. Balaban, *On the History of the Frankist Movement* [H], vol. 2 (Tel Aviv, 1935), 315–320. Even within Habad, doubts have been expressed. R. Shalom Duber himself pronounced the letters copies, not originals (Rafael, "Geniza of Kherson," 138). In 1953, D. Z. Hillman, a Habad Hasid, published a detailed critique of the letters (*Letters of the Author of the Tanya [Shneur Zalman of Ladi] and His Contemporaries* [H] [Jerusalem, 1953], 240–247; and continued in "More on the Matter of the Kherson Geniza" [H], *Ha-Sefer* 2 [1955]: 32–42) concluding that they were not authentic. The late Habad leader, Rebbe M. M. Schneersohn, promised to issue a new edition of the letters that would answer Hillman's criticisms, but this was never done. At an early stage, non-Habad Hasidim, such as the Rebbes of Gur, Belz, and Munkacz, all expressed their refusal to accept the letters as genuine; see Rafael, "Geniza of Kherson," 146–148. Rafael himself hedged over calling the letters forgeries.

63. Rafael, "Geniza of Kherson," 133–135; S. M. Dubnow, *History of Hasidism* [H] (Tel Aviv, 1975), 425–426.

64. D. Assaf, "Rabbi Israel Ruzhin and His Role in the History of the Hasidic Movement in the First Half of the Nineteenth Century," Ph.D. dissertation, Hebrew University, 1992, 94–103, on Rabbi Israel's arrest and detention. Rabbi Israel's papers were confiscated at the time of his arrest, but according to his own testimony, these included homiletic material from his forefathers, not letters, and he said nothing about material from the Besht; see Assaf, "Rabbi Israel Ruzhin," 110–112.

65. Hillman, *Letters.*

66. Ibid.

67. Rafael, "Geniza of Kherson," 143. Partisans of the letters reply to this and other criticisms that the letters are only copies of the originals. In the process

of copying, the paper changed and mistakes and stylistic modifications crept in. This in itself is an admission that the letters are less than authentic. Moreover, if they are copies, why did someone go to the trouble of trying to disguise them as originals, folding and sealing them, adding official-looking stamps, and cataloging information? The contention that these copies were used as decoys to cover up the theft of the originals from the archive and their return to their rightful owner is far-fetched in the extreme.

68. All three letters were addressed in a respectful tone to rabbis and implied recognition and admiration of their achievements in Torah learning. In addition, note the pride the Besht displayed in his letter to his brother-in-law (chap. 6, Holy Epistle par. G) concerning the accomplishments of his grandson, who was a "great prodigy at the highest level of learning."

69. From *SB* to Scholem, there is a long-established tradition of claiming that the Ba'al Shem Tov met with strong opposition in his lifetime. This is most unlikely in light of (a) the sources evaluated here; (b) the Polish sources to be discussed in chapter 10; (c) the probable polemical nature of *SB* (chap. 9); (d) the lack of credibility of Scholem's sources on this point (see chap. 8).

CHAPTER EIGHT. TESTIMONIES

1. Several scholars questioned the Besht's historicity; see A. Z. Aescoly-Weintraub, *Le Hassidisme: Essai Critique* (Paris, 1928), 39–40, 51; I. Schiper, "R. Israel Ba'al Shem Tov and His Image in Early Hasidic Literature" [H], *Ha-Doar* 39 (1960): 525, 531–532, 551–553. These four texts were cited, but not quoted at length, by Scholem in his article, "The Historical Image of R. Israel Ba'al Shem Tov" [H], *Molad* (1960): 337, 341, 343, 352. My interpretations differ from his on several points.

2. TB *Megillah* 6a, an expression connoting great fame and admiration throughout the Jewish world.

3. This is Rabbi Abraham Gershon of Kutów, the Ba'al Shem Tov's brother-in-law, a prominent Talmudist and Kabbalist in Podolia who emigrated to the Land of Israel in 1747. See A. J. Heschel, *The Circle of the Ba'al Shem Tov,* trans. and ed. S. H. Dresner (Chicago, 1985), 44–97.

4. Hayyim ben Berish, *Mayim Hayyim* (Zhitomir, 1857), sec. Yoreh Dei'ah, no. 27; see chap. 7 for translation of the Besht's letter included in the first part of this document.

5. B.-Z. Dinur, *Historical Studies* [H] (Jerusalem, 1954), 205–206, agreed with this assessment; Scholem, "Image," 337, intent on proving opposition, did not accept it; see also E. Z. Zweifel, *Peace Unto Israel* [H], pt. 1, ed. A. Rubinstein (Jerusalem, 1972), 87–88.

6. See chap. 2.

7. See chap. 10.

8. See chap. 1, esp. discussion concerning Mordecai Ashkenazi, near nn. 46–47.

9. Heschel, *Circle,* 98–99.

10. The last four words, literally "may his light shine," are a conventional formula for wishing a person long life; a sign that when this was written the Besht

was still alive. Heschel argued that the emotional reaction to seeing Jerusalem that Rabbi Gershon voiced in the cited passage from this letter is that of a first-time visitor. The tone of the more famous letter, published by Barukh David Ha-Kohen, is much more matter of fact. Therefore, Heschel concluded, the letter cited by Teomim is a different, earlier one; see Heschel, *Circle,* 98.

11. See my analysis of the Rothschild manuscript version of the Holy Epistle, chap. 6, near nn. 24–27. The phenomenon of copying, circulating, and studying the correspondence of Hasidic leaders is very well known in the late eighteenth and early nineteenth century; see Z. Gries, *The Book in Early Hasidism* (Tel Aviv, 1992), 31–35; J. Barnai, *Hasidic Letters from Eretz Israel* [H] (Jerusalem, 1980); N. Karlinsky, *The Hasidic Epistles from the Land of Israel* [H] (Yad Ben Zvi, Jerusalem, in press); R. Haran, "On the Copying and Transmission of Hasidic Letters" [H], *Zion* 56 (1991): 299–320.

12. B. D. Ha-Kohen, *Blessing of the Land* [H] (Jerusalem, 1904), 62–64 (reprinted in Y. Barnai, *Hasidic Letters,* 33–42). Heschel, *Circle,* 44–45, said that he possessed a manuscript copy of this letter but never published the text.

13. These are biblical allusions: I Sam. 17:18; Song of Songs 8:6; II Sam. 1:26.

14. This contrasts with the later traditions—*SB,* 19–22, 26–28, 42, and passim—stressing how Gershon scorned the Besht as an ignorant boor when they first met. If these traditions are accurate, then Gershon eventually changed his mind; see also Heschel, *Circle,* 47–48, 185–186.

15. Heschel, *Circle,* 45–47, 50–52. On Katznellenbogen and ba'alei shem, see chap. 1, near n. 48; on Moses of Kutów, see chap. 7, near n. 37.

16. Probably refering to the Maghreb, that is, the western rim of North Africa.

17. M. Idel, *Kabbalah: New Perspectives* (New Haven, 1988), 75–88: "Weeping as a Mystical Practice."

18. See D. Manor, "R. Hayyim ben Attar in Hasidic Tradition," *Pe'amim* 20 (1984): 88–110, and references there.

19. That is, the group of people who regularly pray together with the Besht.

20. For legends linking the Besht and Haim ben Attar, see *SBF,* 251n.45; see also Manor, "Hayyim ben Attar," 88–110.

21. Ha-Kohen, *Blessing,* 62d.

22. Ibid.

23. See discussion of Jacob Joseph of Polonne, chap. 2, near n. 23.

24. Chap. 2, n. 16 and near n. 22; M. Idel, *Studies in Ecstatic Kabbalah* (Albany, 1988), 141n.5.

25. Chap. 6, Holy Epistle translation, par. E.

26. On this trip, see Dinur, *Historical Studies,* 192–206.

27. A similar tradition concerning a failed trip to Eretz Yisrael relates to the Gaon of Vilna; B. Landau, *The Gaon and Hasid of Vilna* [H] (Jerusalem, 1968), 237–250; see chap. 2, near nn. 40–48, for comparison of images of the Besht and the Gaon.

28. Ha-Kohen, *Blessing,* 64 (reprinted in Barnai, *Hasidic Letters,* 42–46), dated "Monday 17 Marheshvan 5517" (= 10 Nov 1756); this was a Wednesday, not Monday. It is unlikely that a forger would make such a clumsy mistake. It seems more likely that a copyist mistook the cursive Hebrew letter *bet* (signifying Monday) for *dalet* (signifying Wednesday). With regard to the identification

of those close to the Besht by virtue of their relationship to him, see the Polish sources in chapter 10.

29. The book is called *Degel Mahaneh Ephraim* (DME). The place of publication is not mentioned. The pagination of this edition is confused, so references here are taken from the second edition, Koretz, 1810.

30. P. 16a: "I heard from my Grandfather of blessed memory that there are 39 labors which are for the purpose of sustaining human life, but when a person is occupied with Torah he does not need the 39 material labors because the dew [Hebrew *tal*, in numerology equal to 39] of Torah vivifies him." Moses Ephraim also brought a citation he heard from the Besht (p. 87b) that "fear [of God] is primary, the Torah is secondary"—a confirmation of the common Jewish notion that Torah study without commitment to faith is undesirable.

31. Compare, for example, how Pinhas Katznellenbogen wrote about Mordecai Ashkenazi of Lwów who, while originally an ignoramus, was graced by a maggid who taught him enough so that he could write a commentary on the Zohar; see chap. 1, near n. 44.

32. *DME* is laced with citations of interpretations that Moses Ephraim said he heard directly from the Besht or quoted in his name (including citations from Jacob Joseph of Polonne's books); see, for example, pp. 1d, 2b, 4b, 5b, 6b, 8a, and passim. Moses Ephraim also implied that the Besht studied books such as *Brit Menuhah* (by Abraham ben Isaac of Rimmon Sefarad [Amsterdam, 1648]): p. 2b; writings of Maimonides, p. 91a; the Zohar, p. 38d; and the works of the Ari, p. 60c. See also Scholem, "Image," 353.

33. Like Mordecai Ashkenazi; see chap. 1, near n. 44.

34. For examples of parables and stories that Moses Ephraim quoted in the name of the Besht, see *DME*, 58a, 65a, 69d, 71a, 87b, 95c.

35. *DME*, 22c; see also pp. 63d, 87b.

36. According to Moses Ephraim, his grandfather had told him that he did not possess enough power of speech to bring the Messiah: *DME*, 113a; Scholem, "Image," 348. See the later versions of the Holy Epistle about the Messianic process and also the passages in the letter that show him appealing the fate of the Jewish people; and see the statement reported to Moses Ephraim by Jacob Joseph of Polonne (*DME*, 80a): "Sometimes the world is at the high levels, and sometimes the world stands at the low ones. Now that I am in the world, the world is on the high level."

37. *DME*, 7a, 23b, 33b, 85d, 94c.

38. These are standard penitential prayers.

39. *DME*, 113a.

40. See chap. 6, Holy Epistle translation, par. C, where the Besht expressed his fear that he had died while performing his ascent of the soul.

41. These words are recorded in Yiddish, which enhances their credibility.

42. *DME*, 113a; see also Scholem, "Image," 348–349.

43. On the use of these terms and their equivalents by the Besht and those close to him, see A. Rapoport-Albert, "God and the Zaddik as the Two Focal Points of Hasidic Worship," in *EP*, 306–310.

44. *DME*, 58a.

45. On the material dependence of hasidim on the general public, see J. G. Weiss, "The Beginnings of Hasidism" [H], *Zion* 16 (1951): 49–51.

46. S. M. Dubnow, *History of Hasidism* [H] (Tel Aviv, 1975), 484; Scholem, "Image," 339.

47. 1013–1103, a North African scholar who wrote the classic Talmudic digest, *Sefer Ha-Halakhot*.

48. One of the six divisions of Talmudic literature.

49. Died 1798; one of the associates of the Besht, and founder of the Twersky Hasidic dynasty. His book was *Maor Einaim* (Slavuta, 1798); the citation is on pp. 84d–85a.

50. Chap. 7, near n. 44; and see Scholem, "Image," passim.

51. See chap. 1, n. 55.

52. See chap. 1, near nn. 27, 57, 58.

53. See *SB*, 6, and *SBH*, 32–33n.66.

54. Second century Talmudic rabbi, viewed in Jewish tradition as the progenitor of the Kabbalah. This comment is expressing the mystical idea that these great men shared the same soul.

55. See Polish sources in chapter 10 and *SB*, 55, 257.

56. Ostróg 1794, p. 6a.

57. Ps. 19:9.

58. The Urim and Thummim, Exod. 28:28, were an oracle, made out of gemstones, borne on the High Priest's breastplate of gold and fine textiles.

59. Hebrew *hasidut*.

60. Habbakuk 2:4.

61. See chap. 7, near n. 8.

62. See *SB*, 49, 198. On the Cordoveran Kabbalistic roots and theurgic implications of adherence to the letters, see M. Idel, "Perceptions of Kabbalah in the Second Half of the Eighteenth Century," *Journal of Jewish Thought and Philosophy* 1 (1991): 68–76, 90–94.

63. Chap. 2, near n. 48; see also chapter 9, on the Margoliot family tradition regarding the behavior of the young Besht, and the *SB* tradition (p. 34) that the Besht spent years in ascetic seclusion.

64. Version 1: "for the Ba'al Shem Israel of Międzybóż died in 1759 and was famous as a ba'al shem, not as a master of Torah, and all the great ones rejected him, except for a few whose names I remember according to rumor, people without reputation" (S. M. Dubnow, "The Beginnings of Hasidism," in *EP*, 49). Version 2: "Israel Międzybozer, who died in 1759, the year of my wedding, and I remember that he was famous not as a scholar, but as a ba'al shem, writer of amulets, and he did not learn at all . . . and he would walk in the markets and the streets with a pretentious stick in his mouth, a pipe and shank, and speak with the women" (ibid., 57n.57). Scholem, "Image," 352, emphasized Makow's failure to call the Besht by the technical term for ignoramus, *am-ha-aretz*. According to Scholem this omission should "get us thinking," implying that even this enemy of Hasidism was forced to concede that the Besht was not a completely unlearned person. Still, Scholem admits that another virulent Mitnaged, Yisrael Leibl, reported that, according to the Rabbi of Międzybóż, the Besht was "an

empty cistern with no water of Torah" (Scholem, "Image," 351; see also Dubnow, "Beginnings," 47; and J. G. Weiss, "The Kavvanoth of Prayer in Early Hasidism," in Weiss, *Studies in Eastern European Jewish Mysticism,* ed. D. Goldstein
[Oxford, 1985], 100–101, 118n.12). I would refrain from too close an exegesis
of the terms used by these late eighteenth-century enemies of Hasidism. As to the
date of the Besht's death, see Dubnow, "Beginnings," 44, 56n.48, and M. J. Rosman, "Międzybóż and Rabbi Israel Ba'al Shem Tov," in *EP,* 218.

65. Scholem, "Image," 343. The original is in the *She'iltot* appendix to *Tosefet Ma'aseh Rav* (Jerusalem, 1896), 18b, par. 112. This source is problematic. It
appears in a text that is a retelling of traditions concerning bits of wisdom and
halakhic rulings from Hayyim of Volozhin (1749–1821), the Gaon of Vilna's star
pupil. Thus it is hearsay of hearsay. Moreover, as Y. Mondshine (*KH,* 183) notes,
later sources place this assessment of the Besht in the mouth of the Gaon. In my
opinion, this ascription was probably an attempt to harmonize the historical relationship between the two men in order to soften the Hasidic-Mitnagdic antagonism. There is no documented opinion expressed by the Gaon on the Besht.

66. Scholem, "Image," 340, citing Yoel Halperin, *Korei Mei-Rosh* (Berdichev,
1811).

67. See above, n. 65.

68. This is illustrated by the publishing history of *Shivhei Ha-Besht.* This
book began as a manuscript compilation of traditions about the Besht and others, written down some thirty years after the Besht's death. It was edited and aug-
mented and printed by the Habad printer, Yisrael Yoffe, in 1814 and then was
published with additional stories in Yiddish in 1815 (the Yiddish also deleted
many stories from the original collection; see M. J. Rosman, "The History of a
Historical Source: On the Editing of *Shivhei Ha-Besht*" [H], *Zion* 58 [1993]:
175–214). The accretion of traditions as to what the Besht taught continued into
modern times, and the publication of *The Ba'al Shem Tov on the Torah* [H], 2
vols., ed. S. M. M. Wandek (Lodz, 1938; Jerusalem, 1992), which culls teachings cited in the name of the Besht from some 200 sources, represents a climax
of sorts to this process.

69. *Toldot Yaakov Yosef* (Koretz, 1780), *Ben Porat Yosef* (Koretz, 1781),
Zofnat Pa'anei'ah (Koretz, 1782), and *Kutonet Pasim* (Lwów, 1866). A later collection of putative Ba'al Shem Tov teachings is *Keter Shem Tov,* compiled by
Aaron ben Zvi Ha-Kohen of Opatów, and first published in Żółkiew, 1794–
1795. The lack of a direct connection between the compiler and the Ba'al Shem
Tov, the compiler's interpolations in the traditions he cites, and the inclusion of
many traditions stemming from the Maggid of Mezerich and other figures make
this a highly problematic source for deriving original Besht traditions; see G.
Nigal, "A Primary Source of Hasidic Story Literature" [H], *Sinai* 79 (1976):
132–142. Just as unreliable is the so-called *Will of the Besht* (*Zava'at Ha-Rivash*
[Ostrog, 1793]) which is actually a collection of the *Hanhagot* (moral conduct
instruction) of the Maggid of Mezerich; see Z. Gries, *Conduct Literature: Its History and Place in the Life of Beshtian Hasidism* [H] (Jerusalem, 1989), 149–230,
and chap. 6, near n. 29. Each of these two books may indeed contain authentic
Besht teachings, but isolating them is even a more difficult process than it is for
Jacob Joseph of Polonne's books, as will be discussed below.

70. R. Foxbruner, "Habad: The Ethical Thought of R. Shneur Zalman of Lyady," Ph.D. dissertation, Harvard University, 1984, 14.

71. Foxbruner, "Habad," 14; *SB*, 179; Scholem, "Image," 346–347.

72. M. Piekarz, *The Beginning of Hasidism* [H] (Jerusalem, 1978), 20, 27, 29, 31; G. Nigal's introduction to *Zofnat Pa'anei'ah* (Jerusalem, 1989), 10–12. See also Dinur, *Historical Studies*, 195n.13, 198n.30, 203–204n.64; Z. Gries, *The Book in Early Hasidism* [H] (Tel Aviv, 1992), 54–56; and chap. 6, n. 32.

73. See Scholem, "Image," 347–349, 353.

74. Nigal, *Zofnat Pa'anei'ah*, 13. The Maggid wrote nothing down. His teachings have come to us in the form of later written editions of his oral teachings in works such as *Maggid Devarav Le-Ya'akov* and *Zava'at Ha-Rivash*. These texts are quantitatively but a fraction of the size of Jacob Joseph of Polonne's books, and the Besht citations brought in these books are much fewer. See Foxbuner, "Habad," 14–17; and Gries, *Conduct,* 110–181, 292–308.

75. Foxbruner, "Habad," 15.

76. Chap. 6, near nn. 9–16.

77. This practice, the sources for it, and the controversy surrounding it are cited by Abraham Gombiner, in his classic seventeenth-century commentary, Magen Avraham, to the Shulhan Arukh, *Orah Hayyim,* sec. 156, n. 2.

78. Gries, *Book,* 23–27; Gries, *Conduct,* 110–118; and see studies cited in chap. 6, n. 32.

79. Gries, *Book,* 24–26, 49–59.

80. *Maggid Devarav Le-Ya'akov,* ed. R. Schatz-Uffenheimer (Jerusalem, 1976), 3; see also Foxbruner, "Habad," 58, 99.

81. See sources cited by in *KH,* 53; and by Foxbruner, "Habad," 99n.58; see also the comments of Judah Leib, son of Dov Ber, the compiler of *Shivhei Ha-Besht,* near the end of the introduction to his edition of Gedaliah of Ilintsy's homilies called *Teshuot Hen* (Cheers) (Berdichev, 1816).

82. Dubnow, *History of Hasidism,* 52; presumably the same principle applies to the tales.

83. *Hasidism and Haskalah* [H] (Berlin, 1909), 6–7; see also A. Schweitzer, *The Quest of the Historical Jesus* (London, 1956), 333, quoting W. Wrede: "Each critic retains whatever portion of the traditional sayings can be fitted into his construction and rejects the rest." This seems to me to be what Scholem did in his "Image" article and elsewhere.

84. Nigal, *Zofnat Pa'anei'ah,* 13.

85. Scholem, "Image," 349.

86. Foxbruner, "Habad," 13–14.

87. Ibid., 14. Curiously, on the next page Foxbruner seemed to change his mind: "These reservations are least applicable, however, to R. Jacob Joseph's works, which carefully and conscientiously distinguish between what the author actually heard directly from the Besht and second-hand or putative Beshtian teachings." (See, similarly, Nigal, *Zofnat Pa'anei'ah,* 13). I fail to see how these distinctions bear on the problem at hand, which is precisely the problematic nature of the process of transmission of the directly heard word into the form of the printed text as explicated above. "Second-hand or putative Beshtian teachings" are not even under consideration.

88. "The Ba'al Shem Tov and the Beginning of the Hasidic Movement," unpublished paper held in JNUL Scholem Collection, no. 6836.7.

89. J. Vansina, *Oral Tradition as History* (Madison, 1985), 92–108, 114–121; W. J. Ong, *Orality and Literacy* (London, 1982), 48–49, 67, 98.

90. Consider, for example, the disagreement surrounding the Besht's ideas on the study of Torah: J. Weiss, "Torah Study in Early Hasidism," in Weiss, *Studies in Eastern European Jewish Mysticism*, ed. D. Goldstein (Oxford, 1985), 56–62; R. Schatz-Uffenheimer, *Hasidism as Mysticism* (Princeton, 1993), 311–314; M. Piekarz, *The Beginning of Hasidism* [H] (Jerusalem, 1978), 346–347, 358–360. See also A. Green, "Typologies of Leadership and the Hasidic Zaddiq," in *Jewish Spirituality*, vol. 2, ed. A. Green (New York, 1987), 153n.7; A. Green, "The Zaddiq as *Axis Mundi* in Later Judaism," *Journal of the American Academy of Religion* 45 (1977): 339. There is similar controversy over his Kabbalah knowledge; see chap. 11, n. 26. See also Vansina, *Tradition*, 121–123, who delineates certain conditions under which the relationship between tradition and past reality can be assessed. These conditions do not apply in Hasidism, which, despite its strong oral component, was a literate and literarily sophisticated group.

91. Another category of attributions is that of prayer kavvanot. A *kavvanah* is a Kabbalistic tool that held great importance in Kabbalistic-style prayer. The words of holy texts, such as the Bible and the prayer book, hint at various combinations of divine names that, when pronounced as an act of kavvanah, put the worshiper in the proper state of mystical contemplation and empower him to affect the cosmic processes. See Louis Jacobs, *Hasidic Prayer* (New York, 1973), 36–37; Schatz-Uffenheimer, *Hasidism,* 225–230; J. Weiss, "Kavvanoth," in Weiss, *Studies in Eastern European Jewish Mysticism,* ed. D. Goldstein (Oxford, 1985), 95–125, esp. 95–98. For a discussion of how the significance of kavvanot was construed in the eighteenth century, particularly by Hasidic leaders, see M. Idel, "Perceptions of Kabbalah in the Second Half of the Eighteenth Century," *Journal of Jewish Thought and Philosophy* 1 (1991): 68–76, 90–95. Late eighteenth-century texts contain several Kavvanot attributed to the Besht as well as traditions that the Besht advised reciting certain kavvanot at particular times. According to Scholem's identification of the Besht as Shabbetai of Raszkow's teacher, the printed edition of his siddur (Koretz, 1794) contains three such attributions (vol. 1 pt. 1, 20a, 262a [the first p. 262]; vol. 2 pt. 1, 52a) and three traditions (vol. 2 pt. 1, 52b; pt. 2, 7a, 56b), all of which were added by the editor. (See Scholem's handwritten note on the flyleaf of the second volume in the Scholem Collection of the JNUL: R 5010. My thanks to Prof. Moshe Hallamish and Mr. Menahem Kallus for calling the existence of these kavvanot to my attention and to Mr. Kallus for allowing me to read his unpublished analysis of them.) Another kavvanah attributed to the Besht appears as a later addendum to a Lurianic prayer book manuscript written by Moses ben Joseph of Lubomla in Jampol in 1750. (I wish to express my gratitude to Shelomoh Mehudar of Jerusalem for allowing me to peruse the 1750 *siddur* and copy parts of it; I also owe thanks to Prof. Thomas Hubka and Dr. Iris Fishoff for making me aware of the siddur's existence.) The full significance of these seven texts for the development of Hasidism awaits explanation, but it does seem, contrary to what

some scholars have claimed for later Hasidism (see Jacobs, *Prayer*, 74–80; Schatz-Uffenheimer, *Hasidism*, 215–241; Weiss, "Kavvanoth," 98–99, 106–117), that the Besht continued the traditional practice of saying kavvanot.

92. Dubnow, "Beginnings," 26–27; B.-Z. Dinur, "The Origins of Hasidism and its Social and Messianic Foundations," in *EP*, 136; Scholem, "Image," 345; see also M. J. Rosman, "The Quest for the Historical Ba'al Shem Tov," in *Tradition and Crisis Revisited*, ed. B. D. Cooperman (Cambridge, Mass., in press). For more on how the stories have been utilized, see chapter 9.

CHAPTER NINE. LIFE STORIES

1. The text is not divided into story units. Ben-Amos and Mintz, *SB*, identified 251 discrete stories; Rubinstein, *SBH*, thought there were 214.

2. S. M. Dubnow, "The Beginnings: The Baal Shem Tov (Besht) and the Center in Podolia," in *EP*, 26–45; I. Zinberg, *A History of Jewish Literature*, vol. 9 (Cincinnati, 1976), 29ff.; R. Mahler, *A History of Modern Jewry* (London, 1971), 455–458; B. D. Weinryb, *The Jews of Poland: A Social and Economic History of the Jewish Community in Poland from 1100 to 1800* (Philadelphia, 1972), 263–269; B.-Z. Dinur, "The Origins of Hasidism and Its Social and Messianic Foundations," in *EP*, 134–136, 159–160, 196–197, and passim; J. G. Weiss, "The Kavvanoth of Prayer in Early Hasidism," in Weiss, *Studies in Eastern European Jewish Mysticism*, ed. D. Goldstein (Oxford, 1985), 100, 102; S. Ettinger, "The Hasidic Movement—Reality and Ideals," in *EP*, 227–228; G. Scholem, "The Historical Image of Israel Ba'al Shem Tov" [H], *Molad* 18 (1960): 340 and passim.

3. Dubnow, "Beginnings," 27 (my translation of Dubnow's Hebrew text, p. 43, differs from the one in *EP*). This is the metaphorical interpretation alluded to at the end of chapter 8.

4. See L. Raglan, *The Hero: A Study in Tradition, Myth and Drama* (New York, 1936); O. Rank, *The Myth of the Birth of the Hero* (New York, 1964); M. Hadas and M. Smith, *Heroes and Gods: Spiritual Biographies in Antiquity* (New York, 1965), 3; M. Smith, "Prolegomena to a Discussion of Aretalogies, Divine Men, The Gospels and Jesus," *Journal of Biblical Literature* 90 (1971): 186, 191; M. Goodich, "A Profile of Thirteenth-Century Sainthood," *Comparative Studies in Society and History* 18 (1976): 437.

5. *SB*, 13–18.

6. Dubnow, "Beginnings," 28; G. Scholem, "The Sabbatean Prophet R. Heschel Zoref—R. Adam Ba'al Shem" [H], *Zion* 6 (1941): 89–93, 7 (1942): 28; Y. Eliach, "The Russian Dissenting Sects and Their Influence on Israel Baal Shem Tov, Founder of Hassidism," *Proceedings of the American Academy for Jewish Research* 36 (1968): 67–68 (for a critique of Eliach's thesis, see chap. 3, near nn. 68–75).

7. K. Shmeruk, "The Stories about R. Adam Ba'al Shem and Their Development in the Versions of *Shivhei Ha-Besht*" [H], in *Yiddish Literature in Poland* [H] (Jerusalem, 1981), 119–139.

8. B.-Z. Dinur, *Historical Studies* [H] (Jerusalem, 1954), 188–189.

9. Scholem, "Image," 346–356.

10. See chap. 6, near and in n. 5.

11. Scholem, "Image," 338–339 and passim.

12. Ibid., 346–347.

13. *SB*, 179.

14. Scholem, "Image," 347, posited that this pair of tales indicated that one of the main shapers of the Hasidic legends in the generation following the Besht's death was the man who had apparently been responsible for the transformation of this story, R. Gedaliah of Ilintsy.

15. For a short bibliography on the analysis of hagiography, see M. J. Rosman, "The History of a Historical Source: On the Editing of *Shivhei Ha-Besht*" [H], *Zion* 58 (1993): 177n.3, 181n.24.

16. J. Perl, *Uiber das Wesen der Sekte Chassidim,* ed. A. Rubinstein (Jerusalem, 1977), 77–78; for a listing of the various editions and translations of *Shivhei Ha-Besht,* see Y. Rafael, *"Shivhei Ha-Besht,"* *Areshet* 2 (1960): 358–377, 3 (1961): 440–441. Two important additions to this list are *SBF* and *SBH*.

17. It apparently dates from the years immediately preceding the 1814 printed edition (see Rosman, "Source," 183–184); on the differences from the printed text, see *SBF*, 7–18.

18. For my treatment of these problems, see Rosman, "Source," 183–210. For many years some scholars thought that the discrepancies between the printed Hebrew text and the 1815 Yiddish edition printed in Ostróg indicated that the Yiddish was based on an unedited manuscript of *Shivhei Ha-Besht*. This assumption of the existence of some *urtext* can no longer be maintained. Mondshine, *SBF*, 22–47, has demonstrated that these discrepancies are better explained as a result of normal practice in Yiddish translation, while I have claimed (Rosman, "Source," 180–183) that they also reflect typical changes in the translation of any hagiographic work from a literary language such as Hebrew to a vernacular like Yiddish. Moreover, some of the changes in the Yiddish seem intended to solve textual problems resulting from the printer's editing. The Yiddish is clearly based on the 1814 printed Hebrew text, although, in a typical hagiographic development pattern, it incorporates some additional and alternative oral traditions. Note that Ben-Amos and Mintz's English translation (*SB*) does not accurately reflect the placement of parentheses in the text, which makes it more difficult to identify where the printer intervened; see the first printing, which is held in JNUL R 8°35V4001.

19. See, for example, *SB* story numbers 15 and 31, 34 and 35, 37 and 39, 125 and 126. With regard to parallels to stories about other figures, see J. Dan, *The Hasidic Novella* [H] (Jerusalem, 1966), 68–71; G. Nigal, *The Hasidic Tale: Its History and Topics* [H] (Jerusalem, 1981), 25–27; Shmeruk, "R. Adam," 119–139; Rosman, "Source," 202n.93.

20. *SB*, 290–305 (the applicability of some of these categories is questionable).

21. Dinur, *Historical Studies*, 195.

22. All in Hebrew: "A Possibly New Fragment of *Shivhei Ha-Besht*," *Tarbiz* 35 (1966): 174–191; "The Revelation Stories in *Shivhei Ha-Besht*," *Alei Sefer* 6–7 (1977): 157–186; "The Letter of the Besht to R. Gershon of Kutów," *Sinai*

67 (1970): 120–139; "The Mentor of R. Israel Ba'al Shem Tov and the Sources of His Knowledge," *Tarbiz* 48 (1979): 146–158; "Notes on *Shivhei Ha-Besht*," *Sinai* 86 (1980): 62–71; "Concerning Three of the Stories in *Shivhei Ha-Besht*," *Sinai* 90 (1982): 269–279.

23. See *SBF*, 65–67.

24. See I. Etkes, "Hasidism as a Movement—The First Stage," in *Hasidism: Continuity or Innovation*, ed. B. Safran (Cambridge, Mass., 1988), 8–19.

25. An exception to this is Rubinstein's analysis ("Letter," 129–132) of the story about the Besht's ascent of the soul on Yom Kippur 5717. Here Rubinstein compared the details of the story with what is known from outside sources. As a result he demonstrated how the the first trial of rabbinic Judaism instigated by the Frankists in 1757 in Kamieniec-Podolski provided the context for this story.

26. See above, n. 18.

27. I. Bartal, "The Aliyah of R. Elazar from Amsterdam to *Eretz Yisrael* in 1740" [H], in I. Bartal, *Galut Ba-Aretz* (Exile in the Homeland) (Jerusalem, 1994), 34.

28. J. Barnai, "Some Clarifications on the Land of Israel Stories of 'In Praise of the Ba'al Shem Tov,' " *Révue des études juives* 146 (1987): 367–380.

29. Ibid., 379.

30. These names are vocalized according to the way they appear in the Polish documents: EW 41, see chap. 10; see also *SB*, 173.

31. *SB*, 173–175; see also chap. 1, near nn. 29–30.

32. Zev Kutzes and David Purkes came to the Besht.

33. The Besht gave the same lesson he had given in heaven in the presence of the deceased student.

34. See preceding story, *SB*, 173.

35. See chap. 1, n. 64.

36. See chap. 10.

37. Scholem, "Image," 350.

38. See, e.g., *SB*, 46–49, 222–223.

39. The book was by Moses of Satanów, *Mishmeret Kodesh* (Żółkiew, 1746), sec. 5, p. 2a; see G. Scholem, "Two Testimonies about Hasidic Groups and the Besht" [H], *Tarbiz* 20 (1949): 232, 235.

40. This explains the shift from the singular "man" to the plural "They don't speak"; see H. Liberman, *Ohel Rahe"l* (Brooklyn, 1980), 38–49; also M. Piekarz, *The Beginning of Hasidism* [H] (Jerusalem, 1978), 131–141. Piekarz, pp. 306–321, also showed how a second source (Shelomoh Helma, *Mirkevet Ha-Mishneh* [n.p., 1751], introduction [which Scholem, "Testimonies," 232–240, considered to be a critique of Beshtian Hasidim] was in reality a conventional response to general neglect of Talmudic learning and popularization of Kabbalah.

41. See T. J. Heffernan, *Sacred Biography: Saints and Their Biographies in the Middle Ages* (Oxford, 1988), 18–30.

42. Ibid., 4–20, 35, 150–151; R. Boyer, "An Attempt to Define the Typology of Medieval Hagiography," in *Hagiography and Medieval Literature: A Symposium*, ed. H. Bekker-Nielson et al. (Odense, 1981), 128–133; M. Sot, "Arguments hagiographiques et historiographiques dans les 'Gesta episcoporum,' " in *Hagiographie, cultures et sociétés vi–xii siècles* (Paris, 1981), 99–101; P. Maraval,

"Fonction pedagogique de la littérature hagiographique d'un lieu de pélérinage: L'exemple des miracles de Cyr et Jean," ibid., 383–397; B. Cazelles, "Introduction," in *Images of Sainthood in Medieval Europe*, ed. R. Blumenfeld-Kossinski and T. Szell (Ithaca, 1991), 1; M. Carrasas, "Sanctity and Experience in Pictorial Hagiography: Two Illustrated Lives of Saints from Romanesque France," ibid., 41; C. Hahn, "Speaking without Tongues: The Martyr Romanus and Augustine's Theory of Language in Illustrations of Bern Burgerbibliothek Codex 264," ibid., 161–162.

43. *SB*, 5.

44. Ibid., 1.

45. S. Lieberman, *Hellenism in Jewish Palestine* (New York, 1962), xv; J. Neusner, "Judaic Uses of History in Talmudic Times," in *Essays in Jewish Historiography*, ed. A. Rapoport-Albert (Atlanta, 1991), 12–39. S. Zfatman, *The Jewish Tale in the Middle Ages: Between Ashkenaz and Sepharad* (Jerusalem, 1993), 103–104, probably overstated the case when she asserted that a folktale "does not tell anything about the time it occurred, but rather about the time it was told," as historians, anthropologists, and folklorists are engaged in an essential argument over the historical content of traditions; see D. Golan, "Construction and Reconstruction of Zulu History," Ph.D. dissertation, Hebrew University, 1988, 178–179.

46. On the connection between historical events and hagiography, see Bartal, "Aliyah," 7–18; Cazelles, "Introduction," 4–6; Sot, "Arguments," 95–104.

47. *SB*, 3–4.

48. Compare the famous story told by Rabbi Israel of Ruzhin, *Knesset Israel* (Warsaw, 1906), 12a, about how the Besht lit a candle in the forest and said *yihudim* and kavvanot in order to cure a sick person. According to this story, each generation is successively removed from the ability to perform miracles via theurgy, with the last generation ultimately substituting storytelling about theurgy for the acts themselves. For various versions and interpretations of this story, see Idel, *Kabbalah*, 270–271, 397n.92; G. Scholem, *Major Trends in Jewish Mysticism* (New York, 1961), 349–350; M. Piekarz, *Studies in Bratzlav Hasidism* [H] (Jerusalem, 1972), 102–103; E. Wiesel, *Souls on Fire* (New York, 1972), 167–168.

49. For a detailed analysis of the printer's statements on this point, see Rosman, "Source," 198–200.

50. *SB*, 7–32.

51. On the probable reasons for this, see chapter 12.

52. Rosman, "Source," 179–180, 192–194, 208–209.

53. The reasons for this warrant a separate study. By the time the Besht had been dead one hundred years, and Hasidism had spread and strengthened, it reflected well on the Margoliot family to have "discovered" the Besht back when he was an unknown. For analysis of this collection and how it reflects both history and the era of its publication, see M. Altschuler, "*Kevuzat Ya'acov*: Between Biography and Hagiography" [H], in *Proceedings of the XIth World Congress of Jewish Studies*, vol. C2, 153–160; R. Haran, "Ideological Controversies within Hasidism" [H], Ph.D dissertation, Hebrew University, 1993, 62.

54. Chap. 8, near nn. 56–63; see also Scholem, "Image," 352. The *termi-*

nus ad quem for the initial contact is 1737 because that is when Zvi Margoliot died, and it was in his lifetime that his sons Isaac and Meir first came close to the Besht.

55. *Gedolim Ma'aseh Zaddikim,* 13–14.

56. As in *SB* revelation stories concerning the Besht; see pp. 28, 30–31, 34, 45–46.

57. Leib ben Ozer, *The Story of Shabbetai Zevi* [Y/H], trans. and annotated Z. Shazar, ed. S. Zucker and R. Plesser (Jerusalem, 1978), 80–84.

58. G. Scholem, *Studies and Texts Concerning the History of Sabbateanism and Its Metamorphoses* [H] (Jerusalem, 1974), 84–85.

59. S. Maimon, "On a Secret Society and Therefore a Long Chapter," in *EP,* 19–21.

60. See *SB* stories, pp. 49, 165, 198, on the Besht's use of the Zohar for clairvoyance and protection.

61. Chap. 8, near nn. 56–60.

62. See chap. 1.

CHAPTER TEN. LIGHT FROM THE ARCHIVES

1. See chapter 9, regarding attempts to corroborate the *SB* stories—all of which depend primarily on Jewish sources; see also Y. Eliach, "The Russian Dissenting Sects and Their Influence on Israel Baal Shem Tov, Founder of Hassidism," *Proceedings of the American Academy for Jewish Research* 36 (1968): 57–83. The failure of this most famous attempt to place the Besht in the religious context of his time and locale discouraged further research in this direction; see chap. 3, near nn. 68–75.

2. See, for example, his letters in chapter 7 and the stories in *Shivhei Ha-Besht;* also I. Etkes, "Hasidism as a Movement—The First Stage," in *Hasidism: Continuity or Innovation,* ed. B. Safran (Cambridge, Mass., 1988), 21–23.

3. Holy Epistle, chap. 6; Letter to Meir of Konstantynów, chap. 7; Etkes, "First Stage," 21–23.

4. Chap. 6, Holy Epistle, pars. C, F.

5. Chap. 3, nn. 52–53.

6. See the discussion of the Corpus Christi incident in chapter 5, near n. 15.

7. BC 4047 1730; *LJ,* 42–43, 48.

8. M. J. Rosman, "An Exploitative Regime and the Opposition to It in Międzybóż, Ca. 1730," in *Transition and Change in Modern Jewish History: Essays Presented in Honor of Shmuel Ettinger,* ed. S. Almog et al. (Jerusalem, 1987), xix–xxix; and chap. 5, near n. 22; see also *LJ,* 132.

9. *LJ,* 52–66, 87, 192; Rosman, "Regime," xix–xxix; see also G. D. Hundert, *The Jews in a Polish Private Town: The Case of Opatów in the Eighteenth Century* (Baltimore, 1992), 134–155.

10. M. J. Rosman, "Reflections on the State of Polish-Jewish Historical Study," *Jewish History* 3 (1988): 125–126; Hundert, *Opatów,* 43–45, 19–22, 55–57, 104–108; J. Katz, *Tradition and Crisis* (New York, 1971), 29–34.

11. *LJ,* 41–62 and passim; M. J. Rosman, "A Minority Views the Majority: Jewish Attitudes Towards the Polish-Lithuanian Commonwealth and Interaction

with Poles," *Polin* 4 (1989): 31–41; Hundert, *Opatów,* 40–45, 54–57, 61–63, 102–103, 106–107, 134–155.

12. *SB,* 22, 23, 36, and s.v. Index "Gentiles."

13. Chap. 5, near nn. 34–35; chap. 7, Besht's letter to Rabbi Meir of Konstantynów; see also *SB,* 202.

14. Chap. 7, n. 44; chap. 6, The Holy Epistle, pars. C, D; see also *SB* s.v. Index "Governors."

15. A forgery, *Ma'aseh Norah Be-Podolia,* placed him at the 1759 Lwów disputation with the Frankists. M. Bałaban, *On the History of the Frankist Movement* [H], vol. 2 (Tel Aviv, 1935), 295–311, proved that the Besht was not present during this trial.

16. *Shivhei Ha-Besht,* 43–44; petitions in EW 86 Nowa Sieniawa; EW 176 Satanów, Zinków; EW 179 Matjasz Rogola, Jacenty Ordynski, Semian Piasecki, Satanów; EW 525 Szkłów; EW 1509 Iwan, Parzylo, et al.; and see sources listed in *LJ,* 135–136nn.96–100.

17. *SB,* 163–164, 246; *LJ,* 180; J. Goldberg, *Converted Jews in the Polish Commonwealth* (Jerusalem, 1985), 24–40, 73–75.

18. *LJ,* 200–202; *SB,* 202. The town was Bar; the episode involved the Preacher, i.e., Leib. It is probably not related to the incident with the rabbi in Międzybóż discussed in chapters 5 and 7; cf. Hundert, *Opatów,* 144–145.

19. For a description and discussion of the inventories, see M. J. Rosman, "The Polish Magnates and the Jews: Jews in the Sieniawski-Czartoryski Territories," Ph.D. dissertation, Jewish Theological Seminary of America, 1982, 451–457.

20. On the 1764 census, see S. Stampfer, "The 1764 Census of Polish Jewry," *Bar Ilan* 24–25 (1989): 41–59, and bibliography there. The results of the census for the Czartoryski properties, dated 25 December 1764, are held in AGAD Archiwum Potockich z Lancuta 168: RM.

21. BC 4127 1763, BC 4131 1766, RM 124.

22. Sometimes written Hodol, and in RM 124, Judel. Her son, Moses Ephraim, is also listed as Froim together with his wife, Jętel.

23. BC 4111 1752, BC 4114 1753, BC 4117 1755, BC 4121 1758, BC Gospodarcze 308 1760, BC 4127 1763, BC 4125 1767, RM 124.

24. With the exception of BC 4111, the same sources as for Yehiel (n. 23); in RM, Hersh appears on p. 125.

25. The same sources as for Hersh the scribe (n. 24).

26. The same sources as for Yehiel (n. 23) and RM 117. On RM 124, his son, Faywel Kucy Wolfowicz, appears. Wolf is also mentioned in EW 41 3/38/1743, EW 41 1743 Summary of Communal Expenses.

27. EW 41 1743 Summary of Communal Expenses; he is probably one of the several Davids who appear in the inventories with various identifiers (perhaps Dawidko Kaznodzieja [David the Preacher], who lived on the same street as the Besht [BC Gospodarcze 308 1760]).

28. For stories connected to these people, see *SB* Index.

29. *SB,* 125, 206–207; see chap. 7, n. 22; BC 4080 1741, EW 41 1743 Summary of Communal Expenses.

30. *SB,* 108; BC 4080 1741; for other inventories, see n. 23 above; EW 41 expense summaries for various years contain budget allocations for a basista.

31. *SB*, 145–146.

32. C. Kaminski and J. Żukowski, *Catalog of Polish Money* [P] (Warsaw, 1980), 18; A. Popiół-Szymanska, *Polish Monetary Perspectives from the Fifteenth to the Eighteenth Centuries* [P] (Poznan, 1978), 108–109, 114–115. In Hebrew sources, *zloty* is referred to as *zahuv, czerwony zloty* is *adom*.

33. *SB*, 191.

34. See chap. 2, near n. 10.

35. *SBF*, 214. This detail supports the claim that the manuscript is closer both in content and time of composition to Dov Ber of Ilintsy's original compilation of the stories than is the printed version; see M. J. Rosman, "The History of a Historical Source: On the Editing of *Shivhei Ha-Besht*," *Zion* 58 (1993): 183–184, 210, esp. nn. 32, 124.

36. *SB*, 225–229.

37. BC 4117 1755, BC 4121 1758, BC Gospodarcze 308 1760, BC 4125 1767, RM 123.

38. S. Porush, "Międzybóż, City of the Holy Besht" [H], *Nahalat Zvi* 4 (1991): 37.

39. Ed. G. Nigal (Jerusalem, 1991), 15.

40. *SB*, 144ff.

41. Ibid., 20.

42. BC 4067, BC 4079, BC 4085, BC 4121, BC GOSP 308, BC 4127; see also BC 4131 and RM.

43. For discussions of the relationship between the Polish administration and the Jewish communal institutions, see *LJ*, 185–205, and Hundert, *Opatów*, 134–155.

44. EW 41: "Ubogim Żydom w Międzybóżu mieszkaiącym których kahal tuteyszy uznał przezemnie na ten tylko rok są approbowani."

45. See *SB* Index.

46. With regard to the synonymity and interchangeability of the terms Ba'al Shem and Ba'al Shem Tov, see chapter 1. According to the tax rolls and other sources, there were other people named Israel and even Israel ben Eliezer in Międzybóż. One document, dated 25 May 1731 (BC 3822 nr 77)—some nine years before the Besht's arrival in Międzybóż—is an order to Icko Ognisty to appear in court. As guarantors that he would indeed show up, three people signed the document: two Jews and one Christian. The Jews committed themselves, in Yiddish, thus: "I am a guarantor for Mr. Itzik; I am obligated to appear at the castle for the trial concerning the complaints people have against him." One of the signatories was "Yisrael ben Eliezer" (in Polish, Izrael Leyzorowicz), otherwise known as Izrael Niemierzynski.

47. *SB*, 173–174; chap. 1, near n. 29.

48. EW 41 3/28/1743; BC 4125 1767.

49. *SB*, 55; in other stories he is depicted as praising the Besht to his own son and as a person who told stories about the Besht; see *SB*, 6, 176, 203, 257. All of this implies that he was close to the Ba'al Shem Tov.

50. *SB*, Index s.v. "Ze'ev Kotses."

51. *SB*, Index s.v. "David Forkes of Medzhibozh."

52. See chap. 1, near n. 29ff.; chap. 9, near n. 30ff.

53. Not a kloyz, which was sponsored by a private Maecenas; see chap. 2, near n. 10.

54. J. G. Weiss, "A Circle of Pneumatics in Pre-Hasidism," in Weiss, *Studies in Eastern European Jewish Mysticism*, ed. D. Goldstein (Oxford, 1985), 27–42.

55. Weiss, *Studies*, 27–42; B.-Z. Dinur, "The Origins of Hasidism and Its Social and Messianic Foundations," in *EP*, 172.

56. A. Green's comment ("Typologies of Leadership and the Hasidic Zaddiq," in *Jewish Spirituality*, ed. A. Green, vol. 2 [New York, 1987], 154n.7), "the Besht was not a 'Kabbalist' as the term was generally used in the eighteenth century," requires further explanation.

57. See *SB*, 253; M. J. Rosman, "Międzybóż and Rabbi Israel Ba'al Shem Tov," in *EP*, 224n.59.

58. S. M. Dubnow, "The Beginnings: The Baal Shem Tov (Besht) and the Center in Podolia," in *EP*, 35; G. Scholem, "The Historical Image of Israel Ba'al Shem Tov" [H], *Molad* 18 (1960): 337, 342.

59. These lists are not free of methodological problems: some people were omitted, and lists are incomplete. However, whatever is included was put there by the original transmitters of the material.

CHAPTER ELEVEN. A PERSON OF HIS TIME

1. For an enumeration of these contradictions, see the beginning of chapter 1.

2. S. Ettinger, "The Hasidic Movement—Reality and Ideals," in *EP*, 230–231.

3. M. Piekarz, *The Beginning of Hasidism* [H] (Jerusalem, 1978).

4. G. Scholem, "The Historical Image of Israel Ba'al Shem Tov" [H], *Molad* 18 (1960): 353–356; A. Rubinstein, "The Letter of the Besht to R. Gershon of Kutów" [H], *Sinai* 67 (1970): 120–139; I. Etkes, "Hasidism as a Movement—The First Stage," in *Hasidism: Continuity or Innovation*, ed. B. Safran (Cambridge, Mass., 1988), 12–13, 17, 21–23; A. Rapoport-Albert, "God and the *Zaddik* as the Two Focal Points of Hasidic Worship," in *EP*, 299–329.

5. Chapter 4, analysis of Międzybóż Jewish economic structure, and E. Reiner, "Wealth, Social Position, and the Study of Torah: The Status of the Kloyz in Eastern European Jewish Society in the Early Modern Period" [H], *Zion* 58 (1993): 327.

6. See chap. 2.

7. See chap. 3, near nn. 55–61.

8. See the remarks of Solomon Isaac Halpern and Moses ben Yokel of Międzybóż, chap. 8, near nn. 47, 53; and the story from *Gedolim Ma'aseh Zaddikim*, chap. 9, near n. 54.

9. J. Katz, *Tradition and Crisis* (New York, 1971), 109.

10. Rapoport-Albert, "God and the *Zaddik*," 313–314.

11. Chap. 6, near n. 76.

12. M. Idel, "Jewish Magic from the Renaissance Period to Early Hasidism," in *Religion, Science, and Magic: In Concert and in Conflict*, ed. J. Neusner et al. (New York: 1989), 100–106, termed the Besht's modus operandi a variety of "redemptive magic."

13. Chap. 8, near n. 43.

14. Reiner, "Kloyz," 323–326.

15. See chap. 7, near n. 22 and following.

16. *SB*, 46, 48, 164.

17. S. M. Dubnow, "The Beginnings: The Baal Shem Tov (Besht) and the Center in Podolia," in *EP*, 57n.57; chap. 8, n. 62.

18. H. Weiner, *9½ Mystics: The Kabbala Today*, first published by Holt Rinehart and Winston (New York, 1969), reprinted several times since and revised by Collier Books (New York, 1992); Weiner's summation demonstrates the resonance in popular perception of the accounts by Dubnow, *History of Hasidism* [H] (Tel Aviv, 1975), and B.-Z. Dinur, "The Origins of Hasidism and Its Social and Messianic Foundations," in *EP*, 118 ff.

19. It may also be part of an attempt to legitimate later Hasidic leaders; see chapter 12.

20. See chap. 9, near n. 54. In *SB*, the Besht slaughters, but he is never depicted as holding a professional position. We should also recall the hasid of Leipnik (chap. 2, near n. 21), who wanted to become the town's shohet.

21. *SB*, 34–36, 42, 43, 45, 176.

22. *LJ*, 49–51; R. Mahler, *History of the Jews in Poland* [H] (Merhavia, 1946), 248–249.

23. Chap. 8, n. 32. The Besht's Shavuot kavvanah notes the vocalization of the Divine names he coined; see chap. 8, n. 91.

24. Scholem, "Image," 352–356.

25. J. G. Weiss, *Studies in Eastern European Jewish Mysticism,* ed. D. Goldstein (Oxford, 1985), 118n.12 and see p. 100; Scholem, "Image," 353.

26. Scholars have been divided as to the extent of the Besht's mastery of Kabbalah. Weiss, *Studies,* 100; Scholem (as cited by Schatz-Uffenheimer, *Hasidism as Mysticism* [Princeton, 1993], 371n.50); and Green, "Typologies of Leadership and the Hasidic *Zaddiq*," in *Jewish Spirituality*, ed. A. Green, vol. 2 (New York, 1987), 154n.7, were skeptics on this point. Schatz-Uffenheimer, *Hasidism*; and Idel, "Jewish Magic," 100–106, and *Kabbalah: New Perspectives* (New Haven, 1988), passim, had much more confidence that the Besht was knowledgeable in various aspects of Kabbalah.

27. *SB*, 45 and passim; see also Idel, *Kabbalah,* 75.

28. Chap. 7, near n. 43; *SB*, 34, 42, and p. 28.

29. As to his confidence, note the tone of his correspondence in chapters 6 and 7. The cleverness is evident in his plays on words; see chapter 7, letter to Jacob Joseph of Polonne, near nn. 7, 9; see also Green, "Typologies," 154n.7.

30. Chap. 7, near n. 45.

31. Letter to Jacob Joseph of Polonne, chap. 7, near n. 8, and testimony of Meir Margoliot, chap. 8, near n. 57.

32. Chap. 8, near n. 10.

33. Chap. 8, near n. 2.

34. Chap. 8, near n. 64.

35. Chap. 10, near n. 42.

36. Chap. 7, near n. 45.

37. Chap. 8, near n. 2.

38. See Rosman, "Source," 213–214.

39. See the Holy Epistle, pars. C, D.

40. See Etkes, "First Stage," 18–20.

41. See chap. 8, n. 91.

42. Chap. 8, near n. 54.

43. Chap. 2, near n. 28; *SB*, 156. Several scholars have emphasized the Besht's importance in popularizing—if not originating—this approach; see R. Schatz-Uffenheimer, *Hasidism*, 108, 235–236; J. Weiss, "The Beginnings of Hasidism" [H], *Zion* 16 (1951): 69, 89, 93–95, 102; Piekarz, *Hasidism*, 261, 276–279, and passim.

44. J. H. Chajes, "Hasidism's Emergence: Messianism, Asceticism and Theurgy," unpublished paper.

45. See P. Burke, *Popular Culture in Early Modern Europe* (New York, 1978), 70–71; A. Gurevich, *Medieval Popular Culture: Problems of Belief and Perception* (Cambridge, 1988), 2–4.

46. Chap. 7, near n. 9; chap. 8, near n. 57; see Idel, "Jewish Magic," 101.

47. According to *Keter Shem Tov* (Jerusalem, 1968), 22, the Besht also called for attachment to the letters of prayer texts.

48. Y. Liebes, "Shabbetai Zvi's Attitude Toward His Own Conversion" [H], *Sefunot* n.s. 2(17) (1983): 289n.148.

49. G. Scholem, "The Two First Testimonies Concerning the Hasidic Groups and the Besht" [H], *Tarbiz* 20 (1949): 235.

50. See *SB*, 34; and Margoliot description, chap. 8, near n. 59.

51. *SB*, 65.

52. H. Pedaya, "On the Development of the Social-Religious-Economic Model of Hasidism: The *Pidyon*, the *Havurah* and the Pilgrimage" [H], in *Religion and Economics* [H], ed. M. Ben Sasson (Jerusalem, 1994), near nn. 147, 168, traces the development of the Hasidic court directly from the institution of havurah and has asserted that one of the key innovations of Hasidism was the zaddik's assumption of the tasks of host and meal provider for the members of his group. This can be construed as an extension of the conventional role of paterfamilias.

53. I. Etkes, "Trends in the Study of the Hasidic Movement" [H], *Jewish Studies* 31 (1991): 18.

54. See G. Scholem's famous article, "Devekut or Communion with God," in *EP*, 275–298, on how the Besht espoused Divine communion as a possibility for all Jews. Scholem's thesis was significantly qualified by A. Rapoport-Albert, "God and the *Zaddik*," 299–329, showing that a key point in Hasidism was the zaddik's mediation of any communion.

55. A. Green, "Typologies," 130–152, traced various sources and paradigms that were drawn on to create the notion of zaddik; with regard to the element of the priest-healer-holy man in the zaddik persona, see pp. 140–142.

56. The parallels with Jesus as the "founder" of Christianity and Shaka Zulu as the "father" of African nationalism are plain; see A. Schweitzer, *The Quest of the Historical Jesus* (London, 1956); D. Golan, "Construction and Reconstruction of Zulu History," Ph.D. dissertation, Hebrew University, 1988.

57. In a recent unpublished paper, Adam Teller has argued for the plausi-

bility of the story in *SB* (pp. 211-213) placing the Besht in the service of the famous Ickowicz bothers of Słuck. If true, this still does not confirm the Besht's reputation outside of the eastern part of Poland-Lithuania during his lifetime.

CHAPTER TWELVE. FROM THE HISTORICAL BESHT
TO THE USABLE BESHT

1. A. Rapoport-Albert, "The Hasidic Movement after 1772: Continuity and Change" [H], *Zion* 55 (1990): 187-215.

2. Ibid., 235-236, 240-245.

3. See, for example, A. Green, *Tormented Master* (New York, 1981), 265; S. Sharot, *Messianism, Mysticism and Magic: A Sociological Analysis of Jewish Religious Groups* (Chapel Hill, 1982), 180.

4. Rapoport-Albert, "Hasidic Movement," 184, 196-201, 207-208; for the few early examples of protohereditary leadership, beginning with the Lezhensk group in 1786, see p. 235n.204.

5. I. Etkes, "The Rise of R. Shneur Zalman of Ladi to a Position of Leadership" [H], *Tarbiz* 54 (1985): 429-439; I. Etkes, "R. Shneur Zalman of Ladi's Way as a Leader of Hasidim" [H], *Zion* 50 (1985): 321-354; N. Karlinsky, "The Hasidic Epistles from Eretz-Yisrael: The Text and the Context, A Reconsideration" [H], master's thesis, Hebrew University, 1989 [scheduled for publication in 1996 by Yad Ben Zvi), 49-51.

6. Etkes, "Rise."

7. H. M. Hielman, *Beit Rabbi* (Berdichev, 1902), 187; N. Loewenthal, *Communicating the Infinite* (Chicago, 1990), 104.

8. Hielman, *Rabbi,* 104.

9. In its attempt to create the impression of continuity and harmony, Habad historiography glossed over the details of the struggle among the three candidates. Despite this, as R. Elior, "The Controversy over the Legacy of Habad" [H], *Tarbiz* 49 (1980): 166-186, and later in her book, *The Doctrine of the Divine in the Second Generation of Habad Hasidism* [H] (Jerusalem, 1982), 6-14, showed, literary traces of the strife remain. Elior; L. Jacobs, *Seeker of Unity* (London, 1966), 12-13, 21-22, 23-25n.4, 86-88, 115-117, 159-164; and Loewenthal, *Infinite,* 104-141, have all described various philosophical or ideological aspects of the dispute. There was also, however, a political dimension.

10. Jacobs, *Seeker,* 11-13, 23-25; Loewenthal, *Infinite,* 101-103, Elior, *Divine,* 3-21.

11. Hielman, *Rabbi,* 134, 189.

12. R. Aaron, like most Hasidim, identified Hasidism with traditional mystic hasidism. He went a step farther and held up Habad Hasidism as the true embodiment of all Hasidism. This is congruent with the Mitnagdim's opposition to Hasidism on the grounds that it perverted traditional hasidism. The Hasidic response was to insist that there is no turning point, but that the Besht was but one of the great figures in the long history of hasidism stretching back to Judah Hasid in the twelfth century; see chapter 2 on hasidism before Hasidism. The association of the Besht with R. Adam Ba'al Shem (see chap. 9, near n. 5, and below in this chapter) is a good example of this. Once such an identification is made,

it implies that to be chief teacher of Habad is tantamount to being chief spiritual leader of the era.

13. Rabbi Aaron's books, *SYE*, title page and pp. 7b, 8a, 14a; and *SA*, 12b (for both books, the pagination is mine).

14. For detailed explication of his doctrines, see Jacobs, *Seeker*; Elior, *Divine*, 118–125; Loewenthal, *Infinite*, 112–113, 119–120, and according to the Index.

15. R. Aaron's *AL*, pt. 2, pp. 5c–6d; see also Elior, Jacobs, and Loewenthal.

16. *SA*, 13b; *SYE*, 5b, 12b.

17. Cited by Elior, "Controversy," 166–168.

18. S. D. Levin, ed., *Igrois Kodesh* (Brooklyn, 1987), no. 5, pp. 234–235. The forewords to Rashaz's books appear in Y. Mondshine, *Likutei Amarim: The Tanya, Its Editions, Translations and Commentaries* [H] (Kefar Habad, 1982), 62, and Mondshine, *The Halakhic Books of the Old Admor: A Bibliography* [H] (Kefar Habad, 1984), 23–25.

19. S. Katz, "Letters of Maskilim Criticizing Hasidim" [H], *Moznaim* 10 (1940): 269; B. Mayer, *Die Jüden Unserer Zeit* (Regensburg, 1842), 18 (thanks to Dr. Michael Silber for calling this source to my attention); Hielman, *Rabbi*, 113–114; Elior, "Controversy," 167n.10.

20. Elior, "Controversy," 167–168; note how Ruderman's maskilic prejudice against mysticism prompted him to equate it with hypocrisy.

21. Loewenthal, *Infinite*, 104.

22. Hielman, *Rabbi*, 187, 150.

23. See G. Nigal edition, pp. 85–87, 22–25; Elior, *Divine*, 9n.36.

24. Hielman, *Rabbi*, 188–190.

25. The term in Hebrew is *anash,* an acronym for *anshei shlomeinu,* referring to those inside the group and best translated, perhaps, as "the people we care about" or "our crowd."

26. R. Dov Ber's *LB*, 2b; on teaching and preaching, see also pp. 3a, 60a–b, 64b.

27. Elior, "Controversy," 174–186, and *Divine*, 6–14, 289–326; Jacobs, *Seeker*, 85–86, 159–164, and Dobh Baer of Lubavitch, *Tract on Ecstasy*, trans. and ed. L. Jacobs (London, 1963), 11–12, 42–46; Loewenthal, *Infinite*, 119–120, 131–135, 167–170.

28. *LB*, 1, 2a, 9, 65.

29. *LB*, 2a, 11–12, 55b; Elior, "Controversy," 181–186; Elior, *The Paradoxical Ascent to God* (Albany, 1993), 195–197; Jacobs, *Ecstasy*, 13–20, and *Seeker*, 13, 115–116; Loewenthal, *Infinite*, 109–119, 124–131, 159–163.

30. *LB*, 3a.

31. Loewenthal, *Infinite*, 105, 120, 173, 178–187.

32. Levin, *Igrois*, 234–235.

33. Ibid.

34. Hielman, *Rabbi*, 184; Loewenthal, *Infinite*, 103. At the time Lubavici was owned by the Lubomirski family, see *SG*, vol. 5, p. 392.

35. Hielman, *Rabbi*, 188; the letters were written by Rashaz's brother, R. Judah Leib of Janowicz, and by one of Rashaz's associates, R. Pinhas Schick. They are undated, but the subject matter puts them squarely in the period of the contest over the leadership.

36. For publication details, see D. Levin, "R. Dov Ber Schneersohn's Essay on Ecstasy" [H], *Kiryat Sefer* 54 (1979): 829–830. In their final printed form these tracts are called "Introduction to the Essay on Ecstasy," "Essay on Ecstasy," and "Essay on Reflection."

37. See Elior, *Divine*; Jacobs, *Seeker*; and Loewenthal, *Infinite*.

38. *LB*, 3a.

39. Ibid., 60b.

40. Ibid., 64b.

41. Ibid., 66b–67b.

42. Ibid.

43. See n. 18 above; Karlinsky, "Hasidic Epistles," 65–66, 243n.51.

44. Karlinsky, "Hasidic Epistles," 70–75; R. Schatz-Uffenheimer, *Hasidism as Mysticism* (Princeton, 1993), 260–289; I. Tishby and J. Dan, "Hasidic Doctrine and Literature," in *Encyclopedia Hebraica* 17:789–792; R. Elior, *Ascent*, 191–200.

45. Mondshine, *Bibliography*, 23.

46. Ibid.; see also *SB*, 104–105.

47. I. Twersky, "*The Shulhan Aruk*: Enduring Code of Jewish Law," in *The Jewish Expression*, ed. J. Goldin (New York, 1970), 328–329.

48. Mondshine, *Bibliography*, 24: "making it so that every person can read the set law with its reasoning in his way. He will be fluent in it and the casuistry will be left to the enlightened ones only."

49. Mondshine, *Tanya*, 62.

50. Mondshine, *Bibliography*, 25.

51. Z. Gries, *The Book in Early Hasidism* [H] (Tel Aviv, 1992), 50–59; see also exchange between Haran and Mondshine, above, chap. 6, n. 32.

52. Loewenthal, *Infinite*, 139–145, and bibliography of Dov Ber's publications.

53. Y. Y. Schneersohn, "Notations" [H], *Ha-Tamim* 2 (1936): 79; Hielman, *Rabbi*, 10, 149, 213; H. D. Friedberg, *The History of Hebrew Printing in Poland* [H] (Tel Aviv, 1950), 135–137; S. D. Levin, *The History of Habad in the Holy Land* [H] (New York, 1988), 51–52; Levin, *Igrois*, 79, 172–175, 459–463; *SBF*, 19n.37; A. Ne'eman, *Our Hebron* [H] (in press); Karlinsky, "Hasidic Epistles," 75–81.

54. Hebrew acronym for our master, teacher, and rabbi, usually referring to the zaddik, or leader, of a Hasidic group.

55. *Inyan Ha-Hishtathut al Kivrei Zaddikim* (n.p., n.d.). According to A. M. Haberman ("Habad Title Pages" [H], in *Alei Ayin: S. Z. Schocken Jubilee Book* [H] [Tel Aviv, 1951], 339, no. 201), the book was published in Shklov "after 1813."

56. *SYE*, 12b–13a; evidently a reference to R. Dov Ber

57. R. Haran, "Ideological Controversies within Hasidism" [H], Ph.D. dissertation, Hebrew University, 1993, chap. 3; Karlinsky, "Hasidic Epistles," 52ff.

58. This Hasidic leader was a critic of Rashaz; on their rivalry, see A. Brawer, "On the Controversy Between Rashaz of Ladi and R. Abraham the Kohen of Kalisk" [H], *Kiryat Sefer* 1 (1925): 142–159; Schatz-Uffenheimer, *Hasidism*, 256–260; R. Elior, "The Minsk Debate" [H], *Jerusalem Studies in Jewish*

Thought I (1982): 195–199; on Rabbi Abraham in general, see G. D. Hundert, "Toward a Biography of R. Abraham Kalisker," master's thesis, Ohio State University, 1971; Z. Gries, "From Mythos to Ethos: An Outline of the Image of R. Abraham of Kalisk" [H], in *Uma Ve-Toldoteha,* ed. S. Ettinger, vol. 2 (Jerusalem, 1984), 117–146; Haran, "Controversies," chap. 3; Karlinsky, "Hasidic Epistles," 61–62.

59. As to the authenticity of the text, see Karlinsky, "Hasidic Epistles," 75–81; Haran and Mondshine exchange, above, chap. 6, n. 32.

60. Karlinsky, "Hasidic Epistles," 60–62, 74–76, 81–83; see also Haran, "Controversies," chap. 3.

61. See *Peri Ha-Aretz,* the homilies of Abraham the Angel on the unpaginated pages near the beginning of the book, and pp. 2a, 3a–b, 4d, 9c–d, 10a; see also letters 1–6.

62. *Peri Ha-Aretz,* 3d.

63. *SB,* 195.

64. Ibid., 169.

65. Ibid., 147.

66. Ibid., 51.

67. *LB,* 1b, 9b, 65a; see also Loewenthal, *Infinite,* 113–131.

68. *SB,* 55.

69. Ibid., 53.

70. *Sha'ar Ha-Teshuvah Ve-Ha-Tefila* (The Gate of Repentance and Prayer) (Shklov, 1817), 43; see also *LB,* 1b, 11–12; *SBF,* 251; There are several other places where Dov Ber cited exemplary behavior of the Besht that appears in *Shivhei Ha-Besht, SBF,* 254–255.

71. Gries, *Book,* 18–22, 37–40, 64–66.

72. M. J. Rosman, "The History of a Historical Source: On the Editing of *Shivhei Ha-Besht*" [H], *Zion* 58 (1993): 195–196, 207–208; see also W. Iser, *The Act of Reading* (Baltimore, 1978), and *The Implied Reader* (Baltimore, 1974).

73. On the stages and dates of the development of *Shivhei Ha-Besht,* see Rosman, "Source," 177–178, 183–192, 206–207.

74. Rosman, "Source," 197–198; chap. 9, near n. 49.

75. For a technical analysis of how Yoffe emended the text, see Rosman, "Source," 183–205.

76. *SBF,* 153.

77. *SB,* 51.

78. Ibid., 181; in another place, the Besht is referred to as "Israel the son of the midwife," *SB,* 159.

79. *SB,* 9–10. Even this story may originally have been told about Rabbi Adam and not Eliezer; see Rosman, "Source," 202n.93.

80. Hielman, *Rabbi,* 90; *LB,* 67; Levin, *Igrois,* 235; *SB,* 7–11, 12, 16, 17.

81. *SB,* 10–11, 15–16, 19–20.

82. Ibid., 17–18, 31–32; see above near n. 13.

83. See Rosman, "Source," 198–200.

84. *SB,* 31.

85. As noted, he did not do a complete job. The printed collection contains

elements that could be interpreted as going against some of Dov Ber's claims. For example, the story about the Besht opposing the writing down of his teaching (*SB*, 179) might be used to support Aaron's claim that written teaching was not of the essence. However, once Yoffe established the basic argument of *Shivhei Ha-Besht* with the new beginning section, such apparently anomalous passages, occurring deep inside the book, could be ignored or casuistically explained away. In addition, generally known tradition placed a limit on how much Yoffe could change the book. Ideally, the Besht would have received his mystical training from his father. However, most readers knew that the Besht's father was not a famous scholar or mystic. A story that claimed that the Besht received the writings from his father would simply not be credible. Yoffe's solution of assigning the Besht's character to inheritance and his knowledge to transmission was a felicitous compromise. Furthermore, it is not clear to what extent Yoffe succeeded in getting his message across. There is virtually no information as to how Hasidim received *Shivhei Ha-Besht* when it first appeared, except evidence that it was very popular. See Rosman, "Source," 210–212.

86. Heinrich Graetz, *History of the Jews*, vol. 5 (Philadelphia, 1967), 374–379.

87. R. Mahler, *A History of Modern Jewry* (London, 1971), 447–448, 456–458.

88. Harold Stern, "The Testament of the Baal Shem Tov: A Study in the Polarities of the Spiritual Life," Ph.D. dissertation, Northwestern University, 1976, 266.

89. See A. Rapoport-Albert, "Hagiography with Footnotes," in *Essays in Jewish Historiography*, ed. A. Rapoport-Albert (Atlanta, 1991), 119–159.

Bibliography

ARCHIVAL SOURCES

Archiwum Główny Akt Dawnych (AGAD), Warsaw
  Archiwum Potockich z Łancuta 168 (HM 366)
  Archiwum Skarbu Koronnego (ASK) 71/13 (1662) 65/46 (1667)
  Księgi Kancellarskie 115

Biblioteka Czartoryskich (BC), Cracow
  2465, 2532, 2702, 3822, 4047, 4067, 4075, 4078, 4079, 4080, 4085,
  4121, 4125, 4127, 4131, 5758, 5775, 5788, 5796, 5825, 5843, 5870,
  5871, 5881, 5905, 5913, 5929, 5931, 5939, 5948, 5951, 5965, 5987
  Ewidencja (EW) 40, 41, 80, 86, 87, 176, 179, 256, 525, 1509
  Gospodarcze (GOSP) 306, 308, 1566

Central State Historical Archives of Ukraine (CSHAU), Kiev
  Fonds 33, 40, 254

Jewish National and University Library (JNUL), Jerusalem
  Heb 8°5979 (Rothschild Manuscript)
  F 20473 (Oxford-Bodleiana Manuscript 2190)
  F 31652 (Y. Jacobson Collection)

Mehudar Collection, Jerusalem
  Siddur of Moses ben Joseph from Lubomla (Jampol, 1750)

Vernadsky Library of the Ukrainian Academy of Sciences, Kiev Jewish Division
  Or 178 *Sefer Ha-Heshek* by Hillel Ba'al Shem (*SH*)

SHIVHEI HA-BESHT (IN PRAISE OF THE BA'AL SHEM TOV)

Manuscript, ca. 1810, Chabad Library, Brooklyn

Early Printed Editions
  Kopys, 1814 (Hebrew)
  Berdichev, 1815 (Hebrew)
  Lashchov, 1815 (Hebrew)
  Ostrog, 1815 (Yiddish)
  Koretz, 1816 (Yiddish)
  Novy Dvor, 1816 (Yiddish)
  Zolkiev 1817 (Yiddish)

Selected Modern Editions

Ben-Amos, Dan, and Jerome Mintz, trans. and eds. *In Praise of the Baal Shem Tov [Shivhei Ha-Besht]*. English translation (based on the first printing, Kopys, 1814), notes, appendixes, and index. Bloomington, Ind., 1970.

Mintz, Binyamin, ed. *Shivhei Ha-Besht. In Praise of the Ba'al Shem Tov*. With introduction and appendixes (based on the second printing, Berdichev, 1815). Jerusalem, 1960.

Mondshine, Yehoshua, ed. *Shivhei Ha-Besht. Shivhei Ha-Baal Shem Tov*. A facsimile of a unique manuscript, variant versions, and appendixes. Jerusalem, 1982.

Rubinstein, Avraham, ed. *Shivhei Ha-Besht. In Praise of the Ba'al Shem Tov*. With introduction and annotations (based on the first printing, Kopys, 1814). Jerusalem, 1991.

BOOKS AND ARTICLES

Aaron ben Zvi Ha-Kohen of Opatów. *Keter Shem Tov* (Crown of a Good Name). [Żółkiew, 1794–1795] Jerusalem, 1968.

Abraham ben Isaac of Rimmon Sefarad. *Brit Menuhah* (Covenant of Rest). Amsterdam, 1648.

Abrahams, Israel. *Hebrew Ethical Wills*. Philadelphia, 1976.

Adler, Michael. *Jews of Medieval England*. London, 1939.

Aescoly-Weintraub, Aaron Z. *Le Hassidisme: essai critique* (Hasidism: A Critical Essay). Paris, 1928.

Alfasi, Yitzhak. *Entziklopedia Le-Hasidut: Ishim* (Encyclopedia of Hasidism: Personalities). Vol. 1. Jerusalem, 1986.

Altschuler, Mor. "*Kevuzat Ya'acov*: Bein Biografia LeSifrut Shevahim" (*Kevuzat Ya'acov*: Between Biography and Hagiography). In *Proceedings of the XIth Congress of Jewish Studies*, vol. 2. Jerusalem, 1994.

Aron, Milton. *Ideas and Ideals of the Hasidim*. Secaucus, N.J., 1980.

Assaf, David. "R' Yisrael Mi-Ruzhin U-Mekomo Be-Toldot Ha-Hasidut Be-Mahatzit Ha-Rishona Shel Ha-Mei'a Ha-Tesha Esrei" (Rabbi Israel Ruzhin and His Role in the History of the Hasidic Movement in the First Half of the Nineteenth Century). Ph.D. dissertation, Hebrew University, Jerusalem, 1992.

Assaf, Simha. "Iggrot Mi-Tzefat" (Letters from Safed). *Kovetz Al Yad* 3(13), pt. 1 (1939): 122–133.

Bałaban, Majer. *Historja Żydów w Krakowie i na Kazimierzu* (History of the Jews in Cracow and Kazimierz). 2 vols. Cracow, 1931–1936.

———. *Le-Toldot Ha-Tenuah Ha-Frankit* (On the History of the Frankist Movement). 2 vols. Tel Aviv, 1934–1935.

Balzer, Oswald. *Sądownictwo ormianskie w średnowiecznym Lwowie* (The Armenian Court System in Medieval Lwów). Lwów, 1910.

Baranovich, A. I. *Magnatskoie khoziaistvo na iuge Volyni v XVIII v* (Magnate Economy in Southern Volhyn in the Eighteenth Century). Moscow, 1955.

Barnai, Jacob. *Iggrot Hasidim Mei-Eretz Yisrael* (Hasidic Letters from the Land of Israel). Jerusalem, 1980.

———. "Some Clarifications on the Land of Israel Stories of 'In Praise of the Ba'al Shem Tov.' " *Révue des études juives* 146 (1987): 367–380.

Baron, S. W. *A Social and Religious History of the Jews.* Vol. 16. New York, 1976.

Bartal, Israel. "Aliyat R' Elazar Rokeah Le-Eretz Yisrael Bi-Shnat 5501" (The Emigration of R' Elazar from Amsterdam to the Land of Israel in 1740). In I. Bartal, *Galut Ba-Aretz* (Exile in the Homeland). Jerusalem, 1994.

Bartoszewski, Wladyslaw T., and Antony Polonsky. *The Jews in Warsaw.* Oxford, 1991.

Barukh of Międzybóż. *Butzina De-Nehora* (Lamp of Light). Lemberg, 1878.

Barwinski, E. "Zygmunt III i dyssydenci" (Zygmunt III and the Dissidents). *Reformacja w Polsce* 1 (1921): 50–57.

Baszanowski, Jan. *Z dziejów handlu polskiego w XVI–XVII w.: handel wołami* (On the History of Polish Commerce in the Sixteenth and Seventeenth Centuries: The Cattle Trade). Gdańsk, 1977.

Bauminger, Mordecai. "Iggrot Rabbeinu Yisrael Ba'al Shem Tov" (Letters of Our Rabbi Israel Ba'al Shem Tov and His Son-in-Law Rabbi Yehiel Mikhl to Rabbi Abraham Gershon of Kutów). *Sinai* 71 (1971): 248–269.

———. "Od Le-Iggrot Ha-Besht Ve-Hatano" (More on the Letters of the Besht and His Son-in-Law). *Sinai* 72 (1973): 270–282.

Ben Sasson, Hayyim H. *Hagut Ve-Hanhaga* (Theory and Practice). Jerusalem, 1959.

———. *History of the Jewish People.* 3 vols. Cambridge, Mass., 1976.

———. "Ishiyuto Shel Ha-Gra Ve-Hashpa'ato Ha-Historit" (The Personality of the Vilna Gaon and His Historical Influence). *Zion* 31 (1966): 39–86, 197–216.

———. "Takanot Issurei Shabbat Shel Polin U-Mashmautan Ha-Hevratit Ve-Ha-Kalkalit" (Statutes for the Enforcement of the Observance of the Sabbath in Poland and Their Social and Economic Significance). *Zion* 21 (1956): 188–190, 199–200.

Ben-Yehuda, Eliezer. *Milon Ha-Lashon Ha-Ivrit Ha-Yeshana Ve-Ha-Hadasha* (Dictionary of the Old and New Hebrew Language). 16 vols. Tel Aviv, 1948.

Bershadskii, S. A. *Russko-Evreiskii Arkhive* (Russian-Jewish Archive). 3 vols. St. Petersburg, 1903.

Bickerman, Elias. "Das Messiasgeheimnis und die Komposition des Markusevangeliums." In *Studies in Jewish and Christian History,* vol. 3, ed. A. I. Baumgarten. Leiden, 1986.

Birkenthal, Ber (of Bolechow). *The Memoirs of Ber of Bolechow.* Trans. and ed. Mark Vishnitzer. London, 1922.

Bogucka, Maria, and Henryk Samsonowicz. *Dzieje miast i mieszczaństwa w Polsce przedrozbiorowej* (History of Towns and Townspeople in Pre-Partition Poland). Wrocław, 1986.

Bokser, Baruch M. "Wonder-working and the Rabbinic Tradition: The Case of Hanina Ben Dosa." *Journal for the Study of Judaism* 16 (1985): 42–92.

Boyer, Regis. "An Attempt to Define the Typology of Medieval Hagiography." In *Hagiography and Medieval Literature: A Symposium,* ed. H. Bekker-Nielson et al. Odense, 1981.

Brawer, A. Y. "Al Ha-Mahloket Bein Ha-Rashaz Mi-Ladi Ve-R' Avraham Ha-Kohen Mi-Kalisk" (On the Controversy between Rashaz of Ladi and R. Abraham the Kohen of Kalisk). *Kiryat Sefer* 1 (1925): 142–159, 226–238.

———. "Makor Ivri Hadash Le-Toldot Frank Ve-Siyato" (A New Hebrew Source on the History of the Frankists). *Ha-Shiloah* 33 (1918): 146–156, 330–342, 439–448.

Brown, Peter. "The Rise and Function of the Holy Man in Late Antiquity." In P. Brown, *Society and the Holy in Late Antiquity.* Binghamton, 1982.

———. "The Saint as Exemplar in Late Antiquity." *Representations* 1 (1983): 1–25.

Bruckner, Aleksander. *Dzieje kultury polskiej* (History of Polish Culture). 3 vols. Warsaw, 1958.

Buber, Martin. *The Legend of the Ba'al Shem.* New York, 1969.

———. *The Origin and Meaning of Hasidism.* Trans. and ed. M. Friedman. Atlantic Highlands, N.J., 1988.

Burke, Peter. *Popular Culture in Early Modern Europe.* New York, 1978.

Burszta, Jozef. "Zbiegostwo Chłopów znad Sanu w I ćwieci XVIII w" (Desertion of Peasants from the San Region in the First Quarter of the Eighteenth Century). *Roczniki dziejów społecznych i gospodarczych* 34 (1973): 55–84.

Calmann, Marianne. *The Carrière of Carpentras.* Oxford, 1984.

Carrasas, M. "Sanctity and Experience in Pictorial Hagiography: Two Illustrated Lives of Saints from Romanesque France." In *Images of Sainthood in Medieval Europe,* ed. R. Blumenfeld-Kossinski and T. Szell. Ithaca, 1991.

Chirovsky, N. L. *An Introduction to Ukrainian History.* 3 vols. New York, 1981–1986.

———, ed. *The Millennium of Ukrainian Christianity.* New York, 1988.

Clifford, James, and G. E. Marcus, eds. *Writing Culture: The Poetics and Politics of Ethnography.* Berkeley, 1983.

Cyzevs'kyj, Dmytro. *A History of Ukrainian Literature.* Littleton, Colo., 1975.

Dan, Yosef. *Ha-Sippur Ha-Hasidi* (The Hasidic Novella). Jerusalem, 1966.

Davies, Norman. *God's Playground: A History of Poland.* New York, 1982.

Dinur, Ben-Zion. *Be-Mifneh Ha-Dorot* (Historical Studies). Jerusalem, 1954.

———. "The Origins of Hasidism and Its Social and Messianic Foundations." In *Essential Papers on Hasidism,* ed. G. D. Hundert. New York, 1991.

Dobh Baer of Lubavitch. *Tract on Ecstasy.* Trans. and ed. L. Jacobs. London, 1963.

Doroshenko, Dmytro, and O. W. Gerus. *A Survey of Ukrainian History.* Winnipeg, 1975.

Dov Ber, the Maggid of Mezerich. *Maggid Devarav Le-Ya'akov* (Preaching His Words to Jacob). [Koretz, 1781] Jerusalem, 1976.

———. *Zava'at Ha-Rivash* (The Will of the Besht). Ed. J. E. Shohat. [Ostrog, 1793] Brooklyn, 1975.

Dresner, Samuel H. *The Zaddik*. New York, 1960.

Dubnow, S. M. "The Beginnings: The Baal Shem Tov (Besht) and the Center in Podolia." In *Essential Papers on Hasidism*, ed. G. D. Hundert. New York, 1991.

———. *History of the Jews in Russia and Poland*. 3 vols. Philadelphia, 1916–1918.

———. *Toldot Ha-Hasidut* (History of Hasidism). Tel Aviv, 1975.

———, ed. *Pinkas Ha-Medina* (The Minute Book of the Lithuanian Jewish Council). Berlin, 1925.

Eban, Abba. *Heritage: Civilization and the Jews*. Tel Aviv, 1984.

Elbaum, Jacob. *Petihut Ve-Histagrut* (Openness and Insularity). Jerusalem, 1990.

———. *Teshuvat Ha-Lev Ve-Kabbalat Yisurim* (Repentance and Self-Flagellation in the Writings of the Sages of Germany and Poland, 1348–1648). Jerusalem, 1992.

Eliach, Yaffa. "The Russian Dissenting Sects and Their Influence on Israel Baal Shem Tov, Founder of Hassidism." *Proceedings of the American Academy for Jewish Research* 36 (1968): 57–83.

Eliade, Mircea. *Shamanism: Archaic Techniques of Ecstasy*. New York, 1964.

Elior, Rahel. "Ha-Mahloket Al Moreshet Habad" (The Controversy Over the Legacy of Habad). *Tarbiz* 49 (1980): 166–186.

———. *The Paradoxical Ascent to God*. Albany, 1993.

———. *Torat Ha-Elohut Ba-Dor Ha-Sheni Shel Hasidut Habad* (The Doctrine of the Divine in the Second Generation of Habad Hasidism). Jerusalem, 1982.

———. "Vikuah Minsk" (The Minsk Debate). *Jerusalem Studies in Jewish Thought* 1 (1982): 179–235.

Emden, Jacob. *Beit Yehonatan Sofer, Sifrei Pulmus* (The House of Jonathan the Scribe, Polemical Books). Vol. 2. Ed. Barukh Agorek. New York, n.d.

Emery, Richard. *The Jews of Perpignan in the Thirteenth Century*. New York, 1959.

Etkes, Immanuel. "Aliyato Shel R' Shneur Zalman Mi-Ladi Le-Emdat Manhigut" (The Rise of R. Shneur Zalman of Ladi to a Position of Leadership). *Tarbiz* 54 (1985): 429–439.

———. "Darko Shel R' Shneur Zalman Mi-Ladi Ke-Manhig Hasidim" (R. Shneur Zalman of Ladi's Way as a Leader of Hasidim). *Zion* 50 (1985): 321–354.

———. "Ha-Gra Ve-Reishit Ha-Hitnagdut La-Hasidut" (The Gaon of Vilna and Early Opposition to Hasidism). In *Transition and Change in Modern Jewish History: Essays Presented in Honor of Shmuel Ettinger*, ed. S. Almog et al. Jerusalem, 1987.

———. "Hasidism as a Movement—The First Stage." In *Hasidism: Continuity or Innovation?* ed. B. Safran. Cambridge, Mass., 1988.

———. "Heker Ha-Hasidut: Megamot Ve-Kivunim" (Trends in the Study of the Hasidic Movement). *Jewish Studies* 31 (1991): 5–19.

———. *Mei-Havurah Le-Tenuah: Tenuat Ha-Hasidut Be-Reishitah* (From Esoteric Circle to Mass Movement: The Emergence of Early Hasidism). Vols. 9–10 of *Polin—The Jews of Eastern Europe: History and Culture*. Tel Aviv, 1991.

———. "Mekomam Shel Ha-Magiah U-Ba'alei Ha-Shem Ba-Hevrah Ha-Ashkenazit Be-Mifne Ha-Mei'ot Ha-17–18" (The Role of Magic and Ba'alai Shem in Ashkehazic Society in the Late Seventeenth and Early Eighteenth Century). *Zion* 60 (1995): 69–104.

———. *Rabbi Israel Salanter and the Mussar Movement*. Philadelphia, 1993.

Ettinger, Shmuel. "The Hasidic Movement—Reality and Ideals." In *Essential Papers on Hasidism*, ed. G. D. Hundert. New York, 1991.

———. "Helkam Shel Ha-Yehudim Ba-Kolonizatzia Shel Ukraina" (Jewish Participation in the Colonization of Ukraine). *Zion* 21 (1956): 107–142.

———. "Maamadam Ha-Mishpati Ve-Ha-Hevrati Shel Yehudei Ukraina Ba-Meiot Ha-15–17" (The Legal and Social Position of the Jews in Ukraine in the Fifteenth through Seventeenth Centuries). *Zion* 20 (1955): 128–152.

Fine, Lawrence. "The Art of Metoposcopy: A Study in Isaac Luria's Charismatic Knowledge." *Association for Jewish Studies Review* 11 (1986): 79–101.

———. *Safed Spirituality*. New York, 1984.

Farmer, Sharon. *Communities of Saint Martin: Legend and Ritual in Medieval Tours*. Ithaca, 1991.

Fedorowicz, J. K., ed. and trans. *A Republic of Nobles*. Cambridge, 1982.

Foxbruner, Roman. "Habad: The Ethical Thought of R. Shneur Zalman of Lyady." Ph.D. dissertation, Harvard University, Cambridge, Mass., 1984.

Frankel, David. *Iggrot Ha-Besht Ve-Talmiduv* (Letters of the Besht and His Disciples). Lwów, 1923.

Friedberg, H. D. *Toldot Ha-Defus Ha-Ivri Be-Polania* (The History of Hebrew Printing in Poland). Tel Aviv, 1950.

Friedman, Israel (of Ruzhin). *Knesset Yisrael* (The Congregation of Israel). Warsaw, 1906.

Gelernter, H. *Oneg Hayyim Le-Shabbat* (Life Joy for the Sabbath). Munkacz, 1908.

Gierowski, J. A. "Centralization and Autonomy in the Polish-Saxon Union," *Harvard Ukrainian Studies* 3–4 (1979–1980): 271–284.

———. "Kryzys gospodarki folwarczno-pańszczyznianej" (Crisis of the Manorial-Feudal Economy). In *Historia Polski,* Vol. I, pt. 2, ed. H. Łowmianski. Warsaw, 1958.

———. *W cieniu ligi pólnocnej* (In the Shadow of the Northern League). Wrocław, 1971.

Gierowski, J. A., and Andrzej Kaminski. "The Eclipse of Poland." In *The New Cambridge Modern History*, vol. 6, ed. J. S. Bromley. Cambridge, 1970.

Gieysztor, Aleksander, et al. *History of Poland*. Warsaw, 1979.

Gieysztorowa, Irena. *Wstęp do demografii staropolskiej* (Introduction to the Demography of Old Poland). Warsaw, 1976.

Glitzenstein, A. H. *Rabbi Yisrael Ba'al Shem Tov*. Kefar Habad, 1960.

Golan, Daphna. "Construction and Reconstruction of Zulu History." Ph.D. dissertation, Hebrew University, Jerusalem, 1988.

Goldberg, Jacob. *Converted Jews in the Polish Commonwealth*. Jerusalem, 1985.

———. *Jewish Privileges in the Polish Commonwealth*. Jerusalem, 1985.

———. "Poles and Jews in the 17th and 18th Centuries: Rejection or Acceptance." *Jahrbücher für Geschichte Osteuropas* 22 (1974): 248–282.

Gombiner, Abraham. *Magen Avraham* (Shield of Abraham). Dyhernfürth, 1692.

Goodich, M. "A Profile of Thirteenth-Century Sainthood." *Comparative Studies in Society and History* 18 (1976): 429–437.

Graetz, Heinrich. *History of the Jews*. 5 vols. Philadelphia, 1967.

Grayzel, Solomon. *A History of the Jews*. Philadelphia, [1947] 1984.

Green, Arthur. *Tormented Master*. New York, 1981.

———. "Typologies of Leadership and the Hasidic Zaddiq." In *Jewish Spirituality*, vol. 2, ed. A. Green. New York, 1987.

———. "The Zaddiq as *Axis Mundi* in Later Judaism." *Journal of the American Academy of Religion* 45 (1977): 328–347.

Gries, Zev. "Mi-Mytos Le-Etos: Kavim Li-Dmuto Shel R' Avraham Mi-Kalisk" (From Mythos to Ethos: An Outline of the Image of R. Abraham of Kalisk). In *Uma Ve-Toldoteha*, ed. S. Ettinger, vol. 2. Jerusalem, 1984.

———. *Sefer, Sofer Ve-Sippur Be-Reishit Ha-Hasidut* (The Book in Early Hasidism). Tel Aviv, 1992.

———. *Sifrut Ha-Hanhagot* (Conduct Literature: Its History and Place in the Life of Beshtian Hasidism). Jerusalem, 1989.

Guldon, Zenon, and J. Wijacka. "Procesy o mordy ritualne na Rusi Czerwonej, Podolu i prawobrzeżnej Ukrainie w XVI–XVIII w" (Ritual Murder Trials in Red Russia, Podolia and Ukraine in the Sixteenth through Eighteenth Centuries). *Nasza Przeszłość* 81 (1994): 51–84.

———. *Związki handlowe dóbr magnackich na prawobrzeżniej Ukrainie z Gdańskim w XVIII wieku* (Commercial Ties between Magnate Latifundia in Right Bank Ukraine and Gdańsk in the Eighteenth Century). Toruń, 1966.

Gurevich, Aron. *Medieval Popular Culture: Problems of Belief and Perception*. Cambridge, 1988.

Hadas, Moses, and Morton Smith. *Heroes and Gods: Spiritual Biographies in Antiquity*. New York, 1965.

Hahn, Cynthia. "Speaking without Tongues: The Martyr Romanus and Augustine's Theory of Language in Illustrations of Bern Burgerbibliothek Codex 264." In *Images of Sainthood in Medieval Europe*, ed. R. Blumenfeld-Kossinski and T. Szell. Ithaca, 1991.

Ha-Kohen, B. D. *Birkat Ha-Aretz* (Blessing of the Land). Jerusalem, 1904.

Halecki, Oscar. *From Florence to Brest*. New York, 1959.

Halpern, Israel. *Pinkas Va'ad Arba Aratzot* (The Records of the Council of Four Lands). Ed. I. Bartal. Jerusalem, 1990.

———. *Yehudim Ve-Yahadut Be-Mizrah Eiropa* (Eastern European Jewry: Historical Studies). Jerusalem, 1968.

Hanawalt, Barbara A., ed. *Women and Work in Preindustrial Europe*. Bloomington, Ind., 1986.

Hannover, Nathan Nota. *Abyss of Despair* [*Yeven Metzula*]. Trans. and ed. A. Mesch. New York, 1950.

Haran, Raya. "Blil Iggrot Ve-Iggeret" (On the Copying and Transmission of Hasidic Letters). *Zion* 56 (1991): 299–320.

———. "Mahlokot Ideologiot Penim Hasidiyot" (Ideological Controversies within Hasidism). Ph.D. dissertation, Hebrew University, Jerusalem, 1993.

———. "Shivhei Ha-Rav: Le-She'eilat Aminutam Shel Iggrot Hasidim Mei-Eretz Yisrael" (In Praise of the Rabbi: On the Question of the Reliability of Hasidic Letters from the Land of Israel). *Cathedra* 55 (1990): 22–55; 64 (1992): 98–102.

Haskell, T. L. "The Curious Persistence of Rights Talk in the 'Age of Interpretation.' " *Journal of American History* 74 (1987–1988): 984–1012.

———. "Objectivity Is Not Neutrality: Rhetoric vs. Practice in Peter Novick's *That Noble Dream*." *History and Theory* 29 (1990): 129–157.

Hayyim ben Berish. *Mayim Hayyim* (Living Waters). Zhitomir, 1857.

Heffernan, T. J. *Sacred Biography: Saints and Their Biographies in the Middle Ages.* Oxford, 1988.

Heschel, Abraham J. *The Circle of the Ba'al Shem Tov.* Trans. and ed. S. H. Dresner. Chicago, 1985.

Hielman, H. M. *Beit Rabbi* (The House of the Rabbi). Berdichev, 1902.

Hillel, Moshe. *Ba'alei Shem.* Jerusalem, 1993.

Hillman, David Z. *Iggrot Ba'al Ha-Tanya* (The Letters of Shneur Zalman of Ladi). Jerusalem, 1953.

———. "Od Be-Inyan Genizat Kherson" (More on the Matter of the Kherson Geniza). *Ha-Sefer* 2 (1955): 32–42.

Himka, John-Paul. "The Conflict between the Secular and the Religious Clergy in Eighteenth-Century Western Ukraine." *Harvard Ukrainian Studies* 15 (1991): 35–47.

Hisdai, Ya'akov. " 'Eved Ha-Shem' Be-Doram Shel Avot Ha-Hasidut" ('Eved Ha-Shem' [Servant of the Lord] in Early Hasidism). *Zion* 47 (1982): 253–292.

———. "Reishit Darkam Shel Ha-Hasidim Ve-Ha-Mitnagdim Le-Or Sifrut Ha-Drush" (The Emergence of Hasidim and Mitnagdim in the Light of the Homiletic Literature). Ph.D. dissertation, Hebrew University, Jerusalem, 1984.

Homecki, Adam. *Produkcja i handel zbożowy w latyfundium Lubomirskich w drugiej połowie XVII i pierwszej XVIII wieku* (Grain Production and Trade in the Lubomirski Latifundium in the Second Half of the Seventeenth and First Half of the Eighteenth Century). Wrocław, 1970.

Horowitz, Aaron. *Avodat Ha-Levi* (The Levites Service). Lvov, 1842–1861.

———. *Sha'arei Avodah* (Gates of Service). Shklov, 1821.

———. *Sha'ar Ha-Yihud Ve-Ha-Emunah* (The Gate of Unity and Faith). Shklov, 1820.

Horowitz, Elliott. "Eve of Circumcision: A Chapter in the History of Jewish Nightlife." *Journal of Social History* 23 (1989): 45–69.

———. "The Way We Were: *Jewish Life in the Middle Ages.*" *Jewish History* 1 (1986): 78–83.

Hrushevsky, Mykhailo. *A History of Ukraine.* New York, 1941.

Hubka, Thomas. "The Eighteenth-Century Interior-domed Synagogues of Eastern Europe: The Art and Architecture of a Pre-Hasidic Culture." Polin, in press.

Hundert, Gershon D. "The Conditions in Jewish Society in the Polish-Lithuanian Commonwealth in the Middle Decades of the Eighteenth Century." In *Hasidism Reappraised*, ed. Ada Rapoport-Albert. London, 1996.

———. *The Jews in a Polish Private Town: The Case of Opatów in the Eighteenth Century*. Baltimore, 1992.

———. "On the Jewish Community in Poland During the Seventeenth Century: Some Comparative Perspectives." *Révue des études juives* 142 (1983): 349–372.

———. "The Role of the Jews in Commerce in Early Modern Poland-Lithuania." *Journal of European Economic History* 16 (1987): 245–275.

———. "Security and Dependence: Perspectives on Seventeenth-Century Polish-Jewish Society Gained through a Study of Jewish Merchants in Little Poland." Ph.D. dissertation, Columbia University, New York, 1978.

———. "Sheki'at Yirat Ha-Kavod Be-Kehillot Beit Yisrael Be-Polin-Lita" (The Decline of Deference in the Jewish Communities of the Polish-Lithuanian Commonwealth). *Bar Ilan* 24–25 (1989): 41–50.

———. "Toward a Biography of R. Abraham Kalisker." Master's thesis, Ohio State University, Columbus, 1971.

———, ed. *Essential Papers on Hasidism*. New York, 1991.

Idel, Moshe. "Jewish Magic from the Renaissance Period to Early Hasidism." In *Religion, Science, and Magic: In Concert and in Conflict*, ed. J. Neusner et al. New York, 1989.

———. *Kabbalah: New Perspectives*. New Haven, 1988.

———. *The Mystical Experience in Abraham Abulafia*. Albany, N.Y., 1988.

———. "Perceptions of Kabbalah in the Second Half of the Eighteenth Century." *Journal of Jewish Thought and Philosophy* 1 (1991): 55–114.

———. *Studies in Ecstatic Kabbalah*. Binghamton, N.Y., 1988.

Iser, Wolfgang. *The Act of Reading*. Baltimore, 1978.

———. *The Implied Reader*. Baltimore, 1974.

Ish-Hurwitz, Shai. *Ha-Hasidut Ve-Ha-Haskala* (Hasidism and Enlightenment). Berlin, 1909.

Jablonowski, Aleksander, "Wołyn i Podole pod koniec w XVI-go" (Volhynia and Podolia at the End of the Sixteenth Century). *Pisma* 4 (1911): 144–233.

Jacob Joseph of Polonne. *Ben Porat Yosef* (Joseph Is a Fruitful Vine). Koretz, 1781.

———. *Kutonet Pasim* (Coat of Many Colors). Lwow, 1866.

———. *Toldot Ya'akov Yosef* (The Generations of Jacob Joseph). Koretz, 1780.

———. *Zofnat Pa'anei'ah* (Decoder). Koretz, 1782.

Jacobs, Louis. "The Concept of *Hasid* in the Biblical and Rabbinic Literatures." *Journal of Jewish Studies* 7 (1957): 143–154.

———. *Hasidic Prayer*. New York, 1973.

———. *Seeker of Unity*. London, 1966.

Johnson, Paul. *A History of the Jews*. London, 1988.

Judah Leib ben Dov Ber. *Teshuot Hen* (Cheers). Berdichev, 1816.

Kahana, Abraham. "Al Iggrot Bi-Khtav Yad Shel Ha-Besht Ve-Talmidav" (On Manuscript Letters of the Besht and His Disciples). *Ha-Yishuv* 24 (1925): Pt. 3.

Kaidaner, Ya'acov. *Sippurim Noraim* (Awesome Stories). Jerusalem, 1992.

Kaminski, Andrzej. "Poland-Lithuania as a Host Country for the Jews." In *Poles and Jews: Myth and Reality in the Historical Context,* ed. H. B. Segel. New York, 1986.

Kaminski, Czesław, and Jerzy Żukowski. *Katalog Monet Polskich* (Catalog of Polish Money). Warsaw, 1980.

Karas, Mieczysław, and Antoni Podraza. *Ukraina: Teraźniejszość i przeszłość* (Ukraine: Present and Past). Cracow, 1970.

Karlinsky, Nahum. *Iggrot Ha-Hasidim Mei-Eretz Yisrael* (The Hasidic Epistles from the Land of Israel). Jerusalem, in press.

Katz, Jacob. *Halakha Ve-Kabbalah* (Halakhah and Kabbalah). Jerusalem, 1984.

———. *Tradition and Crisis.* New York, 1971.

Katz, Simha. "Iggrot Maskilim Bi-Genutam Shel Hasidim" (Letters of Maskilim Criticizing Hasidim). *Moznaim* 10 (1940): 266–276.

Katznellenbogen, Pinhas. *Yesh Manhilin* (There Are Those Who Bequeath). Ed. I. D. Feld. Jerusalem, 1986.

Klausner, Israel. *Vilna Bi-Tekufat Ha-Gaon* (Vilna at the Time of the Gaon). Jerusalem, 1942.

———. *Vilna: Yerushalayim De-Lita* (Vilna: Jerusalem of Lithuania, Generations from 1495 to 1881). Kibbutz Lohamei Ha-Gettaot, Israel, 1988.

Kłoczowski, Jerzy. *Kościoł w Polsce* (The Church in Poland). Vol. 2. Cracow, 1969.

Kloppenberg, J. T. "Objectivity and Historicism: A Century of American Historical Writing." *American Historical Review* 94 (1989): 1011–1030.

Kohn, Tobias. *Ma'aseh Tuviah* (The Deeds of Tobias). Venice, 1707.

Kohut, Z. E. "Myths Old and New: The Hajdamak Movement and the Koliivshchyna (1768) in Recent Historiography." *HUS* 1 (1977): 359–378.

Kołodziejczyk, Dariusz. *Ejalet Kamieniecki* (The Kamieniec Province: Podolia Under Ottoman Rule). Warsaw, 1994.

Kowaleski, Maryanne. "Women's Work in a Market Town: Exeter in the Late Fourteenth Century." In *Women and Work in Preindustrial Europe,* ed. B. Hanawalt. Bloomington, Ind., 1986.

Kubijovyc, Volodymyr, ed. *Ukraine: A Concise Encyclopedia.* 2 vols. Toronto, 1963.

Kuperstein, Isaiah. "Inquiry at Polaniec: A Case Study of a Hasidic Controversy in Eighteenth-Century Galicia." *Bar Ilan* 24–25 (1989): 25–39.

Kutover, Israel. *Shvil Ha-Emunah* (The Path of Faith). Jozefow, 1878.

Landau, Bezalel. *Ha-Gaon He-Hasid Mi-Vilna* (The Gaon and Hasid of Vilna). Jerusalem, 1968.

Leib ben Ozer. *Sippurei Ma'asei Shabbetai Zvi* (The Story of Shabbetai Zevi). Trans. and annotated Z. Shazar. Ed. S. Zucker and R. Plesser. Jerusalem, 1978.

Leśkiewiczowa, Janina, and Jerzy Michalski, eds. *Supliki chłopskie XVIII wieku z Archiwum Michała Poniatowskiego* (Eighteenth-Century Peasant Petitions from the Archive of Michał Poniatowski). Warsaw, 1954.

Levin, S. D. *Igrois Koidesh* (Holy Letters). New York, 1987.

————. " 'Kuntres Ha-Hitpa'alut' Le-Rabbi Dov Ber Schneersohn" (Dov Ber
Schneersohn's "Essay on Ecstasy"). *Kiryat Sefer* 54 (1979): 829–830.

————. *Toldot Habad Be-Eretz Ha-Kodesh* (The History of Habad in the Holy
Land). Kefar Habad, 1988.

Levin, Y. H. *Aliyot Eliyahu* (Ascents of Elijah). Jerusalem, 1989.

Levine, Hillel. *Economic Origins of Antisemitism*. New Haven, 1991.

Lewitter, L. R. "Intolerance and Foreign Intervention in Early Eighteenth-
Century Poland-Lithuania." *Harvard Ukrainian Studies* 5 (1981): 290–303.

Liberman, Haim. *Ohel Rahe"l* (Tent of R. H. L.). Brooklyn, 1980.

Lieberman, Saul. *Hellenism in Jewish Palestine*. New York, 1962.

Liebes, Yehuda. "Hadashot Le-Inyan Ha-Besht U-Shabbetai Zvi" (New Light on
the Matter of the Besht and Shabbetai Zvi). *Jerusalem Studies in Jewish
Thought* 2 (1983): 564–569.

————. "Keitzad Nithaber Sefer Ha-Zohar" (How Was the Zohar Written?).
Jerusalem Studies in Jewish Thought 8 (1989): 1–71.

————. "Ha-Mashiah Shel Ha-Zohar" (The Messiah of the Zohar). In *Ha-
Ra'ayon Ha-Meshihi* (The Messianic Idea), ed. Shelomoh Re'em. Jerusalem,
1982.

————. " 'Trin Orzilin De-Ayalta': Derashato Ha-Sodit Shel Ha-Ari Lifnei Mi-
tato" ("Two Young Roes of a Doe": The Secret Sermon of Isaac Luria before His Death). *Jerusalem Studies in Jewish Thought* 10 (1992): 113–169.

————. "Yahaso Shel Shabbetai Zvi Le-Hamarat Dato" (Shabbetai Zvi's Attitude Toward His Own Conversion). *Sefunot* n.s. 2(17) (1983): 267–307.

Loewenthal, Naftali. *Communicating the Infinite*. Chicago, 1990.

Lukowski, Jerzy. *Liberty's Folly: The Polish-Lithuanian Commonwealth in the
Eighteenth Century, 1697–1795*. London, 1991.

Maciszewski, Maurycy. *Brzeżany*. Brody, 1910.

Mahler, Raphael. *A History of Modern Jewry*. London, 1971.

————. *Toldot Ha-Yehudim Be-Polin* (History of the Jews in Poland). Merhavia,
1946.

————. *Yidn in Amolikn Poiln in Likht fun Tsifirn* (The Jews of Old Poland in
Light of Numbers). 2 vols. Warsaw, 1958.

Maimon, Solomon. *Autobiography*. Trans. J. C. Murray. London, 1954.

Manor, Dan. "R' Hayyim Ben Attar Be-Mishnat Ha-Hasidut" (R. Hayyim
ben Attar in Hasidic Tradition). *Pe'amim* 20 (1984): 88–110.

Mansoor, Menahem. *Jewish History and Thought: An Introduction*. Hoboken,
N.J., 1991.

Maraval, Pierre. "Fonction pedagogique de la littérature hagiographique d'un
lieu de pélérinage: l'exemple des miracles de Cyr et Jean" (The Pedogogical
Function of the Hagiographic Literature of a Place of Pilgrimage: The Example of the Miracles of Cyr and Jean). In *Hagiographie, cultures et sociétés:
IVᵉ–XIIᵉ siècles*. Paris, 1981.

Marcus, Aaron. *Ha-Hasidut* (Hasidism). Benai Berak, 1980.

Marcus, Ivan. *Piety and Society: The Jewish Pietists of Medieval Germany*. Leiden, 1981.

Margoliot, Meir. *Sod Yakhin U-Boaz* (Secret of Yakhin and Boaz). Ostróg, 1794.

Margolis, M. L., and Alexander Marx. *A History of the Jewish People*. New York, [1927] 1969.

Mayer, Bonaventura. *Die Jüden Unserer Zeit* (The Jews of Our Time). Regensburg, 1842.

Menahem Mendel of Vitebsk et al. *Peri Ha-Aretz* (Fruit of the Land). Kopys, 1814.

Mifalot Elokim (God's Works). Żółkiew, 1725.

Miłosz, Czesław. *The History of Polish Literature*. New York, 1969.

Molchanovskii, N. *Ocherk izvestii o Podolskoi zemle do 1434 goda* (Outline of Information about the Podolian Territory before 1434). Kiev, 1885.

Mondshine, Yehoshua. "Aminutan Shel Iggrot Hasidim Mei-Eretz Yisrael" (The Reliability of Hasidic Letters from the Land of Israel). *Katedra* 63 (1992): 65–97; 64 (1992): 79–97.

———. *Likutei Amarim: Hu Sefer Ha-Tanya* (*The Tanya*, Its Editions, Translations, and Commentaries). Kefar Habad, 1982.

———. *Migdal Oz* (Tower of Strength). Kefar Habad, 1980.

———. "Shnei Ma'asarav Shel Rabbeinu Ha-Zaken" (The Two Incarcerations of Our Old Master in Light of New Documents). *Kerem Habad* 4a (1992): 17–108.

———. *Sifrei Ha-Halakhah Shel Admor Ha-Zaken* (The Halakhic Books of the Old *Admor*: A Bibliography). Kefar Habad, 1984.

Moses Ephraim of Sudyłków. *Degel Mahaneh Ephraim* (The Flag of Ephraim's Camp). Koretz, 1810.

Moses of Satanów. *Mishmeret Kodesh* (Holy Watch). Żółkiew, 1746.

Nadav, Mordecai. "The Jewish Community of Nemyriv: Their Massacre and Loyalty Oath to the Cossacks." *Harvard Ukrainian Studies* 8 (1984): 376–395.

———. *Pinsk*. Tel Aviv, 1973.

Nadel, Ira. *Biography: Fiction, Fact and Form*. London, 1984.

Nadel-Golobic, Eleonora. "Armenians and Jews in Medieval Lvov: Their Role in Oriental Trade, 1400–1600." *Cahiers du monde russe et sovietique* 20 (1979): 345–388.

Nahum of Chernobyl. *Maor Einaim* (Illuminator of the Eyes). Slavuta, 1798.

Ne'eman, Aviva. *Hevron Shelanu* (Our Hebron). In preparation.

Neusner, Jacob. *Development of a Legend: Studies on the Traditions Concerning Yohanan ben Zakkai*. Leiden, 1970.

———. "Judaic Uses of History in Talmudic Times." In *Essays in Jewish Historiography*, ed. A. Rapoport-Albert. Atlanta, 1991.

———. *A Life of Yohanan ben Zakkai*. Leiden, 1970.

Nigal, Gedaliah. *Ba'al Shem Le-Ma'asar Olam* (A Ba'al Shem Condemned to a Life Sentence: The Tragedy of R. Hirsch Frankel). Ramat Gan, 1993.

———. *Magic, Mysticism and Hasidism*. Northvale, N.J., 1994.

———. "Makor Rishoni Le-Sifrut Ha-Sippurim Ha-Hasidit" (A Primary Source of Hasidic Story Literature). *Sinai* 79 (1976): 132–142.

———. *Manhig Ve-Edah* (Leader and Followers). Jerusalem, 1962.

———. *Ha-Sipporet Ha-Hasidit* (The Hasidic Tale: Its History and Topics). Jerusalem, 1981.

————, ed. *Gedolim Ma'aseh Zaddikim* (Hasidic Tales). Jerusalem, 1991.

————, ed. *Zofnat Pa'anei'ah* (Decoder). Jerusalem, 1989.

Novarr, David. *The Lines of Life: Theories of Biography, 1880–1970.* West Lafayette, Ind., 1986.

Novick, Peter. *That Noble Dream.* Cambridge, 1988.

Oles, M. *The Armenian Law in the Polish Kingdom.* Rome, 1966.

Olney, James, ed. *Autobiography: Essays Theoretical and Critical.* Princeton, 1980.

Ong, W. J. *Orality and Literacy.* London, 1982.

Pasek, Jan. *The Memoirs of Jan Chryzostom z Gosławic Pasek.* Trans. and ed. M. A. J. Święcicka. Warsaw, 1978.

Pedaya, Haviva. "Le-Hitpathuto Shel Ha-Degem Ha-Hevrati-Dati-Kalkali Ba-Hasidut: *Ha-Pidyon, Ha-Havura,* Ve-Ha-Aliya Le-Regel" (On the Development of the Social-Religious-Economic Model of Hasidism: The *Pidyon,* the *Havurah,* and the Pilgrimage). In *Dat Ve-Kalkalah* (Religion and Economics), ed. M. Ben Sasson. Jerusalem, 1994.

Pendzich, Barbara. "The Jewish Community of Sluck after the Polish-Muscovite War of 1654–1667." In *Proceedings of the XIth Congress of Jewish Studies,* vol. 2. Jerusalem, 1994.

Perdenia, Jan. *Stanowisko Rzeczypospolitej Szlacheckiej wobec sprawy Ukrainy na przełomie XVII–XVIII w* (The State of the Nobles' Republic with Regard to Ukrainian Affairs at the Turn of the Eighteenth Century). Wrocław, 1963.

Perl, Josef. *Uiber das Wesen der Sekte Chassidim* (On the Nature of the Hasidic Sect). Ed. A. Rubinstein. Jerusalem, 1977.

Piekarz, Mendel. *Bi-Mei Zemihat Ha-Hasidut* (The Beginning of Hasidism). Jerusalem, 1978.

————. *Hasidut Braslav* (Studies in Bratzlav Hasidism). Jerusalem, 1972.

Pinchbeck, I. *Women Workers and the Industrial Revolution, 1750–1850.* London, 1969.

Piwarski, Kazimierz. "Upadek gospodarczy miast" (The Economic Decline of the Towns). In *Historia Polski,* vol. 1, pt. 2, ed. H. Łowmianski. Warsaw, 1958.

Popiół-Szymańska, Aleksandra. *Poglądy monetarne w Polsce* (Polish Monetary Perspectives from the Fifteenth to the Eighteenth Century). Poznan, 1978.

Porush, Shmuel. "Międzybóż, Iro Shel Ha-Besht Ha-Kadosh" (Międzybóż, City of the Holy Besht). *Nahalat Zvi* 4 (1991): 30–42.

Potok, Chaim. *Wanderings.* New York, 1986.

Pritsak, Omeljan. "Ukraine as the Setting for the Emergence of Hasidism." In *Israel and the Nations: Essays Presented in Honor of Shmuel Ettinger,* ed. S. Almog et al. Jerusalem, 1987.

Rabinowitsch, W. Z. *Lithuanian Hasidism.* New York, 1971.

Rafael, Yitzhak. "*Genizat* Kherson" (The *Geniza* of Kherson). *Sinai* 81 (1977): 129–150.

————. "*Shivhei Ha-Besht.*" *Areshet* 2 (1960): 358–377; 3 (1961): 440–441.

Raglan, Lord. *The Hero: A Study in Tradition, Myth and Drama.* New York, 1936.

Rank, Otto. *The Myth of the Birth of the Hero.* New York, 1964.

Rapoport-Albert, Ada. "God and the Zaddik as the Two Focal Points of Hasidic Worship." In *Essential Papers on Hasidism,* ed. G. D. Hundert. New York, 1991.

———. "Hagiography with Footnotes." In *Essays in Jewish Historiography,* ed. A. Rapoport-Albert. Atlanta, 1991.

———. "Ha-Tenuah Ha-Hasidit Aharei Shenat 1772: Retzef Mivni U-Temurah" (The Hasidic Movement after 1772: Continuity and Change). *Zion* 55 (1990): 187–215.

Reiner, Elhanan. "Hon, Ma'amad Hevrati, Ve-Talmud Torah: Ha-Kloyz Ba-Hevra Ha-Yehudit Be-Mizrah Eiropa" (Wealth, Social Position, and the Study of Torah: The Status of the *Kloyz* in Eastern European Jewish Society in the Early Modern Period). *Zion* 58 (1993): 287–328.

Reyerson, K. L. "Women in Business in Medieval Montpellier." In *Women and Work in Preindustrial Europe,* ed. B. Hanawalt. Bloomington, Ind., 1986.

Rosman, M. J. "An Exploitative Regime and the Opposition to It in Międzybóż, Ca. 1730." In *Transition and Change in Modern Jewish History: Essays Presented in Honor of Shmuel Ettinger,* ed. S. Almog et al. Jerusalem, 1987.

———. "Jewish Perceptions of Insecurity and Powerlessness in 16th- to 18th-Century Poland." *Polin* 1 (1986): 19–27.

———. "Le-Toldotav Shel Makor Histori" (The History of a Historical Source: On the Editing of *Shivhei Ha-Besht*). *Zion* 58 (1993): 175–214.

———. *The Lords' Jews.* Cambridge, Mass., 1990.

———. "Międzybóż and Rabbi Israel Ba'al Shem Tov." In *Essential Papers on Hasidism,* ed. G. D. Hundert. New York, 1991.

———. "A Minority Views the Majority: Jewish Attitudes Toward the Polish-Lithuanian Commonwealth and Interaction with Poles." *Polin* 4 (1989): 31–41.

———. "The Polish Magnates and the Jews: Jews in the Sieniawski-Czartoryski Territories." Ph.D. dissertation, Jewish Theological Seminary of America, New York, 1982.

———. "The Quest for the Historical Ba'al Shem Tov." In *Tradition and Crisis Revisited,* ed. B. D. Cooperman. Cambridge, Mass., in press.

———. "Reflections on the State of Polish-Jewish Historical Study." *Jewish History* 3 (1988): 115–130.

———. "Les rôles des Juifs dans l'économie polonaise du XVIᵉ au XVIIIᵉ siècle." In *La société juive à travers l'histoire,* vol. 3, ed. S. Trigano. Paris, 1993.

———. "Ha-Yahas Bein Ha-Hokher Ha-Yehudi Ve-Ha-Atzil Ha-Polani: Ha-Tzad Ha-Sheini" (The Relationship between the Jewish Arrendator and the Polish Nobleman: The Other Side). In *Yehudim Ba-Kalkalah* (Jews in Economic Life), ed. N. Gross. Jerusalem, 1985.

———. *Ha-Yishuv Ha-Yehudi Be-Polin* (The Jewish Community in Poland). Vols. 1–2 of *Polin—The Jews of Eastern Europe: History and Culture.* Tel Aviv, 1991.

Roth, Cecil. "The King and the Cabalist." In C. Roth, *Essays and Portraits in Anglo-Jewish History.* Philadelphia, 1962.

Rubinstein, Avraham. "Al Ketav Yad Mei-Iggeret Ha-Besht Le-Rabbi Gershon Mi-Kutów" (On a Manuscript of the Letter of the Besht to R. Gershon of Kutów). *Sinai* 72 (1972): 189–202.

———. "Al Ma'amadam Shel Ba'alei Shem" (On the Status of Ba'alei Shem). *Alei Sefer* 6–7 (1979): 184–186.

———. "Al Rabo Shel Ha-Besht Ve-Al Ha-Ketavim She-Mei-Hem Lamad Ha-Besht" (The Mentor of R. Israel Ba'al Shem Tov and the Sources of His Knowledge). *Tarbiz* 48 (1979): 146–158.

———. "Al Shelosha Sippurim Be-Sefer *Shivhei Ha-Besht*" (Concerning Three of the Stories in *Shivhei Ha-Besht*). *Sinai* 90 (1982): 269–279.

———. "He'erot Le-Sefer *Shivhei Ha-Besht*" (Notes on *Shivhei Ha-Besht*). *Sinai* 86 (1980): 62–71.

———. "Iggeret Ha-Besht Le-Rabbi Gershon Mi-Kutow" (The Letter of the Besht to R. Gershon of Kutów). *Sinai* 67 (1970): 120–139.

———. "Od Le-Inyan Iggrot Ha-Besht" (More on the Matter of the Letters of the Besht). *Sinai* 73 (1973): 175–180.

———. "Shevah Mi-*Shivhei Ha-Besht?*" (A Possibly New Fragment of *Shivhei Ha-Besht?*). *Tarbiz* 35 (1966): 174–191.

———. "Sippurei Ha-Hitgalut Be-Sefer *Shivhei Ha-Besht*" (The Revelation Stories in *Shivhei Ha-Besht*). *Alei Sefer* 6–7 (1977): 157–186.

Ruderman, David. *Kabbalah, Magic and Science: The Cultural Universe of a Sixteenth-Century Jewish Physician.* Cambridge, Mass., 1988.

Rutkowski, Jan. *Historia gospodarcza Polski* (Economic History of Poland). Warsaw, 1953.

Sanders, E. P. *Jesus and Judaism.* Philadelphia, 1985.

Schatz-Uffenheimer, Rivka. *Hasidism as Mysticism.* Princeton, 1993.

Schechter, Solomon. *Studies in Judaism.* New York, 1958.

Schiper, Yitzhak. "R' Yisrael Ba'al Shem Tov U-Demuto Ba-Sifrut Ha-Hasidut Ha-Kedumah" (R' Israel Ba'al Shem Tov and His Image in Early Hasidic Literature). *Ha-Doar* 39 (1960): 525, 531–532, 551–553.

Schneersohn, Dov Ber (attributed). *Inyan Ha-Hishtathut al Kivrei Zaddikim* (About Prostration on the Graves of Zaddikim). N.p., n.d.

———. *Likutei Beiurim* (Selected Explanations). Warsaw, 1868.

———. *Sha'ar Ha-Teshuvah Ve-Ha-Tefilah* (The Gate of Repentance and Prayer). Shklov, 1817.

Schneersohn, Y. Y. "Reshimat Devarim" (Notations). *Ha-Tamim* 2 (1936): 79.

Schochet, E. J. *Bach: Rabbi Joel Sirkes, His Life, Works and Times.* Jerusalem, 1971.

Scholem, Gershom. "Demuto Ha-Historit Shel R' Yisrael Ba'al Shem Tov" (The Historical Image of Israel Ba'al Shem Tov). *Molad* 18 (1960): 335–356.

———. *Devarim Be-Go* (Explications and Implications). Tel Aviv, 1975.

———. "Devekut or Communion with God." In *Essential Papers on Hasidism,* ed. G. D. Hundert. New York, 1991.

———. *Halomotav Shel Ha-Shabbeta'i, R. Mordekhai Ashkenazi* (The Dreams of Mordecai Ashkenazi the Sabbatean). Jerusalem, 1938.

———. *Major Trends in Jewish Mysticism.* New York, 1961.

———. *Mehkarim U-Mekorot Le-Toldot Ha-Shabbetaut Ve-Gilguleha* (Studies and Texts concerning the History of Sabbateanism and Its Metamorphoses). Jerusalem, 1974.

————. *The Messianic Idea in Judaism*. New York, 1971.

————. "Ha Navi Ha-Shabbeta'i R' Heschel Zoref—R' Adam Ba'al Shem" (The Sabbatean Prophet R' Heschel Zoref—R' Adam Ba'al Shem). *Zion* 6 (1941): 89–93; 7 (1942): 28.

————. "Ha-Pulmus Al Ha-Hasidut U-Manhigeha Ba-Sefer *Nezed Ha-Dema*" (The Debate over Hasidism in the Book *Nezed Ha-Dema*). *Zion* 20 (1955): 73–81.

————. "Shetai Ha-Eiduyot Ha-Rishonot Al Havurct Ha-Hasidim Ve-Ha-Besht" (Two Testimonies about Hasidic Groups and tne Besht). *Tarbiz* 20 (1949): 228–241.

Schweitzer, Albert. *The Quest of the Historical Jesus*. London, 1956.

Seltzer, R. M. *Jewish People, Jewish Thought: The Jewish Experience in History*. New York, 1980.

Serczyk, W. A. *Gospodarstwo magnackie w województwie podolskim w drugiej połowie XVIII wieku* (Magnate Economy in Podolia in the Second Half of the Eighteenth Century). Wrocław, 1965.

————. *Historia Ukrainy* (History of Ukraine). Wrocław, 1979.

————. *Koliszczyzna*. Cracow, 1968.

Sharot, Stephen. *Messianism, Mysticism and Magic: A Sociological Analysis of Jewish Religious Groups*. Chapel Hill, N.C., 1982.

Shmeruk, Khone. "Ha-Hasidut Ve-Iskei Ha-Hakhirot" (The Hasidic Movement and the "Arendars"). *Zion* 35 (1970): 182–192.

————. "Mashma'uta Ha-Hevratit Shel Ha-Shehita Ha-Hasidit" (The Social Significance of Hasidic Ritual Slaughtering). *Zion* 20 (1955): 47–72.

————. "Ha-Sippurim Al R' Adam Besh Ve-Gilguleihem Be-Nushaot *Shivhei Ha-Besht*" (The Stories about R. Adam Ba'al Shem and Their Development in the Versions of *Shivhei Ha-Besht*). In K. Shmeruk, *Sifrut Yiddish Be-Polin* (Yiddish Literature in Poland). Jerusalem, 1981.

Shulman, Nisson E. *Authority and Community*. New York, 1986.

Shulvass, Moses A. *Jewish Culture in Eastern Europe: The Classical Period*. New York, 1975.

Smith, Morton. "Prolegomena to a Discussion of Aretalogies, Divine Men, the Gospels and Jesus." *Journal of Biblical Literature* 90 (1971): 174–199.

Sot, Michel. "Arguments hagiographiques et historiographiques dans les 'Gesta episcoporum' " (Hagiographic and Historiographic Arguments in the "Gesta Episcoporum"). In *Hagiographie, cultures et sociétés: IVᵉ–XIIᵉ siècles*. Paris, 1981.

Spiegel, Gabrielle M. "History, Historicism and the Social Logic of the Text." *Speculum* 65 (1990): 59–86.

Stampfer, Shaul. "The 1764 Census of Polish Jewry." *Bar Ilan* 24–25 (1989): 41–147.

Stancliffe, Claire. *St. Martin and His Hagiographer: History and Miracle in Sulpicius Severus*. Oxford, 1983.

Stanislawski, Michael. *Tsar Nicholas I and the Jews: The Transformation of Jewish Society in Russia, 1825–1855*. Philadelphia, 1983.

Stern, Harold. "The Testament of the Baal Shem Tov: A Study in the Polarities of the Spiritual Life." Ph.D. dissertation, Northwestern University, Evanston, Ill., 1976.

Stuchkoff, Nahum. *Der Otsar fun Yiddisher Shprakh* (Lexicon of the Yiddish Language). New York, 1950.

Subtelny, Orest. *Ukraine: A History*. Toronto, 1988.

Sysyn, Frank E. *Between Poland and the Ukraine: The Dilemma of Adam Kysil*. Cambridge, Mass., 1985.

Tallan, Cheryl. "Medieval Jewish Widows: Their Control of Resources." *Jewish History* 5 (1991): 63–74.

Tamar, David. *Mehkarim Be-Toldot Ha-Yehudim Be-Eretz Yisrael U-Ve-Italia* (Studies on the History of the Jews in the Land of Israel and in Italy). Jerusalem, 1973.

Tazbir, Janusz. "The Fate of Polish Protestantism in the Seventeenth Century." In *A Republic of Nobles*, ed. J. K. Fedorowicz. Cambridge, 1982.

Tcherikover, Victor. *Hellenistic Civilization and the Jews*. Trans. S. Applebaum. Philadelphia, 1966.

Tishby, Isaiah. "Le-Heker Ha-Mekorot Shel S' *Hemdat Ha-Yamim*" (Sources of *Hemdat Ha-Yamim*). *Tarbiz* 25 (1955): 66–92.

———. "Mekorot Mei-Reishit Ha-Meiah Ha-18 Be-Sefer *Hemdat Yamim*" (Early Eighteenth-Century Sources in *Hemdat Yamim*). *Tarbiz* 25 (1956): 202–230.

———. "Ha-Ra'ayon Ha-Meshihi Ve-Ha-Megamot Ha-Meshihiot Be-Tzemihat Ha-Hasidut" (The Messianic Idea and Messianic Trends in the Growth of Hasidism). *Zion* 32 (1967): 1–45.

Tollet, Daniel. *Histoire des Juifs en Pologne du XVIᵉ siècle à nos jours* (History of the Jews in Poland from the Sixteenth Century to Our Days). Paris, 1992.

Tosefet Ma'aseh Rav (Appendix to the Deeds of the Rabbi). Jerusalem, 1896.

Twersky, Isadore. "The *Shulhan Aruk*: Enduring Code of Jewish Law." In *The Jewish Expression*, ed. J. Goldin. New York, 1970.

Vansina, Jan. *Oral Tradition as History*. Madison, 1985.

Velychenko, Stephen. *National History as Cultural Process*. Edmonton, 1992.

Vincenz, Stanislaw. *On the High Uplands: Sagas, Songs, Tales and Legends of the Carpathians*. Trans. H. C. Stevens. New York, 1956.

Volumina Legum. 10 vols. St. Petersburg, Cracow, Poznan, 1859–1952.

Wachstein, Duber. "Sridim Mi-Pinkaso Shel Rabbi Yaacov Yoshua Ba'al *Penei Yehoshua*" (Fragments from the Account Book of Rabbi Jacob Joshua, Author of *Penai Yehoshua*). In *Studies in Jewish Bibliography in Honor of A. S. Freidus*, ed. A. Freimann. New York, 1929.

Wandek, S. M. M., ed. *Sefer Ba'al Shem Tov Al Ha-Torah* (The Book of the Besht on the Torah). 2 vols. [Lodz, 1938] Jerusalem, 1992.

Weiner, Herbert. *9½ Mystics: The Kabbala Today*. New York, 1992.

Weinryb, B. D. "Beitrage zur Finanzgeschichte der judischen Gemeinden in Polen" (Studies on the Financial History of the Jewish Communities in Poland). *Hebrew Union College Annual* 16 (1941): 187–214.

———. *The Jews of Poland: A Social and Economic History of the Jewish Community in Poland from 1100 to 1800*. Philadelphia, 1972.

———. "Reappraisals in Jewish History." In *Salo W. Baron Jubilee Volume*, ed. S. Lieberman, vol. 2. New York, 1974.

———. "Texts and Studies in the Communal History of Polish Jewry." *Proceedings of the American Academy for Jewish Research* 19 (1950).

Weiss, J. G. "Reishit Tzemihata Shel Ha-Derekh Ha-Hasidit" (The Beginnings of Hasidism). *Zion* 16 (1951): 46–106.

———. *Studies in Eastern European Jewish Mysticism*. Ed. David Goldstein. Oxford, 1985.

Werblowsky, R. J. Z. *Joseph Karo: Lawyer and Mystic*. Oxford, 1962.

———. "The Safed Revival and Its Aftermath." In *Jewish Spirituality II: From the Sixteenth-Century Revival to the Present*, ed. A. Green. New York, 1987.

White, Hayden. *Metahistory*. Baltimore, 1973.

———. *Tropics of Discourse*. Baltimore, 1978.

Wiesel, Eli. *Souls on Fire*. New York, 1972.

Wilensky, Mordecai. *Hasidim U-Mitnagdim* (Hasidim and Mitnagdim). Jerusalem, 1970.

Ya'ari, Avraham. *Ta'alumat Sefer* (The Mystery of a Book). Jerusalem, 1954.

Ysander, Torsten. *Studien zum B'estschen Hasidismus in seiner religionsgeschichtlichen Sonderart* (Studies on Beshtian Hasidism in Its Historical-Religious Category). Uppsala, 1933.

Zagorin, Perez. "Historiography and Postmodernism: Reconsiderations." *History and Theory* 29 (1990): 263–274.

Zfatman, Sara. *Bein Ashkenaz Le-Sepharad* (The Jewish Tale in the Middle Ages: Between *Ashkenaz* and *Sepharad*). Jerusalem, 1993.

Zinberg, Israel. *A History of Jewish Literature*. Trans. and ed. B. Martin. 12 vols. Cincinnati, 1972–1978.

Zohar Hadash (The New Zohar). Warsaw, 1885.

Zurbrugg, Nicholas. "Samuel Beckett, Deirdre Blair, *Company* and the Art of Bad Biography." In *Reading Life Histories: Griffith Papers on Biography*, ed. James Walter. Canberra, 1981.

Zweifel, E. Z. *Shalom Al Yisrael* (Peace Unto Israel). Ed. A. Rubinstein. 2 vols. Jerusalem, 1972.

Index

Designer: U.C. Press Staff
Text: 10/13 Sabon
Display: Sabon
Compositor: ComCom, Inc.
Printer/Binder: Integrated Book Technology, Inc.